THE AUTISM DISCUSSION PAGE ON
THE CORE CHALLENGES OF AUTISM

by the same author

**The Autism Discussion Page on anxiety,
behavior, school, and parenting strategies**
A toolbox for helping children with autism
feel safe, accepted, and competent
Bill Nason
ISBN 978 1 84905 995 4
eISBN 978 0 85700 943 2

of related interest

101 Tips for Parents of Children with Autism
Effective Solutions for Everyday Challenges
Arnold Miller and Theresa C. Smith
Foreword by Dr Paul J. Callahan
ISBN 978 1 84905 960 2
eISBN 978 0 85700 818 3

Parenting without Panic
A Pocket Support Group for Parents of Children and Teens
on the Autism Spectrum (Asperger's Syndrome)
Brenda Dater
ISBN 978 1 84905 941 1
eISBN 978 0 85700 958 6

Kids in the Syndrome Mix of ADHD, LD, Autism
Spectrum, Tourette's, Anxiety, and More!
The one stop guide for parents, teachers, and other professionals
2nd edition
Martin L. Kutscher MD
With contributions from Tony Attwood PhD and Robert R Wolff MD
ISBN 978 1 84905 967 1
eISBN 978 0 85700 882 4

Can I tell you about Autism?
A guide for friends, family and professionals
Jude Welton
Foreword by Glenys Jones
Illustrated by Jane Telford
Part of the *Can I tell you about...?* Series
ISBN 978 1 84905 453 9
eISBN 978 0 85700 829 9

Asperkids
An Insider's Guide to Loving, Understanding and
Teaching Children with Asperger Syndrome
Jennifer Cook O'Toole
Foreword by Liane Holliday Willey
ISBN 978 1 84905 902 2
eISBN 978 0 85700 647 9

THE AUTISM DISCUSSION PAGE
ON THE CORE CHALLENGES OF AUTISM

A toolbox for helping children with autism
feel safe, accepted, and competent

BILL NASON

Jessica Kingsley *Publishers*
London and Philadelphia

First published in 2014
by Jesscia Kingsley Publishers
73 Collier Street
London N1 9BE, UK
and
400 Market Street, Suite 400
Philadelphia, PA 19106, USA

www.jkp.com

Library of Congress Cataloging in Publication Data
A CIP catalog record for this book is available from the Library of Congress

British Library Cataloguing in Publication Data
A CIP catalogue record for this book is available from the British Library

ISBN 978 1 84905 994 7
eISBN 978 0 85700 942 5

Printed and bound in the United States

ACKNOWLEDGEMENTS

This book and its companion, *The Autism Discussion Page on anxiety, behavior, school, and parenting strategies: A toolbox for helping children with autism feel safe, accepted, and competent*, were the result of ongoing support and encouragement from the members of the Facebook page I moderate, Autism Discussion Page. The outpouring of encouragement gave me the drive to put all these articles together in a two-volume set to provide a manual for the members as well as countless articles to share with friends, teachers, relatives, and caregivers. Special thanks go out to a handful of early members who have supported and shared my work across the world to spread awareness and understanding. For the early members who advertised and spread the word, without your support these books would never have happened. I owe you an endless debt of gratitude.

I wish to thank my wife and family for all their support and encouragement to enter this endeavor and stay with it through to completion. I am lucky enough to have a patient wife who has put up with me working countless hours to moderate the Facebook page and working endlessly to put these two books together. Thank you, LouAnne! Special thanks to my daughter, Carrie Aldrich, who has been a valuable sounding board for my ideas and has edited my manuscripts. Your support has been very dear to me.

Most importantly, there are many special families and friends with autism who have enriched my life over the years. For all the families who have allowed me into their lives, thank you so much for sharing this journey with me! And last, for all the adults on the spectrum who have shared with me all their comments, suggestions, recommendations, and experiences, thank you so much for providing me with the feedback and guidance to share your unique perspectives. Understanding your world allows me to communicate that awareness to the rest of the world. Thank you so much, and keep advocating your perspectives!

CONTENTS

PART III SENSORY ISSUES IN AUTISM

INTRODUCTION

This is a unique book in that the material was never designed to be a book in the first place. It is a collection of articles that I post on my Facebook page, Autism Discussion Page. I am a mental health professional, with a master's degree in clinical psychology and more than 30 years of experience in treating individuals with developmental disabilities and autism spectrum disorders. Over the years I began to specialize in autism spectrum disorders and developed a strong compassion for these children. In May of 2011 I started this Facebook page to share more than 30 PowerPoint (slide) presentations that I had created over the years of different strategies for supporting children on the spectrum. These PowerPoint presentations consist of a toolbox of strategies for helping children on the spectrum feel safe, accepted, and competent. These strategies provide guidelines for supporting the sensory, cognitive, emotional, and social challenges the children experience, and include parenting and teaching strategies. For those of you who go to the page looking for further information, these PowerPoint presentations can be found in the "Photo (albums)" section of the page.

In addition to these slide presentations, I started posting a variety of text articles on important areas of interest for parents, teachers, caregivers, professionals, and individuals on the spectrum. Little did I realize that this page would take off and grow so rapidly. What I thought would be a membership of a few hundred people blossomed into its current membership of more than 50,000 people from all around the world. In addition to the slide presentations, the members found my daily articles to be very valuable in both enabling them to understand the inner experiences of their children and giving step-by-step "how to" guidelines for helping their children feel safe, accepted, and competent. On this page we have a very supportive group of parents, teachers, professionals, and other caregivers who expand on my articles by sharing their comments, suggestions, and valuable experiences. We continue to grow at a rate of about 2,000 members a month, and with the help of their sharing, we reach an average of 90,000 to 130,000 viewers a week.

This book actually grew out of the members' encouragement to publish these posts in a book format so they could have a hard copy of all these articles in one collection which they could reference and share with others. It would also provide them with a manual for the page, so the members would not have to copy and paste the material and could reference it whenever they desired. So what you will find in this book is a series of short posts/articles that are arranged in chapters by common issues. Most of the posts are designed to stand alone (they do not need to be read in sequence), are written in easy-to-understand language, and can be read in just a few minutes. They provide an in-depth understanding of how the child perceives the world so that the supportive guidelines make natural sense. More than 300 posts are presented in two books:

1. *The Autism Discussion Page on the core challenges of autism: A toolbox for helping children with autism feel safe, accepted, and competent*

    This book provides an in-depth view of the four basic sensory, cognitive, social, and emotional areas of vulnerabilities for individuals on the spectrum. There is a comprehensive view of each area of vulnerability with detailed guidelines on how to support the child through these challenges. When readers are finished, they will have a good understanding of how their children perceive the world, process information, and act the way they do. The book takes you through all the sensory challenges that are common for those on the spectrum, how they process information differently, why they struggle so much socially, and how overwhelming their emotional world can be. From this awareness, it becomes easier to understand and accept those with autism, as well as help them regulate our world. Whether you are a parent, teacher, professional, or someone on the spectrum yourself, this book will be of value to you.

2. *The Autism Discussion Page on anxiety, behavior, school, and parenting strategies: A toolbox for helping children with autism feel safe, accepted, and competent*

    This book covers some of the major challenges that children and families experience during their daily routine and how to address each challenge. We cover stress and anxiety, addressing behavior issues, co-occurring conditions, stretching comfort zones, harnessing strengths and preferences, parenting and discipline strategies, teaching empowerment skills, and a host of mentoring strategies for coaching your child in basic life skills.

Each book, as well each article within, stands alone. Although the second book complements the first, they can be read and understood separately from each other.

Basic premises underlying these books

Before delving into the strategies for helping your child feel safe, accepted, and competent, it is best to outline the basic premises that provide the foundation for the strategies. Every author has their own biases that drive their approach, and it is important that you understand what they are. These premises provide the foundation for understanding the recommendations and suggestions. They may not dictate what procedures are used, but how we apply them. They provide the starting point, the values, and intentions that drive how we perceive the children, understand their needs, interrupt their behavior, and support their growth. The strategies in these books are based on the following premises:

1. *Assume the child is doing the best he can, given the situation he is in and his current skills for dealing with the demands.*

   Dr. Ross Greene, in his book *The Explosive Child*, outlines this basic premise that should drive all strategies designed for helping children. We have to assume that the children will act correctly if they have the right tools to respond competently. Therefore, if they are responding badly or incorrectly, assume that the demands of the situation outweigh the children's current skills for dealing with them. When faced with misbehavior or lack of progress, we have to change our expectations and teaching strategies to better match the child's abilities, build in better assistance to maximize success, and teach better skills for coping with the demands. It is up to us first to change our expectations and strategies, before expecting the child to change.

2. *Understand and validate first, before trying to change.*

   We often make the mistake of jumping in and trying to change the child's behavior before taking the time to understand how the child is experiencing the situation and the meaning the behavior has for him. All behavior has a functional purpose for the child. We must understand the behavior in light of the child's strengths and vulnerabilities before deciding how to change it. When we act without understanding, we often invalidate the child. Understand and validate first, then support and assist the child in learning.

3. *Help the child feel safe, accepted, and competent.*

   In the 30 plus years I have been in the field, I have learned that if I can create conditions so the children feel safe and secure, accepted and valued, and confident and competent, all children grow and develop. Everyone, children and adults, flourishes when we feel safe, accepted, and competent. We are all trying to reach these conditions. There is so much in this world that is chaotic and overwhelming for our children that they often feel unsafe, insecure, and inadequate. When designing strategies to teach the child, always ask yourself: "In what way does this strategy help my child feel safe, accepted, and competent?" If the strategy does not match this criterion, question its worth.

4. *Nothing for the child without the child!*

> The child's perspective and voice should be sought and respected at all stages of designing strategies. All behavior is communication, and we must listen to the child in all areas of training. Whenever possible, the child needs to be a working partner in identifying the goals and objectives, and in designing and implementing the strategies. Strategies should be based on the child's strengths, interests, and dreams, not simply focused on treating their vulnerabilities and weaknesses. Training is more effective when the child is an active agent in the learning process. When we try to impose, demand, and pressure, we force the child to avoid, resist, and mistrust our guidance. We must be a working partner with the children for them to respect us as a trusted guide.

Using these principles will help us understand and validate the child, help the child feel safe, accepted, and competent, and foster greater growth and development. These principles also direct how we set expectations, design treatment strategies, and avoid blaming the child when things go wrong. They also guide where to look when progress stops occurring. These premises give us a framework for identifying where to start, how to go, and what to fall back on when progress halts. At those moments when we are feeling lost and powerless, these premises keep us stable and secure, knowing where to turn and how to evaluate. They are the guiding principles that keep us on the right path. Never fear when momentarily confused. Take a deep breath, slow down, listen, and understand, then try another way! The journey is full of surprises and temporary setbacks, but many celebrations! These principles will provide the path for a fruitful journey! Have fun and support each other in helping the child. Place no blame when things go wrong, but share in the celebration when things go right! The greater the challenge, the sweeter the success!

How to read these books

These books can be read in a variety of ways:

1. They can be read from beginning to end to get a good understanding of all the issues and comprehensive strategies. Although each post can stand alone, they are clustered in series of related topics.

2. The reader can skim through the contents page and pick and choose areas that interest them, isolating strategies that are most relevant to their life and child. The posts do not have to be read in order and a post can often be understood without reading the material before it.

3. The articles are very condensed, packed with information, so it is important not to try to digest all the information at one time. It may be helpful to read the books from beginning to end, while checking off posts and strategies that you can come back to later to focus more on.

4. For parents, teachers, and professionals, these books can be used as reference books for looking up strategies for issues that arise as you move through this journey. These posts and strategies are laid out in an easy-to-find detailed format that provides you with a quick reference to comprehensive guidelines.

5. Since the books do not have to be read from front to back, you can take your time reading each post. If you only have brief moments to read, you can read one or two posts in a few minutes while taking a break from your daily living. You can read as little or much as you want, given the time that you have.

6. For the articles that you would like more information on you can go to our Facebook page, Autism Discussion Page, (www.facebook.com/autismdiscussionpage), view the different slide presentations and follow these same posts that are expanded on by our members sharing their comments, suggestions, and experiences, or message me privately for further information.

7. For members of the Facebook page, you finally have a manual for the page, giving you easy access to all the posts. You no longer have to stress about seeing every new post and trying to copy and paste them as you go along.

8. The appendices provide additional tools to help you support children on the autism spectrum. All the forms included can be downloaded at www.jkp.com/catalogue/book/9781849059947/resources.

Whether you are just starting out on this journey or have been following this ride for a while, you will find new and valuable information in these books. Whether you are a parent, teacher, professional, or a friend of someone on the spectrum, you will find that these books provide you with a better understanding, awareness, and acceptance of those you know on the spectrum.

How to use the strategies

As you read these books, it is easy to become overwhelmed by all the strategies that are compiled in these posts. You will recognize so many of these issues in your loved ones and want to implement many of the strategies. Trying to decide what to focus on and what to implement first can be very overwhelming.

I caution you to work on only one or two strategies at a time. As you read the posts, make a list of the strategies that are pertinent to you and your child. Do not try to implement them all at once. Go through your list and pick one or two to focus on until you have those strategies ingrained into your daily routine. Most strategies require you, as a parent, teacher, or professional, to make changes in your basic daily habits. This is not easy to do and takes time to accomplish. You only have energy to work on one or two at a time. When prioritizing these strategies, I would recommend that you first start off with a couple that would be the easiest for you to incorporate into you current routine. Do not start with the more difficult strategies to implement. Start small and easy and gradually build your way up. The greatest mistake that parents and caregivers make is jumping in and trying too much, never being successful with any of the strategies, and then giving up in despair. Keep it simple and build gradually.

Things to consider

- Like most literature in the field, when using terms autism and autism spectrum disorder I am incorporating Asperger's, PDD-NOS, and classic autism under this label. Occasionally, posts will refer to Asperger's when others are labeling their child that way. But most of the time autism and autism spectrum disorders encompass the whole spectrum.

- Most of the posts will refer to "him" as the person of interest. We use the male pronoun to include both males and females. It gets cumbersome and difficult to read when continually using him/her, he/she, etc. I am not excluding females on the spectrum.

- The material in these books will not flow as smoothly as other books. Since each post (article) was not necessarily written with the others in mind, one post may not easily flow to the next. Although every attempt has been made to group them by subject matter and fill in with material to help them transition together, the material will often read like independent posts. In addition, you may find some principles being repeated several times, since those principles were needed to explain the material of each post.

- Since these books are collections of posts from Facebook, they will not be filled with numerous citations, academic references, and empirical data. Most of the material is based on either common practice or best practiced procedures, but supportive citations will not be occurring here. Such information is way too cumbersome for Facebook posts.

- These books incorporate and integrate many different models of treatment. My work is heavily influenced by sensory integration; cognitive behavior treatment; Stanley Greenspan's Developmental, Individual Difference, Relationship-based (DIR®) Model; cognitive developmental models; Steven Gutstein's Relationship Development Intervention (RDI); Applied Behavior Analysis (ABA): TEACCH; and Ross Greene's Collaborative Problem Solving model. These books do not argue either all for or all against any one model. They incorporate a dynamic mix of many.

- *Disclaimer:* As the author of these books I do not know your child, what his strengths and vulnerabilities are, and which strategies would be appropriate for him. Each of these strategies will need to be individualized to the needs of your child, and I recommend that you seek guidance from those who have evaluated and know your child well. I am not prescribing any specific strategies for your child. Please seek professional guidance.

By reading these books you are taking your first steps into a very supportive, collaborative journey. I invite you all to join the thousands of people on the Autism Discussion Page (www.facebook.com/autismdiscussionpage), to learn, share, and receive supportive guidance. Hope to see you there!

Part I

ACCEPTANCE AND UNDERSTANDING

Chapter 1

ACCEPTANCE AND UNDERSTANDING

Understanding, acceptance, and love!

Autism is a bioneurological difference in how the brain is wired. Simply stated, our brains are wired a little differently. People on the spectrum have areas where their processing is stronger than ours and areas where it is weaker. Not better, not worse, simply different. We experience the world differently and can benefit from learning from each other. However, over the years, behavioral science has thought that by teaching them behavior skills, they will be less "autistic;" they will be "cured." As if autism is a behavior disorder—simply a lack of a skill set. Granted, learning these skill sets make it easier for people on the spectrum to blend in, but don't fool yourself that they are no longer "autistic." Their brain is still wired differently, and they continue to experience the world differently; they are just more skillful in fitting in. We need to respect their world and the gifts that they bring us, and learn to bridge the two worlds.

I have heard of many reports of kids being "cured" of autism. Applied Behavior Analysis (ABA) has done wonders in teaching skills so the person appears less autistic. The Lovaas study used the criteria of being able to function in school without an aid as the criterion of being "cured" of autism. Others have used the learning of an accumulation of skills that makes people look less autistic. If autism is a set of behavioral symptoms, then it is possible to create behavior change so the person looks less autistic. However, the deficits of autism (information processing problems, inability to read nonverbal language, difficulty with reading the intentions and perspectives of others, sensory processing problems, emotional regulation problems, etc.) are things that we all are better or worse at. For example, some of us are good informational processors, some of us are poor at regulating our emotions, and others are poor at social relations. Autism is a neurological, information processing disorder (or should I say a different way of thinking?) that renders the person with fewer abilities on these dimensions; it is not a behavior disorder. No matter how well they learn to compensate for these differences, people on the spectrum will always think and feel a little differently from us. That is not good or bad, but unique to the experience of autism. We can learn a lot from people with autism, as they can from us.

We should strive to bridge our two cultures, learn to accept and embrace our differences in thinking, so we can all grow from sharing our strengths and differences. I have chatted with many adults with autism. Most will tell you that it can be degrading for us to focus on changing their behavior to change them, as if they are something broken that needs "fixing!" As with all children, teach skills to allow each of them to grow and benefit in our social world, not to change them. We can do more good by accepting their uniqueness and fostering their strengths, rather than trying to "cure" them by shaping more "normal" behavior.

Autism! Don't fear it, embrace it!

In the neurotypical world, we tend to focus on the different as negative, rather than unique. We measure "goodness" by how it compares to the norm, and whether it matches our view of value. If the qualities are out of the norm, then we immediately see the negative that blinds us from the positive characteristics. We tend to interpret "different" as a weakness, or deficit, both something to change. We tend to interpret behavior that we do not understand as "bad," not worthy, and needing to be suppressed. We do not look at differences as something to value, understand, and marvel at. These differences may make our world better and enrich our lives. We are so conditioned to wanting to be accepted that appearing different is something to avoid. Unfortunately, we block ourselves off from the true wonders that these differences may bring.

Why is this? Why do we fear differences? Partly, I assume, it is that the unknown scares us. We feel uncomfortable when things do not match what we are used to. How do you relate to it? How do you understand it? Make it change, be like the norm, so I can feel comfortable with it! People have always been uncomfortable, even scared, with things that are different. Difference is not as predictable. It doesn't flow easily with how I regulate. It stands out and will not be accepted! We become anxious, hyper-focused on the negative, and totally blind to the beauty that it may bring. It doesn't fit our "common mode!"

I have been in the field for more than 30 years. I have seen many individuals who are radically different in how they communicate, how they process information, what they attend to, and how they experience the world. I was a "behavior change agent" and employed to change these people; to make them "normal," or at least appear normal. Like everyone else, these differences also scared me, especially since it was my job to suppress and change them. I started out in the back wards of an institution, where people with severe differences were secluded from the rest of the world. People who came from lives of abuse, torment, and despair as a result of neglect and rejection. It was through their eyes that I learned that each had beauty, value, and worth. Once I stopped fearing the unknown and embraced their uniqueness, their differences started to appear not as weaknesses, but as different perspectives and different ways of experiencing the world. Accepting these perspectives allowed me to redefine them not as weaknesses or something to fear, but as strengths and gifts that, if supported, not only benefited their lives but also enriched mine.

I look around and still see our fear of that which is different, and our desire for it to go away. Whether embarrassed or scared, we are definitely uncomfortable with differences, so we immediately interpret them as bad and needing to be suppressed or changed. We do more damage by wanting to change our children than by wanting to support them. If we make them "look" normal, then they will be happier, and so will we. If it is not like us, then it is obviously unworthy. I beg you to resist this viewpoint and try to redefine how you see things. Instead of immediately interpreting differences through a negative filter, try looking at them as potential positives, as different perspectives that, when supported, can be developed into strengths and gifts. Before suppressing the difference, observe and listen to it to understand its value. Look for positive value first, to redefine how you interpret it. My experience is that many of these differences are actually gifts that will enhance our own perspective of the world. Try to resist the urge to smother or change the difference because we simply don't understand it. Try identifying the value in it, validating it, and fostering support for it. You will be surprised how the perceived weed can turn into a beautiful flower!

Your children come with a bundle of qualities. Many may look like ours, but many may not. Try to foster the children to develop all their qualities to see how they unfold. In my experience, if we acknowledge, partner with, validate, and support the natural growth of these qualities, the children flourish, develop strong self-esteem, and truly feel safe, accepted, and competent. Take their interests, regardless of how strange they initially appear, and try to view them from a positive perspective. What are they attracted to? What do they seek out? What do they initiate? What do they find pleasure in? Take their interests and turn them into strengths. Start by assuming that these qualities are gifts and that strengths can occur from them. The children will not only feel accepted, supported, and loved, but will also develop into more competent, self-actualized human beings. In turn, they may change your experiences and possibly enrich your own perspectives. You will see the world totally differently and be happier and more fulfilled as a parent, and as a person.

Feeling safe, accepted, and competent

Parents, school staff, and professionals are often so wrapped up in treating the child's deficits that they often do not see the strengths and gifts that the child offers. Developing a profile of strengths, interests, and vulnerabilities helps people focus on developing the child's strengths and on compensating for any vulnerabilities. People are more focused on "curing" autism than on developing the gifts of autism. For some reason, many do not understand that autism, as a diagnosis, is nothing more than a clinical label for specialized services and research. Those of us working directly with the child need to support him by recognizing his neurological vulnerabilities (sensory, digestive, social overload, etc.), patterning a daily routine that matches the child's profile, and using the child's natural interests to develop his strengths. All children have natural gifts and strengths, which, when supported and fostered, will help them grow into the people they naturally are meant to be. We spend so much time forcing them into a profile that doesn't match them, while we ignore and repress their true essence.

For any child, regardless of their profile or label, if you can identify their natural profile of strengths, interests, and vulnerabilities, and use this profile to help them feel safe, accepted, and competent, they will grow and develop with strong self-esteem and gifts to offer the world. So, any parent, school staff, or professional should be asking three primary questions:

1. What helps my child feel *safe and secure*? What are the major sensory/cognitive/social stressors that overwhelm my child and need to be supported? In turn, what does my child need to feel physically safe, sensorily safe, emotionally safe, and socially safe? The child cannot learn unless he feels safe both physically and emotionally. It is the most fundamental need for all of us. Don't just make a list of what to avoid, but also of what to do to help your child feel safe.

2. What helps my child feel *accepted and valued*? Are the people around my child engaging in ways that helps him feel accepted and valued? What interactive patterns promote the feelings of companionship and safe engagement for my child, so he can feel secure with those around him? Does my child respond best to a soft, slow approach or an animated, upbeat style? Does he require a lot of physical touch or avoid it altogether? Does he do best with a firm, direct approach or an inviting style? Every child is different, and to help each child feel accepted and valued we have to match our interactions to his receptive style.

3. What helps my child feel *competent*? What are my child's strengths, interests, and gifts, and how can we build learning and self-esteem around these interests and strengths? When utilizing their strengths and interests in learning activities, all children can learn, grow, and feel confident and good about themselves. Yes, we need to teach new skills and help develop some of their weak areas, but the emphasis should be on taking their interests and building them in their areas of strengths. This approach provides natural motivation and confidence to grow.

These three principles are basic to all humans, regardless of labels and differences. If we hold true to these principles, we support and foster the development of the child's true essence.

Axiom for teachers and caregivers: Help the children feel *safe and accepted* and they will be attracted to you. Help them feel *competent* and they will follow your lead for ever! The sign of a true leader is one who makes everyone around them stronger!

How can a little child make everyone feel so incompetent?

In all my years in the helping profession, I have never seen emotions as intense as those I experience when helping children and families on the spectrum. Whether it be fighting among parents and caregivers, battling between families and schools, struggling with professionals, or battling with government agencies and insurance providers, the frustrations for all parties become strong and emotions run high. People point fingers, throw names and accusations, and threaten action against each other.

What I realized quite early is that nothing makes parents, professionals, and teachers feel more incompetent than a challenging child with autism. These children often do not respond as favorably to the typical parenting, teaching, and treatment strategies that work so well with other children. Their behaviors are so often difficult to read, and their needs are often hidden and inconsistent. They process information differently from us, so their judgment and reasoning do not match ours. They respond well to one strategy this week, only to fight against it the next. Just when they begin to show progress, they suddenly regress and fall backwards. They can be excited with glee one minute and screaming for their life the next. They can be so unpredictable that the best of minds become flustered in confusion. Nothing makes us adults feel more vulnerable than (1) not being in control, (2) not knowing what to do, and (3) having others demanding that we change.

Whether it be parents who feel the stares, the negative comments, and the accusations that their child's behavior is the result of their poor parenting; the teacher who has to somehow provide strong individual accommodations for one child while trying to meet the needs of the total classroom (especially when no one may know what the problems are); or the professional who exhausts all the common therapy tricks in their toolbox, we all have to admit that no one can make us feel more vulnerable and inadequate than children on the spectrum. They are so consistently inconsistent, and their needs fluctuate from one minute to the next. We all have a great need to feel safe, accepted, and competent, and the challenging child on the spectrum threatens this need in all of us.

The principle often spoken by Dr. Ross Greene, author of the *The Explosive Child* (2010)—that all children do the best that they can given the demands that they are under and their abilities to effectively deal with them—applies to all of us. If someone (parent, teacher, professional) is frustrated, angry, and acting inappropriately, we should immediately assume that they do not feel competent in dealing with the demands they are currently facing. Exactly what we do not want everyone to do with our children (demand, scold, punish), we do with each other. We demand, direct, and pressure others into doing something that they do not know how to provide. They feel inadequate and threatened, then they fight back (just like our children). This is a natural reaction as human beings, whether they are adults or children, on or off the spectrum. When we are faced with uncertainty and anxiety, we feel vulnerable and want to escape and avoid the uncertainty. When we are pressured, our fight-or-flight response kicks in and emotions fly.

We need to remember that this vulnerability affects all of us, and we need to take a deep breath, assume that others are feeling just as frustrated and inadequate as we are, and validate and support each other. Focus on what each of us is doing right, and foster our strengths. Find a common ground and facilitate the positive. Understand and validate before we demand change. Acknowledge that we do not have the answers, and that is OK! If we collaborate together in understanding the child, we will eventually find the path to help. Assume that the journey will be filled with hills and valleys, triumphs and backslides, and that no matter how competent you are, they can always bring you to your knees. This is the life of children on the spectrum, as well as for all of us who love them so much. Let's look behind all the negative actions to understand the vulnerabilities in all of us. In order for us to collaborate effectively, we need to be working partners with each other.

Meet me halfway! Value me if you want me to value you!

We are always in such a rush to help the child with autism that we often try to teach before we understand. We automatically assume we know what is good for them before truly understanding them. We want them to listen to us before we listen to them. We want them to comply without first seeing value. We teach them loads and loads of behavior skills, often without teaching the functions that provide value to those skills. We need first to understand and validate how the child sees the world before trying to teach and change. Most of our professional help quickly jumps to identifying and treating deficits without assessing their strengths and gifts. We identify what *we* don't like or what *we* desire before evaluating what *they* need and what *they* desire.

We often teach them how to talk before teaching them how to relate. We teach them social scripts before teaching them the functional value of relating. We teach them to look at us (eye contact) without teaching the value of referencing others to share information, emotion, and experiences. We call them weak in theory of mind and empathy, unable to read the thoughts, feelings, perspectives, and intention of others, while ignoring what *their* thoughts, feelings, and perspectives are. We often force them to learn correct behavior before understanding what their behavior is saying. We want them to do it our way, to be like us without understanding and appreciating their way. We are often more rigid and inflexible than them, and less empathic and understanding. We need to meet them halfway. Always understand, validate, and appreciate first before trying to guide and assist (change). Value their world first before teaching them to value ours. Be a working partner to become a trusted guide. They will enjoy following our lead when we understand, value, and appreciate them first.

Please see past my diagnoses

I am amazed at the number of co-occurring diagnoses that many children are labeled with. Many of the children have five or six diagnoses that supposedly bring meaning to their challenges: attention deficit hyperactivity disorder (ADHD), obsessive compulsive disorder (OCD), opposition defiant disorder (ODD), bipolar, behavior disorder, anxiety, depression, Tourette's, etc. There is a diagnosis to label any cluster of behaviors children exhibit. Unfortunately, over time, in the eyes of many, the children become nothing more than their labels. "He has behavior challenges! Oh…his OCD and ODD explain that! Let's give him a medication that treats that!"

I have learned to not put much stock in many of these diagnoses. They distract people from seeing the child as a human being who simply has a fragile, disorganized nervous system, which makes the world very chaotic, confusing, and overwhelming. We need to identify those vulnerabilities, isolate out what aspects of the world are overwhelming, provide supports to lessen the stressors, and then teach the child coping skills for dealing with the many irritants our world presents for them. All of these children have vulnerabilities, as well as strengths and preferences that can be built upon. They are all children first, who happen to have fragile nervous systems. Like all of us, they simply seek to feel safe, accepted, and competent. There are more than 40 strategies in the toolbox of strategies in this book that address almost all of these challenges to help the child feel safe, accepted, and competent. Forget your labels when identifying strategies. Simply look at the stressors and vulnerabilities, build in supports for them, and then foster your child's strengths and preferences. Regardless of diagnosis, the same principles apply.

These medical diagnoses lead professionals to treat the symptoms with medication. Professionals begin to see the child only in light of these diagnoses and use these diagnoses as a way of explaining why their treatment strategies are not working. I have to repeatedly catch myself from falling into this trap. All the diagnoses direct people to the child's deficits, not to his strengths and emotional needs as a growing, loving child. None of these diagnoses describes any gifts or strengths. Meetings turn to discussions on all these deficits and which medications to try next. Eventually, people stop looking at how to support the delays and vulnerabilities so we can foster the child's strengths and interests. We focus more on how to stop behaviors and change the child, rather than on how to help the child feel safe, accepted, and competent. Over years, many of the children repeatedly change medications, looking for the miracle drug, while no real positive treatment is given. It is too easy to turn to drugs, rather than on proactive strategies. Medications can help calm and organize the nervous system, which is important. However, rarely do they teach the child skills or help them regulate in this world that is chaotic and confusing for them. These diagnoses and medications do not help the child feel safe and accepted. They do not help the child feel socially connected, loved, and loving.

Diagnoses have their place, and medications can be a very effective tool in helping to stabilize the nervous system. However, at these planning meetings, they should not be the talk of the day. Focus on the stressors that cause the major problems for the child, change the demands of these stressors to match the child's abilities, focus on his strengths and preferences, and for each treatment strategy offered ask: "How does this help my child feel safe, accepted, and competent?" Focus on the child, not the labels. Always respect seeing the world from the eyes of the child, starting where the child is at, and gradually building experiences that will make him stronger and happier! Children are not their labels! They are wonderful children who plead for the world to adapt to their needs to allow them to feel safe, connected, and engaged!

The litmus test for behavior/treatment strategies

This book is developed around a toolbox of strategies to help the child feel safe, accepted, and competent. After 30 years in the field, I have narrowed my analysis down to a foundation that we all have a strong need to feel safe, accepted, and competent. In my job, most people approaching me are seeking help in dealing with a host of social, emotional, and behavioral challenges; almost everyone is feeling vulnerable and inadequate in dealing with these challenges. Every individual comes with his own unique strengths and vulnerabilities, social and emotional challenges, and a past history of repeated failure in trying to integrate into society. In addition, all the people supporting the individual (parents, relatives, teachers, etc.) also are frustrated, vulnerable, and feeling incompetent in dealing with the challenges.

In our drastic attempts to change behavior, some may want to assign harmful intent to the child, and punish, suspend, or otherwise force the child to comply. When we don't understand the conditions presenting the challenges, we turn to modifying behavior by manipulating consequences. Many times, without understanding the issues underlying the behavior, it either doesn't help or makes things worse. It often ends up not reducing the conditions presenting the behavior, and instead invalidates the child. Often we are acting out of frustration when we ourselves are feeling inadequate. Just like the child who needs to control when he feels inadequate, adults will do the same when feeling incompetent.

I've found that if we change the conditions around the child so that he feels safe, accepted, and competent, then he will grow and develop. Problematic behavior occurs when we put the child in situations for which the demands of the situation outweigh the child's current skills for dealing with them. The child feels insecure, unaccepted, or incompetent in dealing with the current demands. When the child feels (1) safe and secure physically, socially, and emotionally, (2) accepted, respected, and valued, and (3) competent in tackling the current demands, then problem behaviors subside and adaptive growth occurs. This is why the current "positive behavior supports" systems are mandated (but rarely used correctly) in our school systems. Positive behavior supports are strategies to lessen the stressors, accommodate for vulnerabilities, match demands to current abilities, and teach better skills for dealing with the social and emotional demands.

So, my request of you is to use this model as a litmus test when evaluating strategies that professionals, teachers, family, and friends recommend to use. Ask yourself (and them): "In what way does this strategy help my child feel more safe, accepted, or competent?" If they want your child to lose privileges, force them to stay in situations that are overwhelming them, suspend them from school, or pressure them into compliance, ask them: "In what way does this procedure support my child to feel safe, accepted, and competent?" If it does not help support one of those three things, then be very cautious. Most likely the procedure will just invalidate the child even more and lead him to feel even more incompetent than he already feels. If the procedure doesn't (1) lessen stressors, (2) simplify demands, (3) accommodate vulnerabilities, or (4) teach better skills, it probably is not a good procedure to use. Whatever strategy is used, ask yourself: "How does it support my child to feel safe, accepted, and competent?" If it does, then you cannot go wrong. Everyone will benefit, feel more competent, and grow more connected with each other. This litmus test is simple and accurate.

Value me, to connect with you!

We spend so much time trying to teach the child to "fit in" to our world. We want them to be as "normal" as possible. So we teach, direct, instruct, push, and pressure them to be "like us." This is all done with good intentions and out of love, but it can be invalidating and very exhausting for the child. Of course, the child has to learn to live and co-exist in our world, just like everyone; however, if you truly want to connect emotionally with your child, you must first value his world, if you want him to connect in yours.

"Value their world." What does that mean? If I want to connect with a child on the spectrum, I watch the child and see what he values. What is he attracted to, interested in? What does he seek out? This includes activities, simple repetitive behaviors, sensory preferences, etc. Usually anything the child self-initiates is a strong preference for him. Whether that be music, movement, stacking things, lining things up, smelling things, sifting sand, etc., identify what the child values and include yourself in it! Join in, alongside the child, side by side, doing it together. Put words to what he is doing: "Wow, I love how you do that. That looks like fun!"

Start out with parallel play, with you copying what he is doing, either sitting across from him or at a 45-degree angle. This way he can see what you are doing, while he is doing it. Try to stay within the child's field of vision so he can reference your face and actions. Show animated pleasure in what he and you are doing. Share the experience together, alongside him, without directing. Let him lead and you copy. Let him feel you enjoying what he values, and share the experience with you. Again, put words to what you are doing, simply describing what you are doing, and talking about the pleasure you are having. Use simple language in short phrases.

If the child resists your attempts to engage, then start by simply watching quietly, until that is tolerated. Once the child tolerates you being with him, then slowly start talking, describing what he is doing. Put words to what he is doing. This allows him to feel that you are interested in what he is doing. Then once the child tolerates that, gradually start to include yourself by copying what he is doing. Take any action, vocal noise, or gesture on the part of the child as an invitation to respond back. Place communication intent into your child's responses and expand on them. Let the child lead, but you imitate and expand. Stay patient, follow his lead, put words to what he is doing, and frequently show animated emotion (enjoyment). Stay within his comfort zone. Do not push or pressure; however, you may have to playfully intrude a little. Keep it safe, keep it fun!

If the child does not engage in any purposeful play, start where he is at! If he rocks or flaps his hands, then join in with him. Copy him and turn it into a "we-do" activity. Try to match the pace and stay in sync with the child. Talk about how it feels and how well he is doing it. Feel the movement pattern and how soothing or alerting it is. Understand how it can be enjoyable. Again, stay within his visual field so that the child can easily reference you. Put simple words to what he is doing, and use a lot of nonverbal facial expressions and animated gestures to share the experience. Again, do not direct or try to lead; simply enjoy.

Once the child allows you to engage in parallel play (copying what he is doing) and is sharing pleasure with you (emotion sharing), then try to expand the play to cooperative play, where you and the child engage in the activity together, taking turns, helping each other out, and adding variations to what you are doing ("I wonder what happens if I do this!"). Remember to play in front of the child, or at a 45-degree angle, so the child can reference your face and actions. Use a lot of nonverbal animated facial expressions and exaggerated gestures. Try to engage in reciprocal, back-and-forth interaction and play. Frequently celebrate "doing it together" and remember not to be too directive. Offer suggestions, but allow the child to pace the activity. Keep it simple, keep it fun!

Including yourself in what the child enjoys and values is the best way to connect emotionally with him. Value what he values, and build engagement around it. He will feel the connection, see you as a working partner who values him, and be more likely to feel safe following your lead to enter into your world. Relating is about sharing the two worlds, not pressing the child to give up his to exclusively join yours. It is about valuing his world and feeling safe entering yours. Relating is about bridging the two worlds, not about abandoning one for the other. It is about understanding and appreciating each other's world.

Although the above is oriented to young children, this still applies to older children (and even adults) as well. The best way to connect emotionally is to engage in "we-do" activities around what they value. Whether it is playing video games, collecting coins, looking up history facts, or keeping statistics of favorite sports figures, do it together and share the experience. Make sure time is set aside to engage in what they seek and do! Show interest, engage along with them, and share emotion around it. Value what they value, and appreciate their world. Relating is about sharing the two worlds!

Don't force, invite! If I don't respond, find out why!

In our own impatience and frustration, we tend to push, prompt, direct, and pressure the child to perform. However, as many of you know, children on the spectrum may freeze, withdraw, and, if necessary, act out if forced to respond. We tend to move too fast for many on the spectrum. They usually take longer to process dynamic information than the time we allow them. Most likely if the child is not responding, he either does not understand what is expected, doesn't know how to perform what you are asking, is overwhelmed and scared, or feels incompetent. If he doesn't understand, we need to clarify and verify. If he is overwhelmed and scared, we need to back up, slow down, and make the demand simpler. If he does not know how to perform what is expected, we need to support and guide.

In almost all cases, if the child is not responding, pressure and force will only produce fear and panic. We need to let the child "pace" the learning and feel safe in knowing we are not going to demand, force, or pressure him to respond. *Invite* engagement. If the child does not feel safe, accepted, and competent enough to respond, back up, understand why, and then provide the support needed for the child to feel safe and competent enough to engage. If the child is not responding, it is our responsibility to change, not his. As impatient as we may be to move on, we have to assume responsibility for not understanding and respect the conditions needed to respond. The more rigid the child's response, the more flexible our approach must be. Listen, learn, respect, and provide. We need to meet resistance with compassion, and listen to what he needs. Unless he perceives us as a working partner with him, he will not accept us as a trusted guide.

What every child wants us to know!

"I would if I could. If I don't, then I can't! So don't blame me, support me!"

Assume that each child does the best he can, given the situation that he is in, and the skills that he has. In times of difficulty, either scale down the demands, or increase the support. It is the adult's responsibility to change, not the child's. If we take this stance, we may not always be right, but we will never go wrong! Understand first, before changing behavior, and most of all do not blame the child. Change the conditions, lower the demands, provide better support, and teach greater skills. This puts the responsibility for change on the adult, not the child.

This is a premise that we have to remind ourselves of every day when tackling the challenges of autism. Because of the deep frustration and our own feelings of inadequacy when parenting/teaching these children, we often blame the child. I have done it, we all have done it. It comes at times when we feel incompetent in helping the child. Just as it applies to the child, it also applies to us! "Assume *we* are doing the best that we can, given the situation we are in, and the current skills that we have." Unfortunately, since we cannot change the demands, we have to (1) gain greater skills and (2) increase the supports to help us out.

ACCEPT, RESPECT, AND CONNECT WITH THE SEVERELY IMPAIRED

The following real-life experiences are examples of developing emotional connections with very vulnerable individuals. They use the principles of acceptance and understanding, valuing and validating, and using the person's strengths to emotionally and socially connect. All human beings deserve to feel safe, accepted, and valued by those around them!

Valuable lessons! Thank you, Jimmy!

Some may disagree with me, but I have learned over the years that a life with no human contact is a life devoid of personal meaning. For the very severely impaired, life can be so chaotic and frightening that they will go to great extremes to escape and avoid all stimulation except that which they can provide themselves. They avoid all contact with other humans, because they do not feel safe or trust those around them.

Starting out my career in the back wards of a large mental health institution taught me the gift of touching the hearts of some of the most vulnerable and challenging individuals. Individuals whose nervous systems were so disorganized and fragile that they tore at their skin, repeatedly banged their heads or bit themselves until they required physical restraints. Individuals who had learned that human contact was demanding and threatening, that eating their own feces was more rewarding than engaging with others. Daily reminders that the best way to avoid human contact was to smear saliva on themselves and vomit on others. These were people, just like you and me, but with lonely, broken hearts that had not experienced the warmth of human touch and the security of human presence.

The very first day of my professional career, I approached a group of individuals who were living in one of the buildings I was going to service. They were all sitting outside enjoying a warm summer day. As I approached, I noticed a young man sitting on the ground, poking a twig into his right eye! I ran over to stop him, listening to the staff chuckling behind me. As I approached, the man poked even harder. I pulled his hand down and was startled that he did not have an eyeball in that socket! Staff chuckled because supposedly he did that for attention, so they ignored it. Consequently, he had lost an eye to that abuse. That man became one of my greatest success stories over that year.

Jimmy also had a host of other nasty behaviors (vomiting, biting himself, slapping himself, and head banging), all of which occurred when others would approach him. I couldn't truly tell if he was trying to draw people to him, or push people away. Every time we approached, he would engage in the behavior. At times it appeared that he would also engage in the behavior to draw you to him. It was obvious to me that the only way that Jimmy knew to deal with his social world was through self-abuse. He did not feel connected any other way. The only time people touched him was to do something to him (personal care). His experience with human contact was negative: others forcing him to do things he didn't want to do, or doing things to him that were uncomfortable.

The only preference that I could tell Jimmy had was food. He would eat just about anything. I wanted to teach Jimmy to welcome our presence and enjoy our touch. I found two staff who were willing to help me on this endeavor. We would approach Jimmy once every 15 minutes with small bits of food. As usual, as we approached he would immediately start to self-abuse. We said nothing about the behavior, gently blocked the abuse, and gave him the parcel of food. We paired the small parcel of food with a gentle touch to the back of his head, and a few nice words. We approached slowly and gently, blocked the self-abuse, and made our presence rewarding. We called these "approach trials," providing frequent, non-demanding, positive interaction at least once every 15 minutes. We did not demand anything of him, or force anything on him. We wanted to teach him to welcome our approach and value our presence.

We did this for most of the day, for two solid weeks—hundreds of rewarding approach trials. Jimmy gradually started to value our presence and would watch for us to approach. We began to initiate all interaction by putting out our hands. Staff would put out their hands to invite Jimmy to put his hands in theirs, then reinforced him with a parcel of food and a soft touch to the back of the head. We were teaching "safe hands," which is a technique I still use today to teach safety in my touch. It communicates "I'm OK, you're OK," and starts off the interaction with a safe connection.

Jimmy began to allow us to sit with him for extended periods of time just to talk and hang with him. He could not speak, but communicated with his warm gaze and soft touch. It wasn't long before he came to value our presence enough that we could stop using food to invite him. He would walk with us, roll a ball back and forth with us, and engage in simple object placement tasks with our assistance. He learned to enjoy our touch, voices, and engagement. Over the next three years, he began to come out of his shell and trust engaging with us in water play, simple music activity, swinging together, and ball play. He no longer self-abused when we approached. He would still self-abuse whenever he was pressed into situations of uncertainty, but he would allow us to interrupt the abuse with the "safe hands" technique with which we taught him to trust. He came to smile, laugh, and give us hugs, and trust us in stretching his comfort zones.

I don't know what happened to Jimmy when he finally left the facility for community living, but I know that he taught me the valuable lesson of human companionship and what life is like without it. Jimmy, thank you so very much. This lesson has stayed with me all these years!

When autism brings multiple sensory impairments!

One of my roles in my professional career has been providing behavioral and psychological services for individuals with developmental disabilities who live in community group homes. Usually my services have focused on developing positive behavior support plans for individuals with multiple challenging behaviors.

I had a request from one of the homes to help out a young lady on the spectrum who was both deaf and blind. Without sight or hearing, her connection with her environment was very limited. Her actual cognitive level was unknown, since her multiple sensory impairments made assessment difficult. This lady was very anxious and insecure. She would become agitated, throw things, hit others, pull hair, grab tightly, and rip the clothes off those trying to help her. She was very strong, and often would grab and refuse to let go, or put staff in a head lock. Consequently, others were very nervous when providing care for this lady, and projected a sense of defensiveness toward her. As can be imagined, staff avoided interacting with Carol, unless they needed to provide care for her. This meant that most interactions were instrumental (bathing, feeding, oral care, toileting, etc.), rather than for relating and having fun together. Most interactions consisted of staff handling her or physically guiding her through actions.

When first observing staff interacting with Carol, I noticed she would seek out deep pressure touch. Of course, being deaf and blind, her sense of touch was very important to her. She would bang on the tray of her wheelchair when she wanted something, but would be very rough in grabbing staff when they approached. Everything she did was very firm and rough. When upset, she would pull staff into her and hold on to them very tightly. If your head was too close, she would grab your hair and hold on until others pried her fingers loose. She didn't know how to regulate her touch. Everything was too hard and rough.

The first step in helping staff to bond with Carol was to institute "approach trials." Since they avoided her unless they had to provide necessary personal care, all contact with Carol was to have something done to her. This made interaction negative and uninviting. With approach trials, the staff's role was to approach Carol at least once every 15–30 minutes simply to relate with her, while placing no demands on her—simply to relate and connect with Carol. No demands, no forcing care, just to relate. The purpose was twofold. I wanted to decrease Carol's fear of the staff, as well as decrease the staff's fear of Carol. She could read the staff's anxiety level and react accordingly. I wanted numerous, non-demanding contact simply to relate with her.

During these approach trials, all staff were instructed first to tap on the tray of her wheelchair to let her know they were there, then to touch Carol's hand for her to reach out and take the staff's hand in hers. Staff would provide deep pressure massage to the palm of her hand, and eventually up her forearm. We also paired this with gentle clapping of her hands with theirs. I had the staff talk quietly to her, sometimes singing, and sometimes talking about what her day would be like. "Why?" they would ask, since she was deaf. Talking is part of relating, and I wanted staff to feel themselves relating with her, to feel relaxed in connecting with her.

Carol liked this and would immediately put out her hand when staff tapped her tray. She learned to seek out the hand and to feel safe with the staff's touch. I call this "safe hands" and teach every individual I work with to trust my touch. Carol learned to allow others to provide deep pressure touch to the palms of her hands, rather than having to grab and hold others tightly. She was learning to let the staff regulate the touch, and feel safe with it. Carol was feeling more safe, and the staff were feeling safer with her. This is a fundamental first step that must be established before any teaching can occur.

Once we felt safe touching Carol, I wanted to probe having her "feel" my voice, so she could further connect with me. I started to put her hand up to my neck, so she could feel the vibration when I talked to her. I had to be very careful with this since she could grab very tightly. I felt that I could do a "pull back release" if I had to. I never had to. This turned out to be the best way to relate with Carol. She would smile as soon as she started to feel the vibration of my voice. I would hum, sing, talk in sing-song, and provide rhythmic vocal patterns. Between the hand massage and voice vibration, Carol was starting to become alert and attend to staff, and respond back in reciprocal fashion. Carol would frequently laugh and make vocal noises; I would go back and forth, from her feeling my voice to her feeling her voice. She learned to tell staff apart by their vibration and touch, which provided more predictability to her world.

In watching Carol, over time it was obvious that much of her acting out was in reference to the uncertainty of the world around her. She didn't know what was coming next and what staff were going to do to her. To help provide greater predictability for Carol, we would use a sequence board to explain to her what was coming up. We used objects for each task, such as a toothbrush for oral care, a small piece of wash cloth for bathing, a spoon for eating, etc. We would Velcro three objects on a Velcro board so she could feel each item in sequence of what would happen. This way it provided Carol with knowledge of what would be coming up. When staff approached her for each task, they would tap her tray, provide brief deep pressure to her palm, and then place the object in her hand. This became the way for staff to communicate a predictable routine for Carol. This, together with the approach trials, greatly reduced her anxiety and made her world more predictable.

Over time, both Carol and the staff learned to relax and enjoy each other's company. They would talk, laugh, and sing by feeling the vibration, clap together, provide deep pressure, and stroke the palms of her hands. Our next step was to have a speech therapist teach staff and Carol how to use manual sign communication in the palm of Carol's hand. This was new to me. I had not seen this before. Staff taught her the manual alphabet. This is when we knew that Carol was much brighter than people expected. Staff become very skillful in using palm signing and Carol was developing a list of receptive vocabulary with which staff could communicate what was coming up for her. Between using objects, voice vibration, and palm signing, her social world was opening up and she was learning to feel the value in relating with others. This was very reinforcing, not only to her but for the others who worked with her each day. Her acting out was reduced significantly, her ability to relate with others grew tremendously, and she became an active participant in her daily routine. She now could find joy in socializing and in her daily routine. Her world changed significantly! She started to feel safe, accepted, and competent in her social world!

Establishing "safety" in human contact

Every person yearns to be engaged with those around them. However, many individuals with severe impairments do not feel safe or know how to connect with others. No matter how impaired or withdrawn a person is, there is always an avenue to their heart. You have to look closely to see it, but if you identify the "safe zone" and become engaged with it, you are on your way.

We had a young man with autism who was nonverbal and very self-abusive. He had a long history of frequently hitting his head when frustrated. Also, staff could not get him engaged in functional activity. He was resistant to following their lead and would refuse to engage in functional activity. However, he would initiate interaction with staff by taking their hands in his and clapping them against his ears. He enjoyed the feel of slapping the hands of others against his ears. Of course, staff would pull away from this because of the fear it would be seen as abusing him. However, this was the one self-initiated interaction he would make. It was the one interaction that he felt safe with. He would seek out others to provide him with this sensory experience.

Staff were amazed when I instructed them to use this "ear clapping" to engage the young man. I asked the staff to put out their hands and let him clap his ears with them. I wanted them to use the one social interaction that he felt safe with, that felt good to him. We used this response to engage him in a "we-do" activity together. We used this interaction to create a social connection. Instead of discouraging it, we embraced it.

We had staff approach him at least once every half an hour and put out their hands for him to clap his ears with. They talked softly to him and provided warm interaction, while he clapped his ears with their hands. Staff gave him their hands and would stand face to face and provide warm interaction while he clapped his ears. This helped him feel safe and connected with staff. We were using the one interaction pattern that helped him feel safe and accepted, by using the sensory stimulation that he enjoyed. He loved this and frequently initiated it.

Once this moment of companionship was established, I requested staff to expand the response from clapping to pressing their hands against his ears to provide deep pressure into his ears. He seemed to enjoy this. It wasn't long before he was seeking the deep pressure, rather than the clapping. Over time we expanded the deep pressure from the ears to the back of his neck. Each time staff would approach him, they would massage the back of his neck while providing warm, positive, face-to-face interaction. This would elicit a warm smile from him.

We next turned the clapping to his ears to just clapping his hands together in a rhythmic pattern. He enjoyed this clapping, and staff could engage him in simple rhythmic clapping. This was another interaction pattern we could do when initiating interaction and soothing him during agitation. Eventually, he would allow us to provide deep pressure squeezes to his hands, which became another calming strategy. This gave staff three interaction strategies (clapping hands, neck massage, and hand massage) that they could use to establish emotional connection.

Over time, this young man became more aware of, and responsive to, staff engaging him in normal, daily activities as long as we started every interaction with "safe hands" (massage to head, ears, or hands). When he was upset and self-abusive, staff could now use "safe hands" massage to interrupt and redirect his hands from hitting himself. He started allowing staff to sooth him with the deep pressure stimulation. This young man became more responsive to others and more engaged in his daily routine. He learned to trust others and to follow their lead. We were no longer people who were trying to make him do things, but people who helped him feel good. Our hands became something to value, rather than something to avoid. It is amazing when you start where the person is at, value what he values, and gradually build the relationship.

These three examples above demonstrate the power of establishing a sense of companionship by understanding, accepting, and valuing the person's unique qualities and interests. We taught that our touch, words, and presence were safe and rewarding. In essence, we entered into the person's world, into their comfort zone, to establish a social connection. We included ourselves in their world to share a valued experience. We redefined what people initially defined as inappropriate and challenging. The behavior became a vehicle for establishing a social connection and eventual companionship. This is the essence of teaching the person to feel safe, accepted, and competent in our presence. To reach out and share experiences with us. To connect, feel valued, and welcome the engagement of others.

Why can't people understand me?

Adults on the spectrum often ask me to explain why neurotypical (NT) people don't understand them, often misinterpret their actions, and seem to lack empathy with what they are experiencing. For those on the spectrum who try very hard to build relationships, regulate with co-workers on the job, and build lasting friendships, it is difficult to understand why NT people often avoid their attempts to relate. In explaining this problem, we focus on why it is difficult for NT people to be empathic with them. As you will see, the information is pretty "intellectual." The great thing about many on the spectrum is that they *are* very intellectual.

Most NT people have a difficult time empathizing with people with ASD. The reason has to do with our brains being wired a little differently, and experiencing the world a little differently. Part of empathy has to do with "like minds" reading "like minds." The person is assuming that the other is processing and experiencing the world in a similar fashion. Part of empathy is also interpreting the other's actions, facial expressions, and body language by comparing the communication to past experiences relating with this person, as well as others. Empathy is not really being able to "read" the thoughts and feelings of others; it is inferring these mental states from the person's words and nonverbal communication. Since the person with ASD does not use nonverbal communication in the same fashion and tends to process information a little differently, the NT person is going to struggle with empathy.

All empathy is inferring from communication (both verbal and nonverbal), based on a general knowledge of what we know about the person already, past experience with interacting with "like" others, and the social context in which the communication is occurring.

Empathy is based heavily on unwritten rules of nonverbal communication. If the person with ASD uses different, or less, nonverbal communication, the NT person will struggle to understand. Yes, to some degree NT people are going to struggle empathizing with people on the spectrum and thus have difficulty understanding the stress and strain that those on the spectrum feel trying to regulate through normal daily demands. All empathy is based on numerous assumptions and unwritten rules common to the person. Empathy improves between people who share common worlds. The greater the differences, the more inaccurate our interpretation. That is one reason why there is always so much friction and war between radically different cultures, like we have now in the world.

The more accurate information the person has about the other, the greater the ability to empathize. It is not so much that the person with ASD can't empathize if they have the right information to infer from, it is more that making these inferences requires the ability rapidly to read facial expressions and body language, understand the words, compare this to like experiences they have had in the past, and interpret it in the social context in which it is being presented.

Part II

COGNITIVE ISSUES IN AUTISM

Chapter 2

COGNITIVE PROCESSING DIFFERENCES

Autism, in its simplest definition, is an "information processing disorder." In many ways it may be argued that it isn't a "disorder," but is a different style of processing information. Simply speaking, our brains are wired a little differently. To understand how people on the spectrum experience the world, and in turn understand their often confusing behavior, you have to know how they process information, how they experience the world. By understanding these qualities, we can help them (and us) to bridge the differences between the two worlds. This series of articles will provide an understanding of the common cognitive processing differences associated with autism spectrum disorders.

As a reminder, you may see some basic principles being repeated in many of these articles. The reason for this is that these articles are posted on the Facebook page, Autism Discussion Page. Since each post is designed to be an independent, stand-alone article, a few basic principles are repeated frequently throughout the articles. They are very important principles, so repetition of them is important.

COMMON COGNITIVE STRUGGLES IN AUTISM

- Problems rapidly processing multiple information simultaneously.

- Delayed processing.

- Focus on details (facts); difficulty seeing the whole picture.

- Interpretation of things literally; blind to context and invisible relationships between the details.

- Poor higher-level abstract thinking/problem solving.

- Rigid, inflexible (black and white) thinking.

- Difficulty shifting gears (transitions, change in plans).

- Poor executive functioning (planning, organizing, following through).
- Difficulty processing rapid change; rigid adherence to familiar routine.

This list summarizes some of the major differences in processing that have been categorized as autistic thinking. As we go through this series of articles, we will take a closer look at most of them. When put together, the way the brains of those on the spectrum are wired makes processing our neurotypical world very difficult and taxing. Their cognitive differences make our world very chaotic and confusing. What makes this a disability is the simple fact that their processing differences do not match the cognitive demands presented by our neurotypical culture. They are literally strangers in a strange land—a land whose processing expectations do not match the abilities of people on the spectrum. However, when placed in a situation that requires processing of static, concrete, factual details, their processing is often superior to ours. That is why they often can be superior in engineering, computer sciences, physical sciences, history, arts, and many other fields that rely heavily on facts, details, pattern analysis, and mechanical and electrical reasoning. However, when it comes to rapidly processing dynamic information, they struggle with processing differences and this can result in the difficulties listed above.

THREE MAJOR CATEGORIES OF COGNITIVE CHALLENGES

1. Information processing problems:
   a. delayed processing
   b. focus on detail, not context.
2. Rigid, inflexible thinking:
   a. absolute vs. relative thinking
   b. black and white, either/or thinking.
3. Executive functioning problems:
   a. poor attention, planning, and organization
   b. poor self-monitoring and impulse control.

This series of articles breaks down the cognitive differences into three main categories: information processing, executive functioning, and flexibility of thinking. The articles will look at these categories separately; however, in reality, these qualities are strongly interrelated and greatly influence each other.

Information processing differences

Like a processor in a computer, our brain is a processor of information. Just as computers come with different speeds of processing, so do our individual brains. Some of us process information differently and more rapidly than others. As you will see, the brains of people on the spectrum are more similar to the processors in a computer than the brains of neurotypical people. This presents both strengths and weaknesses.

Our world is very fast-paced, with continual flux of rapidly changing information flooding our nervous system moment to moment. We are taking in multiple streams of information that must be rapidly filtered and integrated smoothly together. Our nervous system has to filter out what is not important, understand the "invisible context," integrate multiple sources of information simultaneously, rapidly categorize and appraise the overall meaning, as well as evaluate how to respond. We have to multitask all these processes simultaneously, requiring rapid processing of multiple information.

The brains of neurotypical people are more synchronized to process this flux of information. Our culture is patterned this way because we are the ones who dictate the pace of our world. We can rapidly process this information simultaneously, most of it subconsciously with minimal mental effort. Most of this processing—about 80 percent—we do intuitively without thinking about it or even being aware that it is occurring. We quickly scan the information for a few facts and immediately infer the overall meaning. We continually assimilate and accommodate new information and constantly re-adapt our responses to it. We smoothly process rapidly changing information, while focusing our attention on the demands at hand.

To be able to rapidly process and integrate all this information, we have to have good communication between the different centers of the brain. At any given time, we have information coming into different areas of the brain simultaneously. These areas all serve different functions but have to work together, simultaneously communicating with each other to integrate all this information. This is what allows us to rapidly process all this information with little effort. Our brain does most of this subconsciously, with minimal mental effort.

Recent research shows that the brains of people on the spectrum have weak neuropathways (connections) between the various brain centers. The pathways connecting the different brain centers do not allow the smooth communication needed to rapidly integrate dynamic information. This makes it difficult subconsciously to process multiple information simultaneously. Instead, people on the spectrum have to process this information "sequentially," bit by bit, consciously sorting out the details. They have to think their way through the information which we process subconsciously, with little mental energy.

Research shows that this connectivity problem occurs from both under-connectivity in some areas and over-connectivity in other areas of the brain. Either there are fewer neuropathways connecting some areas of the brain, or there are too many weak connections in other areas, scattering overwhelming information chaotically. Either way, there is major interference in the brain centers' ability to communicate and integrate dynamic information.

This weak neuroconnectivity results in different styles of thinking. We tend to rapidly process, integrate, compare and contrast, categorize and appraise dynamic information very smoothly. We tend to infer overall meaning intuitively and smoothly with little conscious thought, whereas people on the spectrum tend to reach meaning by sequentially analyzing the numerous, concrete details. They have to piece together the puzzle, one piece at a time.

We think differently

We tend to look past the details to infer the whole, overall meaning. We infer the invisible relationships between the parts to find the underlying meaning. We define the individual details by the context in which they are occurring. For those on the spectrum, the overall meaning is tied to putting together the individual details. Their brains are stronger at seeing the details, but weaker at reading the context to infer the invisible relationships between the parts. This requires greater thinking through the details, rather than intuitively inferring the meaning. This conscious thinking through requires a lot of mental energy.

Neurotypical people also tend quickly to infer the overall meaning from a few parts, while ignoring many of the individual details. We then use this inferred overall meaning to determine what details are important to focus on. We often gloss over imperfections in the details without even noticing them. People on the spectrum will often not only see the imperfections but may also hyper-focus and get stuck on these imperfections.

Simultaneous vs. sequential processing

When the brain has good neuroconnections, it can process all the multiple information simultaneously, integrating it for one overall meaning. When your brain cannot simultaneously integrate this information, it has to sort through the information sequentially. People on the spectrum often have to consciously figure out what we process intuitively.

This sequential reasoning slows down the processing, leaving the individual missing much of the rapidly changing information. Not only is it difficult to process multiple information simultaneously, but it also results in delayed information processing, sometimes requiring 30–60 seconds (or more) to process what we may process in a few seconds. This is very draining and also often leaves those on the spectrum struggling to keep up with the speed of information. Frequently they are left processing only bits and pieces of the total information, since much of it came and went before it could be processed. So, when you are acting on only pieces of the information, your interpretation and resulting behavior often is out of sync with the rest of us. This is often why the person on the spectrum seems to be a little offbeat with us when interacting.

Many people on the spectrum actually think in pictures, and not in words. They have to rapidly translate our words into pictures before they can interpret meaning. This further slows down and delays the processing.

ASD thinking

- Strengths:
    - Good awareness of detail.
    - Good memory for facts, statistics, and other static information.
    - Literal thinking results in less biased interpretation of facts.
    - Can have very strong photographic memory.
    - Great awareness of sensory patterns.
    - Good concrete, logical reasoning.
- Weaknesses:
    - Slow sequential processing.
    - Difficulty seeing the big picture.
    - Difficulty processing rapidly changing information.
    - Difficulty with vague, multiple meanings.
    - Struggles with abstract reasoning that requires ongoing comparing, contrasting, reflecting and projecting.

As with all thinking styles, ASD thinking has both strengths and weaknesses. People on the spectrum are very good with analyzing detail, memorizing facts, seeing sensory patterns, and seeing mechanical and electrical detail. They are less biased in evaluating, because they tend only to see the facts. However, they struggle in situations that require rapid processing of dynamically changing information, reading underlying invisible relationships between the parts, understanding multiple meanings and vague information, and appraising and evaluating multiple options. People on the spectrum are going to have problems multitasking and filtering out distracting information. They either will hyper-focus on specific, sometimes irrelevant details or get distracted by too much information struggling for attention.

Brain drain

Everything that we do during the day uses both physical and mental energy. As we go through the day, we expend energy and slowly drain our reserves as the day moves along. We eat and sleep to replenish our energy supply to get us through the next day. Our energy fuel range consists of both the human body (physical reserve) and the brain (mental reserve). As we go through the day, we use up both physical and mental energy. The amount of energy (reserve) we start the day with will be determined by (1) how draining the day before was, (2) whether we had a good night sleep, (3) whether we are fighting off an illness, and (4) if we eat a good breakfast. If we are out of shape, in poor health, and/or anxious in general, then our nervous system is disorganized and running hard (out of tune and working too hard). Now, if we slept poorly, do not eat breakfast, have to rush because we are running late, run into a traffic jam on our way to work, or have to return home because we rushed out and forgot something, we are taxing our energy reserves before we even start the meat of our day.

As the day rolls on, the more disorganized and out of sync our nervous system is, and the busier, more stressful, and mentally exhausting the day becomes, the more taxed our system becomes and the more energy gets depleted. The more taxed the nervous system becomes, the harder it runs and the less efficient it is in handling current demands. The person's concentration, cognitive abilities, and coping skills begin to deteriorate. The immediate demands become harder to process, evaluate, and adapt to. Without rest, food, and proper maintenance, the nervous system exhausts itself.

For people on the spectrum, the nervous system is more fragile, disorganized, and anxious. Their nervous system has extreme difficulty processing the very hectic, chaotic flow of our daily routine. Their nervous system has difficulty rapidly processing multiple information simultaneously. Our world simply moves way too fast, with too much information coming too quickly for them to process smoothly. Processing smoothly in our world requires the ability to rapidly process multiple information simultaneously. It requires simultaneous communication between the different brain centers to process smoothly this bombardment of information. In addition, in order for us to be able to concentrate on the task in the moment, our nervous system has to process most of this incoming information subconsciously so as not to distract our concentration, or use up valuable fuel. For neurotypical people, at least 80 percent of this processing is done subconsciously, while using minimal mental energy. Unfortunately, much of what we take for granted and process subconsciously, people on the spectrum have to process consciously (think about), draining precious mental energy. Because the neurological pathways between the different brain centers are not strong, people on the spectrum have difficulty rapidly processing multiple information simultaneously. Instead of smoothly processing this information simultaneously at a subconscious level, they have to process it sequentially, by consciously thinking about it, piecing this information together bit by bit. This slows down the processing and requires extensive mental energy to think through what we usually process without thinking. This taxes the nervous system and drains both physical and mental energy much faster. This means for the child at school, or the adult at work, the typical day of processing and regulating the normal daily demands will require so much more mental energy than it does for those of us not on the spectrum.

This is the normal processing (sequential as opposed to simultaneous) of the person on the spectrum. Now, for those who have extensive sensory processing issues, auditory processing problems, and language processing difficulties, the processing of incoming information is even more delayed and fragmented, taxing the nervous system even more (similar to the car that is out of tune, engine running too fast, and misfiring constantly). To make matters worse, many people on the spectrum have other inhibiting factors such as poor sleep patterns, nutritional problems, weakened immune system, constipation, seizure activity, and high anxiety, so the nervous system is further taxed, depleting their energy reserves even further.

For those with severe sensory, language, and information processing issues, every minute they are interacting in our world is continually depleting an already constricted mental and physical energy reserve. Simply regulating through a relatively normal day can be totally exhausting for them, if they do not get a chance to withdraw, rebound, and replenish their energy reserve. Research has shown that the average amount of stress chemicals in the nervous system of someone on the spectrum is much higher, even in a resting state, than a person not on the spectrum. Their nervous system is often anxious and on high alert, even in a resting state. When you add the difficulty the nervous system has simply processing normal daily activity, it becomes taxed and drained quickly, which reduces its ability to process effectively, further taxing the energy supply. The stress chemicals continue to accumulate as the day goes on, until the system gets overloaded, shuts down, and/or melts down.

Do you ever see that "look"?

Many children, as they start to become overloaded, will show you a "freeze response." They often look away, get a glazed look in their eyes, and "zone out." Sometimes the child may engage in stimming, shut his eyes, put his head down, or cover his ears. This is the temporary moment that cues us in that the child is becoming overwhelmed. Information is coming in too fast, or there is too much for him to process. The brain will initially try to shut down or block out the stimulation to avoid overload. For many children, this freeze moment means to "back off" demands, lower stimulation, and allow them to rebound. Respect this sign, because the child is trying to keep it together by escaping the stimulation that is overwhelming him.

Be careful. When we view the child's unresponsiveness as resistance and noncompliance, we tend to increase our prompting and press him to respond. This will further overload the child who is trying to keep it together and rebound. This temporary "freeze" is just that: temporary! If you continue to press the child, he goes from "freeze" to "fight-or-flight" (panic). The brain, in essence, freaks or panics, and will act out to fight or flee. Then the child is labeled as violent, aggressive, and disruptive!

So please, when you see this freeze response, (1) acknowledge that you see the child getting overwhelmed, (2) back off all demands and lower your voice, (3) reassure him that he is safe and accepted, and (4) allow him time to rebound. Minimize your interaction, to prevent overloading the child. Simply allow him to escape and rebound. Help him feel safe at a time when he is feeling vulnerable. Often the child can rebound simply by pulling away the demands and lowering the stimulation.

Try to analyze the event to understand what may be overwhelming the child. It could be that the demands are too hard or coming too fast or simply that the child is getting exhausted. He could be overwhelmed by the noise or activity going on around him, panic in response to something unexpected, or simply freeze due to task performance anxiety. Once the child has rebounded, be aware that his nervous system is still pretty drained and can be easily overwhelmed again. Minimize demands, break them down into simpler steps, proceed with a slower pace, and provide added assistance to support the child. Many children, if you respect these cues, back off and reassure them, rebound quickly and can continue the activity. Others may need to escape to a safe area to regroup and rebound. If you respect this "freeze" response and support the child, he will trust you and follow your lead!

HOW CAN WE HELP?

When in doubt, let the child set the pace!

I don't know how many of you have noticed! Your child has a processing speed and pace at which he will do things. You cannot rush it. Many kids on the spectrum have delayed information processing and slow responding. We often try to hurry them along, but it never works. They freeze and resist the pressure, which often makes things worse. The harder we push, the stronger they resist. This is because the brain cannot move faster than it processes. It goes into panic, freeze mode, or fight-or-flight. We always need to be respectful of that and let the child pace the speed of action. Unfortunately, it is uncomfortable for us, but it is necessary for him. It is a natural tendency to want the child to match our pace, but that is often not possible. Let him set the pace to feel comfortable and competent!

Reduce confusion: break it down, slow it down, and make it clear

We have discussed how the brains of people on the spectrum are wired differently from ours. Because they have weak neurological connections (pathways) between the different brain centers, they have difficulty rapidly processing multiple information simultaneously. The neurotypical brain can integrate multiple information simultaneously and integrate this information smoothly. The person on the spectrum needs to process this information sequentially, piecing it together, bit by bit, at a conscious level. They have to think through what we intuitively understand. This slows down and taxes the processing, resulting in delayed informational processing.

How can we help? What can we do to support the person when communicating and teaching? How can we bridge the two worlds of processing so we can communicate and relate more smoothly?

Break it down, slow it down, and make it clear!

1. "Break it down!" The first thing we can do is avoid providing multiple information simultaneously and not expect people on the spectrum to multitask several steps or jobs at one time. Break it down into sequential parts. Provide information sequentially, one step at a time, so they can process it and integrate it. Break tasks down into simple steps and lay out the sequence of actions. Lay the information out for them to think it through.

2. "Slow it down!" Because people on the spectrum cannot process multiple information simultaneously and must process it sequentially, slow it down and give them time to process (think it through). Keep your verbal statements short. Slow it down and give extra time for them to process. You may need to allow 10–30 seconds for them to process and give you a response. Let them pace the learning so as to not overwhelm them. When communicating and teaching, break it down and slow it down, allowing plenty of time to process and respond.

3. "Make it clear!" Get to the point and make it clear. People on the spectrum think in concrete, detailed facts. They need very concrete, literal information that is factual, not filled with assumptions and inferences. Get to the point, stick to the point, and make it literal and factual. When possible, present information visually so they can see it. Written words, pictures, diagrams, visual flow charts, and visual models provide a constant resource to reference. Our spoken words are fleeting and easily lost in translation.

4. "Say what you mean, and mean what you say!" Do not beat around the bush, sugar-coat things, or assume anything. Be factual and be consistent. Nothing more and nothing less. People on the spectrum need to know that the information is consistent and predictable. Inconsistencies and unpredictability can lead them into fright and panic. If they cannot understand and predict, they cannot trust.

Our thinking styles and communication styles are radically different. Therefore, we have to provide information so that they can process and communicate in a manner they can understand. Simply speaking, to relate effectively, we need to slow *our* world down. "Break it down, slow it down, and make it clear!"

Clarify, verify, preview, and review

Children on the spectrum fear uncertainty. Much of our world is chaotic and confusing to them. When giving expectations or going into events and activities, prepare them ahead of time by previewing what will happen and what to expect. Lay out a mental map for them to increase understanding and decrease anxiety. When previewing:

1. Clarify

   a. Clarify what he can expect to happen. Explain concretely what is going to happen, how long it will occur, and what is happening afterwards. Make it as predictable as possible.

b. Clarify what is expected of him. Explain what he will be expected to do, how he will be expected to act, what others will be doing.

c. Identify possible difficult times. This may include waiting, conversing with others, sharing with other children. Identify coping strategies to deal with them. Anticipate snags and plan for them. Preview how he can deal with them.

d. Identify an escape route! Make sure he knows how to get out of the situation if it starts to get too overwhelming.

2. Verify

a. Don't assume that he understands; have him verify that he understands it.

b. Go over steps that are confusing until he can verify what to expect and how to handle it.

3. Preview

a. Preview this information when planning the event and then again just before going into the event.

b. Periodically throughout the activity, preview any new developments or changes.

4. Review

a. Following the event, review how it went. Discuss what went right, what went wrong, and what may need to be different next time.

Reduce confusion: provide a "mental map"

We have discussed how the information in our world simply moves too fast for many people on the spectrum. They have to think sequentially about that which we easily process subconsciously. Given these processing differences, our world (culture) can be chaotic, confusing, and literally overwhelming for those on the spectrum. We talked about the importance of breaking it down, slowing it down, and making it clear. Information needs to be very factual, concrete, and literal.

Another concept that is important in supporting those on the spectrum is providing them with a "mental map" to navigate our often confusing world. Many writers who have autism relate that we (neurotypical people) seem to have a mental map to help us navigate our world. We understand the unwritten rules, invisible relationships, and abstract contexts that provide automatic meaning and direction. People on the spectrum do not have this mental map and are lost without it. Consequently, our world is vague, confusing, and unpredictable for them. This creates strong insecurity and anxiety.

Make life predictable; provide them with a mental map!

1. Predictable routines and visual schedules (written or pictures) are very important. Sequencing out the immediate future makes life more understandable and predictable. Scheduling out the day or portions of the day and then writing out the schedule (or using pictures) can provide strong predictability to the day. Whether it be a picture schedule, a written checklist, an appointment book, or smartphone, sequencing out the immediate future is so important in laying out a mental map. Changes can be made more easily when they are presented in advance and made more predictable.

2. For each event on the schedule, prepare in advance by previewing what to expect. For example, what does "going shopping" mean? Where are we going? What will we be doing? How long will it last? What can we buy and not buy? Preparing in advance means previewing what the child can expect to happen, what is expected of him, how long it will take, and what will happen next. Lay out the sequence of events, what is expected, and what boundaries there are (e.g. only purchase what is on the list). Lay out a mental map to provide a clear path. Do not assume anything; make it detailed and crystal clear.

3. Have a backup plan! Not all things in life happen as expected. However, for common snags that frequently occur, have a backup plan! If going to the baseball game could get rained out, then have a "Plan B" for what will happen instead. If an event that requires waiting may take longer than expected, have some filler activity (child's toolbox of a few favorite toys) to occupy his time. Anticipate the snags and be prepared with a backup plan. Identify the backup plans ahead of time so they are predictable when happening.

You will find that by providing a mental map by sequencing out the day, previewing events before they happen, and having backup plans for snags in expectations, you can provide greater understanding and predictability to the child's world, lessening his anxiety and building a greater sense of security. As he gets older, he will need to learn to script out his own day to provide this mental map. Start him out early in life, and include him in your "mapping," so you can empower him to do this for himself as he gets older. Happy mapping!

Reduce confusion: add structure and predictability to daily routine

Since the world can be chaotic and confusing for children on the spectrum, they are often anxious and insecure. Uncertainty scares them, because they cannot adequately appraise it and they feel incapable of dealing with it. They like predictable routines, laid-out plans, concrete beginnings and endings, and knowing what to expect and when to expect it. When there is no predictable structure, they feel anxious and seek to control everything happening to them in order to feel safe.

To reduce confusion and uncertainty in daily routine:

- Provide structure and predictability to daily routine.

- Take away as much confusion as possible.

- Use predictable rituals for daily activities.

- Preview events ahead of time.

- Provide clear, consistent rules and expectations.

- Provide strong, clear boundaries and consequences.

Structured daily schedules

Knowing what is coming in the immediate future significantly reduces anxiety. Structured daily schedules (this event follows this event, follows this event) make the world understandable and predictable. These schedules can be picture schedules, written lists, appointment schedulers, or smartphone apps. They lessen anxiety and strengthen security. They allow the child to relax and be prepared. Such schedules provide the mental map needed to organize his time and make life predictable. It makes "time" and "future" concrete and visual. I can see it, I can process it! Make the invisible, uncertain future visual and predictable. Use visual schedules both at home and at school. As the child gets older, empower him to use appointment schedulers or smartphone apps to provide him with a visual map. You will reduce anxiety and increase certainty!

Build set routines into daily schedules

As we saw earlier, processing through their daily routine can be very taxing for people on the spectrum. The normal daily tasks that we often take for granted can be very draining for them. It is important that we provide as much structure and predictability as possible to their day to minimize the amount of processing and to conserve mental energy. Uncertainty requires increased processing, so providing structure and predictability reduces mental fatigue. Build in structured routines during the day and use visual schedules to make the day predictable. This helps lower both processing needs and anxiety.

The more you can make simple daily routines (getting ready in the morning, getting home from school, mealtime routine, before bed, bathing routines) structured, consistent, and predictable, the more automatic they become and the less processing will be required. We all rely on set routines to do activities automatically without thinking. We dress ourselves, bathe ourselves, and brush our teeth the same way each day without even thinking about it. We do them automatically out of habit. They take minimal mental energy, allowing us to think of other more important things as we are doing them. The more routines become automatic habits, the less mental energy is used to move smoothly through the day. Predictable routines help keep the child from getting overloaded.

Whereas these rituals and routines are important for us, they are vital for those on the spectrum. Routines are the foundation for safety and security. They guide them through the confusion and make life predictable. Disrupt these routines and security comes crumbling down.

Provide consistent rules, regulations, and expectations

Whereas structured schedules and routines give the child clear understanding of what and when to do things, providing clear and consistent rules and expectations give clarity on *how* to do things. They provide the boundaries needed to know what is acceptable and not acceptable. Most rules and expectations are invisible and "assumed." For people on the spectrum, these expectations are either not noticed or are vague, inconsistent, and confusing. Without being able to accurately read these invisible rules and expectations, people on the spectrum are left guessing what is needed. Consequently, what they do and how they do it does not match what we expect. We need to be literal, black and white, and consistent with all rules and expectations. Write them down to make them concrete. Go over them frequently; demonstrate and role-play them. Consistently hold to them so they are predictable for the child. Probably one of the greatest sources of anxiety for people on the spectrum are the vague and inconsistent rules and expectations inherent in our society.

All of these suggestions significantly reduce processing needs, requiring less mental energy and minimizing chance of overload. Simply make the child's world more understandable.

Make the invisible visible!

Much of our world is invisible and assumed. Whether it is what to do, when to do it, how to do it, or how to act, our world is full of invisible expectations that are assumed to be known and understood. Neurotypical people smoothly skate through life, flexibly appraising and following these invisible boundaries. People on the spectrum are stumbling through life, guessing at what is needed and whether they are meeting it. For them, if it cannot be seen, touched, heard, tasted, or smelled, it is vague and difficult to gauge. Once they understand an invisible rule or expectation through consistent repetition, they are fine as long as we stay consistent with them.

As often as possible we need to make the invisible visible! What to do, when to do it, and how to do it need to be made concrete and visual until they become routine habits. Make the abstract concrete, and turn all expectations into visual guidelines. Use picture or written schedules, checklists, and directions to make expectations visual and constant. Take what we assume and make it concrete and visible. Demonstrate and role-play "how to do," and use photo sequence strips to remind them of the steps. Use video and photo social stories, along with demonstration and role playing to teach social rules and expectations. In school or at work, use written instead of verbal instructions and use outlined worksheets and flow charts to provide information. Never assume that which is not concrete and observable. Clarify and verify understanding and provide a visual map of what is expected. When in doubt, write it out, illustrate it, or demonstrate it! Make the invisible visible!

Seeing the big picture (central coherence)

"The whole is greater than the sum of the parts." The invisible relationships between the parts (how they relate together) provide more meaning to the collection of parts alone. Central coherence is the brain's ability to see the invisible relationships between the parts, which give an overall meaning to the whole. The brains of neurotypical (NT) people have a natural ability to seek out overall meaning when looking at an array of details. We seek overall meaning immediately when viewing detail. We immediately search for invisible relationships that provide meaning to the details. When looking at something, our brains scan for a few important details to grasp the big picture. From the first impression, we then tend to use the overall picture to provide the backdrop for defining the individual details. Our brains seek out meaning first, then detail second. We tend to think from general to specific. This is what happens when we immediately see a smiling face out of two dots with a half moon under it. Or when we quickly skim written material, missing misspelled words and reading the meaning without paying attention to the individual words. This also allows us to read the invisible context that provides meaning to how we interpret what people are saying and doing. We often infer meaning quickly when faced with a few details. From there, we go on to interpret all other details by the initial interpretation we assume.

For many people on the spectrum, their brains tend to work the opposite way. Their brains focus on the detail and not the overall picture. They struggle to see the invisible relationships between the parts and have to search for overall meaning by piecing together the details. They are more acutely aware of the fine detail and do not immediately get pulled into seeing the relationships (hidden meaning) between the parts. They first scan the many details and then put them together to form the overall meaning. They tend to think specific to general, rather than general to specific. They see the parts literally, with less bias, and then piece the parts together to form the overall picture.

This difference in processing provides people with autism with many unique strengths as well as weaknesses. They have a much more concise, concrete, literal interpretation of what they perceive. They are very strong detailed thinkers, can perceive detail with minimal bias, and pick out imperfections among the detail. They also can acutely perceive the physical relationships (physical patterns) between the details. They often are superior in perceiving sensory patterns (e.g. visual and auditory patterns) that we may not attend to. For tasks requiring extreme acuity to detail (e.g. engineering), their processing is very strong. Also, their fine attention to sensory patterns can be valuable in arts and music. However, as we will see later, when it comes to interacting and relating, this weak ability to interpret rapidly the overall picture (central coherence) can leave them struggling.

Qualities of weak central coherence

1. Problems seeing the big picture:

    a. Good with detail, not global perception.

    b. Difficulty seeing invisible relationships between the parts.

    c. For us, the whole is more than the sum of its parts. For those on the spectrum, the whole is the sum of its parts.

2. Concrete thinkers:

    a. Difficulty reading context.

    b. Takes things literally.

    c. Doesn't quite get it! Doesn't see the big picture.

3. Misinterprets and misjudges:

    a. Trouble extracting overall meaning of event.

    b. Difficulty with multiple meanings.

    c. Cannot read between the lines.

    d. Often misinterprets and then acts out of context.

It is very important to keep in mind the difficulty people on the spectrum have in understanding the invisible cues, relationships, and context that provide meaning to much of what we interpret. This is why we cannot *assume*. Instead, provide information very literally, and clarify then verify understanding. Do not assume!

Fact vs. inference!

One of the main differences in how our brains (ASD and NT) are wired differently can be seen in how we attend to and process information. In one of the previous posts we discussed the significance of central coherence, which is the neurotypical brain's tendency to look immediately for global meaning when perceiving a few details. We quickly scan the host of details for a few cues that allow us to grasp the overall picture. We look immediately for the underlying meaning between the details, and then proceed to interpret the details by what meaning we assign. This, of course, is very dependent on how accurately we can infer the intended meaning from minimal details. This process allows us to look past the concrete details and process the invisible relationships between the parts, to read between the lines. Socially, when relating with others, this inferring helps us read the thoughts, feelings, perspectives, and intentions of others (theory of mind). This inferring allows us to share mental states and experiences with others, and allows us to think about how others are thinking and predict how they will respond. It helps us pattern what we say and how we act. It also allows us to stay connected both mentally and emotionally during conversation.

The brain wiring for people on the spectrum (ASD) makes it difficult to look past the detail for the overall picture. It is more focused on reading the concrete details (facts). What you see and hear is what you get. People on the spectrum stay more true to the details and analyze the facts to piece together the overall picture. Hence their thought processes can be less biased (although not entirely unbiased) and more true to the facts.

However, without the ability to make rapid inferences about the hidden meanings, those on the spectrum often process what is said and done very literally. Since they do not immediately infer hidden meaning, they also are not looking at the subtle cues (facial expressions, body language, voice fluctuations, etc.) to infer what is meant when something is said. Consequently, our communications move too fast and at a different level from theirs. We are processing inferentially, and they are processing factually. They are looking at the detail, and we are looking at the global meaning. Although they may eventually get to the meaning we infer (by piecing together the detail and facts), it will be delayed in relation to the social processing we are doing. They often have to think through the detail, while we intuitively infer.

Now, when communicating with people on the spectrum, it is easier for us to interact at their level of processing (factual) than to expect them to relate at our inferential level. Whereas we can communicate more literally and factually, it is more difficult, and sometimes impossible, for them to think inferentially. Hence we need to say exactly what we mean and mean exactly what we say! Leave little to be inferred. Say what your thoughts are, explain your feelings concretely, as well as your perspectives and intentions. Do not assume the person is reading your thoughts, feelings, perspectives, and intentions. Spell everything out correctly, and verify understanding when possible. Clarify what you want and what is expected. Since this processing can be delayed, make sure to pause and give the person time to process. In all areas of life, when sharing information, we need to make sure we respect the factual method of processing. When we do, relating becomes much easier.

Social anxiety and central coherence

The term "central coherence" describes our brain's ability to see the relationships between the details of our perceptions, to give meaning to what we are experiencing. It is the brain's ability to look immediately for the hidden meanings and see the big picture that allows us to interpret smoothly what we experience and dictates how we respond. This perceptive ability allows us to apply meaning to a flux of detail, read what is expected, and stay coordinated with the world around us. Seeing the big picture gives us the reference point for interpreting what we are hearing and seeing.

This process, central coherence, is what gives us the ability to "read" two main invisible ingredients necessary for understanding the world around us: (1) the invisible context (situational meaning) for which events are occurring, and (2) the thoughts, feelings, and perspectives of others to apply meaning to what they are saying and doing. Context and perspective taking are the invisible relationships that provide the backdrop to how we interpret and act upon what we are experiencing. All our actions and words change meanings based on the invisible background of the context of the situation. What is said and done has different meanings in one situation compared with the next. We are constantly changing our behavior based on the context in which it is occurring. Kids may swear and talk about sex when together by themselves but turn it down or off when adults walk in. We have to be able rapidly to read the context we are in, and the unwritten social rules of that context, in order to pattern what we do and say. We have to be able to see the big picture to get the gist of what is going on. Without the ability to read the context, we would often be lost and confused.

This ability to read the context (backdrop) also allows us (neurotypical people) to predict the thoughts, feelings, and perspectives of others. The meaning of what we hear and see people saying and doing is determined by the context of the situation. By knowing the context, we can predict what the person is thinking and feeling, which adds meaning to what they are saying and doing. People's actions and words have multiple meanings which we would not understand if we could not effectively read the context around them. A smile can have multiple meanings. Your friend smiling at you in the hallway means something different from when the bully smiles when he catches you alone in the hallway, or when the pretty girl sitting in front of you turns, makes eye contact with you, and smiles. When interacting with others, we immediately read the context and the perspectives and intentions of others to interpret what is going on and what is expected of us. This ability, central coherence, is so important for daily living and a sense of security. It is central to relating in our social world.

Without this central coherence (seeing the big picture), we would often be lost and confused, stumbling through a maze of detail without good meaning. We would not have the hidden backdrop that we use to apply meaning to all the details. The world would be literal: what you see is what you get. However, since our social world is not literal, there will always be uncertainty that we cannot grasp. We would not be able to connect the dots and read the plot behind what is going on. This ability to see the big picture is what gives us our sense of safety and security. It enables us to understand immediately what is going on and predict what will occur. Without this ability, we would be anxious and insecure, unsure of what is going on and needed from us, always reading things literally and misunderstanding what is needed, never really knowing if we "get it" or fit in. Our basic sense of safety and security is vitally contingent upon our ability to read the big picture and match our thoughts and actions to it. Without this ability we would have strong generalized anxiety! This is often the experience for those on the spectrum.

People on the spectrum are said to have weak central coherence. Their brains do not immediately read the big picture. They clearly see the detail, but without intuitively reading the invisible relationships between the details, they are often missing the hidden backdrop that gives meaning to what they are observing. They have difficulty reading both the context and perspectives of others that are required to interpret adequately what is going on, and what is needed. Their brains want to read things literally, and they become anxious with all the hidden meaning that is invisible to them. The fact that the meaning behind our words and actions changes based on when and where they occur (situational context) makes it very confusing and anxiety-provoking for those on the spectrum.

This lack of certainty creates strong anxiety and insecurity. People on the spectrum often misread and act out of sync with what is going on. They cannot accurately predict what is intuitively inferred and expected. Our social world is so dependent on this ability to read context and perspectives. Without strong central coherence, the brain is frequently unsure and anxious in our social world. Social anxiety is very high, as well as task performance anxiety (worrying about meeting expectations). These two together often create ongoing generalized anxiety that permeates their daily living. They are frequently unsure and on guard. The only time they can relax is when they are by themselves and controlling everything around them. The world has to be "literal" to be safe. Unfortunately, there is very little in our social environment that is literal and predictable for them. So, when you wonder why people on the spectrum are so anxious in social situations, remember they are not reading the backdrop that allows them to make sense of what is going on! Slow down, make it more literal, and clarify the context that they are missing.

One of our members had the following question:

 Member's question

My son is nearly 18 and has so many stressors. Crowds, meeting new people, especially doctors, etc., and the stormy weather. It's such a trial that we try to avoid crowed places; however, we cannot really help it if we have to go out in the bad weather or meet a new doctor. He completely freaked out last week as we had to see a podiatrist. Thank God I managed to get him calm before we went and he managed to get through it with no problems.

AUTISM DISCUSSION PAGE

Children on the spectrum get overwhelmed when there is (1) too much detail, (2) too much flux (constant change in the detail), and (3) too much uncertainty! They cannot read the invisible multiple meanings underlying our social behavior, so people and social situations (meeting new people, doctors, crowds, etc.) are very scary for them. They cannot read the situations to grasp the underlying plot of what is going on that gives meaning to what they are experiencing. As you might expect, this uncertainty creates strong anxiety and apprehension. The brain panics when it doesn't know what it is walking into.

To lessen the anxiety, you must reduce the uncertainty by increasing understanding. Help him connect the dots by preparing him ahead of time and interpreting the underlying meanings (plot) as you go along. Your son will see only concrete details, so you have to connect the dots for him by providing the overall understanding of what is going on. When going into events, preview with him what he can expect to happen, what is expected of him, how long it will take, and that he will be safe. Neurotypical people automatically understand the plot that gives meaning and understanding to all the detail. This gives us security. Your son doesn't grasp the plot, so life always represents uncertainty and insecurity. So you have to provide the plot, so the details make sense, and he can feel more safe and secure. Hope this helps.

Connect the dots, define the plots!

We just looked at the difficulties individuals on the spectrum have with reading both the context of the situation and the perspectives of others. These invisible meanings provide the backdrop for interpreting what is going on and how to react. Without reading these invisible relationships, people on the spectrum often do not see the big picture which provides meaning to the details. This leaves them interpreting everything very factually and literally. They live in a concrete world, where relative meanings are difficult to perceive. Unfortunately, in our social world they often do not get it and consequently do not easily fit in.

As parents, teachers, and mentors, what can we do to help the children? How can we assist them in understanding, predicting, and responding to the world when they miss the gist of what is going on? How can we help the "literal" see the "invisible"? Plain and simple, we have to connect the dots, and define the plots for them. We have to make visible that which is hidden, lay out concretely what is abstract. We have to interpret concretely what they do not see. We have to make obvious what is taken for granted by us. Here are some tips for doing that:

- Don't assume understanding. Clarify and spell out the hidden meanings. Pretend your child is a visitor from a different culture and does not understand our customs. Interpret the context around what is happening, and the thoughts, feelings, and perspectives of others. Provide a concrete narrative of what cannot be seen.

- Use concrete, literal language to minimize vagueness or ambiguity. Verify that the child understands.

- Before going into events, prepare the child ahead of time for what he can expect to happen and what is expected of him, and explain any customs that are common to the event.

- As you enter events together, get used to describing the context so your child can pick up the gist of what is going on. All social events have hidden "plots" that provide the hidden meaning to our interactions. This plot also allows us to guess at what others are thinking and feeling.

- In addition to the context, try to discuss what others may be thinking and feeling, and how they are reacting to the situation.

- When entering a new situation, try to spend a few minutes describing the context and norms, as well as defining the whole picture (plot), before actually joining in. Get the child used to observing and investigating first before joining in. This way he can learn to pick up cues that may help him define the context.

- When the event is over, talk about what went on and how it went, and discuss how it falls in line with the context and plot that was predefined. This will help the child reflect on how the big picture was laid out, and if it made sense to him.

Information overload! Overwhelmed by irrelevant detail!

We have discussed how people on the spectrum, because they have weak neurological connections between the different brain centers (different brain wiring), have difficulty rapidly processing multiple information simultaneously. This makes processing much of our fast-paced world very difficult and exhausting. We, neurotyical (NT) people, can process rapidly changing information more quickly because we filter out all of the irrelevant information that is not important to the central theme. This allows us to attend to and focus on only the information that is important to the topic of focus. There are some differences in attention for people on the spectrum that make this filtering very difficult:

- Difficulty sorting out the relevant information from background information. NT people easily filter out 80 percent of information that is not important to the topic at hand. People on the spectrum often take in and have to process *all* the information. They either have difficulty filtering out information (take in all of the information) or they hyper-focus on small detail and cannot get past it.

- Because of the problems filtering out irrelevant detail, people on the spectrum often have difficulty understanding which detail is important to attend to. They can become distracted by all the irrelevant detail and lose sight of what is important to focus on. The important details do not necessarily stand out like they do for us.

- Once information is attended to, NT people immediately categorize it into concepts (files) based on past information and memory. Since people on the spectrum have trouble filtering out irrelevant information, they have to find categories to store and make sense out of all the information. This drastically slows down processing, and taxes, drains, and overloads the brain. The brain cannot categorize all that information as fast as it is coming in.

- Many people on the spectrum have difficulty shifting attention and tend to hyper-focus on information too long, unable to let go and get past it. This drastically slows down processing. Their attention can get stuck on and caught up in the detail, making it difficult to slide through the processing quickly and easily.

- Since people on the spectrum are so hyper-focused on the details, they often do not see the big picture, the overall meaning underlying all the details. Neurotypical people immediately infer from a few pieces of detail what the overall picture is. From there, they use this overall meaning to interpret the individual details. We immediately look for the invisible relationships between the parts that define the whole, often ignoring each individual detail. Our brains immediately look for meaning between the parts, so we can extract the overall big picture and move on. People on the spectrum who have difficulty reading these invisible relationships have to piece together all the details to arrive at the overall meaning. This is why people on the spectrum are good detail thinkers and can do great work in engineering and computer sciences. They can see the imperfections in the details that we often miss. They can focus on all the individual details to a pattern and analyze them concretely.

You can see that these attention differences can drastically slow down the processing speed. When the information is coming in faster than the brain can process and categorize it, then overload occurs and the brain becomes overwhelmed. So, please share this processing speed difficulty with teachers. Slow the information down, to allow the child to process and categorize it at a pace that is comfortable for his brain. It is not about intelligence; it is about speed of processing.

Lost in a sea of details!

Our security is based on our sense of sameness and continuity in our lives and relationships. Our world is full of dynamic change that continuously occurs around us. Fortunately for many of us, we can handle these changes, because we can perceive the stable patterns (whole picture) underlying this flux of change. Our sense of security is based on certain constants (family, friends, job, values, religious beliefs, etc.) that provide continuity and congruency in our lives. We also can see past the little daily snags and challenges that require us to shift gears, to understand that our basic life patterns (whole picture) haven't changed. We can sense the invisible patterns underlying the changes to small details. It is our ability to read between the details to see the overall meaning that allows us to feel secure in the face of these changes. We can adjust and accommodate to unexpected changes because we understand that these surface changes do not disrupt our major life patterns. We can take a deep breath and try a different way when we run into daily snags. We know that it is a temporary setback that simply requires us to try a different way. It hasn't changed what we want to do; we are just taking a temporary detour. The world doesn't collapse, because we can see the underlying pattern in face of the changing details.

This is what we call flexible thinking, the ability to go with the flow, handle the little snags, and shift gears to incorporate changes into our stable life patterns. We can see that the big picture doesn't really change, just some of the surface details. When our usual way to work is blocked, we can simply shift gears and take a different route. We can come home to our house when someone has moved a piece of furniture around and still feel it as the same room. We may get an initial shock, but we quickly realize nothing has really changed. The important overall picture and major themes in our lives stay the same. We can see the underlying current, regardless of the waves above it.

We look past the details to the overall picture to keep our sense of security. We see past the surface details and notice that the underlying meaning stays the same. In other words, we can see the sameness (continuity) in the sea of details. The details can change, without affecting the underlying patterns. We can stay safe and secure, realizing that things look a little different without affecting the overall picture or themes in our lives. We have "same but different" thinking. We understand that we can have change in surface detail, but the big picture remains the same. We immediately look past the surface details to read the overall meaning. This allows us to often ignore simple changes to the details, because we automatically see the overall picture.

For many on the spectrum, this is difficult. They have difficulty sensing the underlying meaning behind the details that provide this "same but different" thinking. They become very dependent on the details, piecing them together to see the whole picture. The overall picture is very dependent on how the pieces fit together. One change in the puzzle and the overall picture changes. For some people on the spectrum, if you make small changes in the details, the overall picture is no longer the same. For some children, if you change your hair color, cut your hair, put on glasses, or make other surface changes, they do not see the same person. Or, if you change the furniture around in the living room, it is no longer their safe and secure home. The stable patterns (relationships) in their lives change based simply on the changes in detail. The same patterns and relationships that provide meaning and security in our life, for them are dependent on the details staying the same. Make one or two simple changes in the details and the whole mountain comes crumbling down. For them, the constants in our lives that help us feel safe and secure are very fragile and vulnerable to simple changes. Take out a piece and the whole comes crumbling down. There is no "same but different"! Only different! The world changes based on the constant flux in details. Their sense of safety and security is threatened by the ongoing changes in details. This results in ongoing stress and anxiety, chronic anxiety that leads to the rigid need for sameness, obsessive compulsiveness, and chronic fear of uncertainty.

In addition, the sensing of the underlying big picture can be very hampered by their hyper-focus on details. For many on the spectrum, their brains cannot filter out the massive flux of details, often leading them to become so overwhelmed that they cannot see the big picture. For example, when talking with others, a person on the spectrum may be so distracted by the noise, lights, and smells occurring around them that they cannot focus on what is being said. Or they may be distracted by an earring reflecting light and not hear what is said. Whereas neurotypical people can filter out all this background noise and stay focused on the interaction, many on the spectrum are so distracted or overwhelmed by the stimulation that they cannot focus on the task at hand. This also tends to set the brain in panic mode (overload), resulting in a tidal wave of anxiety. This again makes it hard for those on the spectrum to feel safe and secure in our world of dynamic flux of change.

We all need constancy in our lives to feel safe and secure. We all need to know that, beneath the surface of ongoing flux, there is sameness and stability in our lives. That even though there are unexpected snags and changes that we cannot control, the important consistencies remain the same. When you have difficulty seeing the sameness underlying the changes to the surface details, you are left vulnerable to the minute changes and snags that our world presents. This lack of central coherence (seeing the big picture) can create ongoing insecurity and anxiety. This is why little changes can set off panic in people on the spectrum. This is one reason why they so strongly need sameness and are resistant to change. This is also why they "freak" when there are minor snags or unexpected changes in their life. Their world of security comes crumbling down when there are unexpected changes in the details of their lives. It is very important that everything stays the same, unless they are the ones making the changes. Unfortunately, our world is a constant flux of change which presents ongoing insecurity and fear in the lives of those on the spectrum.

So, if your loved one on the spectrum needs to have everything the same way and do everything the save way, needs to control all interaction and activity around him, and melts down with small unexpected changes, you can have a little more empathy for what he is experiencing.

Chapter 3

TEACHING DYNAMIC THINKING

Dr. Steven Gutstein, founder of Relationship Development Intervention (RDI), is instrumental in focusing attention on dynamic thinking. In his works, Gutstein (Gutstein 2002a, 2002b, 2009) laid out the differences between static thinking and dynamic thinking, and provided guidelines and activities for facilitating dynamic thinking with children on the spectrum. The following posts were greatly influenced by the work of Dr. Gutstein, with the inclusion of cognitive behavior techniques. For those who wish to learn more about dynamic thinking, I recommend you visit his website at www.RDIconnect.com.

"Process teaching" to strengthen neuropathways!

For many years, scientific research has focused on instructional learning to teach behavior skills. Content learning is taught by rote—repetitive training of discrete skills. This is easier for children on the spectrum, because it does not require a lot of rapid processing and mental engagement. Although these skill sets are very important and of great value, they are difficult to use in the real world. Most regulating in our world requires adjusting our responses to match the unique demands of specific situations. Each time we respond, we have to tweak our actions to match the demands of that setting. This requires rapid processing and ongoing appraising, so that our actions stay synchronized with the dynamic demands of the situation. To help the brain wiring develop so it can process dynamic situations, we need to change our way of teaching.

For some time now, it has been a common belief that our brains are wired differently. Given that, most therapies have been developed to help compensate for these differences (TEACCH, PECS, etc.) or to teach specific behavioral skills (ABA, Social Skills, etc.) to allow the child to cope and live more effectively. Most of the treatments take it for granted that we cannot change the hard wiring of the brain. However, new research on neuroconnectivity (neurological connections between the different brain centers, allowing them to communicate with each other) points to the brain of people with ASD as having weak neurological pathways between the different centers of the brain. This makes it difficult for the brain centers to communicate in order to rapidly process multiple information simultaneously. If that is true, then it could be thought that activity that places the brain in situations that require processing multiple information (using multiple brain centers simultaneously) will strengthen the neuropathways between the brain centers. These activities do not teach a static behavior skill through repetition, but require the brain to think its way through the activity (mental engagement). This is similar to the difference between learning an arithmetic equation and solving a story problem (requiring the use of math skills in problem-solving situations). By doing so, the brain develops more effective connections between the areas of the brain.

Focusing on teaching specific (static) behaviors through rote repetition works well for children on the spectrum, because it doesn't require as much communication between brain centers. It fits the way their brains are wired. That is why discrete trial training is popular in Applied Behavior Analysis (ABA). It is considered *static* learning, similar to memorizing facts, or learning one right response for one specific situation. However, to teach dynamic thinking we want to teach *process* learning—learning through figuring it out, appraising, pondering, contemplating, and evaluating. Teach process rather than content. Putting the child in situations that do not teach a specific skill by rote, but require the child to figure it out, activates better communication between the brain centers. Consequently, by requiring greater integration of the different brain centers we hope to develop stronger neuroconnections.

Although we will look at different examples of these dynamic activities later in this chapter, let's look at one example of using a soccer activity to teach processing multiple information and flexible thinking. I coach soccer and basketball programs for children on the spectrum. Soccer is a very dynamic sport, requiring rapid processing of constantly changing, dynamic information. From moment to moment the child has to continually reference, appraise, and assimilate rapidly changing information, and quickly shift gears and change his actions in response to this information. In this activity I do not teach the child by rote how to stop, turn, or vary the speed of the ball. However, I place the child in activities where the process of successfully completing the activity teaches the skills. The activity teaches him to think his way through, to figure it out. By doing so he is learning how to move and control the ball in response to the demands of the activity (not from rote learning in repetitive static drills).

For example, one activity is called "dribbling on the island." Imagine 12–15 children on the spectrum each dribbling a soccer ball inside a confined circle. Their objectives are to stay within the circle (island), keep the ball close to them, and not run into each other. There is no specific pattern or discrete way of dribbling. The child can dribble in any direction needed to move around, stay within the circle, and not run into anyone. This requires multiple processing of rapidly changing information. The child has to focus on keeping his ball close to him, rapidly appraise the other kids moving in and out of his space, and not go out of the circle. This requires continually assimilating and appraising rapidly changing information and constant shifting of gears and changing directions (stopping and turning the ball, moving faster and slower to miss the other children, etc.). In addition to all this multiple processing, the children also have to listen to and follow the directions of the coach. As they are doing this confined dribbling, I will frequently bark out directions such as "stop and go," "slow and fast," and "switch" (switch balls with someone else). This activity usually ends with, "monsters on the island." One or two of the children will be a monster(s) and chase the other kids on the island, requiring them to work harder and faster, and process even more dynamic information. Since this can be initially overwhelming for the children, we build gradually to allow them to accommodate and adapt.

Now, during this dribbling activity the children are learning how to stop, turn, and control the ball without teaching through rote "static" repetition. They are learning how to do this by referencing, appraising, evaluating, and controlling the ball to match the continually changing conditions of the dynamic activity. This activity places the brain in a situation of multitasking, rapidly processing multiple information simultaneously, requiring the various brain centers to integrate and communicate simultaneously. By placing the brain in situations of thinking it through to figure it out, requiring the brain centers to activate and integrate simultaneously, we are strengthening the neuropathways between the different brain centers. Even children with severe cognitive impairments learn to navigate these challenges successfully.

Even with compensations, our world is a fast-paced, socially dynamic world that is based on the processing mode of NT people. Although allowances and compensations can be built in to make life easier for individuals with ASD, the world will continue to be based on rapidly changing, dynamic information that requires rapid integration and processing.

More recent research on brain plasticity is suggesting that the brain has the ability to change and strengthen neuropathways through dynamic stimulation. It suggests that placing the child in situations that require dynamic thinking might strengthen the wiring of the brain to develop stronger neuroconnections between the different brain centers. This can be accomplished by putting the individual in activities that require the brain to adapt to dynamic processing, gradually developing greater neuroconnections. By doing so, the person develops greater ability to read context (central coherence), read the feelings and perspectives of others (theory of mind), and process ongoing change in stimulation. The individual may be able to better process the dynamic world that is so chaotic and demanding for them.

Teach your child dynamic thinking!

New brain research is suggesting that one of the major deficits in autism is weakness in the neurological pathways which in neurotypical people allow the different brain centers to communicate simultaneously. This allows us to rapidly process multiple information simultaneously, which is required in many of today's life situations. We have to reference, appraise, and evaluate rapidly changing information to adapt effectively to daily demands. We have to think our way through new and similar situations that require us to compare and contrast, reflect and ponder, and evaluate different options of acting. This requires rapid processing of multiple information and simultaneous communication between different centers of the brain.

Because this is a weakness in autism, being placed in situations that require rapid processing often makes the child anxious. Many children panic when they have to think. They want to know the one right way of doing something, or the one right answer to the problem, and have it stay that way each time. That way they do not have to think it through each time, to appraise, evaluate, contemplate. This uncertainty and needing to think it through makes them apprehensive. They want a script, the one right way to do it each time.

People on the spectrum do well with "static" learning, learning facts and skills that stay constant and "right" all the time. And we tend to teach that way: repetitive, rote learning of discrete skills. The bright kids learn tons of static facts and information, but fail continually in using abstract reasoning in daily situations. They panic when placed in dynamic situations that require them to rapidly appraise and think their way through situations. Even seemingly simple situations that require simple appraising often result in panic. Learning static (constant, never changing) facts and skills only works in static situations that do not change. Most daily living situations are not static, but dynamic (always a little different, with multiple options for responding). Life requires dynamic monitoring, appraising, and evaluating of multiple options of responding.

Although the brains of people on the spectrum have difficulty processing multiple information simultaneously, the brain has the ability to develop stronger neuroconnections if placed in situations that require it to process dynamically. Consequently, we need to do more teaching of the children to think their way through situations, rather than teaching them static facts and skills by rote. We need to do more process teaching rather than static teaching. Not jump in and solve all problems for them, but place them in simple problem-solving situations, and allow them to learn new skills by thinking their way through them. Selecting and adapting a response to match a situation can be gradually learned by frequent exposure to simple problem-solving situations. Skills learned by thinking dynamically generalize to new situations, because they are selected and modified by thinking before acting. Simple daily-living activities present many opportunities to monitor, appraise, and evaluate different options for responding. There are many "good enough" ways of doing things, and rarely only one right way of responding. Each situation is always a little different the next time we experience it, requiring us to adjust our actions to meet the demands of the new situation.

Many children on the spectrum panic and actively resist being put in situations that they have to think their way through. Frame the situations so that they present small amounts of uncertainty, with you assisting. Frame the activity that you are doing (simple daily activities) so the child has to think a little to figure it out. Pause frequently during these situations and let the child think about what needs to be done. Don't jump in and do everything for him; give him little challenges and help him think his way through them.

Provide little challenges during the normal events of the day that make the child think (appraise what is needed). Present simple challenges that you can assist him through, but which require him to think about what to do. Give him options, simple barriers, and snags to think through. Pause and make him appraise, evaluate, and contemplate. By keeping it simple and not overwhelming, you allow him to gradually build confidence, thinking his way through things. Repeated exposure to successfully tackling uncertainty by thinking will require processing multiple information, developing stronger neuroconnections between the brain centers and building greater confidence in thinking. So, instead of the rote teaching of discrete skills, place the child in the situations that let the activity teach the skill by thinking.

Think out loud! Model dynamic thinking!

We automatically assume that dynamic thinking skills occur naturally, but when your brain is wired a little differently, this is not always the case. One of the best tools that parents can use, besides giving children time and expectation to think, is thinking out loud. This is a simple process of making your thoughts verbal so the child can hear how you think through things. As discussed in previous posts, the best way to teach thinking is by doing the tasks together. While doing tasks together, verbally talk your way through them, thinking out loud so the child can hear how you think. Whether you are pondering something, contemplating a course of action, appraising the danger in a situation, problem-solving a snag, or evaluating several options, slow down and think out loud. Provide a "map for thinking" by modeling your own thinking. This way the child can learn how you think and begin to transfer that to his own thinking.

This strategy is very valuable. The association (think then act) connects better when the children hear your thinking at the same time as the event is happening (rather than discussing it afterwards). This allows them to connect more easily the thinking to the situational demand (immediate problem), as well as to their behavioral response (how they respond). They learn to stop, think, and then respond, instead of just impulsively acting. They learn how to appraise a situation, compare and contrast, evaluate options, and think about the consequences of their actions, by having you think all these things out loud. By you doing it together, right alongside them, and thinking out loud, they learn how to think their way through things.

The children may not say anything back, but they are listening! They are soaking it in. Just keep it up. Over time you may even notice them responding or saying their own thoughts out loud as they begin to think it out. Eventually, that will all get internalized, so the children have stronger thinking skills. You will notice that as the child develops stronger thinking skills, his anxiety goes down and his confidence increases. The more competent he becomes in contemplating, appraising, and evaluating, the more confident and secure he will feel. Have fun thinking out loud!

The more you "think," the more you "grow!"

Recent brain research reveals that the brain is more "plastic" and flexible than first thought. It was once believed that when the child reached a certain age, the brain was hard-wired and resistant to change. With numerous cases of the brain rewiring itself to adapt to damage and with people regaining skills as the different areas of the brain rewire themselves there is much more optimism about the brain's ability to change and adapt through ongoing learning experiences. We already know that the brain has the capacity for neurological growth through stimulation, and that one part of the brain can take over for other parts that are damaged.

Problem-solving activities and situations requiring you to think through them increase dopamine, which increases neuron development in the prefrontal cortex of the brain. This is the area of the brain that houses our ability to attend, plan, organize, self-monitor, inhibit our impulses, and carry out a plan of action. Further research has shown that the brains of people on the spectrum have weaker neuropathways that connect the different brain centers and allow them to communicate simultaneously. This limits the prefrontal cortex (thinking part of the brain) from influencing the other areas of the brain. This results in slower processing, poor impulse control, weak planning skills, and difficulty with higher order abstract thinking.

It was thought that this brain wiring was permanent, and that the only way to help individuals with weak executive functioning and limited social processing was to teach ways to compensate for this permanent brain-wiring weakness. However, now we are beginning to realize that this is not true. The brain is much more "plastic," and has the ability to develop new and stronger neuroconnections to strengthen many of these skills. These findings also lend support to providing more thinking experiences to stimulate neurodevelopment. Instead of teaching specific behaviors or one right answer by rote, we need to be promoting experiences where the child has to think his way through them to appraise situations, identify and evaluate options, ponder consequences, and monitor effectiveness of actions. What does this mean for day-to-day parenting and teaching?

- Pause and let the children think before giving them the answer or telling them what to do. We get so used to thinking for the child that they simply act how they are told.

- Highlight situations throughout the day where there is more than one right answer, more than one way of doing things. There are many situations in which we respond the same way every day. Instead of automatically responding, pause and discuss the options and the pros and cons of each option. Then once you pick and act on one option, stop and evaluate how well it turned out.

- Preview situations ahead of time and discuss what to expect, and what is expected of the child, and problem-solve any potential problems ahead of time.

- Think out loud. Model your own thinking, pondering, reflecting, appraising, and evaluating by thinking out loud, so the child can experience how you think it through.

- Practice problem solving. Set out a problem-solving worksheet with categories for (1) definition of the problem, (2) possible solutions, (3) pros and cons of each solution, and (4) evaluation of how the chosen option turned out. Make a list of problems that are common for the child and also for you. Practice every day by picking one of the problems and use the worksheet to talk through the four categories. Then, when a problem arises, use the worksheet to help the child problem-solve the situation.

- When watching TV, or watching people in real life, discuss what problems they are experiencing and brainstorm how they could respond. Wait and see how they react, and then talk about how effective it was.

- Keep a journal of situations that you and the child think through together. Review it frequently and reflect on how well the two of you are being social detectives!

- Read children's mystery stories where the child experiences others thinking though, appraising and evaluating, and testing out their options.

- Play problem-solving games, such as mystery games, crossword puzzles, "what if" games.

- The better the child gets at thinking through situations, the more confident he will be at going into new situations. As he learns to appraise and evaluate, he will become more confident in using his thinking skills more often. Highlight these situations and review them frequently.

There are numerous decision-making situations in the day that we automatically respond to in the same way. Take the time to break these down, look at options, and discuss the pros and cons. Try a few different ways to see how it goes. Make sure you reflect on how they work, and which responses to stick with. In essence, build stronger neurological pathways by thinking through things.

Creating situations for dynamic thinking

Static teaching usually consists of learning facts, routines, or scripts that will stay the same and be constant each time. This may be remembering facts about something (e.g. history), learning a scripted routine such as washing your hands (same sequence of steps), or doing something where there is only one correct way of doing it (2+2=4). Usually the information is pretty constant with minimal change, and the answer is usually fairly straightforward. This is what I call "content learning," which is memorizing facts or learning to do a prescribed routine. It requires more procedural memory, but once it is learned it is pretty set.

Dynamic learning (or process learning) usually occurs in situations where there is (1) no one right answer, (2) no one way of doing something, (3) multiple options to choose from, and (4) where the action required may vary based on the demands of the task. Dynamic thinking usually consists of appraising the situation for what is needed, identifying possible options, planning a course of action, monitoring your actions to make sure you are meeting your objective, shifting gears when things are not going right, and reflecting afterwards to evaluate how well you did. In dynamic thinking, you are processing fluid information that may change from moment to moment, and comparing and contrasting multiple information. Your actions may change at any moment based on the changing demands of the situation. Usually these activities require you to think your way through it. Often you do not know the right answer at first, but must figure it out!

Examples of dynamic learning:

- Multiple options, more than one way. Painting/drawing a picture or making a collage, figuring out how to get a large or heavy object from one point to another (use equipment, more than one person, push it, carry it, etc.), making soup out of whatever you can find in the refrigerator.

- Finding different ways you can do the same thing, or use something in different ways. How many different things can you do with a spoon (eat, dig in dirt, scoop something, use to bang on pots, etc.), or how many different ways you can eat soup (spoon, drink it, use a straw, etc.)?

- Making or doing something where you figure it out as you do it. Make something together (e.g. a house) out of blocks (planning as you go, adding and subtracting things, collaborating), clean an area (deciding what to keep, where things should go, what needs to be fixed, who will do what, etc.), create a different ending to a story, play dress-up together.

- Activities that require "on the fly" thinking and problem solving. Playing hide and seek (where each time you have quickly to determine a different place to hide together), problem-solving situations (e.g. some video games) where at each step you have to figure out what to do next, playing "What is this?" identifying things by characteristics (smell, size, feel, etc.).

- Activities that require ongoing appraising and shifting gears, such as playing soccer or basketball against each other, tag, chase, etc. In these activities, the child has constantly to adjust what he is doing by appraising moment to moment what others are doing.

- Teaching "same but different, different but same" by playing catch with different items (baseball, football, rolled-up socks) or playing in different ways, rolling it back it forth, throwing it, bouncing it.

- Pretend play using dolls or pretending one object is another (spoon as a drum stick, stick as a rifle, empty cartoon as a house, etc.). Make up stories and act them out.

- Create barriers and snags. As you do normal things in the day, create little snags or mistakes, then figure out how to get around them. "Oh no, what do we do now!" "How do we fix this?"

- Play games where the two of you use no words and have to use nonverbal language only (facial expressions, gestures, animated actions) to stay coordinated or figure it out. Play charades or "Getting warmer" (hide something in the room, and the other person has to find it as you shake your head yes or no as they get closer), build something together without using words (only gestures, facial expressions), stay coordinated together in action (walking, skipping, running, riding bikes, etc.).

- Teach "good enough" activities. As you do things together, discuss how to appraise in advance what is good enough, and then monitor your performance to know when you get there. When is the room "clean enough"?

- Read the context of social situations and the thoughts, feelings, and perspective of others. Watch TV with the sound off and discuss what might be happening, and what people are thinking and doing, Sit at the park or mall and guess what others are thinking and feeling.

All these activities are examples of using dynamic thinking. Any activity in which the child has to think his way through, where there is more than one right way, or which requires ongoing appraising and evaluating is good for dynamic thinking. Dynamic activities require the child to reference, appraise, monitor, and evaluate in order to continually adjust what he is doing to be successful. Get him to "mentally engage" to promote dynamic thinking! Dr. Steven Gutstein (Gutstein and Sheely 2002a, 2002b) provides further ideas for fostering dynamic thinking. I highly recommend that readers consult these references.

Get them "mentally engaged!"

Many children on the spectrum, because mentally figuring things out can be both scary and exhausting, often seek to avoid activity that presents a lot of uncertainty. They often seek out activity that is familiar and predictable, or activity that consists of very clear expectations and a very concrete path for them to follow.

Children on the spectrum often avoid situations that require them to think their way through. They want the one right answer and to have it be the right answer every time! Unfortunately, our world doesn't work that way. The children often avoid situations that do not provide predictable certainty. They seek sameness and familiarity to minimize the chaos of uncertainty. Usually the children do not trust their own judgment in the face of uncertainty. This leaves them feeling anxious and insecure when tackling uncertainty.

Figuring things out requires multitasking of many steps. It is a dynamic process consisting of appraising what is expected, comparing it to similar situations in the past, looking at possible options, evaluating potential consequences of those options, choosing and initiating the response, monitoring execution, and evaluating effectiveness. In addition, once we begin to act we often face snags that require us to shift gears and modify our response for effectiveness. This dynamic process also requires us to know when our response is "good enough" to meet the objective. Since children on the spectrum struggle with evaluating good enough, they require a perfect response to ensure it is good enough. This need for perfection often drives them to avoid new risks. This dynamic process of appraising, monitoring, evaluating, and modifying can be overwhelming for children on the spectrum.

Given that mentally engaging can overwhelm children and create strong anxiety, we often tend to frame activities so they don't have to think much. We do things for them, or tell them the best ways to do things, to protect them from the anxiety. We do the figuring out for them, and shield them from the insecurity of thinking their way through things. However, by doing so, we reinforce the rigidity of only feeling safe in situations of predictability and certainty.

The best thing to do is to encourage mentally engaging, but provide ongoing safe exposure to it through guided participation. Instead of rushing through daily events, slow them down, do them together, and allow the child to mentally engage with your support. Do the task together, providing guidance as needed to make it successful. With the parent framing the activity to require a little thinking and then providing guidance through it, the parent can scaffold the demands to provide just enough challenge to elicit mental engagement, but not so much as to overwhelm the child, providing the "just right" challenge. By doing the activity with the child, the parent can pause and wait for the child to think and choose, while providing cues or clues if the child freezes. The parent can also think out loud so the child can reference and understand how the parent thinks through things. By enabling the child to think through things with their support, the adult can gradually foster this thinking in the child.

The secret is for the parent to carefully present thinking challenges that are just right (not too easy or too hard). Pause and let the child think, then help out if needed by providing information, but not necessarily the answer. Frame the events to create a thinking challenge, then pause and allow the child to contemplate. If needed, you can give cues to guide the thinking, which lessens the anxiety and teaches the child to feel safe figuring it out. If the child is resisting, then the challenge may be too difficult. Back up and provide smaller challenges and/or give added guidance. If that still seems too difficult, then let the child do it with you: slow it down, do the thinking, but think out loud. This way, the child first references your thinking process before you pause to let him try.

This takes a little time to get used to. We are so used to doing for the child or setting it up so the child doesn't have to think. It is easier and quicker. However, once you get used to slowing things down and sharing the experience, it will become more natural to allow the child to engage mentally throughout the event. Usually, you don't have to create new conditions to teach this; there are plenty of natural opportunities in your typical daily routine.

You cannot learn to think, contemplate, and mentally engage without doing it frequently throughout the day. The routine day for most children is filled with numerous opportunities to appraise, contemplate, monitor, and evaluate. These experiences strengthen the neuropathways needed to develop effective thinking skills and enable the children to feel confident in using them. It helps develop the necessary wiring needed for dynamic thinking. Since children on the spectrum tend to avoid mental engagement, they do not receive the exposure needed to develop strong wiring for dynamic thinking. Consequently, we need to provide numerous safe experiences, with careful guidance from the parent/teacher.

Pause and let them "think!"

We tend to prompt and direct children on the spectrum through daily activities, giving them little time to ponder, contemplate, appraise, and evaluate. These are all part of dynamic thinking that they need to practice. We live such a fast-paced life that we do not want to slow down to "smell the roses." We have to remember that the above components of dynamic thinking, which come naturally for us, have to be taught and practiced for children on the spectrum. This does not require therapy sessions to teach, but can be included in all the daily activities that you do together. Every daily activity can be a learning opportunity to *think*. You simply have to (1) do the activity together, and (2) slow down and let the child think his way through it.

We tend to do an activity for children on the spectrum, or stand behind them and quickly prompt them through it. We don't want them to make a mistake or get anxious, so we give them the right answer, or simply do it for them. However, they have to feel the challenge to elicit thinking in order to master the challenge. It is this process of feeling the challenge—thinking it through, then mastering it—that builds confidence in thinking. Every routine daily activity can be a learning opportunity. This can be taking a bath, baking cookies together, washing the car, playing basketball in the driveway, reading a book together, any daily activity. The important factors are:

- Do the activities together, side by side, sharing the experience.

- Both you and your child have a role to play, each playing your part.

- Try to set up the child's part to be easy, but requiring some challenge to stimulate thinking on his part.

- Add choices and options for him to evaluate, simple snags and barriers to think through, simple mistakes to problem-solve, and a little uncertainty to contemplate. "Oh, I wonder what we do next," "Oops, I did that wrong, I wonder how we can fix that," "Oh, we could do it this way, or that way! I wonder which way is better?" All these little things are typically present in daily activities; however, we often solve them for the child, giving him few opportunities to think his way through.

- Don't be so quick to prompt and direct! We tend to jump quickly in and tell the child the right way, before he has a chance to think about it. As you two are doing something together, try to delay prompting; pause and hold off long enough to allow the child to think it through; otherwise, he will get used to not thinking, knowing you will jump in and solve it for him.

    o Instead of telling him how to do it, say something like "I wonder how we can do that!" and then scratch your head as if you are contemplating. Pause and give the child time to appraise what is needed and make a response.

- If the child doesn't respond, then give him two options to appraise. "I guess we could try _____ or maybe _____." Again, pause and give the child a chance to think and respond.

- If the child still does not respond, verbally appraise each option: "I guess if we tried this way, _____ might happen. However, if we do it that way, then _____ might happen." Again pause, and let him think and respond.

- Start by using examples that are so obvious that they require little thinking at first. For example, when baking something together, in order to move liquid (milk, water, oil, etc.) from one container to another, contemplate whether it would be easier to use a spoon or a fork, then try each one. Obviously, using a fork will not work because the liquid simply pours through the fork, making it impossible to transfer the liquid. Don't tell him, but try each one out and say, "I wonder which one works better." Pause and wait for a response. If there is no response, say, "Which one do you think?" If still no response, then verbally appraise what is needed (transferring the liquid to another container), and then verbally evaluate the pros and cons of each option.

- Get used to slightly stretching the demands of the child's role to make him think a little more. Make the task a little bit harder to make him stop and think about how to adjust what he is doing to make it work. Slowly add new learning, giving a little more responsibility, requiring him to adjust his performance. Let him feel the challenge, think it though, then feel the mastery! Pause and let him try it on his own, before guiding him through it. If there is no response, only give him part of the solution, enough to get him started, but leave still enough uncertainty to make him think.

- Add variations or elaborations to typical daily tasks. Walk to school a different way, pausing at each turn to contemplate the best way to go. Bounce the ball to each other, instead of throwing it. Take the elevator, instead of the escalator. Have the family pass the food around the table to fill their plates (family style serving), instead of filling the plate before bringing it to the table. Take normal daily activities and do them a different way, or add a little variation to them. Again, pause, contemplate out loud ("I wonder"), and give the child a chance to respond!

- Throughout the day, find activities that do not have just one right way of doing them (e.g. vacuuming or sweeping the floor) and pause to contemplate which option to choose. If you have time, do an experiment and try out each option, while evaluating the pros and cons of each.

- Always look for little problems or snags, that you can create to give your child a chance to problem-solve. You may need to highlight the problem, to make it stand out: "Oops…looks like this is not working. I wonder what we can do now!" Pause and give your child a chance to respond. If there is no response, give a clue and pause again.

- When thinking through things together, make sure you celebrate the process. Give each other high fives and thumbs up, with a declarative statement such as "We did it!" "We are good together!" "We Rock!" or "Wow, we thought that one through!" Spotlight the thinking and how successful you were together!

These are just some examples to show how you can build contemplating, appraising, evaluating, and thinking into your child's daily routine. As he gets better at it, add complexity to the thinking. Gradually build stronger and stronger thinking skills!

Increase generalization by switching from static teaching to dynamic teaching

One of the main issues in teaching people with autism is the difficulty they have generalizing (or transferring) the new learning from the training conditions to real-life situations. This is especially true of learning that is dynamically dependent on the context of the situation (where the response varies depending on the demands of the situation). That's why we need to teach skills in the act of dynamic thinking, not by rote or repetitive discrete trial training. Rote training is fine for teaching static skills, such as brushing your teeth or washing clothes, but teaching any functional skills that occur in our social world requires the ability to adjust the new learning to the context (demands) of the situation. This requires dynamic thinking. Flexible thinking cannot be taught in rote learning.

Transfer of learning from *static* situations to the real world of *dynamic* situations requires dynamic teaching, placing the child in situations that require him to think his way through them. Situations that challenge the child to figure his way out present simple challenges that require dynamic thinking. Instead of teaching the child static skills outside the situations they are used in (classroom), teach the child in real-life dynamic conditions. Frame the activity to highlight the objective you are teaching and then provide guided participation to scaffold the learning. Do not teach one right way to do something. Teach the child how to reference and appraise the situation, evaluate options, and organize and execute a response that matches the appraisal.

This type of learning stimulates greater neurological pathways between the different brain centers. Research is showing that children with autism have weak neurological pathways connecting the various parts of the brain. This makes it difficult for the various centers to communicate with each other. Dynamic thinking requires processing multiple information simultaneously, often subconsciously. This requires simultaneous communication between the brain centers. Because of these weak neurological pathways, children with autism have severe problems with processing multiple sources of stimulation simultaneously. They have to process information sequentially, rather than simultaneously, drastically slowing down their processing speed. Our world is simply moving too fast for them to process.

Changing our teaching style from static skills teaching (content learning) to dynamic teaching (process learning), and using activities that require the child to think his way to a solution, requires processing multiple sources of stimulation simultaneously and builds stronger neurological pathways between the brain centers. Dynamic thinking requires greater communication between the brain centers, strengthening the neurological connection between them. We do not want to teach the child just to speak (to say words), we want to teach the child to communicate (share ideas, relate experiences). Young children without disabilities first learn how to communicate (nonverbally) before they learn how to speak. They do not learn to speak words first before learning the function of communicating. The function is learned first, before the skill develops. This provides the foundation for the skill to have meaning.

Because children with autism have difficulty reading context, we have thought we needed to teach the skill outside the context, and hope we can gradually generalize the skill into the context. That has not worked well. We have operated on the assumption that we cannot teach the children how to read context and then pattern a response based on that appraisal. I think making this assumption has greatly limited the learning for children on the spectrum. We end up with an adult who has a good number of splinter skills, but poor judgment and reasoning about how to use them. We end up with the adult who earns a graduate degree with all As, but cannot hold down a job. If we teach the children how to appraise context and think their way to an answer, then the skill they learn has more meaning and flexibility to adapt to daily demands. Dynamic teaching (teaching in context that requires figuring it out), with supportive guidance, teaches the child how to appraise, evaluate, and pattern responses based on the context for which it has meaning. That is what our children need to become fully functioning adults.

Chapter 4

EXECUTIVE FUNCTIONING

The prefrontal cortex of the brain holds what is called the executive functioning skills. These skills allow us to attend to what is important, inhibit our impulses, think before acting, and evaluate the consequences of our behavior. It also allows us to break down a task, evaluate options, plan and organize a course of action, monitor what we are doing as we do it, and evaluate the effectiveness of our actions. These skills also allow us to hold several things in our short-term memory so we can multitask. The executive functions area of the brain is the "conductor" telling the rest of the brain how to work together to appraise, evaluate, and execute action. Without it, we could not function effectively in our day-to-day living.

There are many areas of executive function that people on the spectrum often struggle with. Listed on the next page are some of the common challenges they experience.

WEAK EXECUTIVE FUNCTIONING SKILLS

1. Poor inhibition:

    a. Poor ability to inhibit impulses.

    b. Often impulsive; acting without thinking; interrupting.

2. Attention problems:

    a. Either difficulty focusing or hyper-focused on detail.

    b. Problems inhibiting/filtering out distracting stimuli or picking out relevant details.

    c. Difficulty shifting attention; gets stuck and has difficulty moving on.

3. Shifting gears:

    a. Difficulty shifting from one mindset to another.

     b. Problems with unexpected changes.

     c. Difficulty with transitions.

     d. Rigidly adheres to viewpoint.

4. Planning and problem solving:

     a. Difficulty planning, setting goals, predicting future outcomes, and designing course of action.

     b. Difficulty following sequential steps.

     c. Poor problem solving.

5. Organization skills:

     a. Problems organizing materials, turning in homework, bringing what is needed, and remembering to deliver messages.

     b. Forgetful, disorganized, messy.

6. Working-memory:

     a. The inability to hold information in immediate memory while focusing on a task.

     b. Difficulty shifting attention between task and active memory.

     c. Difficulty with multistep tasks and complex instructions.

     d. Often forgets directions once task is started.

7. Self-monitoring:

     a. Poor ability to monitor and check work.

     b. Poor self-monitoring of behavior.

     c. Tends not to use past experiences to evaluate present actions.

As you read through the different functions, you will notice the difficulties that are common for your child. Poor impulse control, difficulty regulating emotions, trouble concentrating on topics of low interest, difficulty shifting gears, and little snags causing frustration are all very common for children on the spectrum.

Even though the children may be bright, they usually have problems organizing themselves, allowing enough time to do things, forgetting where they are at in the task, and problems completing assignments. They may complete homework and then forget to turn it in. If you tell the child to clean his room, he will freeze and become overwhelmed by the task, not knowing where to begin. These children have problems breaking things down into small parts, getting started, and then sequentially completing all steps of the task.

These children have difficulty multitasking because they have problems holding information in their short-term memory and then shifting their attention from one task to the other. Also, while engaged in action they have difficulty monitoring and evaluating their own behavior, and assessing how their actions affect others. They cannot act and think about how they are acting at the same time. This multitasking job of both acting and monitoring how we are acting is essential when interacting with others.

This chapter will look at ways of supporting these challenges.

Why, why, why?

The most common question I get from parents of teens and young adults on the spectrum is: "Why does my son struggle so much in simple, real-life judgment and reasoning? Why does he know what he is supposed to do, but stumble so much while doing it?" Another one is: "We can preview what to do before he leaves, but he forgets to do it once there!" Another popular question is "Why can't he see the effects his behavior is having on others, and not see when he is out of sync with everyone else?"

The answers to these questions lie in the executive functioning center of the brain (frontal lobes). This area of the brain gives us the ability to appraise a situation, plan and organize a course of action, execute the plan, and monitor how we are doing while carrying out the action. To effectively carry out a course of action that matches the expectations of the demands, you have to engage in multitasking (which is a brain function difficult for people on the spectrum).

To match your behavior to the situational demands, you have to (1) continually appraise the situation, (2) assess what is needed, (3) plan how to respond, (4) monitor how you are doing as you are doing it, and (5) evaluate how effective your actions are. You have to perform all these five functions simultaneously to stay coordinated with the expectations. It requires the abilities to (1) process multiple information simultaneously and (2) multitask the five functions above. This is where the person on the spectrum has difficulty with any social situations that demand them to perform. Plus, when you add the anxiety of performing under such conditions, the ability that they do have to multitask crumbles. In essence, most daily responding that doesn't involve responding by habit requires us to think about what we are doing while we are doing it. We step back and monitor what we are doing as we are doing it. We are constantly appraising, evaluating, and adjusting our actions based on this monitoring. This is very difficult for people on the spectrum.

At best, most kids on the spectrum can learn to appraise what is needed before acting, rather than during the response. They need to plan out a course of action based on that appraisal. However, once they decide to act, they have difficulty monitoring their actions while doing them. They have difficulty continually appraising, evaluating, and adjusting their actions in the midst of doing them. So, if their actions are not in sync with what is needed, they often have no clue that they are off balance. Or, if they feel that they are off course, they do not know why and what to do about it.

How can we help?

1. Prepare the child before entering a situation about (1) what he can expect and (2) what is expected of him. Lay out a script for him. Very literally define any rules and expectations about what to do and what not to do. If possible, role-play and practice any known behavior expectations and how to handle possible snags. Give the child a mental map to follow.

2. Simply providing a mental map ahead of time is not enough. People on the spectrum have problems with working memory. They may understand that what you tell them is expected, but forget it during the acting of doing. They often have a hard time maintaining this information in their working (short-term) memory, and referencing back and forth between this memory and their behavior to keep their actions in sync with what is needed. We think that by telling them what is expected (previewing), they will naturally remember to do it. Then we get mad at them for not following the expectations. We can enhance this previewing by providing them with a more concrete path to follow. The following are possible strategies to use:

   a. Use concrete visual roles and rules. For example, when taking a young child grocery shopping, you have to provide very concrete rules that set a path for correct behavior (otherwise he is all over the place and getting into everything). We need to give the child a role to play (push the cart) and concrete boundaries (path), such as "Hands always on the cart, and walk alongside mom." These two tools, concrete roles and rules, provide the visual map to keep the child on the correct path. If he starts to steer off these boundaries (take hands off cart or walk faster than mom), then we stop the action and redirect him back on track. When children don't have a clear path, they are left to wander haphazardly and get into trouble. We often yell at them to stop doing annoying things without providing them with a concrete path to follow.

   b. Another tool that can help is to connect the child's actions to the sequential steps of the task by providing visual cues to each step. This is where picture sequence routines are helpful. This is a sequence of pictures that show what to do at each step. When "A" happens, you do this, then when "B" happens, you do that, etc. The picture for each step of the task can cue the child what to do next. Scrape the plate, then rinse the plate, then place it in the dishwasher, with a picture designating each step.

c. Another tool for bridging the weak working memory is to provide written instructions as a path to follow. At each step of the task, the child can reference the directions as needed, just as we navigate a map and street signs while driving. This often works well for school tasks, such as writing down steps and directions. This gives a checklist of what to do, step by step through the task.

3. Once the child starts into action, he must learn to monitor (appraise, evaluate, and adjust) what he is doing as he is doing it, to make sure he is doing it right. To help with this, teach the child to break the task/event down into sequential steps, then appraise, act, and evaluate for each step. Appraise what is needed for that step, do the step, then evaluate how he did before moving on to the next step. If the child has difficulty understanding what is "good enough" performance, provide him with a model or picture of what the completed step looks like. This way, he can check his performance against the model. We teach the habit of appraising what to do, doing it, then checking to see if it is right before moving on. So a multistep task will be broken down into sequential steps of appraise—act—evaluate, appraise—act—evaluate. The child will need some coaching to learn how to appraise and evaluate. This can be very taxing and mentally draining for the child. However, over time, the performance will become more automatic (habit).

4. Until the child becomes old enough to do the self-monitoring in step 3, he will need someone to coach him during the action. This is where guided participation is a good technique. With guided participation, the coach and child do the action together, with the child learning by following the lead of the coach. The coach teaches by showing and using assistance to keep the child on the right path. Guided participation provides a very clear path, along with assistance to frame the child's actions to stay on the right path. Once the child understands what is needed, the guide decreases the assistance.

5. Another good strategy used in guided participation is teaching the child what to reference when monitoring how he is doing. Frequently through the action, the coach stops and evaluates how well the action is going (if he is on the right track). This teaches the child to stop and check, as well as *what* to check.

6. Once the action/task is completed, then help the child evaluate how his performance was with regard to the path that was laid out. If he got off the path, discuss what broke down and how you can tighten up on the path.

In conclusion, in order to support the child with poor executive functioning skills, you need preview what is expected ahead of time, provide him with a concrete path to follow, coach him down the path, and then help him evaluate how he did.

Set the parameters to define expectations!
Provide a clear path!

Because our expectations are often vague and difficult to understand, individuals on the spectrum frequently have problems appraising what is needed, as well as evaluating how well they are doing. Since they do not read the unwritten assumptions, they often fail to appraise correctly, and thus act incorrectly. Because their actions do not match what is expected, they frequently elicit negative feedback from others about their actions. This, in turn, creates task performance anxiety because they never know whether their actions are going to meet expectations. Consequently, this inability to appraise correctly and judge what is "good enough" results in perfectionism, where performance has to be perfect or it is failure. For these children, anything but perfection risks not being "good enough." This exaggerates the already stifling task performance anxiety.

To help fight perfectionism, reduce task performance anxiety, and improve the ability to appraise what is needed ("good enough"), we need to define the parameters to better clarify expectations. The following help to do just that:

1. Preview ahead of time what the child can expect and what is expected of him. Demonstrate or provide visual cues if possible. Be sure to clarify what is expected, what is not expected or not allowed, and any rules and boundaries the child must stay within. Do not make up rules as you go along or assume the child automatically understands the rules.

2. Clearly define when something starts and when it is finished. Define the parameters: "We will work on this task until all parts are completed (or until 5p.m.), then eat our snack." The more visual the better: "The activity is completed when we get all the parts together" or a specific time designated by a visual timer.

3. Most importantly, define and contrast what are the minimum and the maximum expectations, to clearly define the parameters of what is "good

enough." This is often what is unclear to the child. The following can help with this:

a.   Clarify the lower and upper limits of what is expected: what the minimum and maximum expectations are. This defines the parameters of what is good enough, so the child doesn't have to be perfect. "We need to complete at least five problems, but can do up to ten." Or, "This boat is good enough when it can float on the water." This makes sure the child appraises what is needed more accurately. It also gives him parameters for ongoing monitoring of his performance to stay within the boundaries. He knows when he is done and when his performance is "good enough." This also lowers perfectionism.

b.   When possible, provide a visual model (picture, demonstration, and model) of what the finished product or performance should look like. This gives a clear, concrete idea of what is "good enough."

Framing activities for success means defining the parameters (rules and boundaries) about how to act and how not to act. It is very important to define and contrast both what is expected and what is not expected before entering the activity. Define time parameters, performance parameters, and behavior parameters. Then, during the activity, provide positive reminders and feedback for staying in the boundaries. This will lay down a concrete path that is easy to see and follow.

Teaching independence: monitoring performance

One of the weak areas of executive functioning skills for people on the spectrum is monitoring their performance as they are doing it. They tend to *do*, without monitoring how well they are doing it. Consequently, they often do things too fast or not completely enough, forget steps, or do a sloppy job of it. They concretely learn how to do things, but do not learn how to monitor how they are doing and check their performance once completed.

It is important to teach children on the spectrum self-monitoring skills. To self-monitor how they are doing requires multitasking, and monitoring how they are doing while they are doing it. This is difficult for children on the spectrum. To monitor how you are doing, you have to have a mental image of what adequate performance is and what the finished product should look like. When we are working on something, we keep a mental image of what the final product should look like and monitor our performance to match that. So, once we learn how to do something, we also have to learn how to monitor our performance to meet expectations (good enough). There are two concrete tools you can use to help with this process. One is to provide a visual model (picture or real object) of the finished product, or the sequential steps of the task (how each step will look when finished). By providing them with a concrete image (picture or model) they can continually reference this model to match their performance to it. The same is true for multiple-step tasks. If they have a picture or model of each step, they can match their performance to these visuals.

The second tool is to use a check-off list, to check if any steps are missed. You can either use a check-off list for each step as they go, and/or a completed checklist to check the final product when done to ensure they have not missed anything. Effective monitoring often combines a visual image (model) of the final product with a written checklist to verify that each step has been completed and matches what is expected.

For example, many kids on the spectrum learn to dress themselves, but they often do not check themselves at the end of the task to make sure that they are neatly dressed (shirt buttoned correctly, shirt tucked in, collar arranged, zipper zipped, etc.). We often teach them a skill, but miss the last step of evaluating their own performance to make sure it is done correctly. Many children on the spectrum are not concerned about dress or appearance, since many do not understand that others judge them based on their appearance. Whether it is basic grooming or dressing, it is important for them to learn self-monitoring skills. This becomes so important when they become adults and try to enter the workforce. Hygiene and dress are among the first major issues that can get the person fired. So, start teaching the importance of personal care early and refine it as they age.

As an example, sloppy appearance is often a problem for people on the spectrum. Dressing and personal hygiene are often listed by teachers or employers as ongoing issues. While dressing, many children on the spectrum do not self-monitor how they are doing. They simply put clothes on without referencing to see if they have done it right. They get dressed and have no clue that things are not right. Neurotypical (NT) people tend to monitor themselves as they go, to continually check accuracy of their actions. Kids on the spectrum often do not check their actions.

One way of teaching this is to have the child dress in front of a mirror (a full-length mirror is even better). This way they can watch themselves doing it and monitor how it looks. On one side of the mirror, place a sequential checklist of the steps for dressing. This way the child can reference the list (or picture sequence) for each step of dressing. On the other side of the mirror, place a photo of the child neatly dressed. As the child puts on each item he can reference himself in the mirror and adjust the clothes as needed. At first the parent may need to stand there with him and cue him to reference the picture to match how he looks in the mirror. He may need help seeing what is done incorrectly, what needs adjusting, and how to fix it. Younger children may also need a picture routine chart to show the sequence of putting on the clothes. Once each item is placed on correctly, you describe what is right about it, making visual reference to it in the mirror and matching the picture. When he finishes all the steps of dressing, the last step should be to look in the mirror and visually check his appearance, matching it to the picture (model). If there are certain things that he misses frequently, then write out a simple checklist (shirt tucked in, zipper zipped, etc.). At first, it is best for you to do the check with him, standing in front of the mirror and going through the checklist. Let him check himself and realize when he has missed something. You eventually want him to be self-reflective, evaluating his own performance. Over time, as the task becomes automatic, with the last step being checking his overall appearance, the use of the visual strategies can be removed.

Using visuals to make expectations clear

The post above shows the importance of using visual strategies for dressing (mirror, photo of child dressed neatly, and visual checklist). Whether the visuals are written steps, directions for each step, or pictures of each step, the use of visuals defines the path for correct execution. Until performance becomes automatic, use visual sequential steps (written or pictures) to define each step of the task and a photo of the completed product so the person can check his finished work to see if it is good enough. This can be used for personal care, household chores, or vocational training. These visual strategies tell the child what to do and how to do it, and provide a visual model to match their performance. Once the task performance becomes automatic, then the visual strategies can be faded out.

These strategies are frequently used when teaching simple assembly tasks in vocational training programs. The child is frequently given a visual sequence board (written or pictures) of each step of the task. The child simply does each step at a time and matches it to the picture, in order, until the sequence is completed. When completed, he can check his performance by matching what he did to the completed photo. These strategies can be used for many task performance activities for daily living. The visual strategies provide the child with a path to follow and a model for checking his performance.

Why can't he get it?

No matter how bright or verbal the child is, he often just can't seem to "get it!"

Many things we do in life we have to multitask, thinking of more than one thing at a time. This is an executive function that is not as strong for people on the spectrum. They have problems thinking about more than one thing at a time. When we are engaging in any action, we have to (1) think about what we are going to do, (2) concentrate on doing it, and (3) monitor and evaluate how well we are doing it. These three cognitive processes have to occur simultaneously.

People on the spectrum have a hard time thinking about what they are doing, as they are doing it.

Monitoring how you are doing as you are doing it is essential to evaluating how you are doing when performing or interacting. In order to continually appraise how well you are doing and adjust what you are doing to stay on track, you have to multitask while you are doing it. This ability to step back and monitor your actions is another aspect of executive functioning. Consequently, these children act without the ability to continually evaluate how well they are doing and what affect their behavior has as they are doing it. They often do not have a clue! This is why they know that they don't "get it" and are not in in sync with others, but cannot figure out why.

What to do?

Teach "appraise, act, and evaluate!"

This multitasking process of monitoring our actions by thinking about what we are doing as we do it is a difficult process for people on the spectrum. No matter how intelligent the person is, he struggles with being able to monitor his actions well enough to accurately match his actions to expectations. He has good intentions, thinks he is synchronized with what is expected, but is often not getting it. In some cases he will not be aware of this imbalance, and at other times he will be aware that it didn't work, but not know why. One reason is due to the difficulty people on the spectrum have reading the invisible cues of the situation (context), and another is because they have difficulty monitoring their actions as they are doing them. Neurotypical people have the (executive functioning) ability to simultaneously step back and monitor what they are doing as they are doing it. They can continually monitor how they are doing and the reactions of others, in order to judge how to modify their ongoing behavior. This self-monitoring is essential to fit in well with our social world.

How do people on the spectrum compensate? How can we help children who are struggling with this problem? Since performing this multitasking process simultaneously (do and monitor doing) is too difficult for children on the spectrum, we can teach these steps sequentially, one step at a time. They can learn to appraise what is needed before acting, next complete the action, and then evaluate how well it is done. In other words, their best approach is to (1) appraise well before doing, (2) execute the action, and then (3) look and see how effective their action is, before moving on to the next step of the task. When doing a task, they need to stop periodically to evaluate how they are doing and then appraise what is needed next. So any given activity would consist of a series of pauses to appraise, act, and then evaluate how they are doing. Since they cannot do these three processes simultaneously (it requires thinking about what you are doing while you are doing it), they have to do them sequentially in order. This is similar to how we learn to do a new task. Since it is new to us, we frequently have to stop to evaluate how we are doing and appraise what is next. We have to stop frequently and check in order to monitor how well we are doing.

Processing and evaluating this way is more exhausting and takes much more mental effort. To effectively coordinate actions with others, people on the spectrum need to continually appraise (figure out) what is needed, act on the basis of that appraisal, and then look for cues on how effective their response was. Doing a task with others requires a series of these "appraise, act, and evaluate" sequences. Although they can become more skillful and quicker at doing this type of processing, it will always be somewhat delayed and require extensive mental energy. We need to be aware of this struggle so that we can slow the action down to allow the person to keep up and more accurately appraise, act, and evaluate.

Parents can help their child by doing the executive functioning work initially for him. The parent can coach the child in appraising the situation (what is needed) before acting, then allowing him to execute the action. Next, immediately following the action, evaluate with him how it went (what cues to look for to measure effectiveness). The parent models the thinking process for the child. The parent acts as a social interpreter and coaches the child on what cues to look for to evaluate what is needed, and then how effective his response was. This is a long ongoing teaching process that will improve gradually as the child gains more repetitive practice.

Write it out! Compensating for weak planning and organizational skills

We frequently discuss the need to use visual strategies (picture schedules, written lists, etc.) to help make the child's life predictable and understandable. Writing it out (or providing a picture schedule) provides a visual, concrete path that not only organizes the child's day, but makes it clear and understandable, reducing anxiety and providing continuity. We all use appointment schedules, weekly calendars, visual organizers, or smartphones to help organize and structure our time. For people on the spectrum, these strategies are even more important.

The abilities to plan, organize, remember what to do, and carry out a course of action are all part of the executive functioning skills located in the prefrontal cortex of the brain. This same area of the brain is also responsible for being able to stay focused on a task, monitor what we are doing and how well we are doing it, and shift gears when things are not going well. Consequently, like people with ADHD, those on the spectrum have problems in these areas. When you have weak executive functioning skills, you need to have strong external executive functions. Until children develop these skills, parents and teachers provide these functions for them. They plan and organize for the children, remind them what to do and how to do it, monitor their actions, and provide them with feedback on how well they are doing. As children get older, and that part of the brain matures, we fade out the external controls (adult monitoring) and expect the children to internalize those skills.

Unfortunately, individuals with weak executive functioning have difficulty internalizing these processes. Because of brain wiring differences, they may never be strong in these areas of planning, organizing, and preparing. However, even though it is not easy to change the brain wiring, we can compensate for weaknesses in these areas by making external what is lacking internally. As the child ages, we need to replace adult monitoring with other external executive functions. This can be accomplished by teaching teens and young adults on the spectrum to use visual models (making lists, keeping a schedule, etc.) to organize themselves.

By using daily planners, written checklists, and visual organizers, these visual strategies can provide the outline needed for planning and organizing themselves. In addition, with the advancement of technology (smartphones, iPad, etc.), these concrete compensations can be made very portable, with auditory reminders to do daily routine events. As children get older, we want to teach them how to use written lists, written schedules, calendars, visual organizers, flow charts, and problem-solving outlines to help organize their time, plan out steps of activities, brainstorm alternatives, and provide checklists for everything from the morning routine, cooking, organizing homework, to going grocery shopping.

In addition to organizing and problem solving, people on the spectrum can use written outlines to prepare for upcoming events. We often talk about preparing the child before events by previewing that activity. Usually this includes previewing (1) what he can expect to happen (in sequential order if possible), (2) what is expected of him, (3) what barriers or problems he may experience, and (4) what strategies he can use to handle any problems. By parents previewing these four things, it prepares the child for what to expect, increases predictability, and reduces anxiety. However, eventually the person needs to learn to preview for himself. He needs to "appraise" situations on his own to identify what is needed, what is expected, and what potential problem situations may arise. This way, he can be prepared for what he is entering into. We need to transfer this previewing from the parents to self-management tools. Using a written outline answering these four questions (what to expect, what is expected of them, what possible problems, and what possible solutions) can be a tool the person can use to outline events before going into them.

It is important that individuals on the spectrum learn to use written schedules, check-off lists, task sequence lists, visual organizers, and planning outlines to help them plan, organize, and prepare themselves to navigate their daily routines.

They can be reliable tools for compensating for areas that may remain weak for their entire life.

Help me, I'm stuck!

Does your child get stuck in an action that he seems to have difficulty shifting away from? This might be a repetitive behavior, vocal noise, activity, or thought. With this problem, the child initiates the behavior, task, or thought and then seems to have difficulty ending it. He continues on and on in a fixated pattern.

Our ability to shift from one activity or thought to another is an executive function of the frontal cortex of our brain. It allows us to initiate, implement, and stop a behavior fluidly, with little difficulty. For many children on the spectrum, these functions are weak. Once a behavior gets started, especially if it is a repetitive pattern that feels good, the child has difficulty shifting gears and moving on to the next expectation. Like a person who doesn't know how to end a conversation, he goes on and on and on.

Sometimes these behaviors are labeled as fixations, compulsive behavior, stereotypic behavior, or perseverations. All of these behaviors/thoughts have in common the difficulty ending the chain once it gets going. Often I see parents and teachers get upset and simply demand the child to stop, only to have the child blow up in an emotional rage. I think we must recognize that many times these behavior patterns are difficult for the child to stop, and they need to transition out of them. I have found the following to be successful in different situations with different children:

- Some kids simply need a warning of when the behavior needs to stop. They are not really stuck, just hyper-focused and thoroughly into what they are doing. These children often respond to a reminding sequence. Parents give five-minute, three-minute, and one-minute reminders that the activity will end and what will occur next. These same children do well with clearly defined start and stop times to the activity. We often use visual timers to clearly define the beginning and ending of the behavior: "Johnny, you can play video games for 30 minutes." Use a visual timer so the child can tell when time is ending, and provide reminders with three minutes and then one minute left. These children also respond well to a picture schedule that lets them see what is coming up next, so shifting gears is easier.

- For behaviors that are compulsive or perseverative, another technique can work well. First, include yourself briefly in what the child is doing, without asking him to stop or directing him to do something else. Talk about what he is doing and do it with him, turning it into a "we-do" activity. This draws the child's attention from the task/behavior and on to you, before redirecting him on to something else. For example, I had a child who would engage in hand-washing motions under the running water. It appeared he enjoyed the sensory stimulation, but would get stuck in the action and have difficulty ending the activity. He would get upset when the parent came in and told him to stop. Instead, we first eased the transition by having the parent go in and include themselves in rubbing their hands together under the water and talking about how good it felt—doing it with the child, turning it into a "we-do" activity. Then, once the child's attention shifted on to the parent, one parent talked about what to do next, turned the faucet off, and moved on. This "including themselves" in the action, interrupted the perseverative response and allowed the child to switch gears.

- In addition to the above, you can also try creating a concrete ending to the sequence. In the example above, you might include yourself in the action first, then count to ten and turn the water off. I do this a lot with behaviors that include repetitive trials of the same behavior. I will say, "OK, we will do it five more times and then stop." Together we count to five, and then move on. Giving the child a concrete stopping point allows his brain to transition.

- Often I find that the person might need gentle touch to shift the brain's focus. So, I will quietly say something to him, and gently touch him on the arm as I include myself in what he is doing. This tactile stimulation seems to jar him from what he is stuck on. This seems to break the neurological feedback loop and allow him to shift.

- Sometimes the child gets stuck because he starts an activity that doesn't have a clear stopping point. These children will get anxious because they do not know when something is good enough or completed. For these children, we usually preview all activity ahead of time and let them concretely know when the task is completed.

- For the hard-to-shift children, we will often follow the behavior that they frequently get stuck on with another favorite activity, so it is more motivating to make the shift. This way we can more easily gain their cooperation in shifting from their perseverative pattern to another activity that they enjoy.

Between the children's tendency to hyper-focus attention on something of interest and the difficulty ending one activity and moving on to the next, it is important to understand that part of this perseveration is a problem in brain functioning. When the child gets stuck in a neurological feedback loop he often needs gentle help in transitioning. However, try to ease the transition, rather than direct the child to stop.

Inability to focus!

Many children on the spectrum struggle with attention, concentration, and organizational skills (similar to children with ADHD). They can at times be hyper-focused on a topic of extreme interest, or be totally distracted and unable to focus on tasks that have little meaning for them. Their attention can also vary widely based on how taxed their nervous system is. If they are sleep-deprived, hungry, not feeling well, sick, or under-aroused, their ability to focus will be greatly hampered.

What we don't realize is that processing normal daily activities for children on the spectrum can be so much more draining for them compared with neurotypical children. They need frequent breaks to regroup and re-energize. As the day rolls on, their mental energy reserve gets depleted, and their ability to attend and focus becomes compromised. If the last activity required strong concentration, they may not be able to focus on the next activity. Giving frequent breaks and providing a sensory diet that maximizes the arousal level can help significantly in maximizing attention.

Kris posted a question about her son's inconsistent attention and concentration. I thought this topic may be of interest to many of you.

 Kris's question

Why is it sometimes my son's light is "on" and other times it is "off?" This is especially true when it comes to writing and focusing. Either he does a nice job or he's totally tuned out and unresponsive. Any suggestions for what we can do? He's a smart young man, but this is a major road block.

AUTISM DISCUSSION PAGE

Attention and concentration can be major deficits for children on the spectrum. They are either "on" or "off." Sometimes it has to do with the activity itself and whether it has purpose and meaning to them, or if it is a preferred interest of theirs. The children can be very hyper-focused on tasks of high interest and when the activity has valued purpose for them. However, they frequently cannot focus long on tasks that have little value for them. So, with your son's writing, try to keep a journal of each assignment. What time of day, where is he writing at, what is he asked to write about, and how long the project is. You may pick up patterns and learn to predict which circumstances increase his concentration and which do not. Then you can learn to maximize the circumstances which increase success for your son. If the topic has little interest for him, then you may need to break the assignment into smaller parts, and work for short periods at a time until it is complete. You may also need to build in reinforcement for completing the assignment to increase his motivation.

Loss of concentration and inability to attend can also occur if the child is distracted by something else and/or is perseverating on another activity. He may already be preoccupied with something else and cannot focus. Also, the child's ability to focus can be determined by how much mental energy he has at that time. Most daily activities require a lot more mental energy for kids on the spectrum, and they can get drained quickly. Their mental reserves can be influenced by anything else that has happened that day, if they had enough sleep, if they are hungry, or if they are sick or tired. So, when their energy reserve is drained, they will lose their attention and do poorly. They cannot focus when they are drained.

So, try to have homework completed at the same time of the day and done in the same calm, quiet place each time. Allow the child time to rebound after coming home from school to re-energize. If your child appears more drained and less into it, try to break the task down into short parts and keep the sessions brief with frequent breaks. If the child simply cannot focus, try again later. Sometimes it may help to assist the child in getting started, then help him through the activity. For some children it may be good to skip it for the night, go to bed a little earlier, and do it in the morning. As a last resort, when in need, build reinforcement to motivate completing the task (e.g. computer time).

Sometimes, because of sensory processing issues, the children have problems with their arousal levels. When under- or over-aroused, they have difficulty concentrating. When they are over-aroused it is best to give them time to escape, calm, and organize themselves before working on tasks. If they are under-aroused, they often benefit from physical, up-and-moving activity that will increase their arousal level and keep them alert and focused. A child may attend better when listening to music through an MP3 player, sitting on an exercise ball, or chewing gum. A good sensory diet will help with that. In general, if the child is eating a good diet, sleeping well, and getting plenty of exercise, he can consistently focus better.

Some children have true ADHD, and concentration can come and go based on biochemical imbalances. For these children, medication can help. I would try everything else first.

It is important that as the child gets older he learns what affects his concentration and what accommodations he can make to maximize his attention and concentration. Many adults have to feed their nervous system alerting stimulation (drinking from a straw, eating something crunchy, chewing gum, listening to music, standing instead of sitting, etc.), take frequent up-and-moving breaks, break the tasks down into smaller parts, and move to a distraction-free setting to stay focused. When the task is boring for that person, it often helps to build in self-reinforcing strategies to increase motivation. By learning to regulate his own arousal level, the person becomes more empowered.

Taking responsibility for your actions!

Many children on the spectrum have difficulty claiming responsibility for their actions, especially if the effects of their behavior were not what were expected. Lindsey, one of our members on this page, had a great question which I thought would make an interesting post for everyone!

 Lindsey's question

Do you have any previous posts regarding kids on the spectrum taking responsibility for their actions? My son has a difficult time with this. A good example would be accidents. If someone accidentally hurts him, he gets upset and says they did it on purpose and if he hurts someone, he gets angry when they cry because it's an accident. This is a goal on his IEP, and he reaches it only 45 percent of the time. My concern is that this is too difficult a goal. If you have any suggestions, I would really appreciate it. Thanks!

AUTISM DISCUSSION PAGE

To take responsibility for one's actions and to assume intent in others are two different processes. To understand the intent of others would take perspective-taking skills which you would have to teach. I am assuming the school is not doing that. Also, when he does something to hurt someone else, he probably feels that it was an accident. Not the behavior per se, but the fact that it hurt someone else. He probably is not anticipating that his action is going to hurt someone else, or that he was expecting the consequence of that behavior to happen (e.g. break something when too rough). He may be responsible for the behavior, but doesn't feel responsible for the consequence (someone getting hurt or something getting broken). He doesn't want to take responsibility for the consequence that he didn't intend to happen. He would only take responsibility for something that he intended to happen. He also doesn't see, or connect, the consequences that were not the expected results of his behavior. So, he may deny that his behavior event resulted in that consequence.

To take responsibility he needs to be able to (1) appraise what he needs to do in a situation, (2) monitor how he is doing as he is doing it, and then (3) evaluate the effects that his behavior has after doing it. Most children on the spectrum are poor at all three. So, to help the child learn to take responsibility, you need to (1) help him appraise a situation before acting (talk it over), (2) anticipate what effects his behavior will have (both on what he intends and on others), and then (3) help him evaluate the effects of his behavior after doing it (both on the intended result and on others).

So, I would recommend that, before you expect him to take responsibility for his actions, talk about what "taking responsibility" means and that the consequences (effects) of his behavior may not always be what was intended; that taking responsibility doesn't necessarily mean doing it on purpose, and it can be an accident. So it can be an "accident" and he still takes responsibility for an accident. However, you will have to connect the "unintended" effect directly to his actions for him to see how he created it.

Look for opportunities throughout the day to talk about what he is doing, what effects his behavior has, whether it meets his intended objective, and how others are interpreting or experiencing his behavior. He is not looking at the unintended effects of his behavior, only the intended objective. Help him see how his behavior affects his surroundings and others around him. Remember, he probably does not even think others have a different perspective from his.

There are three situations in which you can discuss this: (1) talk about your actions as you are doing them (what you intend, how effective it is, and what effects it has on others), (2) discuss the actions you see of others around you (watch what others are doing and talk about what others are thinking and feeling, and the effects of their actions), and (3) help him appraise (ahead of time) and evaluate (after behavior) the effects of his own actions.

When discussing this, make sure you evaluate what intended effects his behavior had (whether he reached his goal) and discuss the effects his actions had on others (how they think and feel about it). If possible, try to also do this before he acts (what do you want to do, what effects will it have, and how others react). This social cognition does not develop on its own, in the way it does for some NT children. You have to do the cognitive processing externally (talk out loud) at first. You have to be his inner voice, until it becomes more automatic for him.

Compensating for executive functioning issues

People with executive functioning issues usually have difficulties in the areas of attention, impulse control, working memory, planning and organizing, monitoring one's own actions, and multitasking. Neuroscience is in the infancy stage in the area of brain plasticity and strengthening the wiring in the areas of the brain that have weak connections. So, for individuals with ADD and ASD, most strategies have focused on finding ways to compensate for those weaknesses, building in strategies to work around the issues. These usually include (1) changing the physical environment to make the skill easier, (2) making modifications to the task itself, and (3) teaching the individual coping skills to help him compensate for the given weakness. For example, in the area of attention/concentration, these three areas may consist of:

1. Physical environment: making modifications to the classroom to minimize distractions, sitting the child to face away from activity that may distract, using partitions if needed to do work, taking the child out of the classroom for tests, etc.

2. Tasks modifications: breaking the task down into smaller parts, presenting only one portion at a time, using page rulers/templates, giving/providing/using written outlines to highlight important information, etc.

3. Individual coping skills: sitting on an exercise ball, chewing gum, and listening to an MP3 player to facilitate attention; using visual schedules to do lists, and task sequence lists to keep the child oriented to what to do and when to do it; setting auditory cues (alarms) on watches and smartphones to cue the child into what and when to do something; and using problem-solving/task completion worksheets to outline the steps to complete.

To compensate for weak executive skills, we usually need to provide the function externally to substitute for what the brain cannot do internally until we can teach an automatic routine (habit) to take its place. The habitual routine takes the place of the need for the cognitive thinking skill the person lacks. When someone has good executive functioning, we assume he has the ability to inhibit his impulsive response long enough to use his thinking skills to appraise, evaluate, and execute what is needed. When the brain does not do that naturally, we have to provide that function externally (e.g. using the previous strategies) until we establish a set routine that becomes automatic (habit). For example:

1. We may use a picture routine to cue someone into doing his morning routine, until it is repeated enough to become habit. Once the routine becomes automatic, the picture routine can be faded out. However, for every new routine, we may need always to start off with a visual schedule until the routine becomes habit. As the person becomes older, he learns always to set up a visual list (checklist, written steps) when starting new routines, until they become automatic habits. We use a habitual routine to by-pass the executive functioning (think it through) process.

2. A child who impulsively blurts out comments while the teacher is talking can be taught (with prompts and practice) to raise his hand before talking. The teacher has to prompt, practice, and reinforce until it becomes habit. We might also place a visual cue card for raising the hand (no talk, raise hand) on his desk to visually remind him. Once this behavior becomes habit, we can remove the cue card.

3. A child who has difficulty rushing through tasks and is doing a sloppy job may be given a visual model or photo of the finished product to match his work to. He matches what he does to the visual model. Once he can complete the product accurately, we can fade out the visual cue card.

As you can see, in all of these examples, we are not necessarily improving the executive functioning skills, but providing the missing function externally until it becomes a habit, which by-passes the need for the cognitive (thinking) mediation. We all need to develop strategies to compensate for our weaknesses. By focusing on developing our strengths and compensating for our weaknesses, we grow stronger!

When in doubt, schedule it out!

Many people with ADHD and autism have difficulty doing chores around the house and tackling big projects; these consist of simply too much organizing, planning, and multitasking for many on the spectrum. The more they think about it, the harder it gets. When faced with a large task, the thought of physical exertion and organized planning overwhelms them. In addition, if the task is boring, they cannot initiate that first step to jump-start themselves. For many on the spectrum, or those with ADHD, if the task is boring they will struggle maintaining attention on it. However, the longer they wait, the more it piles up and the more depressed and anxious they feel about it.

I have found two strategies that often help. Only do short, simple tasks at a time and schedule these tasks into their daily routines. Break the tasks down into simple parts and only do short periods of work at a time. For example, for house tasks, schedule short 20–30 minute tasks, once or twice a day, usually at the same time every day. That way the tasks are short and easily managed. If they are boring and it's difficult to maintain their attention, make the task even shorter. Take larger projects (e.g. clean house) and break them into one short task every day (clean bathroom on Mondays, vacuum on Tuesdays, etc.). Make the tasks routine in their daily schedules. We all are creatures of routine. Once you establish the routine (which usually takes about six weeks of doing it consistently each day), it becomes a habit and easier to do.

Keep the task short enough that they can maintain their attention through it, and schedule the tasks prior to doing preferred activities (favorite interests). I prefer to do one load of laundry each morning, rather than waiting and doing a lot of laundry once a week. If they cannot clean the house as a total project, break it down into simple concrete tasks that can be completed quickly and give them a sense of completing something. Follow it with a preferred interest (read, computer, video game, etc.) that motivates them to complete the chore again. Always do the brief, non-preferred tasks before allowing them to engage in preferred activity (first do fun this, then the activity). They get rewarded twice: the sense of accomplishing something plus getting to do what they enjoy.

It is all about how they view it. Focus on what they do complete, rather than what they don't finish. If they do a big project (clean house) and only get a third of it done, because they cannot stay organized long enough, they then see what they didn't get done, feel depressed, and are less motivated to do it again. However, if the objective is only to complete one simple task, they complete it and feel good about themselves. Quit while they are ahead, and don't tax them. Don't keep working until they are exhausted or dreadfully bored. They will remember that the next time and talk themselves out of doing it. Keep it short and simple!

Also, for many on the spectrum, judging the amount of time needed to do something is often poor. They look at a block of time and think they might easily complete a lot of work. They inevitably think they can complete more work in a period of time than they typically complete. They get rushed, become anxious, and then depressed when they do not complete it. If you think it will only take 15 minutes do to something, give them 30 minutes to do it. When making out your schedule, add at least 15 minutes to every task that you think will take 30 minutes to complete. They will get them done, without rushing, and they will feel good about themselves, and be more productive!

Remember, a little amount done completely is much more rewarding than a lot left uncompleted. Just do a little at a time, give them more time than expected, and follow it with a preferred activity to enjoy and rebound. They will feel happy about what they do complete and actually be more motivated to do more in the future.

Break it down, schedule it out! Testimony

Ashley, an adult on the spectrum, describes her experiences with organizing and completing household chores. This is a good example of the strategies in "When in doubt, schedule it out!" Thanks, Ashley!

ASHLEY

I usually break up all the things that need to be done into small tasks, and keep them all in a list. When I think of something that needs to be done, instead of trying to think about when I will do it, I just add it to the list on the spot and put it out of my mind. I have a set of things that automatically add themselves to my list once a week, or once a fortnight, etc. Because they're all so small, the barrier to starting one feels much lower, but then once I complete that first small task I often end up feeling enthused I got it done and will go to my list for another small task. I essentially trick myself into a state of mind where the starting barriers matter less than the feeling of having just achieved something. Four tasks of 15 minutes each feels like you've achieved a lot that day (wow, I got four things done!), while one task of 60 minutes tends to be harder to maintain, easier to rationalize not starting, and more likely to hit a focus barrier. Since I keep all the tasks in the list, I usually end up ticking off three or four when I planned to only do one. So instead of a "do X on Monday" item, I have a "check my list and do one item on Monday" routine. It makes my process more flexible, but keeps the barriers low enough that I still actually get them done! Because most things add themselves to the list periodically the general stuff tends to keep up to date, but because it's not a locked in a "do X now" system the more reactive needs get done reasonably well too. Because even the smallest most mundane tasks can be put on the list, ticking them off and realizing you actually did complete things helps avoid the depressive/anxious feeling of not getting something done as well.

Chapter 5

RIGID, INFLEXIBLE THINKING

People who are flexible are able to see different perspectives, consider different options, and easily shift gears when things don't go as expected. Generally speaking, people who are flexible are by the far the happiest people. They can go with the flow and bend with the wind. They do not get easily anxious and have minimal difficulty seeing different options or trying different ways. They do not get disturbed by simple snags, minor frustrations, or initial setbacks.

To live successfully in our world, you must be flexible! In order to be flexible we need to understand that everything is relative, based on the demands of the given situation and the options available to us. We all have known people who hold on to rigid beliefs even in the face of strong evidence against those ideas. We are all different in our degree of flexible thinking. Most people on the spectrum have difficulty with flexible thinking. Rigid, inflexible thinking is at the heart of much of their anxiety. Listed below are some of the qualities of rigid/inflexible thinking.

RIGID, INFLEXIBLE THINKING

- Autism thinking is very concrete, literal, and absolute.

- Rules, regulations, and expectations are black and white, and right or wrong, with little room for interpretation.

- Thinking can be rigid and inflexible, with little tolerance for variability.

- Variability creates insecurity and anxiety.

- Child may hold on to rigid beliefs and expectations, and melt down if things are not going as expected.

- Child feels safer with concrete, predictable rules and laws that remain constant.

When your thinking is very literal and tied to the facts, thinking tends to be very black and white, either/or and right/wrong, with little room for gray area. This type of thinking leads to the person applying rigid rules to situations that require variability and flexibility. Rarely do rules and regulations (especially social rules) apply rigidly without variation across situations and settings. Unfortunately, when you cannot read the fluctuations between situations, then you cannot adjust your thinking and must hold tight to your rules and expectations. Our world is way too relative for most people on the spectrum. What applies in one situation doesn't necessarily apply to the next situation. This results in anxiety, misinterpretation of situations, out-of-place behavior, the need to control all situations to match their expectations, and extreme anger when things don't go their way. Things have to be the same and stay the same each time, or the world falls apart.

Black and white thinking

- Things are either right or wrong, good or bad, with little in between.
- Cannot see gray area.
- Needs one right answer.
- Difficulty with multiple alternatives.
- Difficulty with evaluating "good enough."
- Inflexible, hard to change mind.

Black and white thinking consists of two extremes on a continuum of variability. When you cannot read the gray area, you need to have one right answer. For people on the spectrum, multiple options that need to be appraised and evaluated can cause extreme anxiety. They prefer one right way of doing something. That way, once they learn it, it is constant. However, most of the world does not operate that easily.

Many of these children are strong perfectionists, who melt down if they are not perfect at something the first time. They are unable to evaluate when a response is "good enough" and must get it perfect. Hence, they are rarely satisfied and may spend countless hours trying to get it right. They have a very difficult time changing their mind, even if what they are doing is not working. They may freak if you try to interrupt them or offer them a different way.

Cognitive distortions

For some of these children, their rigid/inflexible thinking is often based on rigid belief systems, called cognitive distortions, which taint everything they do. We all can relate to one or more of these cognitive distortions.

Catastrophizing	Exaggerates the importance or negative aspects of things: "It is horrible that…"
Over-generalizing	Views one negative event as a never-ending defeat: "I suck!", "I will never be able to…"
All-or-nothing thinking	Black and white thinking. "I have to be perfect or I am a failure."
Mental filter	Picks out one single negative detail and obsesses about it, darkening the whole event.
Emotional reasoning	Negative emotions can overwhelm rational reasoning.

Cognitive distortions are rigid, inflexible ways of viewing the world. They are at the base of much anxiety, whether on the spectrum or not. We can recognize these cognitive styles in all of us to some degree, but they are more exaggerated in autism spectrum disorders. Which ones apply to your child? Black and white thinking lends itself to cognitive distortions.

Related behavior challenges

As you can imagine, this rigid, inflexible thinking can lead to a host of behavior challenges. The anxiety that rigid thinking generates can be expressed in the following behavior challenges:

- Rigidly seeks predictable, static routine/activities.

- Actively resists change.

- Must control all activity and interactions.

- Seeks rigid routine and self-controlled activities to avoid chaos/confusion.

- Shows strong resistance to following the lead of others.

- Exhibits compulsive, repetitive, ritualistic, self-absorbed, oppositional behaviour; self-stimulation and tantrums.

Of course, this rigid/inflexible thinking results in a lot of the acting-out behavior that we see in our children. When the world doesn't go exactly the way they view it, they can melt down very quickly. Now, the biggest problems occur when a rigid/inflexible child meets a rigid/inflexible adult! All hell breaks out! The more rigid the child, the more flexible the adult has to be. Since the adult supposedly has better self-control and is "wiser," they should become more flexible to hold off major confrontation.

For many of you, your children must control all activity and interaction to feel safe. Uncertainty creates strong anxiety, and they resist following your lead. To keep sanity in the household, you usually have to give in and follow the child's lead. This rigid/inflexible thinking can control a whole household, holding everyone in it captive.

In addition to sensory issues, rigid/inflexible thinking is at the heart of much of the anxiety experienced by those on the spectrum. It creates major stress, both for the child and for the people around him. The world has to be his way, or it crumbles. This inflexible thinking can be very difficult to change. The adherence to rigid beliefs, rules, and rituals helps reduce the chaos and confusion. It also serves as a defense mechanism to reduce uncertainty and anxiety. To help teach greater flexibility, we must start where the child is at, help him feel safe, and then gradually stretch his comfort zone. The following posts will suggest ways to promote flexible thinking, reducing both anxiety and challenging behaviors.

Dealing with snags: rigid, inflexible thinking

Individuals on the spectrum often have trouble with rigid, inflexible thinking. Everything is black and white, right or wrong, either/or, good or bad. They also have trouble shifting gears when things don't go as expected. Adding to the fire, they also have a hard time with relativity. For us, there are different degrees of importance that little snags have for us. We judge our emotional reaction based on the degree of importance, or threat, that the snag means to us. Kids on the spectrum have trouble with relativity. They go from 0 to 100 rapidly and often over little snags that amaze us. Part of it is their poor ability to judge the degree of conflict the snag represents, and part of it is their strong feeling of incompetence in dealing with unexpected conflict. Now, given the way they think and react with raw emotion, this all gets worse with anxiety. The stronger the anxiety, the greater the rigidity. The world has to stay the same, very predictable, and go the way they expect. If it doesn't, they collapse in insecurity.

Given the difficulties children on the spectrum have, there are ways to teach greater flexibility:

1. Teach the concept of "same but different." Children on the spectrum can hold rigidly to routine, creating meltdowns when things change a little. To help develop greater flexibility, have fun figuring out how to do things in different ways. For example, with smaller children we might

figure out how many different ways we can play catch. We may play catch with a small ball, large ball, football, tennis ball, rolled-up socks, pillows, rolling a ball, bouncing a ball, tossing a high ball, etc. You can build this into everyday activities (go different ways to school, eat with different utensils, take an item and figure out how many different ways you can use it, etc.). If you go out for ice cream or a snack, try a different place or different flavor when you get there. This helps build flexibility. Make sure you talk about it before doing it. This makes it fun and takes the anxiety out of it.

2. Teach more than one way to do things. Children with inflexible thinking often see only one right way to do something. Throughout the day, as you do things together, talk about different options for doing things and solving simple problems. Discuss pros and cons, but don't focus on any one being necessarily better than the other. Focus instead on having more than one right way to do things. Get him to try different options instead of rigidly holding to one. If the child refuses to budge and demands his way, then try to compromise. Try the new way, then he can do it his way. Make it fun and see how many different ways you can do things.

3. Teach "good enough" thinking. Kids on the spectrum often see responses as good or bad, with no gray area in between. This develops into perfectionism and the need for everything to be perfect. While focusing on different ways to do things, talk about what performance will be "good enough" to meet what is needed. In the game of basketball, the objective is not to make every basket, but just to make more than your opponent. When doing things, identify what would be good enough and then only perform until you reach that objective. Focus on how it doesn't have to be perfect to get the job done.

Readers who want more ideas and activities for fostering "same but different" and "good enough" thinking are recommended to read the works of Dr. Steven Gutstein and Rachel Sheely (2002a, 2002b). They have published extensively on fostering flexible thinking.

4. Teach the child to rate, or gauge, the intensity of things. Use a visual thermometer or rating scale to measure emotional reaction or intensity of a problem. Are we a "little bit" upset, "moderately" upset, or "a lot" upset? Or use a four- or five-point scale to rate the intensity of emotions, difficulty of something, or degree of conflict a problem causes. Kari Dunn Buron and Mitzi Curtis introduced us to the "5 Point Scale" in their book *Incredible 5 Point Scale: The Significantly Improved and Expanded Second Edition; Assisting Students in Understanding Social Interactions and Controlling their Emotional Responses* (2012). Work with the child to rate some of

the common things that upset him. Let him rate the degree of threat or intensity that issues actually pose for him. Then discuss how he can handle them, and cue him in ("Remember this is only a 2") when the conflict arises. As you both experience things during the day, discuss if you are a little bit happy, sad, or mad, and if a problem is a little snag, so-so snag, or big snag.

5. Teach the child a coping response for when snags occur. Teach a specific phrase like "I'm OK, I can handle this." Take a deep breath, count to ten, and look for alternatives (or talk to an adult). Tailor the coping response to match the child. Practice the response, doing it together. Role-play it, and use it frequently during the day.

6. Once the child becomes more competent and confident dealing with rating the intensity of events and learns coping skills for dealing with them, then start building snags into his daily routine. Start by building in one or two small snags into the child's day. Tell him that something in the event is not going to go as expected, but don't tell him what. Remind him of the coping strategies, and then praise him for using them during the situations. Make it fun and allow him to feel competent by handling it. Gradually build up to bigger snags.

7. Sit down with your child and make a list of least to most disturbing events for him. Use common situations that often upset him (typical snags). Discuss "plan Bs" for each snag and how to cope with each. Make an index card for each event, with three things listed: (1) the snag, (2) the coping skill for handling his emotions, and (3) the "plan B" for solving the problem. Review it ahead of time and preview it just before going into the event. Help him through it and praise heavily when he is successful.

8. From the list of "least to most" anxiety-provoking events, tackle the least anxiety-provoking first. Provide repeated exposure to the snag and prompt/reward using the coping strategy. Gradually build up to bigger snags. If he has a meltdown, do not dwell on it; simply back up, break it down, and try it again.

9. Have the child keep a competency journal. Every time he is successful at tackling snags or handling a difficult situation, have him write it in a journal, keeping a log of successful times dealing with uncertainty. Take photos and make picture stories of tackling difficult snags! Review it with him and discuss how he handled it successfully. When snags occur, remind him how he has handled similar situations before.

Does your child display perfectionism?
Must be perfect, or a failure!

Perfectionism is a natural by-product of "black and white," "all or nothing" thinking that many children on the spectrum display. They tend to see things as either right or wrong, displaying difficulty reading the gray areas in between. Most situations in life are not right or wrong, good or bad, but vary in degrees depending on the context in which we are acting. In our world, most situations do not have one right way of doing things, but several responses that can work given the demands of the situation. When doing a task, we need to know when our response or performance is "good enough," or know which option among the alternatives is "good enough." Over time, people become competent in measuring what level of competence is good enough. From this appraisal they can match, monitor, and modify their behavior accordingly.

For example, if a person wants to get an A in his class, he may realize that if gets a 90 percent or better the teacher will give him an A. This means on a test of a hundred questions, he can miss up to 10 to get an A. So, he doesn't have to be perfect. To win in a soccer game, the players do not have to make 100 percent of their shots but only one more than their opponent. Any percentage of shooting will be good enough, as long as they score more than their opponent. "Good enough" is measured by matching your performance to meet the objectives of the task at hand. This is called "good enough" thinking.

"Good enough" thinking is being able to evaluate when a response is good enough to meet the demands of the situation. Some people on the spectrum have trouble with "good enough" thinking. It is either right or wrong, with little room for gray area. This difficulty sensing when performance is good enough leads to a strong need to be perfect. They interpret any performance that is not perfect as failure. If you are anxious, and already struggle with self-esteem, then anything other than perfection is seen as failure. Hence, such high expectation is impossible to reach, so the person gathers strong feelings of incompetence, anxiety, and depression (feeding further the drive for perfectionism).

Teaching flexible thinking with multiple options

Children with inflexible thinking often have difficulty with facing multiple options. They usually want there to be only "one right way" so they are certain to be correct. Situations that present multiple ways of doing things make them uncomfortable since they have to appraise and evaluate each option, and there is no way of doing it. There is no way to be certain that their option is the right (best) one.

We work with children on this by placing them in activities that do not have one right answer, or activities that are impossible to get right every time (such as shooting baskets in basketball). Many young children want to know the one right way of doing things. I place them in situations where there is no one right answer. We have to figure out which option will work the best. Once children learn one way of doing things, they tend to rigidly adhere to that way. So, by placing them in situations for which there is more than one right way, they begin to cognitively appraise the options available. Now, this will not happen immediately. The children will often pick out one of the options and rigidly adhere to that option. This is natural, since it lessens uncertainty and avoids the anxiety of deciding among alternatives. In these cases, we will (1) block that option, (2) pause to give the child a chance to choose another option, and (3) point out alternatives if the child doesn't choose one without support. This also encourages the child sometimes to pick an alternative that is not perfect, but is good enough to meet the objective.

For example, I love teaching "multiple options" and "good enough" thinking in my sports programs for children on the spectrum. For soccer, in the beginning, I will first let the child dribble down and shoot the ball into the goal (SCORE!). This is fun and establishes an objective. Then I start standing in their way to create a barrier for the child to have to go around me to score. Some children will automatically pick one side to go around me and will stay with that option over and over if I let them. So, once I see that they are consistently going one way, I will overplay them to that side so it forces them to go the opposite way. This creates a little anxiety at first. They want that one way to work at all times. When blocking them, I pause and give them a chance to figure it out on their own. If they freeze or get too anxious, I will gesture for them to go the other way. I try to use gestures first, before verbally telling them. By using gestures, they have to mentally engage more and think it through to interpret what the gestures mean. So, as they get better at getting past me, I will put a little more pressure on them, making it harder and harder to get around me, and never the same way. This requires them to shift gears several times before they are successful. Once they are comfortable with this, I will up the ante by stealing the ball from them, requiring them to steal it back. Each time I up the ante, it creates a little bit of anxiety, enough to alert them to shift gears, but not enough to overwhelm them. It requires them to mentally engage and figure it out. These are the dynamic thinking tools they need to tackle uncertainty and reduce rigid thinking.

This is similar to "exposure therapy." By scaffolding the activities to maximize success and providing repeated, successful exposure to figuring out what is good enough, we help the children learn to evaluate options when they reach road blocks. In this process we also teach the children the principle of "fail to succeed." You make mistakes until you practice and get better. If you don't make mistakes, you are not stretching yourself and learning to get better. Mistakes are expected and acceptable for learning.

Just as in soccer and basketball, once they begin feeling more competent at one level, I will up the ante, creating minor snags and mistakes so they see that these "accidents" simply mean they need to re-evaluate and try a different way. Some children actually learn to enjoy the challenge of tackling these barriers, to not fear making mistakes, and to learn how to shift gears and choose alternatives when mistakes happen. You teach them that they often have to fail to succeed, which is the principle that you have to experience failure (when tackling new challenges) in order to succeed—that failure means learning what didn't work to find out what does work. Or it simply means more practice is needed to be successful. We first struggle to succeed before we gain competence. Mistakes are often necessary to gain success. This is not a principle they learn by simply having it explained to them. Many parents try to convince their children of this. The children have to feel it by doing it. You have to put them in life situations for which they feel the challenge to feel the success.

As the children get older, we will sit down and cognitively evaluate each task to define what responses are good enough. They have to identify what the goal of the activity is and how good the response has to be to reach that goal. This allows them to cognitively structure the behavior needed to succeed at the goal, without needing to be perfect. For teens and young adults, we use cognitive behavior therapy. Perfectionism is one of the cognitive distortions that underlies anxiety and depression. So, we teach the individual to evaluate the difficulty of the task, the worst that can happen if not successful, the probably that these consequences will occur, and then access the options available.

Perfectionism and "fear of failure"

Perfectionism in autism is often self-expectation, not a need to match the unrealistic expectations of others. Yes, trying to meet the expectations of others is anxiety-producing and can be an ongoing problem for people on the spectrum, but that is not usually what drives perfectionism. For kids on the spectrum, perfectionism is usually a self-driven expectation based on their inability to perceive what is good enough. Since the person cannot read what is good enough, perfection is required!

Perfectionism is often not an "other" driven dynamic, when people put too much pressure on the child to meet their expectations. It is not developed by over-demanding parents or pushy teachers. For many children on the spectrum, it is an internally driven need to match their own unrealistic expectations. Since they feel very fragile in their own sense of competency, if they are not doing it correctly they believe they are failing. It is often called a cognitive distortion. The person exaggerates their appraisal of what is needed to be "adequate." For them to feel adequate, they have to be perfect. Perfect is the only thing that is good enough.

In addition, the need for perfectionism often results in fear of failure. This person often needs to do it completely correctly the first time or they get very anxious about failing. For these children, the fear of failure will make them give up immediately and refuse to try, or they will obsessively do it over and over again (the same way since they don't know how to modify what they are doing) while getting angrier. Some kids avoid trying in the first place, to avoid the anxiety of not being able to do it perfectly the first time. They often cannot (1) appraise what is needed to succeed, (2) understand that practice is required before succeeding, and (3) understand that you often have to fail in order to succeed (make mistakes while practicing). They do not know how to appraise what they need to work on and how to practice. Consequently, their whole self-worth is based on doing it perfectly the first time (because they don't know how to practice), and anything short of that is failure. In addition, some people on the spectrum may even project these unrealistic expectations on to others and get angry when others do not meet those same expectations. This interferes greatly with being able to make friends, because they often demand the same performance out of others as they do of themselves.

Fighting perfectionism: teaching flexibility

Perfectionism often comes from the either/or, all or nothing, black and white thinking. This comes from difficulty evaluating context and assessing "good enough." This also results in wanting to know the one right way of doing something and having difficulty understanding several options and multiple meanings. This also drives the desire for concrete rules and laws to govern behavior. My experience is that social stories are good for teaching concrete rules and norms, but to teach flexible thinking you need to put children in activities that lead them to think flexibly. There are severe ways to teach flexible, relative thinking:

- Put the children in simple situations where there is no right way of doing it. Don't tell them how to get through it; however, do the activity with them and help them think their way through it. Help model for them by thinking out loud and evaluating different options. First, ask yourself out loud, "What is my main purpose here?" This way, the children learn the global outcome that they are looking for. From there, don't tell them any one way of getting that global outcome. However, while thinking out loud, help guide them to problem-solve, see different options, and evaluate which options are good enough. By doing the activity together as a team, there is less performance anxiety on the child.

- Teach "same but different" and "different but same" (Gutstein and Sheely 2002a, 2002b). Do simple things like play catch with a ball, then vary the way you are doing it. Start by changing the item, playing catch with different balls, rolled-up socks, or pillows. Then think of different ways you can play catch. Throw the ball high, bounce it, throw two balls at one time. Have fun thinking of different ways you can play catch.

- Perfectionists tend to see minor mistakes as devastating. Teach by example. Get involved in simple activities with the children, and again think out loud as you have them help you do the activity. Purposely make a mistake or run into a snag. Create minor irritations. While thinking out loud, problem-solve your way through it. Pretend to be confused and say, "I wonder how I am going to make this work." Pause and wait to see if one of the kids will recommend a way through it. If not, come up with one of your own, so the children see how mistakes, problems, and snags can be mastered, with the outcome being good enough.

- Design situations where the children have to evaluate together when the response becomes good enough. "The purpose is to build a platform strong enough to hold the weight of this block. Once it can hold this block without collapsing (regardless of what it looks like or how strong it is), then it is strong enough." Once that is decided, stop when it is good enough, not perfect. Have fun deciding when the outcome is good enough. "We need to shovel the snow off the sidewalk so we can easily walk down it. We do not have to clear every flake of snow off the sidewalk—just enough so we can walk down it without getting the tops of our shoes snowy." Shovel the snow, but don't scrape it perfectly clear.

- Have fun playing "opposite" games. Actually practice doing something the "wrong" way. If you are playing catch, practice missing the ball. Have fun and exaggerate doing it wrong, and see how "goofy" you can do it wrong.

I coach soccer and basketball for children on the spectrum. I am working on these concepts in all activities. I do not teach the children specific, step-by-step skills. I put the children in activities, whereby the activity itself leads them into flexible thinking. I do not teach them one right way to do something. For example, in soccer, to teach the children to keep the ball close to them while dribbling and to shift gears in different directions, I simply put them in a small circle and have each child (usually 12–15 kids) dribble their balls inside the circle without running into each other. This activity alone teaches them how to keep the ball close to them and to shift gears and turn the ball quickly, in order to avoid running into each other. I start with a large circle and gradually make the circle smaller as they become more skillful. They learn that there are many ways of moving and turning the ball, all being good enough.

The most important thing is to take attention off task performance and teaching a skill. Most teaching in autism has been centered on discrete trial learning and teaching specific skills and scripts. We need to focus more on teaching function and process, and not skills. Learning skills becomes natural once you learn the function and process for getting there. Once you become aware of your objective, there are always different ways of getting there—all potentially good enough.

Perfectionism: teaching how to "cognitively appraise" what is needed!

Perfectionism in people with autism can occur for a variety of reasons: black and white, all-or-nothing thinking; task performance anxiety; fear of failure; inability to adequately appraise expectations. To help children feel less anxious about doing things perfectly, it is important to help them learn how to cognitively appraise what is good enough. Since most actions in life do not have to be done perfectly, the child needs to learn how to appraise when actions are good enough. The child often (1) misappraises what is needed (thinks it has to be perfect), (2) underestimates his ability to do it, and (3) over-exaggerates the consequences if he does it wrong (makes a mistake). The following are ideas for helping the child better appraise these three variables:

1. *Define your objective.* Before doing tasks together, discuss what the goal and objectives are for doing it successfully. Discuss what is good enough to meet the objective of the task. Talk about what response is good enough to be successful. Define both what is the minimum performance needed and what is the best expected. In actuality, the child simply wants to be successful. However, since he has a hard time appraising what is needed, he thinks he has to be perfect. Remember he thinks in all-or-nothing extremes, so you have to lay it out for him so he can see the gray area. What is the least performance required to be meet the objective?

2. *Define your steps.* Before starting the task, talk about what he can expect and what is expected of him. Discuss how you will do the task together, breaking it down and clarifying exactly what is expected and how it will be accomplished. Usually these kids have no idea of what is needed and how to do it. They often just jump right in with no clue, and then freak when failing.

3. *Monitor your performance to match your objective (what is good enough).* While doing the task, continually appraise (evaluate) how close you are getting to the "good enough" response (objective). Monitor your performance as you go along. Frequently pause and evaluate how you are doing

in relation to your defined objective. These children have a hard time thinking about what they are doing as they are doing it. They have a hard time monitoring how they are doing as they are doing something, in order to keep their performance in line with the expectations. Slow things down and continually monitor out loud (1) what is needed and (2) how close they are to good enough. Once you reach good enough, stop and discuss how you reached the goal. Emphasize how it didn't have to be perfect (in fact, mistakes may have been made along the way) to be good enough.

4. *Do it together.* When doing the task, do it together and highlight steps when there are decisions to be made. Discuss each option and how to go about picking one. If it doesn't work out, then we go back and choose a different alternative.

5. *Preview before beginning.* Before starting, make sure to discuss what snags, possible mistakes, and alternative ways of doing things might occur along the way. Always talk about snags and mistakes as simply being accidents that can be corrected. Snags and mistakes are expected, so highlight working through them together to eventually meet the "good enough" response. As you make a mistake or reach a snag, think out loud so the child can understand how you are thinking and feeling. This gives him your perspective on how you handle mistakes (try to minimize the swearing!).

6. *Review when finished.* When finished, go back and review how it went. Talk about each step of the way and how it went, how you corrected mistakes and handled snags. Discuss what was good enough and how you can get there even with mistakes.

Encourage practice to succeed

Many children have difficulty with tasks that require practice in order to become competent. They want to be perfect from the start and frequently shut down if they cannot meet this standard the first time. For an activity that requires ongoing practice to get better, approach it this way:

1. If it is a new behavior, discuss how it will take some time to learn it. Try to break the new skill (behavior) down into simple steps (short-term objectives) that he can learn one at a time. This way you are sequencing out a series of short-term, easy objectives that will lead to the final goal. This gives him easy objectives (expectations) that he can comfortably meet quickly. If he needs assistance from you to meet them at first, talk about that before doing it. Kids do not like others helping them if they

are not expecting it ahead of time. Keep the objectives simple and easy, building one step at a time. Clarify simply, literally, and concretely what the expectations are for successful (good enough) performance.

2. For behavior that will need to be practiced or learned in steps, remember that the child often sees only the final goal (end step) and doesn't see the objectives (steps) building up to it. He jumps in and expects to perform at the goal step immediately. Then when he doesn't meet it, he freaks and melts down. So lay out the steps concretely (pictures, checklist, and visual reminders), and try to project how long it may take to get each step down. "Let's say it may take us ten practices to get this step right." This way, he understands that the expectation is not to do it right at first, but to learn it by so many repetitions. (Of course, make the number estimated high enough so that he is sure to learn it.)

3. Write down each step (expectation) and how he can practice to learn it. The emphasis is on practicing. Provide guided participation at first to maximize his success (remember to talk about this guidance before you give it so it is expected). Focus on praising his efforts, not the actual task performance. Make the expectation the number of repetitions (tries) he will do (or time practicing) to meet success for the day. Practice for shooting for 15 minutes, or for 30 shoots. That way the expectation is the amount of practice, not how good his performance is.

4. Focus on what little steps he is making in performance, so he begins to see that practice produces better performance, one step at a time. So, he can feel good (1) meeting his practice goal of so many repetitions or practicing for a certain amount of time and (2) seeing how he is improving with baby steps.

Have fun teaching your child to feel competent tackling new challenges!

Living in a world of extremes!

We have discussed the all-or-nothing thinking style of many people on the spectrum. This trait is represented in many areas of their life (sensory, cognitive, emotional, and social). They often fluctuate from one extreme to another, having difficulty staying in a moderate range. They have difficulty regulating their cognitive and emotional responses to stay in a range that matches the demands of the situation. It is as if their processing has an "on and off" switch, but not a volume control switch. Most neurotypical (NT) people have a volume switch that allows them to regulate the intensity of sensory stimulation, their emotional reactions, and behavior responses to match what the situation demands. This allows us to regulate and match our cognitive, emotional, and behavioral reactions to the current demands, not to overreact! From moment to moment, for a person to stay regulated and in sync with his surroundings, he has to be able to turn the intensity up and down, depending on the current situational needs. If the sensory stimulation is too loud, the brain will turn it down. If a daily snag initiates an anger response, our brains will immediately tune it down to not overreact. We constantly adjust the volume of intensity to adaptively match the situational demands. When possible danger is present, we become hyper-aroused to increase our alertness to react, and then quickly turn it back down when the danger subsides. When we need to go to sleep, we lower our arousal level so we can fall asleep. People on the spectrum have difficulty raising and lowering their arousal level, emotional responses, and cognitive interpretations to respond adaptively to the immediate demands. This is why they are frequently out of sync with their social surroundings.

People on the spectrum seem to have faulty volume control and react with an all-or-nothing response. They have an on/off switch, but not a volume control knob. They are either all on or all off, reacting in the extreme ends of intensity. We frequently see this in sensory processing, where the person can be sensory-defensive (over-responsive) or hypo-sensitive (under-responsive), over-aroused (hyper-alert) or under-aroused (slow and sluggish). Their nervous system reacts quickly to the fight/fight/freeze, panic response, or they may not notice the stimulation altogether (e.g. not feel typical pain). Their nervous system either filters out too much stimulation or lets in overwhelming stimulation. This leaves the nervous system on guard—nervous, anxious, and on high alert!

This "all or nothing" also affects the extremes of emotional reactions. The children may overreact emotionally to minor irritations, or show minimal emotional reaction at all. They are either calm or angry, happy or sad, with little in between intensities. When they are happy, they are excited; when mad, very angry. Unfortunately, they frequently interpret any negative emotion with fear and panic, and this can escalate quickly. They also have a hard time rebounding once the situation subsides. Little snags can set their brains into a spin, or the brain shuts down to avoid overload. Once again, an all-or-nothing response.

Cognitively, these extremes are also seen. They think in black and white, right or wrong, either/or extremes. They have difficulty perceiving the gray area or flexibly adjusting to variability in thought. Rules are black and white, with little room for bending. They interpret things literally and have difficulty with "good enough" thinking. In regard to attention and concentration, they either are easily distracted with problems attending or hyper-focused to the point of blocking out the rest of world. They have difficulty shifting attention based on moment-to-moment priorities. This leads to major problems with multitasking. They are either totally focused or unfocused.

Behaviorally, they are either unmotivated for tasks that provide little meaning to them or hyper-focused (even to the point of obsession) for topics of interest. They are both committed and dedicated to action (even when evidence points otherwise) or totally indifferent. This all-or-nothing thinking often creates obsessive perfectionism or stifling fear of failure. They have difficulty understanding what is good enough. The world of moderation is difficult to grasp.

Unfortunately, our world is built around flexibility, variability, fluctuations, and moderation. Most of the world operates in the middle ground, fluctuating occasionally from one extreme to the other, only to quickly modulate back to moderation. Most NT people get annoyed and even scared by people operating in the extreme ends. People out of sync with the rest of the crowd, and whose reactions do not stay coordinated with others, make us feel uncomfortable. Not only does the person with autism not understand our relative processing, we do not understand their all-or-nothing reasoning. This lack of matching makes it difficult for people on the spectrum to fit in. Often they do not understand why they don't get it, which only increases the anxiety, further decreasing the ability to regulate.

However, if those close to people on the spectrum can remember that they are operating from the extremes, then it is easier to understand their behavior and help them regulate. Awareness of why they are reacting so extremely helps us accept their differences. Understanding this all-or-nothing reasoning helps us stay calm during emotional turmoil, understanding when they don't get it, accepting when they are rude, and remaining patient when they are obsessive. Understanding that they see the world differently from us allows us to live together more cooperatively and appreciate the gifts that come with these differences.

Turning deficits into assets! Rigid inflexibility expressed as commitment and dedication!

Many differences that we often call deficits can be true benefits. Many people on the spectrum tend to have all-or-nothing thinking, which is often labeled as rigid, inflexible thinking. This is often thought of in negative terms, because it leads to difficulty in times when flexible thinking is required. Things are viewed very black and white, either/or, or right or wrong, but this type of thinking can also be an asset. When the person on the spectrum likes something or is committed to something, he will go all out for it. He will commit wholeheartedly to whatever his passion or endeavor seems to be. Therefore, he can excel in a preferred vocational interest or favorite topic, be very disciplined in practicing, and persevere in the face of adversity. This all-or-nothing thinking can be very favorable when channeled in the right way. With the hyper-focused attention, strong passion for detail, and drive for perfection, our technology, personal lifestyles, and economy have benefited greatly from this type of thinking. Why change it? Develop it!

The same is true for friendships. Even though relating can be difficult for them, most people on the spectrum, once they befriend you, will be among the most dedicated friends you will ever have. They will support you, help you out, and stand by you when things are not going well. If they are going to be your friend, they will be a *good* friend. If they like something, they *really* like something. They don't go halfway.

Most of the so-called deficits in autism are simply differences. For many of the traits, we can either view them in a negative light (since they are not like ours) or we can view them in a positive light (strengths that we do not have). Why not redefine them and develop them into strengths? They grow stronger, and we grow wiser! A win–win situation!

The more inflexible the child, the more flexible the adult needs to be

Dr. Ross Greene, author of *The Explosive Child* (2010), goes into detail about how to use his collaborative problem-solving approach for parents of rigid/inflexible children. In this book he states that it is not just the rigid and inflexible child who causes the most problems, but it is when the rigid/inflexible child meets a rigid/inflexible adult that the greatest problems arise.

Ross Greene takes the stance that children do the best that they can, given the situation they are in and their current skills for dealing with it. This presumes that if a child is acting out, then there is a good chance that he does not have the skills needed for dealing with the situation that we put him in. Due to sensory, cognitive, social, and emotional issues, the expectations are usually greater than the child's abilities to deal handle them. In these situations, the adult needs first to look at changing the demands/expectations to better match the child's abilities, then provide added assistance to support the child through the situation, and eventually teach better skills for dealing with the expectations. This assumption usually means that the responsibility for change starts with the adult first, before expecting the child to change. This is hard for many of us to accept. Since the child is acting out, we instinctively tend to place the blame on the child and expect him to conform.

When the child is acting out, we often demand for him to stop and then get frustrated when he doesn't cooperate. Often he simply cannot stop on command. This leads us to get more upset, frustrated, and punitive. We often say and do things we wish we hadn't. We may pressure, demand, and try to force the child to comply, without first looking at what we need to change. This often occurs because the adults do not understand all the processing problems the child has, and also the adult may not know how to support the child.

The more rigid and inflexible the child is, the more patient, understanding, and compassionate the adult has to be. Easier said than done; I have been here many times myself. We need first to listen and understand before demanding that the child changes. We need first to look at what is going wrong in this situation and what changes we need to make in the conditions presenting the behavior. Does the child have the sensory, cognitive, social, emotional, and behavioral tools to meet our expectations? What changes do I need to make? Is there extra assistance I could give? Or maybe I should just validate the child's feelings of uncertainty, fear, and frustration before supporting them? This does not mean that we have to give in to the child and let him always have his way. It just means we have to understand and validate, while providing the guidance needed.

So remember, when the heat is on, try to remain calm, understand and validate first, and then move on to trying to support the child. After the storm is over and everyone is calm, try to analyze the situation to identify what you may be able to change in your expectations to better match the child's abilities, and/or what assistance you can provide in helping him to be more successful in meeting the expectations. Take a deep breath, try not to react out of frustration, and be willing to change first before asking the child to change. You will have fewer battles and more successes.

Picture schedules and flexibility

Visual picture schedules are frequently recommended to provide structure and predictability to the child's day. However, many people worry that picture schedules tend to reinforce rigid, inflexible thinking in the young child. When changes occur that disrupt the set routine, the child melts down. In actuality, visual schedules can be used to teach greater flexibility. Using visual schedules is a way of organizing time and activity, so the world is more predictable and understandable. Using visual schedules can be used to take away the chaos of flexibility. You can use set schedules (where the routine stays the same) or variable schedules (where the activities vary or the order for which they occur varies). With the variable schedule, you sit down every day and map out what the day will be like. The schedule is used to organize the time, making it predictable and understandable. Once you establish a visual schedule, you can build in more and more flexibility. The security comes from using the visual schedule to structure the child's time, not necessarily keeping a rigid schedule.

Different types of variability

- *Change in routine.* If you use set routines, then you simply make these changes on the visual schedule (picture or written) and discuss them. Some people will put a different colored change card on the schedule, just above where the change will occur. This tells the child that a change in activity will occur and what activity it will replace. Some people prefer to put the new activity on the schedule in place of the normal activity, and put the normal activity right alongside the new added activity, to show that this new activity will occur in place of the normal activity.

- *Plan Bs.* If you are going to schedule activity that may not occur for some reason (e.g. get postponed because of rain), then have a plan B (a picture of what will occur instead) placed right next to the scheduled activity. This can also be used as an either/or technique for the child to choose between two activities.

- *Move from specific to broad categories.* You can build in variability by first starting with a specific activity (e.g. take out the trash, then go on the computer) and then moving on to general activity (e.g. chore, then "free choice" activity). With the general activity, we put up pictures of general categories of activity (chore, homework, leisure activity, etc.) and then have visual menus (pictures or written chore menu, leisure activity menu, etc.) that have choices for the child to pick from. So when it comes to do a chore on the schedule, the child looks at the chore menu (which has several chores to pick from) and picks out what he wants to do. Same for the "free choice" menu: he can pick out if he wants to play on the computer, play with Lego®, ride bike, etc. This way, he knows what general activity he will be doing on the schedule, but can pick out the specific activity to do. This gives the child a general idea of what is coming up, but also gives him choices of what to do. It builds variability and flexibility to the schedule. The parent has to make sure that if there are limited choices for that day the menus only include those activities. So, if riding bikes cannot occur at that time, it is not included on the menu.

- *From specific to variable schedules.* As discussed above, families can choose to use specific structure routines, for which the routines are consistent (set) from day to day, or use variable schedules where the parent and child sit down each day and make out their schedule for the day (may vary from day to day). Either way, you are providing the child with a structured routine that gives him predictability for his day. Often families have some set routines built around a more flexible schedule.

Whether you use very set, structured daily routines or a more variable schedule depends upon the needs of the child and the family. Some families simply cannot hold to set routines, so they need to use more variable schedules. Often, however, we try to build in some structured routines within variable schedules, with set routines for (1) getting up in the morning, (2) getting home from school, and (3) getting ready for bed. These are prime transition times that work out better with set routines. Then, between those times, we build in more variability.

In addition, the rigidity of the child will determine where to start. For younger or more rigid children, we often need to start with very firm routines and schedules, and then build in greater flexibility over time. So, as you can see, pictures or written schedules can be used to build in greater variability by moving from set to variable schedules, and also from more specific to general schedules. By doing so, you teach the child to use schedules to organize his time and make it more predictable, so that he can handle flexibility. It provides predictability to flexibility. So, use visual schedules to build greater acceptance of flexibility.

Part III

SENSORY ISSUES IN AUTISM

Chapter 6

COMMON SENSORY ISSUES

Fasten your seat belts!

We are going to spend some time discussing the sensory world for those on the spectrum. Sensory differences vary greatly for people on the spectrum; however, most of them experience the sensory world quite differently from neurotypical people. People on the spectrum frequently have difficulty in all areas of registering, integrating, and processing sensory experiences. For some, these sensory issues dominate everything they do. When the outside world is constantly assaulting their nervous system, they are on high alert and always anxious.

First it is important for us to gain an understanding of the different types of sensory issues that can be affected. Although there are many shades to sensory vulnerabilities, the several listed below are the main ones. It is important to be aware of how the child processes sensory information, what sensory preferences he is attracted to, and what sensory sensitivities he avoids. Knowing how your child experiences the world will allow you to modify his environment to minimize sensory overload, change your interaction style to foster engagement, and build learning opportunities around his sensory preferences. You can use the child's sensory preferences to soothe and calm him when overwhelmed, and arouse him when slow and sluggish. Parents, caregivers, and teachers need to be aware that sensory processing issues can be one of the biggest challenges people on the spectrum experience. The more we understand how the person experiences his sensations, the better we are in accommodating and compensating for these vulnerabilities.

Common sensory issues

- Fragmented or distorted perception.
- Hyper- or hypo-sensitivity.
- Sensory defensiveness.
- Problems integrating multiple senses.
- Mono (single channel) processing.

- Delayed processing and sensory overload.

- Modulating arousal level.

People with autism spectrum disorder can experience a variety of sensory issues. The most common, and the ones people recognize the most, are sensory defensiveness (hyper-sensitive to stimulation) or sensory overload (when too much stimulation is bombarding the child). In addition, problems can occur in the actual registering of stimulation, integrating the various senses together, and regulating the amount and intensity of stimulation provided to the brain. We will look briefly at a few of these problems.

Fragmented or distorted perception

Fragmented perception is common in autism. The neurotypical (NT) brain automatically takes in and organizes all incoming information (sensations) into one overall perception. We integrate all of our senses smoothly with little conscious awareness of this process. We take in what we see, hear, smell, taste, and feel, and smoothly integrate all this information into one flowing perception. Our ongoing experiences consists of a dynamic flow of sensory information continually integrating and assimilating to keep a steady stream of experience that allows us to interact with and adapt to the world around us.

However, some individuals on the spectrum have fragmented perception. They only perceive parts or fragments of the perceptual field at one time. For example, people typically can look at a face and see the overall face in one perception, integrating the shape of the head, eyes, nose, ears, hair, mouth into one perception of a face that we recognize. For people with fragmented perception, they may only be able to discriminate parts of the face (eyes, nose, mouth, etc.) at one time and have to piece together each part sequentially, like a puzzle. Some have "face blindness" which means they do not recognize faces at all. For many, they will pick one aspect of the face, such as your hair or your glasses, to remember you by. Consequently, if you cut your hair or get new glasses, they may not recognize you.

For people with fragmented or distorted senses, their perceptions do not come in overall smooth patterns. Instead of their brain integrating all the details into a whole picture, they are overwhelmed by a sea of details that often seem to conflict with each other. In a steady stream of confusing stimuli, they pick up on bits and pieces, without perceiving all the information. This can cause faulty perception by not gaining the whole picture. At best, it can result in delayed processing, since the bits and pieces have to be put together sequentially, like a puzzle, instead of simultaneously.

Of course, we can imagine how stressful that could be, especially when the stimulation is fleeting (changes quickly) or the situation demands quick responding. Much of our daily experience requires us to rapidly process dynamically changing information. It requires our brains to rapidly process multiple stimulation simultaneously. For those with fragmented perception, piecing together the fragments might not give the whole complete picture, rendering their responses out of sync with what is required. Children with these difficulties will usually categorize things by one or two fragments, rather than the whole picture. They may remember a person only by their hair, a room by a certain piece of furniture, or an object by its shape, color, or feel, but not all three. This can make the world more fragile for the child. When the one characteristic they recognize changes (person cuts her hair, furniture is moved from the room, etc.), this can throw the person's sense of security out of whack!

Less common, but more troublesome, are distorted perceptions. For individuals with this problem the distortions can vary across a variety of dimensions (size, shape, depth, movement, etc.). Objects shake, distort in size, or move and stretch. Since these distortions may not stay consistent, their field of vision or hearing can fluctuate, making judgment very difficult. You might see delayed processing plus hesitation in responding with these children. They may have problems navigating objects around them or feel that everything is moving. They have to proceed slowly, sometimes freeze, or shut down completely. Again, their ability to process stimulation will be weakened under periods of stress, fatigue, illness, or hunger, rendering their perceptions unreliable.

Hyper- or hypo-sensitivity

Heightened acuity or hyper-sensitivity is very common. These individuals register stimulation at a much greater sensitivity. They can hear frequencies and intensities of sound that most people cannot register, see minute particles or distinct details, sense smells that others cannot pick up on, and feel the slightest stimulation to their bodies. This can be distracting and overwhelming, and at times painful. Their brains may not be able to filter out background noise, and they may get so distracted by meaningless details that they miss the important elements. Imagine seeing the flickering of fluorescent lights, feeling the magnetic and electromagnetic waves of refrigerators and microwaves, or hearing people near you breathe. This heightened acuity, or hyper-sensitivity, can be a strength (jobs requiring observation of detail), but more often it is a distracting nuisance. It can be overwhelming and make concentrating very difficult.

Some individuals can be hyper-sensitive in one sense and hypo-sensitive (poor awareness) in another. With hypo-sensitivity, the person does not register normal levels of stimulation and often does not feel, hear, see, or smell common sensations unless they are intensified. This is the child who stumbles around because his body does not "sense" the contact with the floor and objects around it. He may be really rough with things because he does not sense how firm he is being. In addition, this person may not feel pain at normal levels and may be prone to injuries (broken bones, cuts, etc.) without awareness of the injury.

Sensory defensiveness

Often occurring with hyper-sensitivity is sensory defensiveness. With this condition, the child may be oversensitive in one or more senses, often causing uncomfortable and sometimes painful sensations. For him, soft touch can feel like pins and needles, or certain frequencies and intensities of sounds can be amplified numerous times. The buzzer at school may be tormenting, or the phone ringing can shock his nervous system. Typical smells can make him nauseous, and common lighting can be overwhelming. His nervous system is constantly anxious and on high alert. He panics easily. This child will often try to escape or avoid common sights, sounds, tastes, and touch that may put his nervous system in a frenzy.

These children are often on "high alert," anxious, and oppositional, because they are on guard for possible threatening stimulation. They need to control everything that occurs around them to control the level of stimulation. Imagine sitting in a classroom where the hard seat is painful, your clothes are uncomfortable, the fluorescent lights overwhelm you, you can hear the person behind you breathing heavily, the smell of the markers and paste make you nauseated, and the scratching sounds of all the pencils irritate your ears. Then try to concentrate on what the teacher is discussing!

Problems integrating multiple senses

Some on the spectrum may register each sense adequately but have problems integrating all their senses into one overall perception. Whereas our brains take in multiple senses (seeing, hearing, feeling, smelling, etc.) and integrate them together simultaneously, people with integration difficulties are bombarded by competing sensations that are not integrated effectively. For them, all the sounds, smells, and sights compete with one another and do not get integrated simultaneously. They often need to block out one sense in order to focus on another. For these individuals, our normal stimulating world can be very overwhelming. Often they need to process each sense sequentially, one at a time, and then piece all the information together. As can be expected, this can be very draining.

Mono (single channel) processing

Those who have a hard time integrating their senses often have a dominant sense that they use to interpret their world. They may need to touch and manipulate everything they are processing, smell everything first before eating or engaging with it, or explore things visually before engaging with them. For them, their other senses are too competing for them so they may try to block out the other senses, so they can concentrate on their dominant sense. So, the child who is a visual processor may frequently cover his ears to block out noise so he can focus on his vision. We need to identify what sense (vision, hearing, or touching/ manipulating) the child primarily uses to explore his world, and then tailor learning around that sense.

Delayed processing and sensory overload

As you can imagine, if you cannot filter out background noise, have fragmented or distorted sensations, or cannot integrate all your senses simultaneously, your sensory processing will be delayed. While sorting through all the jumbled sensations and piecing together all the details, the child's processing is delayed and often overwhelming. When you are hyper-sensitive to stimulation and cannot adequately integrate your competing sensations, the brain becomes overwhelmed and panics easily. The person is always on high alert, anxious and insecure. This child can appear resistant and oppositional, and have a high need to control everything around him. When the brain starts to become overloaded, it may start to shut down, blocking out stimulation to avoid being overwhelmed. The child may become glassy-eyed, or close his eyes and lie his head down. However, if the stimulation is coming in too much and too fast, the child may melt down (act out).

Modulating arousal level

Lastly, many children with sensory processing difficulties have trouble modulating their sensory input to stay aroused. They are either over-aroused and overwhelmed easily, or under-aroused and bouncing off the walls to increase stimulation to stay alert. They either filter out too much stimulation to stay alert (the hyperactive child) or do not filter out enough stimulation and become overwhelmed by the stimulation coming in. For these children, staying calm, organized, and alert is a difficult task. They may either be slow and sluggish or fidgeting and moving constantly to stay alert. These children are often labeled hyperactive and have trouble concentrating. These individuals benefit from a sensory diet (discussed later in this chapter) to provide them alerting stimulation when under-aroused and calming stimulation when over-aroused. An occupational therapist who specializes in sensory processing disorders will develop a list of sensory strategies for the child to engage in throughout the day to keep him calm and organized.

As you can see here, sensory processing issues can dominate the lives of many people on the spectrum. These issues can make the world chaotic, confusing, and very overwhelming. These differences can lead to a host of challenging behaviors (acting out, compulsive behaviors, self-stimulation, oppositional resistance, rigid inflexibility, etc.). These difficulties can be very overwhelming and taxing to the brain, leaving it drained and irritable. We need to be very aware and respectful of the individual's sensory needs.

Sensory sensitivity: hyper- and hypo-sensitivities

For many children on the spectrum, their sensory world can be very unpredictable and often overwhelming. This leaves them feeling threatened and helpless, creating fear and strong anxiety. Understand their sensory world and you will understand their behavior. Understand how they process their senses and you will be better able to support them!

The nervous system of people on the spectrum may react differently in how sensory stimulation is registered. People with autism often register stimulation in extremes; they are either hyper- or hypo-sensitive. It is as if they have an on/off switch, but not a volume control knob. They may display hyper-sensitivity in one or more senses, whereby they have a heightened awareness of stimulation, often to the point of discomfort, pain, and even nausea. In milder forms, this hyper-sensitivity can be annoying and distracting, but for many it can lead to severe sensory overload, causing their sensory processing to become overwhelmed and break down. Children with hyper-sensitivity are usually motivated to escape and avoid the stimulation, which can be misinterpreted as resistant, oppositional defiant behavior. They often overreact to the stimulation (noise, light, touch, smells) to the point that panic sets off the fight-or-flight response.

At the other extreme, some children have hypo-sensitivity in one or more senses. For these children, their sensory threshold for registering stimulation is very high, whereby they often have difficulty even sensing the stimulation. They need much stronger intensity of input for their nervous systems to respond to it. This is the child who may not feel pain, does not get dizzy after spinning, or does everything too roughly! They often seek out high levels of the stimulation, simply to register it. They tend to be overactive in seeking stimulation and are often called sensory seekers. Whereas people with hyper-sensitivity may try to escape and avoid simulation, many children who are hypo-sensitive often are sensory seekers, to the point of being distracting to both themselves and others.

Sensitivity can vary!

As with many characteristics in autism, sensitivities can be consistently inconsistent. Sensitivity may stay the same or vary across senses or within each sense from day to day, moment to moment. They can be hyper-sensitive in one sense, and hypo-sensitive in another. Or they can be hyper-sensitive to certain frequencies or intensities in one sense, and hypo-sensitive to other frequencies or intensities in the same sense. These sensitivities can vary from day to day and be extremely affected by any stress to the nervous system, such as fatigue, lack of sleep, stress, hunger, or illness. They can seem oversensitive and avoid the stimulation one day and hypo-sensitive and seek it out at another time. This can lead to heightened arousal, hesitation, and anxiety due to the unpredictability of the child's sensory experiences. For those who are hyper-sensitive to stimulation, events that have multiple sensory stimulation (often crowded, noisy situations with a lot of activity) can be totally overwhelming, rendering their processing dysfunctional. This can be very frightening and create panic.

Hyper- and hypo-sensitivities
Tactile (touch)

Hyper-sensitive

- Dislikes light touch.
- Resists hugs and kisses.
- Dislikes wearing hats.
- Resists getting hands messy.
- Is fearful when others approach.
- Is picky about clothing.
- Pushes up sleeves or pant legs.
- Resists grooming.

Hypo-sensitive

- Needs strong touch to be registered.
- Tries to handle or touch everything.
- Insists on holding an object in hand.
- May touch too forcefully.
- Craves touch; is clingy.

Visual

Hyper-sensitive

- Is very sensitive to bright lights and sunlight.
- May be sensitive to certain colors.
- Has very fine vision, seeing particles in the air.
- Direct vision may be too overwhelming for child.
- May squint, or look with peripheral vision.

Hypo-sensitive

- Is very attracted to visual stimulation, often stares at light.
- Seeks out intense visual stimulation.
- Loves turning lights on and off.
- Loves mirrors, shiny objects, reflecting surfaces.

Auditory (hearing)

Hyper-sensitive

- Is sensitive to loud noises.
- Can hear frequencies others cannot hear.
- Covers ears with hands.
- Is distracted by background noises.
- Becomes agitated in large groups.

Hypo-sensitive

- Speaks loudly.
- Is a very noisy person.
- Turns volume up loud.
- Hums or makes vocal noises constantly.
- Loves items/activities that have distinct sounds (motors, pounding, etc.).

Tastes and smells

Hyper-sensitive

- Finds many common tastes and smells repulsive.
- Can be overwhelmed very easily by normal daily scents (perfumes, natural odors, chemicals, foods).
- Sensation of smell goes directly to the limbic system (emotional brain).
- May gag or vomit easily.
- May be a very picky eater.

Hypo-sensitive

- Needs to smell or taste everything.
- May seek out strong smells and tastes.
- Will often identify people and objects by their smells.
- May put inappropriate objects in their mouth, smell others' hair, or want to lick things.

Vestibular (movement)

Hyper-sensitive

- Shows gravitational insecurity.
- Has strong emotional reaction to unexpected movement.
- Resists movement activities.
- Gets dizzy and nauseous from simple movement.
- Feels strong need to sit or keep feet on ground.
- Is often very anxious, insecure.

Hypo-sensitive

- Is very active, always on the move.
- Craves movement, climbing, falling, and spinning.
- Makes fearless, impulsive movements without regard to safety.
- Rarely gets dizzy.
- Has difficulty sitting still.

Proprioception (stimulation to joints and muscles)

Hyper-sensitive

- Places body in strange positions.
- Often has difficulty manipulating small objects (e.g. buttons).
- May turn whole body to look at something.

Hypo-sensitive

- Is often unaware of body position in space.
- Is awkward and clumsy.
- Is floppy, with poor muscle tone.
- Often needs to lean on objects and people.
- Often bumps or crashes into things.
- Craves pushing, pulling, banging, crashing.

Sensory defensiveness

With sensory defensiveness, the child is hyper-sensitive to stimulation. For this condition, the child's nervous system overreacts to the stimulation, lowering the threshold for the fight-or-flight panic response. For these children, light touch can feel torturous, specific sounds and frequencies can be deafening, normal intensity of light can be blinding, and smells can be overpowering and noxious. For these children, the world can be overwhelming and alarming. The child's nervous system is often on high alert and on guard in anticipation of unexpected assaulting stimulation. These children are frequently insecure and highly anxious, and are often motivated to escape and avoid any situation of uncertainty, since the nervous system is worried about being assaulted. The child frequently has to control all activity and interaction to feel safe from unexpected stimulation.

Usually, the children are not sensitive in all senses. They can be oversensitive in one sense and not in others. They can also be oversensitive to some stimulation but not other stimulation, within the same sense. For example, their hearing may overreact to high-pitch frequency, but be under-aroused by low pitches. They may be able to listen to a loud, pounding rock concert, but not be able to handle the siren of an ambulance. These sensitivities vary depending on the status of their nervous system. If the child is tired, fatigued, ill, or hungry, sensitivities increase. The more taxed the nervous system, the greater sensitivity to stimulation. Also, when they are in "sensory loud" environments (a lot of activity, noise, lights, etc.), their nervous systems can be overwhelmed and sensitivities increased to heightened levels. These poor children are always anxiously anticipating the bombardment and panic attack.

The effects of sensory defensiveness can be felt across all areas of living. The child's nervous system is often on guard, anxious about the next, unexpected assault. This child is frequently nervous, apprehensive, and easily overwhelmed.

He often panics at unexpected sensations and becomes anxious in anticipation of what may be coming next. This defensiveness can often be seen in the child who needs to control everything around him and resist following the lead of others. He is often seen as resistant and oppositional. In turn, sensory defensiveness can weaken the child's sense of security, emotional stability, self-identity, and social connectiveness. It is hard to act with confidence when constantly on guard and ready to flee. The littlest snag can send him into a whirlwind.

Sensory defensiveness and anxiety

With sensory defensiveness, the nervous system tends to overreact to moderate levels of stimulation (light touch can hurt, normal daily sounds can be painfully loud, smells can be overwhelmingly nauseous, sunlight can be blinding, etc.). The child's nervous system overreacts and sets off the fight-or-flight response. In addition, the child can be oversensitive at one moment and under-register at other times. For the child who is oversensitive, normal daily sensory stimulation can be overpowering and overwhelming. These sensitivities can vary from moment to moment and day to day. The nervous system is on guard, anxious, and on high alert. The child frequently has high levels of stress chemicals in his nervous system and is often in a defensive mode. The child feels anxious and insecure, and cannot trust his nervous system's reactions to events occurring around him.

This anxiety from sensory defensiveness can result in a variety of challenging behaviors. The child can be resistant and oppositional, very rigid and inflexible, and need to control all stimulation and activity around him. Since he is nervous and on guard, he can melt down at the drop of a dime or with simple snags in routine. He may engage in repetitive behavior to block out the painful stimulation, or shut down (tune out) in order to escape the assaulting environment. When in an environment that he cannot control and is unpredictable for him, the child may be on high alert and very apprehensive. He will be running scared from the anticipation of unexpected, painful stimulation.

Sensory overload

Sensory overload occurs when the nervous system is bombarded by too much or too intense stimulation for it to process effectively. Although sensory defensiveness can influence sensory overload directly, sensory overload can also occur from the inability of the brain to filter, or tone down, the stimulation coming into the brain. For many of us who do not have sensory processing problems, our brain filters out much of the stimulation bombarding the nervous system. It filters out much of the background noise (sensory distraction) that is unnecessary for us to be aware of, so we can concentrate on the task at hand. This allows our brain to comfortably integrate the important information so we can process it smoothly and effectively. We can attend to what we need to because we block out what is irrelevant at the moment.

However, for some people with sensory processing problems, this filter does not function effectively and allows too much stimulation into the brain, taxing and overloading it. The individual is not able to block out the background noise (their clothes scratching them, sound of the refrigerator turning on and off, smell of the perfume or deodorant of people near them, flickering of sunlight coming through the blinds, conversation going on nearby, scratching sound of the pencil, etc.). Their nervous system is unable to filter out or tone down the stimulation. Too much stimulation coming into the brain at too high an intensity results in sensory overload. Rather than necessarily being defensive to one sense, as in sensory defensiveness, overload can come from too much stimulation bombarding the brain at one time.

For these children, the average day at school can be full of sensory assaults. They cannot adequately filter out all the conflicting sensory stimulation. The bright lights may give them a headache, or the humming of the lights may distract them. Their seat may be too hard and they cannot avoid attending to it. Their clothes irritate them, the sound of the chalk on the board screeches in their head, the whisper of other students distracts them, smells of the markers and glue may be nauseating, and the sound of the bell may be overwhelming. With all these sensory distractions and irritations, the nervous system is in an escape/avoidance mode, making learning almost impossible. When the brain feels insecure, it goes into survival mode, focusing on protection, not learning. If the stress chemicals build slowly, the brain will often start to shut down to avoid being overwhelmed. During shutdown the child may look "out of it," be unresponsive, and sometimes lay his head down and fall asleep. This shutdown is the way the brain protects itself from sensory overload. If the stress chemicals build too fast, the child may melt down, acting out to escape and avoid the assaulting stimulation, as well as to release the stress chemicals. Either response is the result of the fight-or-flight stress response kicking in. The brain is in survival mode, not in a learning readiness mode.

Treating sensory defensiveness and sensory overload

For children who are sensory defensive, it is important that we are aware of their sensitivities at all times. There are seven main ways of helping the child avoid overload.

1. Modify the environment to minimize overload

Turn down the lights, reduce the noise, avoid unexpected touch and scratchy clothes, and minimize foods and smells that are untolerable. Parents need to get used to scanning the immediate environment to appraise for sensory threats to the child. It is up to us to monitor and modify the child's environments to reduce the amount of sensory bombardment. Whether it be at school, at home, or in the community, it is important to think ahead about the type of stimulation that may assault the child's nervous system. Fluorescent lights, mechanical noises, chemical smells, scratchy materials may all need to be modified to match what the nervous system can handle. As the children get older, they need to understand their own sensitivities, be able to appraise situations for the level of sensory threat, and build in modifications and coping skills for dealing with sensory overload.

We may need to build in accommodations and adaptations into the school IEP, as well as at home, to minimize defensive overload. Some common accommodations may include switching to unscented soaps and detergents at home, building in special air filters, eliminating fluorescent lighting at home and in the classroom, purchasing seamless socks, removing tags from clothes, and eliminating certain fabrics to pacify the nervous system. Each child's sensitivities will be very individualized, needing modifications to match their sensory needs.

2. Use adaptations to filter down the level of stimulation

When the environment cannot be modified, then sunglasses, ear plugs, head phones, MP3 players, sun visors, and so on can be used to help filter the stimulation. If the stimulation cannot be filtered, then sometimes favorite activities, such as hand computer games, music, or reading can be used to temporarily distract the nervous system and to minimize overload. Parents usually get used to carrying around a "toolbox" of sensory filters and temporary distracters for times when they cannot modify the environment to tone down the stimulation. It is important to use these filters to prevent overload, rather than wait for the child to get overwhelmed before using them. Often, once they are overwhelmed, such adaptations will not work.

3. Allow the child to control the stimulation

When the child is defensive to stimulation, you can reduce anxiety tremendously by allowing the child to control the type and intensity of stimulation. Usually, when it is predictable and under their control, they can dictate the intensity of stimulation they can handle. Let them control the pace and intensity of interaction, activity, and stimulation around them to feel safe and secure.

4. Give frequent breaks to rebound and regroup

To keep the stress chemicals from overloading the children, give them frequent breaks during the day to unwind, release stress chemicals, and re-energize. Some children need to go to a quiet area to regroup, some prefer to engage in solitary activity such as listening to music or reading, and others prefer physical activity to release the stress chemicals and reorganize. Know what your child can handle. We often keep them in events too long, or jump from one event to another without giving them time to rebound. Gauge how much and how long the child can handle the stimulation. This is especially true in fun, highly stimulating activities. Parents and teachers often think if the child likes it he can handle the stimulation. But this is not true. Spending the day engaged in fun, ongoing, highly stimulating activities (especially if it requires socializing with others) can be just as stressful as activity that is not enjoyable. Like most children, they will not want to stop the preferred activity when they start to become disorganized. We need to know what they can handle, arrange the activity to be as sensory-friendly as possible, and only expose the children for short periods at a time.

5. Sensory diet to keep nervous system calm and organized

A sensory diet includes controlled presentation of sensory stimulation throughout the day to keep the child calm, alert, and organized. Usually, an occupational therapist can evaluate the child and recommend sensory activities that can help him process stimulation better, alert him, and soothe him when overwhelmed. This may include chewing gum or drinking water through a straw to help the child focus and stay calm and alert in class. It also may include sitting on an air cushion or therapy ball to keep him alert and organized, or giving him physical activity periodically throughout the day to release stress chemicals and regulate the nervous system. We will discuss sensory diet more a little further on in this chapter.

6. When he is overwhelmed, back off and let him escape

When the brain is in sensory overload, we must immediately remove as much stimulation as possible. Let the child go to a quiet area, remove all demands, and talk very little. Some children will allow an adult to use deep pressure strategies to help soothe them, but often the child needs you to back off and give them time to rebound. These strategies will be presented in more detail when discussing meltdowns and emotional regulation challenges. Children may appear calm before their nervous system is actually ready to engage again. Give them plenty of time. When returning to normal routine, be aware that overload can occur again very easily. Evaluate the situation to determine what stimulation/activity may have resulted in overload. Often it is ongoing participation in a highly stimulating/demanding activity.

7. Corrective therapies

Depending on the type of defensiveness (touch, sound, smells, etc.), there are several strategies that have been used, with varying degrees of success, to help desensitize sensory defensiveness. Occupational therapists will often use a technique called Wilbarger Protocol, which consists of two steps: (1) briskly brushing the arms, hands, shoulders, back, legs, and feet with a surgical brush, followed by (2) providing joint compressions to the joints of the arms, shoulders, wrists, fingers, legs, ankles, and feet. During the course of treatment, this procedure is used approximately once every two hours. It is easy to implement, but must be done under the guidance of an occupational therapist trained in this approach. Occupational therapists also use a variety of sensory integration strategies (sensory diets, gradual exposure to stimulation, etc.) for decreasing sensory defensiveness.

There are a variety of therapeutic listening therapies to help reduce auditory defensiveness, and vision therapies to help correct visual sensitivities. Psychologists will also use graduated exposure therapy to desensitize defensiveness. These strategies are too complex to be covered here. I would recommend that parents approach their specialists for guidance in these areas.

Sensory overload: personal experience

One of our members on this page shares her experience with sensory overload.

 ? Member's question

Sensory overload for me can come from sound, light, the movement of other people, and maybe other things I'm not even aware of at this point. I've seen it described as one's central nervous system "vibrating," which I think is a great way to describe it to someone who is unfamiliar with it. I often want to cry, or need something tactile when I'm overloaded, so I'll hit my hands into something (usually my legs, each other, or my head—but not in a self-injurious way) or shake them pretty hard. Deep pressure helps too, because it's soothing in general. And, of course, getting away from whatever is bothering me is a good idea.

AUTISM DISCUSSION PAGE

Thanks for sharing! Yes, what you describe are common sensory sensitivities for many on the spectrum. For those who are tactile defensive, light touch is usually very annoying, even painful, especially if they don't know it is coming. Usually, I find that most people are much better with the touch as long as they are controlling it. It is mostly when others are touching them. So, in therapy, I will always have the parents invite the touch, but let the child control the touch. This way the child can regulate how they want it. Also, yes, frequently when sensitive to light touch, they often like deep pressure touch. Tactile defensiveness is in the sensory receptors in the surface of the skin, so light touch activates those sensitive receptors. Deep pressure touch goes past the surface and into the receptors deep in the muscles, negating the surface receptors.

Usually with desensitization procedures, we start with the deep pressure touch (or any touch within the child's comfort zone) and gradually lighten the touch until he can tolerate light touch without activating the fight-or-flight response. Also, we usually start by providing the touch on parts of the body (e.g. shoulders) that are usually less sensitive. As the child learns to tolerate the touch, we gradually work our way to more sensitive areas, until the child is tolerant to touch on most of the body. The thought is that we are gradually resetting the nervous system's threshold for the fight-or-flight response. That is just a theory; there is no physical evidence to prove it.

You also seem to have problems with filtering out unwanted sensory stimulation, being distracted by background stimulation. This is also common for people on the spectrum. The brain has a hard time focusing attention on one source, while filtering out background stimulation. It tends to bounce around across all stimulation. For people like you, it is better to lower the stimulation level around you so you can focus on the task at hand.

Something that is not talked about as much, that you mentioned here, is the "movement actions of others" as a problem. I hear that mentioned frequently, but usually from self-reports, rather than the literature. Sensory overload can come from two sources: (1) oversensitivity to a given simulation, and (2) not specific sensitivity to any one sense, but becoming overwhelmed by multiple sources of stimulation (noisy, busy, confusing setting) coming in at one time. Too many different sources of sensory stimulation (noise, bright lights, overpowering smells, etc.) are bombarding the brain at one time. The first one (defensiveness) is the intensity of the stimulation, and the second one is the amount of stimulation coming in from multiple sources at one time (not defensiveness, but a modulation issue).

Also thanks for sharing what strategies you use to regulate in such situations. You mentioned strong proprioceptive input, like hitting/banging body parts and shaking your hands hard. Yes, strong input into the joints (banging, push, pull, snapping as in shaking/flapping hands), muscles and tendons helps to (1) release stress chemicals and (2) calm and organize the nervous system. Deep pressure touch also helps a lot. Also, any repetitive, rhythmic sensory patterns help to regulate the nervous system, as well as help tune out unwanted outside stimulation. So, the self-stimulation that many people display can help to (1) calm and organize the nervous system, as well as (2) block out unwanted stimulation so the nervous system can rebound.

Explaining the touch avoidance/seeking paradox!

Children who experience tactile defensiveness display strong avoidance reactions to touch. They may pull back defensively when others touch them, struggle during personal care, refuse to wear certain clothing, avoid touching certain textures, and feel the need to control all interaction occurring to them. However, paradoxically these same children can show strong seeking of deep pressure touch, often craving it. They can be very clingy, grabbing and holding on to mom and dad at all times. These two conditions seem contradictory if the child is sensitive to touch.

If you look closely at many of the children who are tactile-defensive, it is *light* touch that they are usually sensitive to. It is the nerve endings at the surface of the skin that are very sensitive, and set off a quick fight-or-flight response. However, the nerve receptors deeper into the muscles are usually not oversensitive, so deep pressure touch cancels out the negative effect of the touch to the surface of the skin. Deep pressure touch goes past the surface, activating the receptors in the muscles and tendons. Deep pressure touch also has a calming effect on the nervous system and can help calm and organize the often anxious nervous system of those who are tactile-defensive. So, when touching children with tactile defensiveness, use firm touch to avoid activating the fight-or-flight response.

Now, for the children who are grabby and clingy, these children may also want to seek out constant touch. They grab and hold on tightly to you and pull on you. They may be touching everything in sight to explore and get tactile feedback. Again, if you look closely, there are two qualities: (1) the child is controlling the touch—he is touching you, rather then you touching him—and (2) it is usually firm touch, not light touch. Even with light touch, the children can often handle it if they are controlling the touch. These same children may seek out soothing tactile stimulation by smearing feces or saliva on their skin. This controlled stimulation can be soothing to the anxious nervous system.

Touch is a basic human need, and often the sensory-sensitive child will crave touch, but have to (1) control it and (2) seek it firmly. They can be tactile avoiders on the one hand and be tactile seekers on the other. This often seems paradoxical. However, when interacting with kids with tactile defensiveness, my recommendations are:

- Warn them before touching them, or ask if it is OK to touch.

- If possible, let them control the touch (let them hold your hand, instead of you holding theirs).

- When touching, use firm pressure touch, instead of light touch.

- Invite touch; do not force it on them. I use "give ten" to celebrate a lot. However, I always reach out my hands, and allow the child to touch me, rather than touching him. Keep it safe, but let the child control it.

- Understand what parts of the body are more sensitive than others. Often the hands, feet, and face are very sensitive, whereas the back, shoulders, arms, and legs are usually less sensitive. Give physical affection firmly to those areas.

- Most importantly, be respectful of the child's sensitivity. Immediately withdraw your touch if the child reacts negatively, reassure him, and then proceed with caution only with his permission. Work with the child, respect his sensitivity, and allow him to control as much as possible.

- I also teach people who are tactile-defensive that briskly rubbing the surface of the skin will temporarily dull the sensitivity. So, if they know that someone (e.g. doctor) is going to touch them, they can rub that spot vigorously just prior to them touching there. This will temporarily dull the sensitivity.

Competing sensations!

A common sensory processing problem for many on the spectrum is poor integration of all the senses. People with good sensory integration easily integrate all their senses simultaneously into one overall perception. For some individuals, these different sensations (vision, auditory, touch, smell, vestibular, etc.) do not integrate into one comprehensive perception. As you can imagine, if all the sounds, sights, smells, and touch are not synchronized into one perception, they will be competing with one another for attention. Consequently, the bombardment of competing senses can be very distracting and overwhelming.

Many individuals on the spectrum who have problems with integrating their senses will favor one sense over others as their primary method for making sense of the world. This is called "mono-processing." For some it may be vision; for others hearing, and others touch, taste, or smell. These individuals, if the other senses are bombarding them with competing sensations, cannot filter out the sensations and will become overwhelmed. They may try to block out other competing sensations in order to focus on their preferred sense. For example, if the child uses vision as the primary sense, he may cover his ears to block out auditory stimulation if it is competing with his vision. Often we may misinterpret this as the child being auditory-defensive, when he is really just trying to block out one sense (hearing) to focus on his preferred sense (vision).

Neurotypical (NT) people integrate all of their senses simultaneously and subconsciously with minimal effort. However, those on the spectrum who cannot integrate their senses have to piece each competing sense together sequentially at the conscious level (think it through). They have to consciously make sense out of the competing senses that we process with ease. This takes a lot of mental energy and easily taxes the brain. As you can imagine, the more sensorily "noisy" (combination of all sensations) the environment is, the more taxing and overwhelming it is to process. Sensory overload is a major problem for many on the spectrum. All the artificial lights, noises, smells, and textures in our environment often tax and overwhelm the nervous system.

So, be very cognizant of how much sensory information we are bombarding the children with when engaging them throughout the day. Try to determine whether they have a preferred sense. If they do, try to use that sense to teach, relate, and engage around. Try to make that sense stand out, while minimizing the amount of other distracting sensory information. Try to tone down, modify, or mask the other competing stimulation. If your child is primarily a visual processor, you may want to give him ear plugs when entering into a noisy setting. This will help him filter out the competing noise, so he can better use his vision. If he starts to get agitated for no apparent reason, there is a good chance he may be experiencing overload from the sensory bombardment around him. Try to turn it down, or allow the child to pull back to regroup. If the child has sensory integration problems, be very respectful of this vulnerability. Sensory overload will quickly set off the fight-or-flight panic response. It represents a major threat to the nervous system and must be treated immediately by removing the stimulation until the nervous system has a chance to regroup and rebound. The more aware we are of this vulnerability, the greater we can adapt the environment to be more sensory-friendly for our children.

Sensory sensitivities: artificial vs. natural

Of the many people on the spectrum who have shared their experiences with me, many seem to be more sensitive to all the artificial sensory stimulation in our world today, and less so to the sounds and sights of nature. This is not true for everyone. Some can still be very oversensitive to sunlight, wind, or sounds of bugs flying, but in general they tend to be more overloaded by all the artificial sounds, lights, smells, and textures in our highly stimulating culture. Whether it is the fluorescent lights that flicker and hum, chemical smells of perfume and cleaners, scratchy feel of our synthetic fabrics, high-pitch noise of machinery, or other sensory bombardment, the poor child who is sensory-sensitive is often left overwhelmed.

Many adults move to the country as they get older. It allows them the comfort of escaping many of the artificial sights, sounds, and smells of today's world. Many of the sights, smells, and sounds of nature can be very soothing for those who have sensory sensitivities. Children are often attracted to natural body odors, many of which we try to cover up with artificial smells.

So, if you work with kids on the spectrum, please be conscious of all the artificial sensory sights, sounds, and smells in the environment around them. Try to avoid wearing perfumes and smelly deodorants. Also, try to allow access to natural smells (grass, dirt, flowers, etc.).

Regulating arousal level
Keeping the nervous system calm, alert, and organized!

Our nervous system needs an optimal amount of stimulation to stay alert and ready to meet the needs of the moment. The nervous system has a built-in regulator that adjusts the amount of stimulation needed to match the immediate demands of our environment. We each have an optimum level of alertness that allows us to feel calm but alert, able to relax and focus. When under-aroused we may feel slow and sluggish and find it difficult to focus, and when over-aroused we may feel overwhelmed and anxious. Throughout the day we may experience both extremes, but we tend to regulate to stay in the optimal range of arousal. When a little sluggish, we tend to increase the stimulation level to alert ourselves. We may fidget, chew gum, eat something, or stand up and go for a short walk. We doodle or twirl our hair, or play with our earlobes to stay alert. When over-aroused, we tend to back away, take a break, or tone it down a bit to avoid being overwhelmed.

Many children on the spectrum have difficulty regulating the amount of stimulation their nervous system needs to stay optimally aroused. Their internal regulator is not regulating the incoming stimulation well enough. When under-aroused, they may seek out added stimulation, but not be good at gauging how much stimulation they need. They may feed themselves too much stimulation and become overloaded, or not have enough to maintain focus. For some children, their poor nervous systems are constantly disorganized and either seeking out or attempting to avoid stimulation to establish optimal arousal.

The brain has a built-in filtering system (diencephalon) that acts to regulate how much stimulation is distributed across the brain. It acts as a filtering system, at any given time determining what type of stimulation and how much is needed to stay alert and focused on the task at hand. Our nervous system is constantly being bombarded with multiple stimulation, some of it important for us to attend to, but much of it irrelevant for the immediate task. For example, I am currently sitting at McDonalds working on this document. There are multiple sounds, sights, and smells all around me. For my nervous system to focus on the task at hand (focusing on what to type), it has to tone down or block out many of the noises (people talking, sounds of the equipment, cars going by, etc.), sights (actions of others, lights, distractions out the window, etc.), and the constant smells of the food. My nervous system constantly adjusts the amount of stimulation coming in to feed my brain what it needs to stay alert, but also to block out all the irrelevant stimulation that may be distracting. It is filtering out over 80 percent of incoming stimulation so I can attend to the task. Those who cannot adequately block out the irrelevant stimulation will be distracted, overloaded, and unable to focus.

For many of the children on the spectrum, their brains do not filter well. If the brain does a poor job of filtering out stimulation and lets in too much, it is distracted by all the irrelevant stimulation and becomes disorganized and overwhelmed. It cannot attend to the important information (constant distraction) and is anxious and on high alert.

However, if the brain is filtering out too much information, it will not be able to get the stimulation it needs to stay aroused. These children will become sluggish and may seek out increased levels of stimulation (hyper-activity) to increase their arousal level to stay alert. These children may seek out continuous stimulation (cannot sit still) in order to stay alert. When you try to get them to sit quietly, their nervous system becomes under-aroused and anxious, again seeking out stimulation. However, if you allow them to sit on an air cushion or therapy ball, chew gum, or fidget with small items to increase stimulation to the brain, they may be able to stay focused. The secret is finding ways to keep their nervous system in the optimal level of arousal and eventually teaching them how to establish and maintain optimal arousal.

Throughout the day we can move in and out of the optimal arousal level. We are most effective when we can recognize and regulate the intensity of stimulation to keep ourselves in the optimal range. When we hover in one extreme or another, we have difficulty. Children who tend to become over-aroused easily (brain filters too little) are often on guard and anxious, and melt down easily. Their stress chemicals are high, they are hyper-alert, and they panic easily. They are insecure and seek to avoid overload at all costs.

The child who is under-aroused may show this in two radically different ways. They may appear slow and sluggish, with little energy and poor muscle tone, or they will be overactive (bouncing off the walls), trying to increase the stimulation level to stay aroused. In either mode, they will not be in a state of readiness for learning.

Please be aware that the children are held captive by their nervous system. Before the brain can focus on learning, it has to pacify the nervous system. Regulating its arousal level is a high priority for the brain. When these needs are not met, the brain will feel threatened and start to panic. All attention is then focused on stabilizing arousal. When the nervous system is not getting what it needs, the brain's focus will turn toward re-establishing maximum arousal level.

It becomes high priority. Many of the behavior challenges we see in children on the spectrum are the nervous system's attempt to satisfy its need for increasing or lowering the arousal level. The better we get at recognizing this and helping the child to modulate his arousal level, the more calm, alert, and organized the child will be.

One of the ways to help the child regulate his arousal level is through implementing a sensory diet. When using a sensory diet, we are giving alerting stimulation when under-aroused and calming stimulation when the nervous system is over-aroused. The child learns to regulate his nervous system by feeding it stimulation to keep it organized.

Sensory diets
Helping the child feel calm, alert, and organized

Autism is a neurological condition that often leaves the nervous system out of sync with the environment around it. This is very evident in the difficulties the nervous system has in processing sensory input. As discussed earlier, there are a host of difficulties that this condition can present to the individual. Since the nervous system has difficulty processing sensory information effectively, it is often left agitated, disorganized, and overwhelmed. As mentioned above, the child (and adult) often has a hard time regulating the amount and intensity of stimulation to keep the nervous system calm, organized, and focused. He can be under-aroused and sluggish one moment, and overwhelmed and anxious the next. Because of this problem balancing what the nervous system needs, occupational therapists trained in sensory processing disorders often develop sensory diets to calm and organize the nervous system and keep it within the optimal range of arousal.

A sensory diet is a carefully scheduled routine of sensory activities given throughout the day to help keep the nervous system calm, organized, and focused, and within the optimal range of arousal. This lowers anxiety, increases focus, and maximizes the child's ability to learn and adapt to daily demands. Usually, the sensory diet is a set of activities to calm and organize the nervous system when over-aroused, and alert the nervous system when under-aroused. When the child is over-aroused, calming and organizing activities are given to stabilize the nervous system. When the child is under-aroused, alerting activities are given to increase the arousal level. Once the nervous system is in the optimal range of arousal, then a steady dose of organizing stimulation can maintain that state of readiness.

Usually, as part of a sensory processing evaluation, the occupational therapist will develop an inventory of sensory preferences and sensitivities that defines a sensory profile for the child. Although most therapists use one of the several published sensory scales, in Appendix A I provide a sensory inventory that I often use when doing behavior assessments. From this profile the therapist identifies what stimulation calms the child (e.g. deep pressure, slow rocking), what stimulation alerts the child (e.g. jumping, swinging, chewing crunchy snacks), what stimulation the child seeks out (preferences), and what he avoids (sensitivities). From developing this profile, the therapist can design a schedule of activities into the child's daily routine that will calm and organize his nervous system. Often a set of activities are recommended to be used on a set schedule each day (frequently, every couple of hours) as standard practice to keep the child organized, and then provide either calming or alerting activities as needed based on the child's arousal level. Although a thorough discussion of sensory diets is beyond the scope of this book, some of the general sensory activities are listed as follows.

General calming activities

- Deep pressure massage.
- Sitting on bean bags, large body pillow.
- Sandwiching, pillow press.
- Lap pads.
- Deep pressure or weighted vest.
- Bear hugs, neutral warmth.
- Slow rocking.
- Lotion rubs.
- Soft lighting.
- Soft, slow music.
- Joint compressions.
- Stretching.
- Chewing gum.
- Sucking.
- Fidget toys.
- Calm, rhythmic movement patterns.
- Physical relaxation exercises.

General alerting activities

- Brisk rubbing.

- Tickling.

- Chewing gum, chewy food.

- Any push/pull, run, skip, jump, heavy lifting activity.

- Fast, irregular movement (swing, trampoline, therapy ball).

- Kick, bounce, and throw a ball.

- Strong tastes and odors (peppermint, perfumes).

- Bright lighting.

- Loud, fast music.

- Cold water play.

- Fidget toys.

- Drinking carbonated drinks.

- Sitting on T-stool or air cushion.

- Physical exercise.

- Dancing.

Deep pressure, proprioception, and vestibular stimulation

Three popular types of sensory stimulation that provide necessary input in sensory diets are deep pressure touch (e.g. massage), proprioception (resistance to joints, tendons, and muscles often found in gross motor activity), and vestibular (usually consisting of moment activities, movement of head in space). The general sensory effects of these types of stimulation are:

- *Deep pressure* tends to calm the nervous system.

- *Proprioception* (resistance to muscles and joints) tends to organize the nervous system. Can be used to either calm or alert the nervous system.

- *Vestibular* (slow movement) tends to calm, while fast movement tends to alert.

In general, in all three categories, slow, soft, rhythmic stimulation tends to calm, and fast, intense, irregular stimulation tends to alert. However, children with autism have strong sensory sensitivities with wide individual variations. These diets have to be individualized based on the child's specific preferences and sensitivities.

Although the above three groups are very common in sensory diets, rounding out many diets may consist of a variety of calming and alerting tactile (touch), auditory (sound), olfactory (smells), and gustatory (taste) simulation. Below are examples of tactile/deep pressure stimulation, proprioception, and vestibular activities.

Tactile/deep pressure activities

- Brushing.
- Hand massage.
- Pillow press/ sandwiching.
- Neural warmth, wrap.
- Lotion rubs.
- Snuggling in blankets, pillows, bedding.
- Rubbing with different textures.
- Finger painting.
- Water play.
- Finding objects in rice, sand, beans.
- Play-Doh.
- Painting with shaving cream or whipping cream.
- Making sand castles, mud pies.
- Feeling different textures.

Proprioceptive activities

- Joint compressions.
- Stretching.
- Wall push-ups.
- Squeeze ball.
- Run, jump, skip.
- Lifting, carrying, push/pull.
- Chew, suck, blow.
- Vacuum, sweep.
- Leap frog, tug-of-war.
- Wheelbarrow walking.
- Hit, kick, bounce, throw ball.
- Climb, crawl, scoot, pull self.
- Rolling/kneading dough or clay.
- Outdoor work (raking, sweeping, mowing).
- Rough-housing, wrestling.
- Crashing on bed, beanbags.
- Pillow fights.
- Weighted vests, lap pads.

Vestibular activities

- Jumping, bouncing activities— trampoline, bed, ball, etc.
- Swinging—swing set, suspended swing, glider, hammock, etc.
- Running, skipping, riding activities.
- Turning, rotating, spinning—Sit 'n' Spin, swivel chair, swing.
- Scooter boards, wagon rides.
- Rolling, tumbling.
- Playing on slides, teeter totters, trapezes.
- Hopscotch, tag, chase.
- Rocking prone on therapy ball.
- Rocking chair.

Developing a sensory diet

Complete a sensory profile

When developing a sensory diet, consult an occupational therapist with experience in sensory processing disorders. In Appendix A is a sensory scale that I use when assessing sensory preferences and sensitivities for developing a sensory diet. Any sensory profile is going to explore the following:

- What types of stimulation does the child seek/avoid?

- What stimulation calms: deep pressure, slow movement, soft lighting, rhythmic chatting, etc.?

- What stimulates, excites, and holds the child's attention: fast movement, rough play, animated facial expressions, etc.?

- What helps organize and regulate: allows the child to feel relaxed, alert, and attuned to you?

- What stimulation should be avoided? What distracts the child?

How to identify sensory preferences?

Since children on the spectrum are attracted to, and often seek out, sensory stimulation they enjoy, it is important to know what their preferences are. Once we identify these preferences, we can build social, leisure, and learning activities around these preferences. Consider the following when trying to identify sensory preferences.

1. Ask the child! Sit down and fill out the profile together.

2. Watch the child. The child will tell with his actions.

   a. Play (run, bounce, sing, etc.).

   b. Self-stimulation (spin, rock, vocalize, etc.).

   c. When upset (hit, throw, bit, bang, etc.).

   d. To calm self (wrap up in blanket, rock and hum).

   e. What does he seek out? What does he avoid?

3. Systematically sample stimulation (smells, tastes, different touch, etc.) and note reaction.

4. Ask family and support people close to the child.

5. Use sensory assessment scales to help identify profile.

6. Direct assessment of stimulation by an occupational therapist trained in sensory processing disorders.

Putting it together!

Once your profile is developed, the occupational therapist can develop a routine schedule of sensory activities to keep the child's nervous system calm, organized, and focused. Usually, the diet will include routine activities to do at different times of the day, as well as sensory stimulation to be used as needed to calm and organize the nervous system. This diet should be used throughout the day, both at home and at school. A sensory diet may look like the following:

James's sensory diet

At home

Morning: Massage, joint compressions upon waking. Jumping on trampoline after morning routine (while watching TV). Chewing gum with MP3 player on the bus going to school.

After school: Trampoline or climbing/swinging on playscape.

After dinner: Exercise bands with dad, wrestling, heavy work activity, or trampoline.

Before bed: Deep pressure massage, compressions, weighted blanket.

At school

First thing: Group exercise/gross motor activity.

Circle time: Sit on ball or swivel board.

Mid-morning: Sensory break—trampoline, swing, jump or climb.

After lunch: Group exercise/gross motor activity.

Mid-afternoon: Sensory break—trampoline, swing, jump, or climb.

Before bus: Wear heavy backpack while sharpening pencils for teacher.

Throughout the day: Weighted lap pad, chewy tube, and air pad to sit on.

The murky area of sensory diets!

Autism is a bioneurological condition that leaves the nervous system fragile for regulating our very fast-paced, chaotic world. For many on the spectrum, their nervous systems are often going either too fast or too slow and are frequently out of sync with the environmental demands (physical and social). When this occurs, the nervous system is usually taxed and struggling to maintain effective processing. It becomes drained very easily, which hinders its ability to process even more.

Fundamentally, the connection between our nervous system and the world around us is through our senses. Through our basic five senses, we stay connected to the external world to functionally adapt to the environmental demands placed upon us. If we get mixed messages from these senses or they do not get integrated well, then we misread what the environment is requiring and respond incorrectly. In addition to regulating with the external world, we also have to stay connected with our internal world—what is occurring inside our bodies. We have to be aware of what our bodies are doing both in time and space, while coordinating all of these body parts together in unison. This awareness often comes through the proprioceptive (input into our joints, tendons, and muscles) and vestibular (movement of head in space/inner ear) senses. These two senses, in combination with touch, are fundamental to our sense of safety and security, as well as to establishing our sense of self.

When these three senses are not processing and integrating well, children (and adults) feel anxious and insecure. It will affect both their awareness and sense of security in their own bodies, as well as their security in interacting with the external environment. This leaves the person feeling apprehensive and on high alert for possible threats. Often this not only results in poor ability to appraise and match what is expected of them by others, but also leads them to be resistant to the demands of others, have a strong drive to escape and avoid any uncertainty, and feel the need to rigidly control everything around them. It is vital to their own sense of safety and security. This often leaves parents with a very scattered, disorganized, hyperactive, and highly resistant child.

The use of sensory diets to help regulate the nervous system is more of an art than a science. It is very difficult to evaluate exactly what the nervous system needs, when to provide it, and how much to provide. There is no exact protocol that objectively identifies and maps out a definitive course of treatment when developing sensory diets. There are some general guidelines, but activities need to be highly individualized. Also, the sensory diet is not the only variable that is needed to calm and organize a nervous system. For many of our kids, nutritional diets, sleep, and exercise are equally important in stabilizing the nervous system. So, when it comes to designing and evaluating the effectiveness of sensory diets, the path can be very murky at best. Finding the right sensory diet is very individualized to the child's unique nervous system and requires knowing the sensitivities and preferences of the child. It is also not something that can be imposed on the child. It very much depends on being a working partner with the child, making him an active participant in designing and monitoring his sensory diet. It requires observing and listening closely to the child (both what he is saying and how he is behaving) to understand what his nervous system needs. Between the therapist, parents, and child, it is important to try out and sample different sensory activities while closely observing the child's reactions and listening to his reported feelings. Only by letting the child control and pace the stimulation can the child learn to regulate his own nervous system.

However, all this takes time, close observation, and continuous tweaking of the diet to match the current needs of the nervous system. There is no one-size-fits-all sensory diet or standard protocol that matches each child. Right now it is more of an art than a science, with little reliable data to measure the effectiveness of this approach. It is hard to standardize in order to measure. The effectiveness of sensory diets is very much determined by the ability of the therapist to observe and read the actions of the child in order to appraise the needs of his nervous system. Also, most sensory diets are not used alone. They are built into overall comprehensive treatments consisting of behavior strategies, environmental accommodations, nutritional guidelines, and other social/emotional strategies. A sensory diet alone may not show strong effects in isolation in making environmental modifications to better match the external demands on the child's processing abilities, and teaching the child better strategies for coping with these social and physical demands.

In conclusion, no therapist can say with certainty what sensory activities will definitely work for your child. It is a sensitive process of sampling, observing, and then appraising the type, pace, and intensity of stimulation to match what the child responds best to. It takes a very close relationship between the therapist, parents, and child, always allowing the child to be an active voice in the process.

Chapter 7

SHARING DIFFERENT SENSORY WORLDS

When talking about how neurotypical (NT) people see the world and how people with autism experience the world, one of the differences may be the foundation for how we interpret our sensory experiences. Many people with autism report that they are acutely aware of and in tune with their sensory sensations. What they see, hear, smell, taste, and feel is often very vivid and intense. Some think in pictures rather than words, and others tend to categorize their world based on how it feels, smells, tastes, or moves. As we will discuss here, this is radically different from how NT people process their world.

When an infant is first born, he has no language to define what he sees, hears, feels, tastes, or smells. The world is a series of raw sensory data coming together to eventually form familiar patterns (e.g. mother's face). Eventually, as children develop language, they start to categorize their experiences based on language concepts. Over time, these language concepts are used to define our sensory experience, redefining how we process and perceive our experiences. Language concepts become a filter that helps shape for us what we see, hear, feel, smell, and taste. Over time, our perceptions are biased by our language-based filtering, defining for us what we are experiencing.

Processing for people with autism stays more sensory-based, with less language filtering. They tend to experience their sensory experiences as the raw sensory data presents itself, with few language-based concepts. They do less filtering before interpreting. They tend to use fewer language concepts to interpret what they see, hear, feel, etc. Therefore, their thinking is more sensory-based than language-based, more literal and concrete in their sensory perceptions. They experience the world more true to their raw sensory experiences, rather than first redefining it by language-based concepts.

For people with autism, perceptions are more true to their sensations. Sensation is the raw sensory input, and perception is how we interpret what we see, hear, smell, etc. With neurotypical people, sensory sensations are mediated by language-based concepts, defining how we perceive the experience. We interpret what we sense through words, language concepts that we use to interpret what we experience. People with autism tend to perceive more closely what they sense, experiencing the raw sensations. The perceptions of neurotypical people are more biased by inference, whereas the perceptions of people with autism are more true to the raw experience. However, since people with autism can have a variety of fragmented and distorted sensations, their perceptions are not necessary a factual representation of reality. When they have sensory registration problems that can vary from moment to moment, it can drastically affect what they perceive. However, if they don't have these challenges, their acute sensory perception can be a strong asset in tasks and vocational areas that favor very unbiased observation of sensory detail (art, music, engineering, etc.).

This sensory- versus language-based processing is not either/or, but most likely on a continuum with varying degrees of language mediation. Most likely, the degree of sensory- versus language-based processing varies from person to person, and within the same person from day to day. For those who have learned to use language mediation, it quickly falls apart under stress or sensory overload. Although not verified, I suspect that the less language the child has, the more sensory-based the processing will be. However, there are many people with autism who have strong language skills and also stay very sensory-based in their processing. When it comes to communicating their experiences, they have first to translate their experiences into words.

Now, based on the two ways of processing, NT people tend to interpret and then categorize their experiences in memory by language. We use language to define what we experience and then use language to categorize the experience into memory. People with autism tend to perceive the raw sensations with less language mediation and then have more sensory-based memories (categorized and stored by sensory characteristics rather than language concepts). These memories can often be very vivid representations of the raw sensation. This also affects the encoding of emotion to raw sensation. Consequently, the emotional reaction associated with the raw sensory sensation is often attached to the memory of that event. Thus, when those raw sensory sensations occur again, it can elicit strong emotions that were initially associated with that experience.

Language thinking vs. sensory thinking

We (NT people) tend to be language-based thinkers, processing and interpreting the world via language concepts. Children with autism tend to be sensory thinkers, processing their world by literal sensory perceptions. They categorize people, things, and experiences by their sensory qualities, by the shapes, smells, tastes, sounds, or how they feel. For example, mom is someone who smells, feels, or looks a specific way. Consequently, if mom changes her perfume, deodorant, hair style, or glasses, the child may not recognize mom. They are tied to the sensation. In addition, children with autism often favor one sense over the others, using that sense to interpret their world. For example, if the person uses smelling as a dominant sense, they frequently smell everything that they come in contact with. If touch is their main sense, then they have to feel everything.

When it comes to thinking, many people with autism can be sensory-based thinkers (often thinking in pictures). When communicating with others, they have first to translate their sensory based concepts (e.g. pictures) into words, before communicating with others. And when listening to others, they have to translate what they hear into pictures. This can cause delayed processing when trying to communicate with others. Since our experiences and thoughts are already language-based, no translation is needed. This is similar to two people with foreign languages trying to communicate.

The costs of learning to speak! One member's experience!
Moving from nonverbal (sensory-based) processing to verbal (language-based) processing

In the post above, I explored the mental processing differences (especially nonverbal) for people on the spectrum. Many on the spectrum process the world on a sensory level, whereas neurotypical people use language-based processing. Of course, as the person on the spectrum gains speech, he often incorporates more language-based processing. However, as one of our members on the spectrum describes below, this often comes with a price. She took great effort to explain to all of us how this moving from a sensory-based to language-based processing played out for her as she learned to talk. She also explains how draining it can be to communicate in our verbal world.

MY THOUGHTS ON SENSORY VS. VERBAL THINKING

Sorry it took me so long to go about writing this, but it took me a while to process and word my response. I wanted to make sure I took the time to really think on it. I may have also been a bit nervous about how people may respond to this. I want to thank you for letting me share this.

Your slide show on verbal vs. sensory thinking in my opinion is very well done. I really like how it broke down the differences between verbal and sensory thinking and puts it into simple terms so most people can understand it.

I also really liked how you used the differences in thinking to explain many of the symptoms of autism. That was very well done!!! I especially loved the example with perfume! So few people realize how traumatizing a sensory experience can be, especially when it is something they don't notice at all!

I really loved this slide show. I feel it matches very closely to my own personal experiences. Below I have written of my experience of going from being nonverbal to verbal.

I had a moderate speech delay when I was little in spite of the fact I received early intervention since the age of eight months old. When I was little my predominant method of thinking was sensory-based. This was also the major source of my memories. I used to use people's scent, sound of voice, and hair to recognize them as I couldn't recognize faces. The truth is I still use these features to identify people. However, all my thoughts as a child were based in sense and experiences. While reading your slides, one memory in particular came to mind and that was the first time I saw those huge round light bulbs they used to put around mirrors in salons as well as some stores. It fascinated me! It was bright and it smelt different to the lights we had at home. Curious, I reached out and touched it with my fingers. And I remember the feel of the burn on my fingers and a sensation that went from the tip of my fingers up my arm and to my tongue. I know it sounds strange but it kind of had a taste or feeling in my tongue. In fact many types of injuries have feelings or tastes in my tongue or a smell-like feeling in my nose. It isn't exactly a literal smell but a sensation that is smell-like. I'm not really sure how to explain it. I used my senses to understand and navigate the world. I used them to have an idea on the time of day and where I was. I know it sounds crazy but I remember being able to pause what I was doing and focus and have an idea of the time of the day. A lot of my memories are based on the look, feel, smell, and sensation of objects.

Growing up I received a lot of therapies and slowly I went from having very minimal communication skills to being highly verbal. I think the peek hit around 14 or so. For me, sensory thinking and verbalization/verbal understanding had two separate compartments in my brain. The verbal compartment seems to have been linked to the auditory compartment. As a child, the more I used words, the less aware I became of my senses and environment. In fact over time I became kind of "detached." My brain can't seem to juggle understanding the world for what it is and using verbal communication at the same time. Temple (Grandin) once explained that with autism we don't have enough wiring to support all the parts of our brain and I do feel this is very true. When I had little to no speech, all of the wires in my brain were linked to my sensory thinking. With therapy more and more wires were moved to verbal thinking and processing. Slowly, over time I began to lose a lot of my sensory thinking and it was being replaced with verbal thinking. However, unlike sensory thinking it does not feel natural and I think for me it manifests differently than for those who are natural verbal thinkers. My process seems a lot more jumbled.

This is the best way I can demonstrate it below.

Sensory sensation → sensory sorting *processing* → understanding (now more it is more like partial understanding) *This is where it would end as a child before much of the speech therapy*→ search for and match with previously spoken sentences/scripts → dissection and mixing of scripts to match thought or experience → raw mental verbal translation → apply scripted additives for sentence structure→ adding pre-translated phrases and scripts from past experiences→ transition of verbalized translation of thought/experience from brain to body (this step might best be understood by imagining the verbalized translation sliding from the brain down nerves or something to the back of the mouth) → coordinating verbalized thought into physical movement of tongue and mouth → physical verbal communication.

This is kind of a raw idea of how communicating works in my brain but there are more complicated aspects I can't word. This very draining process can take anywhere from a minute or two to days, weeks, or years depending on what I'm communicating. It is almost as though my original sensory thinking had many extra tedious and draining steps added to it. This processing is kind of like a big puzzle in my brain. In a general back and forth conversation this takes a few minutes as I am often sifting and rearranging our scripted translation. However, this takes a lot from me to do and I will often become nearly completely unaware of my environment, as my body focuses all its mental processes to this one task. This also makes conversation very difficult for me as I have to constantly do this. Often I don't know what to say to keep a conversation going and after we have run out of things I can quickly script or run into something I have not yet scripted or need to process, the conversation falls short. Keeping the topic on my interest makes it much easier to communicate and to keep my attention in conversations. After all, I have plenty of pre-scripted information to exchange in conversation.

It used to be I would only have to go through this processing while having a conversation or when in class if I wanted to participate. However, slowly over time and the more I was expected to communicate verbally, the more this process began to take over. As though my brain is constantly in this exhausting process to prepare itself for surprise conversations. As I said, this is a very stressful and tiring process for me and can even be painful. Constantly having to do this makes the world feel dead to me. And in spite of the fact that my brain is almost always stuck in this loop there is still so much I will never be able to communicate, so much that remains trapped inside of me. Even if it has been translated I can't seem to get the translated signal to travel to the next step.

Honestly it feels like I traded the frustration of being nonverbal, not being able to find the words and not really being able to communicate, for a very stressful and draining and frustrating process, depression. And still struggling to communicate but having the demands and expectations that I communicate verbally in spite of how stressful, tiring and frustrating it tends to be.

While a large amount of my sensory processing has been taken from me, I still need a lot of sensory input when thinking and translating. Especially if my brain is trying to formulate complex concepts or process big events. Sometimes my brain will start this translating process while I'm walking. This has lead to me losing track of where I am and finding myself in a sort of wandering state.

Even though I have lost much of my sensory understanding, my senses are still heightened and I can easily become overwhelmed and overloaded. I think for me this process is almost like a sense in that I become overwhelmed and overloaded a lot easier during it. Some days I would do anything to make it stop because of how tiring, draining, and stressful it can be.

However, there are times where I can stop this cycle and turn it off. When this happens I am nonverbal but in a good way, a way that is not caused by stress, overstimulation, or anxiety. During these times I feel much happier and for a while things feel right again. This last year I have undergone two surgeries that both times left me nonverbal for about a week or so. During that time I discovered a few things. One, I was a lot happier during the time I couldn't speak as I didn't have to start that cycle up as I used AAC apps to communicate. Two, I communicate a lot better typing and using these apps than I can talk. Three, I feel higher-functioning and can manage conversations and social interactions better with my apps.

For me, becoming verbal took a lot of hard work but has also become something of a burden. It is something that came with new and unexpected challenges. There is a part of me that wishes to give up speaking and just use my apps, but this is something I know many would never support and would think poorly of me for it. I know there are many who are nonverbal that would love to have my ability to speak. I know many parents who read this would give anything to have their kids be able to speak. I honestly often wish I could give this to someone else who could appreciate it more. But I can't and so I'm left trying to figure out what to do next.

I wrote something explaining the negative effects becoming verbal has had on me. If you would be interested in reading it let me know. I can't thank you enough for letting me share this with you. I love your page so much. I honestly believe this specific slide show should be given to every parent when their child receives a diagnosis!

Strong "associative" memory

Children with autism have strong factual, associative memory, being able to encode the exact sensory memory that was associated with an experience. These sensations, and the emotions attached to them, are memorized in association with the event. Consequently, any future events with similar sensory sensations may set off the same emotional reactions. Johnny is very sensitive to perfume. When his aunt, who was wearing a blue dress, hugged him tightly, the smell of her perfume made him nauseous and he panicked. Now, when he sees women wearing blue dresses, he automatically smells the same perfume (even though they may not be wearing any), panics, and runs away. Strong emotions get attached to sensory experiences, to be relived over and over again.

Here again, in more detail, is the link between sensory memory and emotions associated with the encoding of the raw sensory experience. These can be very vivid memories, with intense emotions attached to them. Hence, when the same raw sensations occur again, they can elicit the same strong emotion, which may not seem to fit the occasion. This can explain some of the emotional regulation problems in children with autism. Since NT people's experiences are more filtered first by language, their emotional responses are often toned down by the language-based mediation. Hence, when encoded into memory, the emotion attached to it is not as strong. This allows NT people to more easily regulate their emotional responses.

Parents, caregivers, and teachers need to be very aware that sensory stimulation can elicit very strong emotional reactions, with very vivid memories. At the same time, when children become sensorily overwhelmed, they may become emotionally upset very quickly. When there is no language mediating the sensation, you have direct emotional reactions.

PTSD and autism

It has amazed me how long it has taken for the field to accept sensory processing dysfunctioning in autism spectrum disorder. For years, the field of psychology practically ignored sensory issues. Applied Behavior Analysis ignored it while forcing children to obey and stay in situations that were overwhelming for them. If the children acted out, we made them stick it out, so their acting-out behavior was not reinforced by escaping the unwanted situation. More than 20 years ago when I first started incorporating sensory processing strategies into my behavior plans, the behavioral psychologists all looked down on it because you could not observe it and measure it. Agencies would try to stop me from using the strategies because they were not evidenced-based. Sensory processing problems were not real. The agencies were in the business of changing behavior. Treating autism was nothing more than changing their behavior. The child's internal experiences were not recognized, considered, or valued. The ends (changing behavior) justified the means (punishment, forcing compliance). Sensory processing issues were not "real." Even though adults on the spectrum were writing extensively about these traumatizing experiences, the behavioral psychologists still claimed they were not real.

Sensory dysfunction in autism is being recognized now. Finally, after many years of people on the spectrum speaking out and demanding to be listened to, these experiences are being taken seriously. However, another topic not mentioned much in autism spectrum disorder is post-traumatic stress disorder (PTSD). Since most PTSD is caused by extreme sexual or physical abuse and wartime emotional trauma, it is not often suspected in ASD. However, I see evidence of it, and many of the reports from adults on the spectrum relate experiences that seem very similar to post-traumatic stress. Post-traumatic stress occurs when there is severe insult to the nervous system. It results in both changes in brain chemistry and in suspected structural changes in the brain. The person exhibits generalized anxiety, depression and isolation, panic attacks for no apparent reason, and sometimes rages.

PTSD can come from one or more emotional traumas, or long-term distress from severe sensory processing dysfunction. Many nonverbal people on the spectrum, who also experience severe sensory defensiveness, are often experiencing intense physical and emotional trauma from the overwhelming sensory insult to their nervous systems. The child never knows when the sensory bombardment is going to occur, and it often attacks without warning, leaving the child helpless in defending against it. The constant fight-or-flight panic reaction has long-term effects on the nervous system, leaving the individuals battling stress and anxiety for many years. Each time the nervous system experiences intense sensory bombardment, the stimulus characteristics of the event become associated with the severe panic response. At other times in the future, when these common stimuli occur again, it can produce an immediate panic reaction that was originally associated with the traumatic event. For these individuals, immediate panic occurs for no apparent reason. Neither the person nor those around him may understand why the panic reaction occurs. This response can occur in response to a given sound, color, or smell that was originally associated with the traumatic event. Our sensory memories are very intense. When your sensory experiences are very intense and inconsistent, like those of people with sensory processing disorders, such overwhelming emotion can be associated with, and set off easily by, simple sensory memories.

So, when working with severely impaired individuals on the spectrum, tread very lightly. Be very respectful of their comfort zones. Be very careful how you touch them, talk to them, and press them. Their nervous systems are very vulnerable and easily traumatized. Their reactions can be very guarded and intense. They can be very emotionally reactive and need you to be very calm, gentle, and compassionate. Always be looking for defensive reactions and immediately pull back when you see them. Never press children into situations they are scared of. Guide them, but let them pace their actions. Let them feel in control so they can immediately end any situation of panic. Learn what touch, words, actions, and stimulation help them feel safe and secure. Always listen and understand first, before intervening and redirecting their actions. Always assume that underlying their defensive reactions is intense emotional upheaval. Be respectful and compassionate, allow them to pull back, escape, and rebound. Teach them coping skills for dealing with these intense experiences, but most importantly teach them to feel safe in your presence and to trust in following your lead.

Cognitive mediation of emotional control

With neurotypical people, our emotional reactions to events are mediated by language concepts. We tend to match our emotional reaction to the cognitive interpretation of the potential threat of what we perceive. Instead of reacting impulsively to raw sensation, we appraise it first. This allows us first to check our impulse to fight-or-flight, cognitively appraise the actual threat, then tone down our reaction (both emotionally and physically) to match the perceived threat.

People who are sensory processors tend to react emotionally to raw sensations with little language mediation, and often over exaggerated, impulsive reactions. Their fight-or-flight panic reaction sets in before they can cognitively appraise the actual threat. Emotions come on strong, often like a tidal wave, and rebound slowly.

The ability to use language to mediate, or appraise, before we emotionally react to our sensory sensations allows us to better regulate our emotions (think before we react). This language-based mediation becomes very important in first inhibiting an emotional impulse and in using forethought before responding. Thus, regulating one's emotional reactions often requires language-based mediation to (1) check our emotional impulse, (2) evaluate potential consequences of our reactions, and then (3) choose how to act. Without this language-based mediation, the child goes from zero to one hundred very quickly. Since this does not come naturally for the child with autism, it takes a lot of practice. Although they can get better at using cognitive mediation, many children and adults can still be prone to quick emotional reactions when their coping skills break down under sensory overload. This is why it is important to teach cognitive mediation techniques (five-point rating scale, self-talk, thought scripts, etc.) to help the child learn to use cognitive coping skills to help him regulate his emotional reactions (much more on this in the chapter on emotions).

Fragile sense of security

When the way you process the world is tied to raw sensory perception, your sense of safety and security is weak and vulnerable.

Because many children experience sensory processing problems (hyper-sensitivities, sensory overload, delayed processing, fragmented perceptions, problems integrating senses, etc.), their primary way of interpreting the world is unreliable. When you cannot trust your senses, you become anxious and insecure. You cannot trust and need to control all interactions and activity around you. You become very dependent on predictable, ritualistic behavior and routines.

Many children with autism experience strong anxiety and insecurity. Since their emotions are strongly attached to their sensory sensations, with less cognitive mediation, their emotional reactions are tied directly to their vivid sensory experiences. Unfortunately, many children with strong sensory processing difficulties often experience sensory overload, which elicits their fight-or-flight panic reaction. When their sensory processing is not consistent and reliable, then they are left feeling anxious and emotionally insecure. That is why it is important to provide sensory integration therapy as early as possible, and provide ongoing accommodation to reduce sensory chaos and overload.

What does understanding this sensory processing mean for us?

We can use the knowledge of sensory processing to support and soothe the child when upset, and use sensory preferences to build social/emotional engagement with others and build learning around the child's sensory strengths and preferences. Since sensory-based processing is the foundation of the child's experiences, we need to start there and build on his processing strengths. We also need to think sensory processing when interpreting emotional outbursts, explaining self-stimulation, and understanding sensory-based fixations. Think sensory when soothing, modifying undesirable behavior, motivating and engaging the child, and building learning opportunities around their interests.

- We have to stay aware of this difference in perceiving so we are sensitive to how they interpret the world.

- For those with sensory sensitivities, their world can be very chaotic and overwhelming when intense sensory stimulation is present.

- Artificial lights, sounds, and smells can be very overwhelming. When the child is resistant, having trouble concentrating, or acting out, look for possible sensory bombardment.

- Be sensitive to the perfumes you wear, deodorants you use, and the lights, smells, and sounds that are around you.

- Build strong associations with the feel of your touch, the smell of your presence, the sound of your voice, the sight of your face. Use these sensations to build strong memories of feeling safe, accepted, and loved.

- Build familiar holding/cuddling/rocking patterns, singing/chanting/ soothing voice patterns, predictable perfume/soap/shampoo odors, and predictable visual signs (glasses, hair style, earrings, jewelry, etc.).

- Appeal to his senses to connect to his emotions. Use his sensory preferences to emotionally engage with him. Build simple interactive play around his sensory preferences.

- Identify the sensory preferences to soothe the child when upset and alert the child when under-aroused.

- Build "I love you rituals" around sensory preferences.

- Build on his sensory strengths. Design learning experiences around his sensory preferences.

- Encourage him to develop these strengths in sensory-based activities (music, drawing, visual puzzles and games, mechanical design, etc.).

- Develop his keen sense of detail into leisure, academic, and vocational skills.

- He can sense, feel, and think in ways that we cannot. Don't stifle this, develop it!

Sensory patterns!

Since many people on the spectrum have very sensitive sensory systems, they often have vivid attraction to sensory patterns. These patterns can be visual patterns (visual movement patterns—waves, ripples in water, leaves waving in the wind or gently falling from the trees, hand waving in front of eyes, etc.), auditory (sound patterns, music rhythms, voice patterns, etc.), tactile (feel of sand or water flowing through their fingers, pulsating deep pressure massage, etc.) or kinesthetic (repetitive body part movement—hand flapping, rocking, head rolling, etc.).

People on the spectrum are more sensitive to, and more acutely aware of, these sensory patterns. They can often see, hear, and feel sensory patterns that neurotypical people do not register. For example, they may hear the humming of florescent lights, or see the lights' endless flickering, whereas most of us cannot sense these frequencies. They may also see particles floating in the air, which we are not sensitive enough to pick up. They may hear sounds, frequencies, pitches, and low volumes that neurotypical people cannot hear. They also can feel vibrations that may be too low for many of us to notice, or the slightest smells can make them nauseous. As you can imagine, these sensory sensitivities can be very distracting and overwhelming.

Although these same hyper-sensitivities can present alarming sensations, they also can present very vivid, pleasurable experiences. The visual, auditory, and tactile rhythmic patterns can be very soothing and attractive to the nervous system. Given that these sensations are so vivid and important to emotional stability, these sensory patterns also become important in how people with autism categorize their experiences into memory.

Hence, many people with autism are very attracted to and can be distracted by sensory patterns. They often use sensory patterns to soothe themselves when overwhelmed, or to block out unwanted stimulation. We often label self-directed sensory patterns as self-stimulation—the repetitive movements or vocal patterns that are commonly seen.

At the same time, people on the spectrum so vividly experience subtle sensory patterns that they can be extremely talented in music, art, photography, and other fields that involve sensory patterns. They can have very accurate associative memory and can reproduce visual images and music (sound) patterns that others cannot.

Whether it be the horrific bombardment of unpleasant sensations or the glorious enjoyment of pleasurable perceptions, the sensory world of those on the spectrum is second to none!

What kind of sensory patterns are your children (or you) attracted to? What catches and holds their attention, often mesmerizing them? Have you ever sat with them to try to share their experience?

To touch their "hearts," love with your "senses!"

Whereas we live in a world of language, children with autism live in a world of senses. They think, feel, and experience through their sensory preferences. They live intense sensory experiences, where they explore, process, and categorize their world based on vivid visual, auditory, tactile, and olfactory images. They encode these sensory memories and use them to build their sense of safety and security, connect with others, and organize their experiences.

Since these children tend to experience the world through their senses, we need to use these sensory pathways to communicate our love for them. Children on the spectrum are attracted to sensory patterns, which are visual, auditory (sound), tactile (touch), vestibular (movement), and olfactory (smell) patterns. These patterns may be movement patterns, such as rocking, swinging, swaying back and forth, or auditory patterns such as humming, chanting, singing, and whistling. Probably the most interpersonal senses are touch and smell. Whether it is deep pressure massage, soft stroking, simple hand games, or rhythmic brushing of the hair, the medium of touch can establish those sensory memories that build strong bonds of love. In addition to touch, smells are very powerful for building emotional memories. Smells go directly to the limbic system, the emotion center of the brain. The smell of your hair, the perfume you wear, the hand lotion you use, or just the natural smell of your skin become highly associated with strong emotion.

To help your child connect with you, use his sensory intuition to encode strong episodic memories of safety and security, love and belonging. Develop a sensory profile of your child to identify the sensory patterns that will help him feel safe, accepted, and loved. Learn which patterns calm and soothe the child, alert and organize him, as well as those that scare and overwhelm him. Associate your presence with his favorite sensory preferences. Incorporate his favorite smells into your lotions and perfumes, or avoid them altogether if your child is defensive to them. Be conscious of the shampoos, deodorants, lotions, soaps, and perfumes you use, and the reactions they receive from your child. Try to use only one scent on a consistent basis rather than varying your scents, or wearing multiple scents (deodorant, perfume, lotion) at one time. Find the scent they prefer and wear it consistently. Pair this with your child's favorite touch: stroking, brushing, massaging, snuggling. Again, this will depend on his sensitivities, as well as his preferences. Avoid his sensitivities and identify his favorite tactile (touch) patterns. Pair these favorite touch patterns with his favorite smells and you are on your way to establishing strong sensory memories of you.

To make this emotional connection even stronger, pair your tactile/smell associations with your child's favorite auditory and movement patterns. Identify what movement patterns (slow rocking, swinging, dancing, etc.) and auditory patterns (simple little chants, sing-song phrases, singing, humming, etc.) attract your child. Make an inventory of all these little smells, touch, movement, and auditory patterns that can be combined together to build simple "I love you rituals" that can be repeated several times a day. Begin the day with a sensory pattern "I love you ritual" (Baily 2000); use them to ease transitions, soothe difficult times, and end the day with sensory connections. Stay with them, keep them consistent, and use them to establish stronger bonds. Touch your child through his senses to captivate his heart.

Match your interactions to the child's sensory preferences!

Once you determine your child's sensory profile (what he is attracted to, what he avoids, what calms him, and what overwhelms him), then you want to match your style of interaction to the sensory comfort zone of the child. What interaction style does your child respond best to? What does he feel safest with? What will best facilitate engagement? Often his sensory preferences will dictate how interaction should be given. Does he respond best to an upbeat, animated style, or a slow, calm style? If he is sensory-defensive, he may often get overwhelmed by excited, loud, animated people, and respond best to slow, calm, and quiet interaction. If he is a sensory seeker, he may tend to like more upbeat, quick-paced, animated interaction that alerts him.

The three main interaction tools are your hands, voice, and physical presence (body posture and facial expressions). It is important to identify how to use each of these tools to establish greater connections with your child. How does he respond to touch? Does he seek out and respond best to physical contact, or pull back and avoid any touch? What type of touch does he respond best to? Soft, light touch, or rough and deep pressure touch? How can you use your touch to calm and soothe him when upset, and to excite him when under-aroused? Does he pull away from touch or draw into your attention when touched? Do you initiate touch or invite it and let him control it? Touch is the most intimate human contact we can provide. It is important to know how to give it.

Your voice also has prime importance. The way in which you use words, the length of your sentences, and the speed, tone, and volume of your voice all have a major impact on drawing your child's attention and establishing a safe connection. Many children on the spectrum have auditory processing problems and strong auditory sensitivities. Many respond better to soft, slow, quiet voices, while others need loud, exciting voices to keep them stimulated. Many respond well to sing-song, chanting-type speech and like rhythmic vocal patterns. Others may like short phrases, spoken in slow, quiet voices, and become totally overwhelmed with fast-paced, excitable types of voice patterns.

Next, your physical presence and facial expressions play a major role. What is your child's need for physical space? Does he prefer a large physical space, and feel uncomfortable if you get to close to him? Or, does he like to cling, hug, or climb on you? Does he get overwhelmed with animated facial expressions and exaggerated gestures, or does he perk up and attend to animated styles of interaction?

These preferences can seem inconsistent depending upon the state of the nervous system. When the child is calm and organized, he may respond well to touch, excited voices, and animated interaction. However, when his nervous system is stressed and drained, he may pull away from such intensity and want more space, quieter voices, and limited touch. We need to match the level of interaction to the state of the child's nervous system.

Once you identify his sensory preferences, you can identify how to combine your touch, words, and facial expressions to help your child feel safe, accepted, and engaged with you. Teach people around your child how to relate with him in a way that he feels safe and engaged with.

Combine sensory preferences with rhythmic patterns!

Using sensory preferences for promoting attachment, emotion sharing, and reciprocal engagement.

Just as we try to compensate to accommodate for the child's sensory sensitivities, we also want to identify and use his sensory preferences to engage the child. Use them to play interactive games with each other, and build them into learning experiences. If the child loves jumping and climbing, play interactive games around the stimulation that attracts him. If he likes deep pressure touch and crashing, then build those into interactive play. If he grooves to music, then play interactive games around music.

The two elements that I find children most attracted to are (1) appealing to their sensory preferences and (2) building these sensory preferences into repetitive, rhythmic patterns. Using repetitive, rhythmic sensory patterns draws the children into feeling safe and engaged with you. This may include singing nursery rhymes while rocking back and forth, tapping a balloon back and forth, bouncing on your leg to a favorite song, clapping to music together, crashing on the bed together after saying "Ready, set…crash!" and sitting face to face, holding hands, and rocking back and forth to "Row, row, your boat." The activities are endless!

When building sensory motor patterns into interactive play:

- Identify one or two sensory preferences (e.g. singing, bouncing, swinging).

- Build those sensory preferences into simple interactive play patterns that are short and repetitive (e.g. clapping hands together while singing, holding hands while crashing on to the bed together). See Appendix B for a list of possible sensory patterns.

- Involve minimal toys or items in the play. You become the main element in the play—just you and the child, if possible.

- Sit face to face at eye level, so the child can easily reference your face. You want your face to be the center of attention.

- Use your hands, face, and voice to happily engage the child. Use animated facial expressions and exaggerated gestures to draw in the child's engagement.

- Respond to every communicative intent or reciprocal play by your child with excited feedback.

- Place emphasis on the sensory stimulation that your child is attracted to. Accent it and make it stand out (exaggerate the bouncing, singing, etc.).

- Build back-and-forth, reciprocal engagement so the child feels himself being an active participant in the activity.

- Frequently celebrate doing it together with high fives, thumbs up, and bump knuckles!

The next section gives an example of how I used sensory motor play to engage a young child who often resists engaging with others. Appendix B gives further instructions on how to implement sensory motor interactive play, a list of potential play activities, and a sample plan for using these strategies throughout the day. Just remember to build the child's sensory preferences into repetitive rhythmic patterns!

The power of sensory preferences

Many of you have children who are rigid and inflexible, have to control everything around them to feel safe, have poor emotional regulation, and tend to melt down over minor snags in their expectations. These characteristics are very common in young children on the spectrum. Many of these children do not know how to regulate themselves. They do not know how to stay calm and organized. They often jump from one thing to another, seeking stimulation, but without really knowing what they need and how to provide it to themselves. They are lost but refuse to let others help them regulate. They do not feel safe letting down their guard and following the lead of others to guide them. It is very challenging and frustrating for the parents, as well as for the child.

All infants have poor ability to regulate their needs and emotional responses. It is only through feeling safe giving up control and letting the parents regulate their needs (both physical and emotional) that they learn what it feels like to be regulated, and eventually learn how to self-regulate. The ability to self-regulate only comes from first allowing others to help regulate you. Self-regulation is born out of loving emotional attachment. Unfortunately, because of strong sensory sensitivities and sensory overload, many children on the spectrum never learn to feel safe giving up control and allowing the parent to help soothe and regulate them. They never learn to trust following the lead of others. Uncertainty, especially social uncertainty, is very scary for them. They need to control all interactions in order to feel safe. Consequently, they never learn to successfully regulate their emotional responses and usually overreact emotionally to minor snags in their daily living.

For such children, build simple interactive play patterns (repetitive, rhythmic patterns) around their sensory preferences. These play patterns help them feel safe and accepted, and emotionally connected to their caregivers. If the child likes to swing and jump, then I build simple interactive play around swinging and jumping.

I had a little eight-year-old girl come into the sensory clinic. Like many kids on the spectrum, she was cute as a button, with wide, beautiful eyes that just made you melt. She came in anxious, scared, and crying. She ran around, jumping from one piece of equipment to another, initially refusing to do anything we wanted her to do. The father and occupational therapist eventually got her to calm down and try some of the swings. She would not follow their lead, and would only stay with an activity for approximately one minute before running to another. As long as she was leading, she would allow us to interact a little. Once we tried to lead, she would become resistant.

From interviewing mom and dad, I found out that she enjoys bouncing and loves singing simple nursery rhymes. I stepped in and decided to build some interactive play around bouncing and singing nursery rhymes. My objectives were to teach her to relax and follow my lead, engage in coordinated play with me, reference my face to share pleasurable moments, and learn to allow me to regulate her through repetitive, rhythmic, sensory patterns—in essence, to share the experiences with me, and trust engaging with me to relax and stay organized.

The first activity was playing "Humpty Dumpty" by bouncing on an exercise ball. I would position her on the therapy ball, kneeling face to face, at eye level. I would calmly bounce her on the ball while saying "Humpty Dumpty sat on the ball, Humpty Dumpty…had a great fall!" as we slowly fell sideways off the ball into a crash pad. Again, as we fell, I stayed right with her so I could keep her referencing my face, to share the pleasure. She initially wanted to bounce very fast and haphazardly, but I would stop her and set the pace for her. She was a little anxious the first couple of times, but then would jump up and want "more!" When I slowed her down and set a nice regulated pace, she would reference my face for information, as well as to share emotion (pleasure). She was feeling safe with letting me regulate the activity and her emotion. She would look at me and smile in anticipation, and laugh with me as we went crashing into the pad. She let down her guard and would let me lead her to stay regulated. She also stayed with the activity until I wanted to shift to something else. She was able to focus, stay regulated, and stay on task with someone else leading. She also was feeling emotionally connected to me.

Next, I wanted to see if she could maintain this connection for a long regulatory pattern. I wanted to stay with the two preferences (bouncing and singing) so I sat her on my legs, facing me. We played a simple interactive activity called "This is the way the cowboy rides." I held her hands and moved them in a circular fashion, as I bounced her on my knees in a slow rhythmic pattern to "This is the way the lady rides, lady rides, lady rides. This is the way the lady rides so early in the morning!" Again, my face was at eye level, so she could reference my animated facial expressions.

This activity goes through three phases, with each phase increasing the tempo and intensity of the bouncing. From the "lady rides" to "gentleman rides" (little more intense), to "cowboy rides" which is high tempo and intensity. This was a much longer pattern and required a lot more trust. She loved it! She giggled, referenced my face to share pleasure, and followed my lead. After each time she would immediately return for "more!" She followed my lead, relaxed, and allowed me to pace it. She let me keep her regulated for at least five to ten minutes. I finally had to quit because I was worn out!

The father was excited to see how his daughter could relax and feel comfortable engaging with me, stay regulated by following my lead, and reference my face to stay emotionally connected. He learned how I took her two main sensory preferences, bouncing and singing, and built rhythmic, repetitive play patterns around these two preferences. From these sensory motor play patterns she let me pace her in cooperative play and stayed focused and regulated throughout. By using these two sensory preferences we allowed her to relax and be attracted to our engagement.

This is the beginning phase of teaching emotion sharing and sharing an experience with another: to stay coordinated in play while following the lead of the other, to feel calm and regulated by allowing the adult to "pace" the activity.

Helping your child regulate with sensory play

Many of our children have disorganized nervous systems that are always seeking out sensory stimulation to try to calm and organize themselves. At our sensory clinic I saw a 13-year-old, nonverbal young lady who is one such child. She was a charming girl, with a warm smile. She could not sit still or focus on any one activity for more than a minute without having to get up, literally bounce around the room, jumping, stamping her feet, and loudly clapping her hands together. She was not upset, but she just could not stay regulated. She appeared happy and enjoyed attention, but simply could not regulate. She would continually seek out strong proprioceptive stimulation (pressure and resistance to her joints and tendons by jumping and clapping). She could not control this. We could engage her for approximately a minute before she had to do her running around. Instead of sitting, she would squat with her knees and back compressed to add stretching and compression to her joints.

As strong as this sensory input was, it was a much-improved adjustment to what she was displaying four years ago when she was constantly pinching, slapping, and biting herself and others. Her sensory seeking was less intrusive since she had substituted strong hand clapping with the jumping to provide the sensory input.

This girl was very charming in that she smiled a lot and loved to share emotion with us. As active as she was, when we offered her our hands, she would stop briefly, take our hands, smile, and bring her face close to ours. Then within ten seconds she was back to jumping and clapping. Since she was seeking strong proprioceptive input (resistance to her joints by jumping and clapping), I decided to do some sensory motor interaction that provided joint input. We sat on the floor together, facing each other, holding hands with outreached arms, and rocking back and forth, in a "Row, row, row your boat" fashion. This allowed us to pull and stretch our arms and shoulders, which provided strong sensory input. She referenced my face the entire time, smiled, and seemed to enjoy both the sensory input and the emotion sharing from my animated facial expressions. She was allowing me to regulate her, by engaging in a "we-do" (back-and-forth) activity together. She could only handle this for about two minutes, before she needed to get up and do her bouncing, jumping, and handclapping. During these times I would also calming clap with her.

Next, I provided compressions to her legs by doing a rhythmic pattern of pressing her folded legs up and in toward her chest, which we call leg presses. She relaxed to this while calmly referencing my face. She was experiencing what it felt like to have another person help her feel relaxed. During this time she was referencing my face to share the experience of calming, soothing input that came from someone else, along with a nice warm smile, and good inviting eye contact.

For most of her young life, this girl had always loved to sift sand through her fingers, or transfer small objects from one hand to another in self-stimulatory fashion. At home she would do this throughout the day, for only a minute or so, and then back to bouncing, jumping, and clapping. When she went anywhere, the group of small objects went with her. She had them on the floor at the clinic. Frequently throughout our session, after bouncing and clapping, she would return back to her collection of objects and briefly squat and stim with them.

Mom reported that her daughter did not usually let others engage in this stimming with her. She would resist if others tried to intrude in this play. However, this was one activity in which she felt safe and competent, so I wanted to try using it to engage her. I sat down in front of her, stated how much fun she seemed to be having. I showed great excitement in her transferring these small toys back and forth, from one hand than the other, then back to the floor. Each pattern was the same: pick them up, transfer them back and forth, and then let them slide back to the floor. When she picked them up again, I reached out my hand and said "My turn!" She looked up at me but did not give me the items. Once she let them drop back to the floor, I gently cupped my hands around the items and slowly picked them up in my hands, while saying "My turn." I quietly chanted, in a sing-song voice, "Back and forth, back and forth," as I transferred the items from one palm to the other, twice, and then laid them gently back down on the floor. Next I stated quietly "Your turn!" with an animated facial expression. She looked up at me and smiled, taking the items and repeating the pattern. Once she laid them back on the floor, I would again state "My turn!" and pick up the items, then repeat my pattern "Back and forth, back and forth, back to the floor." She was a little nervous at first, but calmed quickly once she understood the interactive pattern.

During this play, she became calm, relaxed, and engaged with me for probably about ten minutes. She went from squatting to sitting quietly and did not get up to bounce, jump, and clap. She was calm, alert, and regulated, feeling what it was like to be engaged and letting someone else pace and regulate her. After every few turns, I would reach my hands out, she would place her hands softly into mine, and I would gently bring her hands up to my face as we smiled warmly at each other. She was relaxed and regulated, following my lead and pacing herself to stay engaged. She was smiling, referencing my face to share emotion, and calmly following my lead at that point. She felt safe, accepted, and competent sharing the experience with me.

At that moment she did not need to bounce, jump, and clap her hands to stay regulated. She went ten minutes while engaged in a calm, regulatory pattern with another person. She is not capable of regulating herself yet, but she was feeling safe allowing someone else to pace it for her. For her to eventually learn to self-regulate, she would first need to allow others to help her regulate. All children need to first let others regulate them, before learning to self-regulate. They learn to regulate themselves by allowing others to help them regulate. If the young child with autism is too overwhelmed to allow her parent to regulate her, then she will struggle with ever being able to regulate herself. Hence, at the age of 13, this young lady is not able to do so.

How did I do this? Three main tools! I used her sensory preferences (proprioception) to engage her, used my hands, face, and words to help her feel safe, and built a calming, regulatory pattern around her favorite activity (sifting). I initially helped her feel safe by giving her proprioception through rowing and leg presses together, then engaged in reciprocal, back-and-forth, repetitive play around her object play. I used soft words (sing-song chant), gentle facial animation, a warm smile, and gentle touch (holding hands and bringing her hands to my face) to relax her. I also used a repetitive, rhythmic, back-and-forth pattern of toy play to create "we-do" engagement where she followed my lead to pace her to regulate. These are the beginning stages of learning to allow others to help you calm, organize, and stay regulated. She was feeling what it was like to be engaged, connected, and regulated with another person—a great feeling to experience, for both of us.

The lesson here is (1) identify what stimulation helps your child feel calm and organized, (2) begin by following your child's lead engaging in their preferred activity (even if it is self-stimulation), and then (3) slowly build a calm, soothing regulatory pattern (rhythmic, repetitive, back-and-forth) around that activity. The child follows your lead to pace herself to stay regulated. Use your words (often sing-song chanting), touch (if not defensive), and facial expressions to pull the child into feeling safe, accepted, and competent following your lead. Help the child feel regulate and engaged *through you*, by doing *with you*.

Chapter 8

THE WORLD OF SELF-STIMULATION

A discussion about autism rarely occurs without someone referencing the association of autism and repetitive, self-stimulatory behavior. Whether it is rocking, hand flapping, twirling, vocal stimming, twirling objects, whatever the repetitive patterns are, the frequency of self-stimulation is evident. As many on the spectrum will report, their self-stimulation is often their best friend. They use it to stay calm and regulated and would be lost without it. The topic of self-stimulation and whether to eliminate or regulate it is often up for heated debate. The following posts should help you understand self-stimulation, what drives it, the important functions that it provides, and the ethical questions that surround trying to eliminate it. Some of the posts below focus on hand flapping; however, the issues apply to other forms of self-stimulation.

Stimming to regulate!

Stimming (self-stimulatory behavior) is a way for children to help regulate their nervous system. Hand flapping is a common self-stimulatory behavior in autism. We all have an optimum level of arousal for our nervous system to stay alert and organized. When the child is under-aroused (slow and sluggish), he will stimulate to increase his arousal level. When he is over-aroused (excited, anxious, scared), he will stimulate to calm his nervous system. Whenever the child's nervous system is excited, startled, bored, or overloaded, his nervous system seeks out the stimming to regulate it. Stimming works well because it provides rhythmic sensory input that he can control. You will find that the stimming looks a little different depending on the function it is serving (calming, organizing, alerting, etc.). In addition, many children need to feel their body in action in order to feel connected to it. Because their internal sensory cues do not provide good feedback, they often need to stim to feel aware of their body.

Children with autism tend to seek out stimulation that feels good to their nervous system, as well as regulates it. We all engage in self-stimulation (foot rocking, nail biting, gum chewing, hair twisting, smoking, cracking knuckles, etc.), but usually hide it under more socially acceptable behavior.

If you notice a big increase in stimming, the child's nervous system may be more disorganized for some reason. A strong sensory diet of jumping, lifting, pushing, carrying, or any major gross motor activity can help organize the nervous system. Hand flapping is very common because it provides very strong proprioception into the wrists and joints of the fingers. The fast flapping provides strong rhythmic, pulsating input into the wrists that feels good. The faster you flap, the more intense the input. Occasionally, if the child does it a lot, the stimulation almost becomes addictive, because it is "feel good" chemistry.

For many children on the spectrum, stimming is the only tool they have for controlling the stream of stimulation coming in from the world around them. It allows them to control the surge of emotions that often overwhelm them, and to maintain a sense of connection to their body. When you restrain the child from stimming, you leave him without the one tool he has to protect his sense of safety and security. We can help the child by recognizing what his nervous system needs and providing a good sensory diet that helps the nervous system stay calm and relaxed. We can also recognize and reduce the environmental demands that tend to overwhelm the child. Until the child learns more socially acceptable ways of regulating his nervous system, stimming is an adaptive response for him. It serves a very strong functional need. Please respect the need for stimming and do not punish the child for doing it. It is a lifeline for many children. As they get older, their nervous system matures and stimming often decreases. They also learn to provide less obvious and more socially acceptable forms of stimulation (like we do). However, they will almost always need to use stimming occasionally throughout their lives when their nervous system becomes disorganized. Next time you are anxious, disorganized, and alone, try it—you may like it!

Hand flapping! Encourage or discourage?

Hand flapping has been associated with autism for years now. We have discussed the function that it plays for children on the spectrum, but what about the stigma that is attached to it? My experience is that many people do not see it as big deal for young children (just an expression of excitement), but as the children get older and more mature, many feel that they should be able to refrain from such stereotypic behavior. It only makes them stand out and become open to being ridiculed, teased, and possibly bullied. There is a lot of truth to all those arguments. As the children mature, the part of the brain that regulates behavior— the executive functions—gets stronger. Usually this means, as the person ages, he gets better at checking his impulses and finding more socially acceptable ways of satisfying his nervous system. We may bite our nails, twirl our hair, crack our knuckles, tap our feet. So, as the child matures, some may expect him to refrain from such "excitable" behavior and be able to cognitively mediate it. I think, that like most neurotypical (NT) people, children on the spectrum who are more socially aware and more concerned about "fitting in" do learn to substitute more socially acceptable ways of satisfying their nervous system. However, those who are less socially aware, or less motivated to fit in, may continue to seek out this stimulation. In essence, there is nothing wrong with stimming: it provides needed regulation and keeps the person feeling organized.

Whether something should be done about hand flapping is an issue for debate. It doesn't harm anyone or infringe on the rights of anyone else, but it does make the person stand out and appear childlike. It does leave them open to ridicule and harassment, and it does make others feel uncomfortable. There are some who feel that people have every right to do it if they choose, and since there are no laws against it, they have every right to feel that way. That is my personal viewpoint. However, there are others who feel we need to teach the children how to refrain from immediate gratification of urges and learn more socially acceptable behavior. After all, most young children have little self-stimulatory behaviors that we teach not to do in public.

Personally, I do not see a problem with teaching the child to (1) inhibit the hand flapping in public over time, while (2) teaching them other ways to regulate their nervous system, especially if they choose to want to control flapping in the community, just as I tend to bite my nails for self-stimulation, but refrain from doing it while interacting with others. We can respect people's need to regulate their nervous system, without engaging in obvious repetitive behaviors that stand out and make others feel uncomfortable, which may leave them open for even more negative social feedback. Many adults on the spectrum learn to inhibit the immediate need to stim until they can go off privately to meet those needs. They learn when and where it is appropriate to flap their hands, rock and hum, or engage in other more obvious forms of self-stimulation. They learn that they don't have to give it up completely, but learn when and where to do it. When in public, they learn other less obvious and more socially appropriate ways to substitute for hand flapping. We can respect the need for regulating the nervous system, while teaching more socially acceptable ways of doing it. I don't see it as an all-or-nothing, either/or issue like many people do.

What type of self-stimulation do you use? Learn about yourself to understand your child!

Now let's turn the attention on ourselves! We engage in self-stimulatory behavior ourselves. Smoking is an oral stim (as well as a self-injurious behavior). Chewing gum, twirling our hair, and biting our nails are all self-stimulatory. We will do them if we are anxious or over-aroused, and we will do them to alert us when sluggish or bored. Nibbling (eating) is also self-stimulation.

What type of self-stimulation do you use to calm or alert yourself? I have an under-aroused nervous system. I cannot read for more than ten minutes without getting drowsy. I have to be chewing on something, drinking liquid out of a straw, riding the exercise bike, or listening to my iPod to stay aroused well enough to read. One of the best ways to understand how to calm and organize our children's nervous system is to first understand our own. What little forms of stimulation do you use to calm yourself when over-aroused, and alert yourself when under-aroused?

The more we understand how we engage in self-stimulation to meet the needs of our nervous system, the easier it is to understand why the children need it. Their nervous system is still developing, so they need more of it. As they get older and their nervous system matures, they likely will need less of it. However, even adults on the spectrum need some self-stimulation. They learn more socially appropriate forms of stimulation when in public and save the odd self-stimulation until they are home alone. They may also feel the need to use it when they are very anxious or very excited.

How many of you chew gum? This is a strong self-stimulatory behavior. For me, chewing gum is not rewarding. The taste is gone after a minute, so I spit it out. If you continue to chew the gum after the taste is gone, it is because of the organizing effect it has on the nervous system. It will calm you when you are over-aroused and alert you when under-aroused. It provides proprioception that both calms and alerts the nervous system, depending on what it needs. Smoking also serves the same purpose, both to calm when over-aroused and alert us when under-aroused.

Keep an eye on yourself and determine what you use in your own sensory diet!

Sensory "seekers": understand it, use it, and engage it!

Many of the children are sensory seekers. Why is that? Should we discourage it or accept and go with it? As mentioned in past posts, the sensory world of children on the spectrum is a vivid component of how they experience the world and process information, and a vital component for their safety and security, as well as their self-identity. For many, it is the primary way they connect with our world. As we have seen, even though this is their primary form of connection, it is often highly variable, unstable, and overreactive. At one minute they can be calm and organized and the next moment they can be anxious, insecure, and overwhelmed.

We have seen how the children can be hyper-sensitive and defensive to stimulation, and frequently experience sensory overload. Just as their sensory experiences can frighten and overwhelm them, the sensations that feel good to them are extremely pleasurable. They intensively seek out stimulation that feels good or they are hypo-sensitive to. Many children have preferences (movement, repetitive self-stimulation patterns, frequent banging/pounding, repetitive vocal noises, etc.) that they seek out and engage in repeatedly.

Sensory seeking serves many adaptive functions for the child:

- Children will frequently engage in preferred sensory stimulation to calm and organize their nervous system. There are many sensory, cognitive, social, and emotional demands that irritate the children's nervous system. They can seek out preferred rhythmic sensory patterns to block out unwanted stimulation and to calm and organize their nervous system.

- Engaging in repetitive, rhythmic sensory patterns can release stress chemicals from the nervous system, keeping the children from reaching overload and meltdown. This is especially true of proprioception, which is any resistance to the muscles, joints, and tendons. Crashing, banging, feet stomping, hand flapping all provide strong resistance (proprioception) to the child's joints. This releases stress chemicals, which helps to keep the child calm and organized.

- Many children have trouble "modulating" the overall sensory input to their nervous system. Our nervous system requires an optimum level of stimulation to stay calm, alert, and organized. If our system is under-aroused and sluggish, it will seek out increased stimulation (twirling hair, biting our nails, doodling, tapping our feet, etc.) to alert ourselves. Also, if our nervous system is over-aroused, our system will increase the filtering of stimulation to avoid being overwhelmed. Many children on the spectrum have faulty filtering systems, making it difficult for them to regulate the amount of stimulation at the optimum level. Sensory seeking allows them to arouse themselves in order stay alert and organized. They often need to be feeding their nervous system stimulation in order to focus on the task at hand.

- Children who have hypo-sensitive senses need to seek out frequent and/or intense stimulation to feel connected to that sense. Some children feel disconnected from their body unless they are frequently moving or tapping/banging body parts on themselves or objects around them. They may stomp their feet, hit their hands, wrists, elbows, or ankles on nearby objects to feel connected to their body. The sensory receptors in their body are not providing them with adequate input to feel connected to their body parts. By moving or banging, they feel connected. In the same way, many children need to keep eliciting sensory feedback from their environment to stay connected to their world. They may need to touch or smell everything to stay connected with things around them.

- Finally, the children may simply enjoy the stimulation that makes their nervous system "feel good." Many children experience extreme pleasure from the stimulation that feels good to them. This stimulation releases feel-good chemicals in the nervous system, and the child will actively seek out and may become fixated on this feel-good stimulation.

As we can see, sensory seeking plays important functions for the children. It is the children's way of providing their nervous system with what is needed. We need to (1) identify what they like, (2) recognize what it provides for them, (3) allow them the sensory input, and (4) build in a sensory diet of frequent calming and alerting stimulation to keep their nervous system organized. If the sensory seeking is inappropriate or disruptive to others, we need to look for other stimulation that can be substituted for it. We need to allow the children to regulate their nervous system and teach them how to use the stimulation to keep themselves calm, alert, and organized.

Also, we need to use the children's sensory preferences to engage them, relate with them, and to build learning opportunities around these preferences. For children who are self-involved and difficult to relate with, try engaging yourself in their sensory seeking. Become part of it! If they like movement, use movement play to engage them in reciprocal interaction. Use their preferred stimulation to calm and soothe them when upset. If the child needs frequent proprioception, engage in active play including running, jumping, climbing, wrestling, crashing, pillow fights, push-and-pull activities. Not only will you calm and organize their nervous system, but it will also increase social/emotional engaging with you.

At school, have the occupational therapist develop and use a sensory diet (calming and alerting sensory activities) throughout the day to keep the child focused and organized. Allow him fidget toys, air mats for seats, gum to chew, and frequent activity that gets him up and moving to satisfy his nervous system.

In conclusion, any sensory stimulation that the child seeks out, or even is fixated on, plays a major function for him. Do not abruptly suppress it. Understand what function it serves for the child and find more acceptable ways for the child to continue to regulate his nervous system.

Sensory "seekers!" When should I interrupt, and how should I modify it?

As discussed in the previous posts, the seeking of stimulation usually is an attempt to satisfy and regulate one's nervous system, and is very important for children with autism. However, like all good things, it needs to occur in moderation, be effective, and be exhibited in a socially acceptable manner. Most sensory seeking is harmless, except for self-injurious behavior or dangerous climbing and jumping. Usually, it is not so much the behavior that is unacceptable as the time, place, and/or frequency of the behavior. So, it usually means defining when, where, and under what conditions the child will be allowed to engage in the preferred sensory behaviors, and substituting more acceptable forms of sensory seeking at other times. The following are times when it is most appropriate to limit sensory seeking:

- When the behavior is potentially dangerous and needs to be eliminated or reduced for safety reasons. This will occur for children who are hypo-sensitive to touch or proprioception. These children may engage in hitting, biting or digging themselves, or head banging. When you need strong stimulation to feel connected to your body, it can become dangerous over time. For example, if the child seeks out frequent slamming, head banging, and hitting or biting himself, this often needs to be interrupted. If not interrupted, it can become more frequent and intense, to the point of being addictive. Such intense stimulation can release endorphins in the nervous system. This feels good and the child can become addicted to it (seek out at high cost). The brain has a tendency to habituate (become numb to) stimulation that occurs regularly. So, when the brain habituates to the strong stimulation, the child will have to do it even more strongly to activate the release of endorphins. This is especially true of behavior that scars the surface tissue (skin and underlying tissue). For example, if the child digs at his skin to create stimulation to "wake up" his body (feel his body), the stimulation can release endorphins. The endorphins feel good and can become addictive. The frequent digging will eventually create scar tissue which will have less feeling. The child will have to dig deeper, with more intensity, to elicit the same sensation. Not only does the brain habituate and become more tolerant of the stimulation (raises the threshold for feeling it), the scar tissue at the surface will also dull the sensation. Hence, the child slowly increases the intensity of the digging until it becomes gouging. So, any behavior that represents potential injury needs to be modified (not necessarily eliminated), so that it is no longer injurious.

- Often sensory seekers have trouble modulating stimulation (knowing exactly how much their nervous system needs). They frequently tend to be "all or nothing," seeking it to the extreme and often dysregulating themselves. For example, a child may need frequent movement to stay alert and organized, but goes overboard and provides too much, or too intense movement, actually causing himself to become disorganized. He does not have a "volume control" that lets him know what is just right. In these cases we need to regulate the intensity and frequency of the stimulation so that it organizes the child but does not dysregulate him.

Usually it means pacing the child so he is providing his nervous system with organizing stimulation, without overwhelming it.

- Sometimes the child may become fixated on the sensory seeking so that it drastically interferes with engaging in functional learning opportunities. In other words, the sensory seeking interrupts and interferes with participation in other daily activities. Then it is appropriate to put controls on when, where, and how frequently the sensory seeking occurs. For these children, we usually identify times of the day (sensory breaks) when they can engage in their sensory seeking, and then build in other forms of substitute stimulation when they need to focus on a task (e.g. gum chewing, fidget items, air cushion, iPod, etc.). This way we are (1) substituting more appropriate stimulation to promote organization and (2) allowing the preferred sensory stimulation in "free time" sessions to rebound and re-energize.

- Not only can sensory seeking interfere with child's participation in functional learning opportunities, but it can also interfere with the activity of others. If the child's sensory seeking is interrupting or significantly distracting everyone around him (e.g. vocal stimming), then we need to look at (1) substituting more acceptable stimulation and (2) giving the child sensory breaks where the sensory seeking is acceptable. There is a time and place for everything.

- Finally, sometimes the child is simply engaging in the sensory seeking because it "feels good." It is not necessarily helping him connect or regulate his arousal level, but simply occurs because it feels good. However, we have seen that these children often do not have volume control and find it hard to turn off the sensory seeking once it is turned on. If children are engaging in the feel-good stimulation in excess, it may be because it feels good and they are fixated on it. Not only do they have poor volume control, they also have trouble stopping a feel-good behavior once it gets going. In these cases we need to set limits.

Now, how do we modify inappropriate sensory seeking? We do this in several different ways:

- Set limits by defining when, where, and for how long the child can engage in the stimulation. We may also have to define how intense the sensory seeking can be, so the child doesn't get dysregulated by the sensory seeking. For example, the child may have specific times during the day at school where he can go to the resource room, or to another private area, and engage in time-limited sensory seeking.

- During times when the preferred sensory seeking is not allowed (task assignment), we can provide more appropriate substitutes (gum chewing, chewy tubing, fidget toys, air cushions to sit on, MP3 players, etc.) that provide stimulation in the areas (tactile, auditory, proprioception, etc.) that the child is seeking. In doing so we are substituting an acceptable stimulation for an inappropriate stimulation.

- We also can reinforce the child for *not* engaging in the sensory seeking. Actually, we often use their preferred sensory seeking (the behavior we are trying to limit) to reinforce time without it. For example, if we want to stop the seeking during functional activities, we can reinforce the child for not stimming during functional activities by giving him free time to stim afterwards. So, if the child sits with his hands on his lap quietly for ten minutes during circle time, he earns five minutes of hand flapping (away from the group) after circle time. We have even used token programs where the child earns tokens for lack of stimming during activities, which he can later use to buy the sensory seeking.

- Once you identify the function of the behavior (what it is providing for the child), then you can identify a more acceptable substitute that provides the same function. This is where we may substitute gum chewing for chewing on his clothes, or fidget toys to provide tactile and proprioceptive stimulation to keep the child from picking at his skin. We might provide music via an MP3 player to reduce vocal stimming.

- If the child is doing the behavior to alert himself when under-aroused, then we provide other, more acceptable stimulation to arouse him (sensory diet). Or, if he is engaging in the behavior to block out stimulation that overwhelms him, then we need to modify the environment so it is less sensorily noisy. Turn down the amount of stimulation in the environment.

I am sure I may have missed one or two other ways of modifying unacceptable (dangerous or interfering) sensory seeking, but these tend to (1) respect the child's need for stimulation, (2) help the child learn when and where it is appropriate, and (3) provide the child with more appropriate sensory substitutions. Notice that I don't use punishment for modifying the behavior, or try to eliminate sensory seeking without providing a substitute. This is because these techniques (1) do not respect the child, (2) do not provide the child with what he needs, and (3) do not teach the child appropriate ways of satisfying his nervous system. We want to satisfy what the child needs, while framing it in acceptable and adaptable ways.

Sensory addiction

Many children have fragile nervous systems that can get excited, anxious, and overwhelmed easily. Sensory (self) stimulation is a very functional tool for regulating the nervous system, keeping it from getting overwhelmed, and helping the nervous system to rebound once it is overwhelmed. However, for many children, sensory stimulation can feel very good to the nervous system and can become addictive simply because it feels good! Such stimulation, if it occurs continuously for long periods of time, creates feel-good brain chemicals (endorphins). Over time, the brain develops neuropathways that seek out the continuation of that stimulation. At these times the brain will seek out this repetitive, sensory stimulation, simply because it feels good, not because the brain is overwhelmed or under-aroused. Usually at these times the child engages in the behavior a lot, for long periods of time, and seems to become totally engulfed in the stimulation, for no other reason than because it feels good. Usually for these children the self-stimulation occurs so often that it interferes with engaging in functional daily activities and inhibits learning opportunities. It is no longer just a mechanism to protect from overload, but takes on a compulsion of its own because it simply feels good.

For these types of sensory stimulation, we need to identify under what conditions and for how long it is appropriate for the child to engage in the stimulation. To decrease the compulsive sensory seeking, we usually try to define where and when the child is allowed to engage in the stimulation, then build in sensory breaks where the child is allowed to seek the stimulation. In some cases, we even use engaging in feel-good sensory stimulation as reinforcement for engaging in other daily activities. For example, once a child finishes several school tasks, he gets to have a sensory break to engage in his sensory stimulation. This way we do not take the feel-good stimulation away from him, just structure when, where, and for how long he can stim. Some parents simply remove the object of self-stimulation to eliminate it totally. However, if the child goes into withdrawal, you will need to fade it out gradually. Since the stimming is not a "safety tool" for regulating arousal or minimizing overload, you can usually reduce or eliminate it without a problem.

Verbal stimming and thinking!

Verbal stimulation (repetitive spoken words or phrases) can be both a sensory and cognitive form of sensory stimulation. It is a higher form of stimulation than just motor stimulation. The brain needs to keep an optimum level of stimulation, so verbal stimming can occur when bored or under-aroused, just like we daydream. It allows them to provide stimulation when needed and is also a way of withdrawing into their own world of scripting when the outside world becomes too chaotic for them. Verbal stimming can also be a fun way to play with words, practice pairing words together, and thinking out loud. This process displays a beginning stage of mental engagement and pretense.

At the beginning stages of vocal stimming, the child may hum or make repetitive sounds. They like the sound of the vocalizations, but more importantly the vibrating feeling in the inner ears helps alert them. This is really obvious when the children cover their ears when humming. It provides more internal vibration, which feels good. As they get older, they begin to use words. They often report liking the sound and feel of saying certain words, and will play with certain words and phrases to explore the sound and feel.

Many children also begin thinking in words by talking out loud. This gives them auditory feedback. Many children on the spectrum think in pictures, so they actually need to practice thinking in words. To help with thinking, model your own thinking (think out loud). When doing things with the child, think out loud so your child hears your thoughts. Many children on the spectrum do not realize others have thoughts and feelings different from their own. When you think, contemplate, ponder, and problem-solve out loud, the child not only learns that you have these processes, but he also learns by hearing how you think. As you are doing things together, problem-solve out loud and then purposely present a snag. Say, "I wonder what I should do now" or "Oh no, I goofed, I don't know what to do!" Pause and wait to see if the child will give you a suggestion. This allows him to feel competent in learning to think through your modeling. It also is great fun!

Placing boundaries on vocal self-stimulation!

Vocal stimming (sounds not words) can occur for a variety of reasons. Depending upon the vocalizations, if it has a rhythmic pattern to it, many children simply enjoy the sound of the vocalizations. Some children enjoy the vibration they feel from vocalizing, and the cause and effect of being able to control the rhythmic pattern of stimulation. For other children, vocal stimming can be used to calm them when over-aroused, and alert them when under-aroused. It can occur when they are over-excited, or again when bored. It is used to calm and organize the nervous system. It can also be a coping skill for blocking out unwanted stimulation. I find that vocal stimulation is often just an enjoyable rhythmic pattern that is fun to produce, listen to, and feel. It is predictable and easy for the child to control. In some cases, where the vocal stimming is repeating words or phrases, it can also be a way for the child to practice saying words in fun patterns.

Self-stimulation is one of those behaviors that is not inherently bad but may be annoying or interfering at certain times and under certain conditions. For example, it may be fine to vocally stim at home, but not at the movies. It is not the behavior itself that is bad; it is just undesirable at certain times and places.

What you want to do is teach the child under which conditions it is allowed (at home, when alone, etc.) and which conditions it is not allowed (classroom, movies, group activities, etc.). Help the child to learn when it is allowed and when and where it is not appropriate. You don't have to stop the behavior, just teach when and where it is appropriate.

- Make a few rules about engaging in vocal stim. You might want to write a social story about when it is appropriate and when it is not. Make sure to acknowledge and validate the importance the stimming has for the child, while teaching him when and where it is appropriate.

- Review these rules frequently, especially before entering into events where vocal stimming is not acceptable. Let him know when it is not acceptable, but also when and where it will be allowed. If the setting or activity has a place and time for the child to engage in the stimming, then review that with him.

- At times when vocal stimming is not appropriate, try to provide an oral substitute such as chewing gum. If you frequently use chewing gum, then it can become a cue: "When I chew gum I do not stim." Tell the child to chew instead of vocalizing. Stay close by and periodically praise the child for not stimming. If the child starts to stim, calmly redirect him to stop and chew his gum instead. If the child is older, you might want to use a gestural cue such as putting your finger to your mouth to signify "stop stimming." If he stops, wait a minute and then praise him for not stimming. If he keeps stimming, stop the action until he stops, or briefly move him away from the fun activity until he stops. Over time the child learns when it is appropriate and when it is not appropriate to stim. However, I tend not to use punishment, but only redirect and reinforce desired behavior.

- When entering stressful situations, if the vocal stimming is used either to mask or avoid stimulation or to cope with being overwhelmed, identify a safe area where the child can go to stim and regroup as needed. Be very aware of your child's state of being and whether the vocalizing is for fun or coping with stress. Respect the need for the stimulation before trying to suppress it.

I usually try to attack an issue cognitively, emotionally, and behaviorally. So, in this case you want to (cognitively) work with him in understanding the effect his behavior has on others (social story) and that there is an appropriate time and place for stimming, recognize the (emotional or sensory) function the behavior serves for him, and try to provide an appropriate alternative behavior (e.g. chewing gum) to take its place.

Many children on the spectrum are attracted to repetitive, rhythmic patterns. The rhythmic sound and vibration, and the sense of controlling it, are very inviting. For these children, this holds strong sensory value. At the times when the vocal stim is allowable, try engaging in the vocal stimming with your child. Use it to engage with the child by imitating and animating his vocalizations. This shows the child you value what he is attracted to and wish to share the experience with him. Once you have his interest, try to add little variations to it, and see if you can get him to copy you. Try to expand the pleasant vocalizations for greater enjoyment.

We all have our own forms of self-stimulation (biting nails, playing with our hair, doodling, tapping our feet, humming, smoking, etc.), which serve the function of regulating our nervous system. Most self-stimulation, unless it is injurious, is functional and adaptive, and not inherently bad and something to suppress. However, over time the child learns which self-stimulation is allowable in public and which stimming needs to occur in privacy. Never stop the behavior without providing a substitute, and teach when and where it is appropriate. We will all live more comfortably while respecting each other's individual needs.

Teaching boundaries for self-stimulation with cognitively impaired children

Many of you had questions with the last post on placing boundaries on vocal stimulation: essentially, teaching children when and where the stimulation is allowed and not allowed. In that post we talked about focusing on teaching from a cognitive, emotional, and behavioral approach, such as using social stories or teaching cognitively when and under what conditions the stimming is appropriate.

Some of you questioned how to do this with a child who is either too young, nonverbal, or too cognitively impaired to understand the teaching strategies. Teaching rules and boundaries can be taught both cognitively and behaviorally, and it is best to combine the two when possible. Yes, it is great to understand why the behavior is not appropriate in one setting but allowable in another. Yes, it is great when you can teach the child to cognitively appraise the situations and rules so they can make those kinds of decisions. However, even for the more cognitively able, don't assume that they are going to be able to appraise and understand the social context of why it can occur in this setting and not in that setting. They are not going to learn this simply by socially understanding. They have to be taught rules for governing this behavior, just like all behavior.

First, let me give you some guidelines that I implement when working with nonverbal and supposedly more cognitively impaired children (although I am not equating being nonverbal necessarily with lower cognitive abilities).

1. First, don't assume that because they do not talk, they do not understand. Most children understand much more receptively than they can communicate expressively. So, just because they cannot talk, it doesn't mean that they don't understand what you say. Keep your statements short and to the point (literal and clear), and when possible pair them with visual information (pictures, video, demonstration, etc.). Unless it is a distraction to the child, I usually give brief explanations to nonverbal children, because repetition often sets in.

2. Many nonverbal children have auditory and language processing delays, so I frequently use pictures to communicate simple information. For example, if I am trying to communicate that it is OK to hum here, then I show him a picture of a person talking or with mouth open and demonstrate the vocal stimulation for the child to associate the picture with the vocalization. Same goes for having a picture to represent "not OK" to hum (screech, etc.): a photo of a person with mouth closed and hand over mouth, or the red "no" sign over the humming photo. I use these pictures when communicating to the child to stop humming (screeching, etc.) and when it is OK to vocalize. This has to be taught. I put a picture of the "OK" photo in the entryway of each room that it is OK to vocalize (hum), and a photo of the "not OK" picture in the entryway of rooms where it is not allowed. We practice daily going back and forth from one room to the other, pointing to the photo, and practice vocalizing together for the room where vocalizing is allowed, and then going to rooms where it is not allowed, pointing to the picture of the "not OK" photo, shaking head no, and putting the quiet hand sign (for shush) by our mouth. Next, I have both parents model this for the child. When entering the "not OK" rooms, I might have one parent start to do the vocalization (imitate the child) and then the second parent showing the photo, shaking head no, and giving the "shush sign" over their mouth. They may also briefly state, "If you want to hum (screech, etc.), then go to your room (or other "OK" room)." We implement repeated trials of pairing the picture to our words and gestures.

3. Once the areas have been set up, then we run repeated practices doing it together. If the child still needs extra help, then I will actually reward the child, with concrete reinforcers, for vocalizing in the "OK" room, to show him that it is desirable to vocalize there. When the child is vocalizing there, then I will frequently reinforce him for doing it in the right room.

4. Until the child learns the distinction, whenever entering the rooms the parent immediately reminds him by pointing to the picture and telling

him that it is either "OK" or "not OK" to vocalize here. This cues him in to the rule as soon as he enters the room. If the child starts to vocalize in the "not OK" room, then the parent immediately shows him the picture, shakes head no, and/or gives the shush sign, or tells him that if he wants to do that, he needs to go to his bedroom (or other OK room). If the child stops, the parents praise him. If the child continues to do it, the parents immediately redirect him to an "OK" room.

5. If the child is at school and we want to give both a location (where) and time (when) the behavior is allowed, we place the photos in the appropriate spots and give the child a visual schedule of when he can go to that area and vocalize. This way the child learns when he can have stimming breaks during his daily routine. We can show the child that when you complete circle time then you can go to the stimming area. In the "OK" area, we may have a visual timer that we set so the child can see how long he has to stim.

For these procedures, the child does not have to be verbal or have a cognitive understanding of why he can or cannot engage in the self-stimulation. We simply teach behaviorally where and when it is allowed. The child can be nonverbal and cognitively delayed. It may take many repetitions and practice, but if you are consistent, over time the behavior will fit the rules. These strategies can be used for any self-stimulation. It tells the child that the behavior is OK, but also where and when it is OK.

When self-stimulation does not work!

Our nervous system needs an optimum level of stimulation to stay alert and organized. When it is not getting enough stimulation, we become under-aroused, have difficulty focusing, and will feel sluggish or anxious. On the opposite end, when over-aroused the nervous system will become overloaded, disorganized, and anxious. So, the nervous system is always seeking that optimum level of stimulation that helps it stay calm but alert and organized.

Many children on the spectrum have fragile, disorganized nervous systems that have difficulty reaching and maintaining the optimum arousal level. They are frequently seeking, or avoiding, a variety of sensory stimulation to pacify their nervous system. Their nervous system does not know how to regulate the type and amount of stimulation that it needs. Their internal regulator is not working well. Usually they stumble upon the type of stimulation they need (movement, smells, proprioception, tactile, etc.) but may have difficulty regulating the amount and intensity they need. These children may seek out more than they need, give it too intensely, or have difficulty stopping once they get started. For them, having a structured sensory diet where they have controlled doses of sensory stimulation can be beneficial. It can provide the "just right" doses of stimulation to keep the children in their optimum range of stimulation. They need to have the amount and intensity regulated for them until their nervous system becomes reset and they can regulate themselves.

However, for some children, the nervous system is further taxed by biomedical imbalances that irritate and aggravate the nervous system so that it is rarely in a state of equilibrium. Their nervous systems may be over-aroused, on high alert, leaving the children feeling anxious and insecure. When the nervous system is out of balance, these children seek out ongoing stimulation, often in intense forms, to the point that they cannot learn or may possibly injure themselves. For them, even steady doses of sensory input provided by a structured sensory diet will not stabilize their nervous system. The nervous system is in constant flux and rarely balanced. When this occurs, we need to look closely at what may be aggravating the nervous system (digestive problems, allergies, biochemical imbalances, etc.) and treat the underlying cause of the irritation/imbalance. This may consist of regulating their diet, providing necessary supplements, or seeking medication to balance neurotransmitters. A sensory diet alone will not work. Usually these children are seeking out intense proprioception (banging, hitting, biting, etc.) or frequent movement. They cannot sit still and focus; they are driven to seek out stimulation. Often these behaviors are hard to redirect and difficult for the children to control. They feel driven to act, although the actions do not seem to satisfy them. They seek out very high doses of stimulation, to the point that it drives all actions and makes it difficult to concentrate in learning activities. It dictates what they do and when they do it. For these children, medical attention will often be needed. There is a chemical imbalance or medical/biomedical issue that needs to be resolved. The families will need to seek out a biomedical doctor, neurologist, or psychiatrist for added assistance. However, this process can be a long, trial-and-error period of assessments and treatments before the vulnerabilities are identified and effectively treated.

Hand banging!

Does your son or daughter frequently tap or bang his/her hands or feet on objects? I have seen this in children who need strong proprioceptive input. Jamie, one of our members asked this question a while back.

> **?** Jamie's question
>
> My daughter "bangs." She uses the inside of her wrist to bang whatever she can. She has broken windows, walls, doors, TV or VCR. You name it, she's banged it 'till it broke or her hand went through it. We have targeted this "behavior/stim" over the last five or six years a million times, but it's usually replaced with high-pitched screaming which I guess gives her the same sound satisfaction and attention-seeking satisfaction or it's replaced by something worse (if you can imagine). But the "banging" always comes back. We've tried to get her to only hit pillows, but it doesn't provide the same function. She likes the feeling and the noise. It's so hard to live with. And her wrists are calloused over. I'm shocked her wrists aren't broken. The rest of the house is. She does it for a myriad of reasons: attention, dissatisfaction, lack of verbal communication, and also, for no reason we can discern, while completely alone. Any suggestions?

AUTISM DISCUSSION PAGE

Jaime, you first need to identify what function the behavior serves for your daughter. I have known many kids in the past who need to bang their wrists or ankles on objects around them. Yes, they do like the sound, as well as the strong proprioception (jarring to the joints and tendons). However, there are often other functions involved:

- Usually these children have poor registration of proprioceptive stimulation (need high intense input into their joints). Their nervous system needs a higher intensity of stimulation for the brain to register it. The behavior usually needs to be stronger to feel the stimulation. They tend to be sensory seekers to arouse their nervous system. Now, they will use the same behavior to calm themselves when overwhelmed, and also to alert themselves when under-aroused. In these cases we give the child a sensory diet of strong proprioception (jumping, pushing, pulling, carrying, lifting, strong resistance to the joints and muscles). We are giving them activities frequently throughout the day to feed their nervous system proprioception to keep them regulated.

- If your child has an under-aroused nervous system, she needs to be feeding her nervous system this intense proprioception to stay alert and connected to her body. When the proprioception doesn't register well, she will often feel disconnected from her body. Providing the strong banging wakes up her nervous system and allows her to feel briefly reconnected to her body again. If she doesn't do it, she starts to lose focus and awareness of her body which makes her feel anxious. For these children, it can help to place ankle or wrist weights on them to increase the proprioception in those areas. We also give activities that provide strong input into their wrists, such as playing with clay, rolling dough, or squeezing something. Bouncing a basketball and hitting a large exercise ball around with a bat provides good input into the wrists. Next, we give them an alternative hand-banging behavior, which is reinforcing them to slap the back of their hand into the palm of their other hand. This gives the strong jarring into the joints, plus added stimulation into the other hand. We have practice sessions where both the child and adult practice doing the hand banging. Then when the child starts hand banging, we redirect him to smacking his hand into his palm. Once this behavior is substituted, we teach the child to gradually lighten the slaps to make it more subtle.

- If the child has an anxious, disorganized nervous system, then strong proprioception will release stress chemicals from the nervous system. For these children, their nervous system is anxious and continually developing stress chemicals. They will feed their nervous system strong jarring/banging to their joints to release the stress chemicals. We provide them with a strong sensory diet of proprioception (gross motor activity) throughout the day to release accumulated stress chemicals.

- When the behavior (banging) occurs a lot, it can release strong endorphins, which feels good. This can become addictive, resulting in the child continually engaging in the behavior to release the endorphins. This can make the behavior very resistant to change. Also, the power the child feels from the cause and effect of hearing the strong sound, breaking objects, and getting strong reactions from the people (attention) around them can be very reinforcing. The behavior can be maintained (reinforced) by many variables (sound, feel, sight of things breaking, the reaction of others, proprioception, etc.). This can make it more difficult to reduce the behavior.

When the behavior injures the child, injures others, or damages property, regardless of the function, it needs to be stopped or modified. The child needs to feel that we recognize the need he has. Try to substitute other behavior that will serve the same function, but place strong boundaries on not accepting the unsafe behavior. We block, interrupt, and redirect the behavior immediately. Autism can explain why a behavior may be occurring, but it doesn't excuse a behavior that is destructive.

Part IV

SOCIAL STRUGGLES IN AUTISM

Chapter 9

FITTING IN

So far we have discussed the cognitive and sensory issues in the world of autism; however, the social issues stand out as one of the major challenges for people on the spectrum. Since they think and experience the world differently, trying to regulate the day-to-day interactions in our social world can be exhausting, overwhelming, and invalidating. It is hard to feel competent and confident when you don't fit in.

COMMON SOCIAL STRUGGLES

- Difficulty reading and interpreting social cues.
- Impaired ability to read the thoughts, feelings, perspectives, and intentions of others.
- Difficulty understanding the unwritten social rules.
- Hard to initiate, co-regulate, and repair interaction.
- Poor awareness of how their behavior affects others.
- Difficulty establishing and maintaining relationships.
- Often teased, bullied, or taken advantage of.
- Strong social anxiety often leads to isolation/depression.

In the following articles, we will explore some of the cognitive (social processing) differences that lead to these common struggles. You will understand how these social struggles are tied to the three cognitive processing differences (information processing, central coherence, and rigid/inflexible thinking). It makes sense that the way we process information (the world around us) will directly affect how we relate to others.

One of the cognitive differences in autism is the difficulty of rapidly processing multiple information simultaneously. Our brains are continuously taking in a rapid flux of information simultaneously. Our brains have to register and integrate all this information simultaneously, most of it subconsciously with minimal mental effort. As we saw in the articles on information processing, this rapid processing requires simultaneous communication between the different areas of the brain in order to integrate the flux of information effectively. People on the spectrum often have weak neurological connections between the different brain centers, which make this rapid integration of information difficult.

The social processing underlying relating requires this rapid processing of multiple sources of information simultaneously. We have to process the following information simultaneously:

- Hearing and interpreting the words spoken.

- Interpreting nonverbal communication (facial expressions, body language, voice fluctuations, etc.).

- Reading thoughts, feelings, perspectives, and intentions of others.

- Understanding the context in which interaction is occurring.

- Deciding how to respond.

- Referencing others' feedback to our response.

- Staying coordinated in back-and-forth flow of interaction.

The dynamic process of interacting with others leaves the person on the spectrum multitasking this very rapid flux of very vague information. "What did he say? What did he mean? Why did he frown? What is his intention? Did he understand me? What do I say next?" Trying to read the continuous interplay of verbal and nonverbal language, comparing it to the context of the situation we are in, reflecting back on what is already known about this person, appraising how to respond, and so on requires way too much rapid processing for people on the spectrum. Relating requires rapid shifting between listening and responding; we have simultaneously to listen, interpret, plan a return response, and read the person's reactions to our response. For those who cannot process this simultaneously, trying to attend to all this information is exhausting.

In the following posts we will explore these social processing issues, the challenges they present for those on the spectrum, and helpful ways of bridging these difficulties.

He can't have autism, he likes people!

I don't know how many times I have heard doctors say, "Your child can't have autism because he is interested in others." There often seems to be confusion about the degree of social interest in children with autism. The social desire of children on the spectrum can range from seeking isolation to seeking frequent, ongoing, social attention. The degree of social interest is not the discriminating factor; it is the child's ability to co-regulate interaction with other children, especially those their own age. Individuals on the spectrum, even if they a have strong desire to interact with others and have friends, struggle with being able to read the thoughts, feelings, perspectives, and intentions of others, and have difficulty coordinating play with peers. It is not so much that they are not interested as they simply don't know how. They have difficulty with coordinating the back-and-forth cooperative play, maintaining purposeful interaction, and repairing breakdowns in relating.

The children often want to either lead the play or sit back and stay passive. They do not understand social boundaries and can become overbearing or intrusive in their play. They probably will not be able to take turns, stay in sync with peers, and understand all the social rules of the play. They may want to dominate the interaction or dictate the rules of play. They may want very badly to connect, but just don't get it.

So, social interest itself is not a deciding factor; it is the ability to engage effectively in the back-and-forth reciprocal play. By the way, the child on the spectrum often feels much more comfortable playing with children much younger than him or with adults. He struggles much more with children his own age.

Unless the child can learn to (1) read the nonverbal communication that makes up 80 percent of relating, (2) read the thoughts, feelings, perspectives, and intentions of others, and (3) read the contextual cues of the social situation, he will struggle with relating with NT peers as he gets older.

I find that children with ASD can relate really well with others on the spectrum who have the same interests to relate around. This works well since neither person is using or reading nonverbal language. Nonverbal language is not as important in this interaction.

I also find that relating with neurotypical (NT) peers can go well, as long as the peer has a good awareness of how and why the child acts, or does not act the way he expects. The problem arises when the NT child feels uncomfortable because he does not know how to read the ASD child's behavior or cannot understand the lack of response. When he understands how to relate with the child and what to expect, then the children can have fun with each other.

Autistic but social!

There often seems to be confusion about the degree of social ability in children with autism. Social *ability* should not be confused with social *interest*. Many people still think that people on the spectrum are not interested in socializing. The image is of someone who is withdrawn and indifferent to others. Although there are some people on the spectrum who are not really interested in connecting with others, there are many who are very socially motivated. It is not so much the social interest that distinguishes them from others as it is their social abilities that make relating difficult.

There are many children on the spectrum who try very hard to connect with others and want very much to have friends and close relationships. Unfortunately, their difficulties with reading the thoughts, feelings, and perspectives of others, problems in understanding the social context and unwritten social rules, and difficulty engaging in back-and-forth, reciprocal interaction make establishing and maintaining relationships very difficult.

Children on the spectrum, even if they have a strong desire to relate, will usually find it hard to fit in. They have difficulty with coordinating back-and-forth cooperative play, maintaining purposeful interaction, and repairing breakdowns in communication. They may recognize this difficulty and tend to play along the outside of the group, or not recognize this problem and try to dominate the play. They may not understand social boundaries and become overbearing or intrusive in their play. They may not be able to take turns and understand all the social rules of the play. They often will try to dictate what is played and how they play. They may assume that others will want to do exactly the same things and in the same way as them. They will have difficulty understanding the perspectives of their playmates and will struggle to co-regulate the play with them. As the child gets older, this inability to recognize, consider, and collaborate in play becomes aggravating to other children, who tend to avoid or tease the child.

So, social ability, not social interest, is more the deciding variable in autism. Because of this, we need to provide these children with numerous opportunities to learn how to (1) reference and read the perspectives and intentions of others, (2) reference and read nonverbal language, (3) initiate and maintain back-and-forth, reciprocal interaction, and (4) read the unwritten rules of relating given the context they are in. Without these skills, the child is left helpless in the very confusing world of "relating" to others. This leads to strong social anxiety and eventually depression from years of trying to fit in and not getting it. Even if the child doesn't have a strong interest in relating, these skills are necessary for fitting in and co-existing with others in order to play, work, and live successfully in our social world. However, we need to listen to and respect the social desires (degree of interest) the children have. Many children are not really interested in socializing, and many find socializing to be very draining. Let the child's social interest determine how much exposure you give him. Do not force him to be more social than his social interests dictate. It will be difficult and exhausting for him, and socializing will become associated with negative experiences.

As they become adults, it is not the lack of academic skills that affects quality of life for those on the spectrum; it is the lack of social functioning that makes it difficult for them to relate in a very social world. Many individuals on the spectrum can achieve graduate degrees but cannot hold down a job because of their inability to handle the social demands of the setting. We need to make social relating skills a higher priority in the developmental years to provide those on the spectrum with the tools needed to relate successfully with others. From the early grades on, we need to establish the teaching of pragmatic social skills as a priority in educational planning. Give these kids numerous opportunities for facilitated play, such as group recreation, boy scouts, dance class, adapted sports, and other social situations for learning and practicing social skills. We need facilitated interaction and peer mentoring throughout the school years to teach social skills in a real social context. Make learning to relate a necessary priority so the child can feel safe, accepted, and competent in the social world.

A word of caution for parents. You may have a desire for your child to be social and have a lot of friends; do not assume that he has the same desire. Children on the spectrum often do not desire the same level of relating as you do. Some do, but many do not. Some like a little social exposure around their activities or topics of interest. Others want a lot of exposure. Also, try not to throw the children into unstructured group play. They will most likely feel very incompetent because they do not know how to process and regulate with more than one or two children at a time. We tend to think that by throwing them into a lot of group social activities, the child will naturally develop stronger social skills. That is not true. It is better to start out with just one-on-one play dates to make relating easier. Keep socializing short and simple. It takes a lot of mental energy to try to regulate with others. Start simple, build gradually, and let the child pace the amount of exposure.

To reach out, but be rejected!

They try, but they can't! They reach out, but cannot grasp! They strive to fit in, but are often left out! Almost every parent has seen it; almost every parent has felt it. To try to connect, but to be turned away! It hurts us, it hurts our kids, and it represents one of the greatest barriers for people on the spectrum. I have yet to meet someone on the spectrum who will not connect with others, if they are made to feel safe and accepted doing so.

If social ability means social acceptance, then why don't we focus more on fostering social abilities? It is true that we can foster greater social acceptance of people who relate differently, but that will not lead to stronger friendships and close relationships. From the early years on, we need to place major emphasis on teaching social cognition—the ability to read the mental, emotional, and social states of others, interpret social context and the unwritten social rules, and the ability to continually reference others to stay coordinated with them—as well as the social/behavioral skills needed to initiate and maintain relationships. We need to have a curriculum with facilitated social activities that involve supported inclusion. This is not just placing the child in with neurotypical children, but with support that facilitates successful interactions. To do this, the child needs to learn how to read nonverbal language. He needs an interpreter who can explain the perspectives and intention of others, help to appraise what is expected, help choose how to respond, and give feedback on the effectiveness of his responses. Until the child is capable of reading social situations, appraising what is expected, and monitoring how effective his actions are, he needs to have mentors who can provide these interpretations for him.

Although the facilitation is guided by adults, the true mentors must be peers. Children can be the best helpers, when carefully selected and with appropriate awareness. From the first days at school, awareness training needs to be provided for all the children to help support the child with ASD. This includes concretely clarifying what their perspectives, intentions, and expectations are and giving adequate feedback so the child learns how to coordinate his actions with others. From the early grades on up, schools can provide long-term goals with short-term objectives, to develop the child through progressive steps of perspective taking, social context reading, and coordinating interactions with others. Between the natural social settings of the lunch room, playground, recess, middle school dances, and high school basketball games, peer mentors and facilitated support can foster the social cognition and interaction skills necessary to build friendships and maintain close relationships.

To teach relating, we need to make it easier for neurotypical kids to understand and guide children on the spectrum. Relating is a two-way street. Like us, kids avoid or make fun of that which they do not know. Facilitating this understanding will not only increase acceptance but also set the stage for children to mentor those on the spectrum. When you grow up supporting each other, you learn to relate to each other. This needs to be the next direction in providing social support for people on the spectrum. For all children who want so badly to connect with others, we owe them the guidance to teach them how to do it.

Now, saying all this, we have to realize that socializing is very draining and often exhausting for people on the spectrum. It doesn't come naturally, so it has to be learned through repetition and repeated exposure. Because of this we need to facilitate, not pressure, children into socializing and learning social thinking skills. We need to match the encouragement to the social interest of the child. If the child shows strong social interest, he is going to want more social exposure. If he is not attracted to others, keep the interaction brief and allow him to control the flow. Try to build social activities around activities of interest to him. He will often feel more competent and motivated to relate when the activity centers on his specific interests.

Since socializing is taxing for children with ASD, they need time to rebound and re-energize. The more drained they become, the longer break-time they need to regroup. Learn to read your child well, and remember that the experience of socializing is one of the most exhausting activities people on the spectrum have to live with. Match exposure to the child's interest to engage, and give plenty of rest time afterwards! Keep it fun and engaging!

Cognitive processes underlying social deficits

One of the major difficulties in relating for many people on the spectrum is their difficulty with rapidly processing multiple information simultaneously. People on the spectrum do well in static systems, where information is constant, logical, and predictable. Dynamic systems are any system whereby the information is rapidly changing and the meaning is relative to the context in which it is occurring. Such dynamic systems require reading between the lines for hidden meanings and rapidly processing multiple channels of information. The meaning of this information is relative to the context of the situation, requiring strong central coherence (seeing the big picture). Since many on the spectrum have difficulty grasping the invisible social rules and understanding subtle nonverbal communication, the best they can do is watch and imitate others in hopes of fitting in. This can be very taxing.

The ability to simultaneously process multiple information is important for central coherence (seeing the big picture), which is important for theory of mind (being able to read and understand the thoughts, feelings, and perspectives of others). This ability to read the inner experiences of others is what provides rhythm to our interaction. It allows us to reference and provide meaning to what the other is saying and doing, and in turn pattern how we respond back.

The latest brain research suggests that this problem is due to poor connectivity between the different areas of the brain. Individuals on the spectrum seem to have weaker neuropathways between the different areas of the brain (either underdeveloped or overdeveloped but scattered connections). This leads to poor communication between the different brain centers. Simultaneous communication among brain centers is required to reference and process multiple changing information (registering and integrating the information, comparing it to the context of the situation, evaluating it to past experiences and future expectations, applying meaning, responding to it, and then evaluating the effects of the response).

Social interaction (relating in the NT world) requires simultaneously processing numerous information (words, pragmatics, facial expressions, body language, intentions and perspectives of the other, multiple meanings relative to the context of the conversation, past experiences with that individual, etc.). At the same time that we are referencing and evaluating what the other person is communicating, we are also simultaneously deciding how to respond back, next executing the response, and then referencing how the other person is reacting to our response (do they understand, how are they taking it, etc.). Being able to interact effectively in dynamic conversation requires this ability to coordinate this back-and-forth, rapidly changing interaction. You have to be able to figure out what to say, how to say it, and how to maintain and repair breakdowns in communication. This multitasking is almost impossible for those on the spectrum.

People with ASD often do better in instrumental conversation, usually centered on sharing information about a specific topic. Usually, this is sharing facts that are constant and static. This is easier to process and follows specific rules. Often the information is predictable, or at least logical, and doesn't require processing of dynamic flux. Interacting for sharing information is much more concrete and easier than interacting to *relate*, which is not predictable or static. If neurotypical people could find a way to communicate with words only, and say exactly (literally) what they mean without relying on nonverbal cues, then relating for people with ASD would be much easier. Unfortunately, that is not how we relate. Our interactions are filled with vague hidden meanings which are often communicated by our facial expressions, body language, and intonation/fluctuations in our voice.

How do we help make conversation easier?

1. Speak very literally, saying what you mean, leaving very little room for misunderstanding. Don't use vague language filled with multiple meanings, innuendos, sarcasm, analogies, etc. Say exactly what you mean, and mean exactly what you say.

2. Use a lot of concrete examples to clarify what you are saying. Then verify that the person understands it correctly.

3. Slow down the information you are giving, allowing the person to process what you are saying and meaning. Present information sequentially rather than giving multiple information simultaneously.

4. Try not to jump from one topic to another without giving a clear indication that you are doing so.

5. Make sure you get clarification that the person understands before moving on further in the topic. Don't assume that the person understands your position, especially your thoughts, feelings, and perspectives on things. You have to verbally say them.

By no means should this be viewed as condescending to the person on the spectrum. It has nothing to do with intelligence, but communication styles and processing differences. It would be similar talking to someone from a different country who doesn't know your language very well. You have to slow it down, keep it simple, use very concrete, literal language, and make sure to clarify and verify what is said and meant. This allows everyone to interact and relate on safe grounds. Most of all, it allows both parties to be more comfortable relating.

Autism is like being an actor in a play, with no prepared script!

Adults with autism learn how to be effective actors, often living in pretense in an effort to fit in, or at least not stand out. When it is difficult to grasp the unwritten social rules around you, understand the thoughts, feelings, and perspectives of those you are with, and rapidly process the conversation occurring around you, you often have to pretend to understand, fit in, and blend in with others.

In order to be successful, many people on the spectrum learn to imitate those around them. When entering into a social event, they immediately scan those around them to see how they are acting. From this they learn to copy their behavior after what they see others doing, so they can blend in. If the conversation is with one person only, they may be able to regulate it pretty well. If the conversation is between several people, the children get lost very quickly. For people on the spectrum to be successful in such situations, they have to become very clever social scientists, often copying behavior which they don't understand. As years go by, they accumulate a lot of "scripts," which they can adapt to many situations. They learn scripts for introducing themselves, topics for small talk, being pleasant, and so on. The older they get and the more situations they experience, the better they get at it.

However, this social acting takes its toll over time. Socially, people cannot be themselves; they have to fake it. Since we develop a sense of self from our relations with others, it tears at their self-identity and self-esteem. When you have to pretend all the time, you get anxious, angry, and depressed. It is also very draining. Even for those who are good at it, trying to copy others requires extensive mental energy and can only be done for short periods of time.

Prepare ahead of time

The worst thing for children on the spectrum is being thrown into social situations with little preparation. Make sure you prepare the child ahead of time. Talk about what he can expect, what social graces are expected of him, and what to do if he gets confused and/or overwhelmed. The more he knows ahead of time, the more prepared he is going in. If the child is responsive, role-play and practice common scenarios. Be very literal with him. Let him know what social games may be going on at that specific event. Unfortunately, since these children have difficulty self-monitoring their own behavior, they cannot read how they are doing as they try to fit in. This is where a peer mentor (buddy) comes in. With a mentor there to coach, interrupt behavior that is off key, and be a tour guide to help navigate the maze of interactions, the child can learn to hope to effectively regulate socials situations. When you don't have the executive functioning skills to effectively monitor, appraise, and evaluate social behavior, it is good to have an external guide. It can help put the child at ease and enable him to enjoy the event. The more accepting peers become, the more the children can relax and be themselves.

When relating with people on the spectrum, please try to respect how hard these situations are. Be respectful of "out of sync" behavior, as well as the emotional needs of the person. When we can understand what they experience, we can change our behavior and acceptance to make it more relaxing for all of us.

Copying others to "fit in!"

Copying others seems to be the number-one skill that many people with high-functioning autism and Asperger's use to fit in. It can be a very effective tool, if (1) the person has good referencing skills and can accurately imitate those around him, and (2) he does not lose his self-identity while doing it. All people, both on and off the spectrum, use copying (imitation) at times when entering into situations in which they do not know what is expected and how to act. We watch those around us and reference what others are doing. From there we copy and match our actions to be in line with those around us. This is a very effective learning tool.

This copying strategy can be a very effective social strategy for those on the spectrum, as long as they choose it as a way to fit in and co-regulate with others, and not feel invalidated by doing it. Many people on the spectrum have low self-esteem and weak self-identities, due to years of trying to fit in but failing. They also have been teased, ridiculed, and bullied for being different. This often leads to poor self-esteem and a weak sense of self. For them, constantly copying others is a way of developing an alternative self, one that is accepted by others. This can have negative effects, typically resulting in ongoing depression.

Also, we need to realize how mentally draining it is for people on the spectrum to use the copying strategy. It involves continuously reading what others are doing and then trying to copy, modify, and refine their responses. This takes a lot of energy and is very draining. This strategy needs to be one that the child wants to use; he should also control how much of it he does.

So how do we teach children to successfully use copying as an effective tool, while protecting their self-identity? I think children need to be taught that we all have differences, some private and some social. We all have our social self and our private self. These private differences are not bad, but are just not meant for everyone to see. When we are out in public, we put on our social mask, and we take it off when we are at home. We are not defined by our public mask, but use it to fit in with others. We all have certain self-stimulatory behaviors, rituals, and fixated interests that we leave at home and those that we can freely use when with family and friends. We can still accept and validate the child's unique differences, but there is a time and place for all tendencies. We can feel comfortable with this and do not find it invalidating. Many people on the spectrum think that neurotypical people do not have to copy and act differently to fit in, but we all do to varying degrees. Some of us are better at it than others. However, it is not invalidating to use this copying strategy to fit in with the group. Actually, the better you are at it, the easier socially relating is. However, once home, allow the children to be themselves and express their needs, wants, and desires in their own unique ways. We all need to feel free to be our true selves when at home and away from the group. This is true for all people, both on and off the spectrum. By allowing them to do so, we can protect their identity and self-esteem.

Once children learn how to observe others to pattern their own behavior, then I recommend teaching them how to use this referencing others to effectively read social expectations and how to act. We can slowly teach the child what to look for, both in reading the expectations of the situation (context) and the behavior of those around him. When entering into situations together, discuss with the child what you see going on, how others are acting, and how to use this information to decide how he should act. While doing so, objectively read the body language, facial expressions, and actions of others, as you talk about how others are reacting to each other. Have the child try to size up what he can expect and what is expected of him. Help him practice imitating so that he can effectively copy the behavior of others. Have fun with it; make it a game. Be careful, because this act of appraising and copying can be exhausting. It is for all of us, but much more so for people on the spectrum. It comes more naturally to us, but requires a lot of processing for them. They can only do it for short periods of time. It affects each person differently. Some can use this technique relatively easily, and some find it too exhausting. It is important to teach the child he is not trying to be something that he isn't (invalidating his autism), but simply learning how to socially fit in with others.

Copying others! When, what, and how!

We have discussed how many children on the spectrum often listen, observe, and then copy the behavior of those around them when trying to fit in. This is commonly used by all children when trying to learn what to do to fit in. We watch what others are doing, then watch the reactions that those actions get from people around them. From this information we determine how we should act. The child watches what the other children are doing. If it is getting a good reaction from others, then the child tries to copy that same behavior. All of us do that when we are in new situations for which we do not know what is expected. We first watch, then follow along.

Unfortunately, many children on the spectrum do not know how to appraise the context of a situation to understand which behavior to copy and which not to copy. Since they do not pick up on the unwritten rules, invisible context, and thoughts and feelings of others, they do not understand the intent and social meaning of the behavior they are copying. They simply copy and imitate, without much awareness of the social meaning. If it gets them a favorable reaction, or avoids an unfavorable reaction, then it is the best they can do.

However, copying behavior without understanding it can cause problems for children on the spectrum. They often copy the behavior of the wrong children and get themselves in trouble. They often do not understand what is good behavior and bad behavior, but copy that which helps them fit in. This can get them into real trouble. Why do they copy the behavior of the problem children instead of the good children?

- The children often do not know how to appraise a situation to understand if the behavior is desirable or undesirable. They just see others doing it and want to fit in, so they copy what others are doing.

- The children will often copy the behavior that they see getting the greatest reaction out of others. The attention from others and intensity of reaction is what guides them. Often undesirable behavior gets a greater reaction from others than positive behavior. Since the negative behavior of one child may get laughing from other children, as well as strong emotional reactions from the adults around them, they often think that behavior is favorable.

- The children do not know how to appraise whether the behavior is desirable or undesirable; they simply do it and watch the reaction. They cannot appraise how their behavior will affect others or what the consequences of their actions will be. If other children laugh, they think it is favorable. They get confused when adults scold or punish them for behavior that other children laugh at.

- Since their behavior often does not match that of the children around them, children on the spectrum are frequently rejected by the more favorable peers. Consequently, this makes them attractive to the more problematic peers. They are easy targets for teasing and usually naïve with respect to the intentions of others. This makes them attractive to the wrong crowds of children. They can be talked into doing things, with little awareness of the consequences and effects of their behavior.

- Children on the spectrum cannot read social context to tell if a behavior is appropriate for the given situation. What may be funny and appropriate in one situation may get an unfavorable reaction in other situations. What may be funny to other children on the playground may get unfavorable reactions from others in the classroom. They copy and imitate without awareness of when and where to do it.

The act of copying others is not without drawbacks. If children cannot understand the social meaning behind the behavior and appraise when and where the behavior is appropriate, then they are left very vulnerable to negative reactions from others. They are literally engaging in behavior while blind to its consequences. Therefore, the children learn to only copy what they see occurring at that moment, and only at that moment, not to trust using it again unless they see others doing it.

How can we protect the child?

- First and foremost, we have to educate the adults around the child as to why he is copying like this, and that he does not understand the social meaning (effects on others, consequences of behavior, etc.) behind the behavior. Educate the adults around him that these are teachable moments, not punishable moments. When the child is doing something wrong, don't assume intention, but assume misunderstanding. It is a time to teach, not punish.

- Educate the adults around the child to watch for this copying and then help the child understand why the behavior fits and when and where to use it. Try to connect the behavior to the context by telling the child why it fits or why his behavior does not fit. Try to make it concrete to the specific context (situation), so he can connect the dots.

- Educate the adults to look out for the child and steer him away from the wrong children to copy. The adults should be very specific about which children and what behavior to copy. This is why it is good to encourage the use of peer mentors to help coach the children in social situations and to give them good models to copy. The best mentors are other children.

- Teach the peers around the child how to help him fit in. Help them understand how the child has a hard time understanding what to do, why his behavior is often "off," and how to coach him to copy correctly.

- Identify a few good children to be peer mentors. They will not only help coach good behavior and provide the child with appropriate models, but also help protect him from bullying and falling in with the wrong crowd of children.

Navigating this confusing world can be very difficult for children on the spectrum. When you cannot understand the invisible rules around relating, you fall back on copying those around you. Like any strategy, it is not perfect and can mislead the child. However, with appropriate support around the child, copying (imitation) can be a good tool for children to use. They have to learn when to copy, who to copy, and how to clarify and verify if their copying is effective.

Interacting is mentally draining!

I think what neurotypical (NT) people (especially teachers and parents) need to realize is that part of the main reason why children (and adults) on the spectrum have difficulty interacting and relating is their neurological differences. Our neurotypical brains have strong neurological connections between the different brain centers that allow the different centers to communicate simultaneously with one another. This is what allows us to process multiple information simultaneously, most of which is done at a subconscious level, requiring minimal mental energy. On the other hand, for people on the spectrum, the neurological pathways between the brain centers are not well developed, making it harder for the centers to communicate effectively with each other. This makes it difficult to process multiple information simultaneously. Whereas NT people can multitask, rapidly processing information at a subconscious (intuitive) level, people on the spectrum have to process this information sequentially, a little at a time, at a conscious level. They have to think through what we do intuitively without thinking. They can eventually arrive at the same understanding, but it takes at lot longer (delayed processing) and requires a lot more mental energy (since they have to consciously process it).

This is similar to what we (neurotypical people) do when placed in a social event which we have never experienced before. It is like being in a different country and not understanding their language and social customs very well. Without understanding the social rules, we watch and read what others are doing, appraise what is needed, and then try to copy it. This requires us to concentrate, analyze and appraise what is expected, act based on that information, and then evaluate how successful we are. This concentration is exhausting. What usually comes naturally with little conscious thought now requires concentrated effort. This is what it is like for people on the spectrum on a daily basis. Just trying to regulate a typical day at school can be so draining for them. Spending two hours at a birthday party can be totally exhausting for children on the spectrum.

These processing differences drastically affect interacting with others (relating). When we interact with someone we have to rapidly process multiple information simultaneously. While listening to the other person, we are simultaneously processing the words he is saying and the context they are being spoken in, the tone and inflection in his voice, facial expressions, physical gestures, and body language to understand what the person said, as well as his thoughts, feelings, and intentions. At the same time that we are processing what the other person is saying, we are formulating how we think and feel about it, plus how we are going to respond back. Then as we are responding back, we have to read the nonverbal cues of the other person to see if he understands us and is staying interested in what we are saying.

In order for us to focus on the topic of conversation, we have to process most of this nonverbal information (facial expressions, body gestures, fluctuation in voice, etc.) subconsciously, with minimal mental energy. This allows us to relate with others effortlessly. However, people on the spectrum have to process all this information sequentially, at a conscious level, thinking it all through. This processing is delayed and only parts of it get processed, making it difficult to get the big picture. They can only process bits of information at a time, often missing much of the meaning, as they try to keep up with the conversation. Sometimes, by the time they have processed what was said and formulated a response back, the interaction has moved on to a different topic. Consequently, between not getting all the information and having a delay in processing it, their responses are often out of sync with others. For people on the spectrum, this can be very mentally and emotionally draining. This inability to process multiple information simultaneously is a major reason for many of the social struggles people with ASD experience.

This social processing issue is common across all people on the spectrum. They can be very bright, but still have these processing problems. This is hard for people to understand. If the child is very verbal and bright, they assume that he must intentionally choose to misinterpret instructions and act differently from others. For the more verbal and cognitively able children, this disability is more hidden, masking their difficulties. That's why awareness training for significant people in the child's life can be important.

Teach your child to be a "social detective"

When the facts are not clear, you investigate. The social world will always be a mystery for many on the spectrum. It will always be a maze that is difficult to navigate. However, one of the strengths of many on the spectrum is a strong attachment to logic, rules, and facts. They use these facts and rules to make sense of a chaotic world. Given this, we can use their ability to look for facts and details to socially investigate situations they are in—to be a "social detective!" Michelle Garcia Winner (2008) first coined this term in her book *You Are a Social Detective* (2008) and has been the leader in the field in the area of social thinking.

From the early years on, teach your child to be a social detective, to always be investigating, compiling facts and data. Many children on the spectrum are great with facts and data. Use that to increase social understanding. Turn them into social scientists. Teach them to look methodologically at the interactions around them, to size up situations by looking for social detail. Questions such as: What situation am I in? What is the context (why are we here, what are we doing together)? Are there any social rules for this situation (e.g. talk quietly in library)? What is the topic of conversation (girls, sports, music)? What can I expect, and what is expected of me? Teach them to observe, listen, and understand first, before jumping in, and to clarify when they don't understand. What does their body language tell me? Listen first, then talk. The child should learn to seek information and clarification about events before entering them (what I can expect, what is expected of me—context, common themes, sequence of events, etc.?) and learn how to observe, listen, and clarify during interaction so that they can stay synchronized with the interaction.

During the early years, the parents need to be the detective for the child, thinking out loud ("I wonder how that person is feeling? I bet that made him sad"), as well as the social interpreter, explaining and clarifying the unwritten rules, perspectives and intentions of others. The parent can model the methods of the social investigating, creating a hypothesis of what is going on, what can be expected, what is expected of them. Seek to observe first, then clarify and verify. Do not assume: check it out! Teach the routine of look, listen, and clarify, then respond. The parent can think out loud to size up the situation (what is occurring, what is expected), describe what others may be thinking and feeling, discuss how to respond, and then help the child evaluate the effects of his responses on others (how are they reacting?).

In the early stages, it may just be the parent narrating this investigation with minimal participation from the child. You model the investigation. Don't worry if the child is not an active participant; he will gradually pick it up. He is listening! You are providing him with a framework for analyzing social situations. As the child becomes more engaged, expect him to be an active participant with you, collaborating and investigating together. Over time the child internalizes a routine of observing, verifying, monitoring, and evaluating when navigating social situations.

For more information on social thinking, Michelle Garcia Winner has developed a whole curriculum around social thinking. Please visit her website at www.socialthinking.com.

Reading the mental states of others!

Many children on the spectrum are so literal that they rarely think about how others are thinking or feeling. They do not look past the spoken words to read the perspectives and intentions of those speaking the words. What they see and hear is all there is. They often do not consider what other people are thinking and feeling.

To relate effectively with others, we have to look past the spoken words and think about how others are thinking. Next, based on this appraisal, we (1) predict what the person will do, and (2) pattern how we will respond.

Ongoing interaction consists of continually thinking about how the other is thinking, predicting his behavior and then patterning our behavior based on this assessment. This ongoing appraising is essential for staying coordinated with others in interaction.

Since children on the spectrum do not think about how others are thinking (or are weak at doing so), they are not using this information to add meaning to what others are saying and doing. They are reacting to what others literally say and do, rather than appraising, predicting, and projecting on what will happen in the interaction.

Teaching the child to look past the literal

1. First start with thinking about how others are thinking. Think out loud to model this thinking process for the child. Later on, this process can extend to thinking about how others are *feeling* as well as thinking, connecting how the person may be feeling based on what he is thinking: "I bet Johnny is sad because he thinks that Jenny doesn't like him." Many children do not make the connection between their thoughts and feelings. However, this comes later when the child has a good knowledge and language base for identifying and labeling emotions. Unless the child has gained that knowledge, only start with what the other is thinking.

2. During the day, watch what others are doing together and talk about what is literal (what you see and hear happening); then talk about what the people are thinking. Help the child learn to look at the body language and facial expressions, and what is going on in the situation, which helps us determine what the person is thinking. Do it together, modeling how you do it. Then talk about what evidence leads you to the guess (body language, facial expression, situational factors, etc.). Practice "watch, listen, think (about what they are thinking), and then predict (how they will respond)." Use this "watch, listen, think, predict" model for practicing together.

3. There are numerous ways of practicing this. Go to the mall or park and watch others interacting. First, list what you see and hear (literal), then what are they thinking. From this assessment, predict how they will act based on what they are thinking. You can also do this while watching TV or movies, and also while reading stories together. Use picture books so you can discuss how the characters are thinking from what you see, and use this information to predict how they might respond.

4. Keep it simple at first. Just focus on what the person is thinking. Once the child gets used to that, then you can move on to what the person is feeling.

From there you can start guessing at what the person's perspectives and intentions are. The final goal, over the long term, is for the child to think about the other person's thoughts, feelings, perspectives, and intentions, and use this appraisal to (1) predict what the person will do, and (2) pattern how he will respond. This process will take years to develop, but each step in that direction is valuable.

5.   When making these appraisals, be sure to discuss what evidence the child is using to make the guess (facial expressions, body language, actions, situational factors, etc.). This way, when in doubt, he will have a few tools to use to make an appraisal.

6.   As the child gets older and more skillful, the appraisals can also include how others think and feel about him and his behavior. "Jim, when you let Johnny borrow your toy truck, how do you think that made him feel?" "Jess, what do you think Tommy was feeling (or thinking) when you took his ball?" This way they can get better at monitoring how others are responding to their actions. This requires more abstract reasoning and can only be mastered after first learning to appraise the perspective of others.

Be sure to have fun while doing this. Get used to thinking out loud as you evaluate social situations during the day. The "thinking out loud" strategies can be used to teach the child that people have different thoughts, feelings, and perspectives. For more information and strategies for teaching perspective taking, refer to Michelle Garcia Winner's books (2003, 2008) and website, www.socialthinking.com.

The world is a two-way street!

Many children on the spectrum have difficulty seeing the perspective of others and understanding that others may view the world differently from them. They literally have difficulty reading the needs of others, so they often are not considering what others need or how their behavior affects others. The children often see the world only through their own eyes, and expect the world to revolve around them. They want what they want, when they want it. This is also driven by the anxiety that is created by their sensory vulnerabilities, cognitive overload, and social confusion. The world can be very chaotic and overwhelming for children on the spectrum. They are often operating on high alert, anticipating what dangers lie ahead in the uncertainty around them. To reduce anxiety, many children have to control all activity and interaction to feel safe. They see the world only through their eyes and demand that their needs be met, regardless of the effects on others.

To lessen anxiety and minimize meltdowns, we often cater to their needs to help them feel safe. We follow their lead and "do for them" to help them feel calm. Since trusting the uncertainty of others is scary for them, they have difficulty letting down their guard and trusting to follow the lead of others. Because we are so used to following their lead and doing for them, the children have difficulty getting past the "world according to me" phase. All children start off in this egocentric mode, but gradually develop reciprocity, the understanding that what I do affects others, and that I do for others as they do for me; that when doing things with others, I need to meet their needs as they help meet my needs—that the world is a two-way street.

Reciprocity (recognizing and mutually meeting the needs of both self and others) is the foundation of relating and co-regulating with others. This begins very early in life when the parent and child engage in back-and-forth emotional interactions (cooing, animated facial expressions, patty cake, peek-a-boo, etc.). Most daily activities consist of the parent and child engaged in give-and-take, back-and-forth, reciprocal interactions. The child learns that "You respond to me, and I respond to you"; that there is value in meeting your needs, as well as you meeting mine—that interacting is a two-way street.

This reciprocity can be learned; however, it does not come as naturally for children on the spectrum. It has to be spotlighted and taught. We get so used to doing for them and meeting their needs that we do not highlight the need to return the favor! When the child doesn't naturally reciprocate, the parents become used to not expecting it. It is not something that parents usually have to teach. However, I find that when reciprocity becomes an objective to spotlight, parents find it fun and rewarding. Every parent craves the emotional reciprocity from their child that feeds their desire to relate.

The main strategy for teaching reciprocity is to expect it, highlight it, and then help it happen! In all your interactions throughout the day, make them a two-way street! Ensure the child has an active part to play in all interaction and activity. Any time you respond to the child, pause and wait for a response back. In all activity that you do with the child, give him a small role to play and require him to do his part in turn. If you rub his back, have him rub your back! Don't do *for* the child: do *with* the child! Give him a small role that he has to coordinate with you to complete the action. If you roll him the ball, he has to roll it back. If you tap the drum, he has to tap the drum also! If you feed him a chip, have him feed you a chip! We share! Do *for* and do *with* each other! Help each other and share the experience together.

This should become ingrained in all your daily interactions. Even when praising, I use reciprocal reward. The child is reinforcing me, as I reinforce him! I give "five" a lot. I invite it by putting out my hand, and the child completes it by giving me five! I open the interaction, and the child finishes it. The child is an active participant in reinforcing me as well as me with him. When I give thumbs up, I pause for him to return the gesture! If I provide soothing sensory stimulation, I encourage him to give it back! We do it together, giving each other soothing sensory stimulation. We build this reciprocal interaction around many daily activities. We may be unloading the dishwasher together, raking leaves, or reading a story (child turns the pages, or I am one character and he is the other, etc.). I respond, pause, and wait for his response. The child learns that the activity does not keep going unless he does his part to maintain it. If he forgets, I pause and look at him. When he looks back at me to see why I have stopped, I give him a facial expression or simple gesture to show that I am waiting for his response. If the child forgets, then I will cue him in and stop the action until he is back on track. Of course, to teach this I start with simple activities that the child loves to do, so he will be motivated to keep it going. That way when I pause, he is motivated to do his part to keep the interaction going!

Parents can have fun playing little games with this. If your child loves ice cream, sit down with him with one bowl of ice cream and one spoon. Give the child a bit of the ice cream, then give him the spoon and have him feed you a bit of ice cream. Animate your enjoyment of tasting the ice cream, then give him a bit and show animated anticipation of his enjoyment. Again, give him the spoon and point to your mouth with excited anticipation! For children who get sensory brushing, I might play a game where I brush their arm, then they brush mine, and we go back and forth around the body. Everything we do during the day incorporates elements of this back and forth, give and take, taking turns and responding to each other.

In addition, it also helps to talk about what you are experiencing. Label your feelings, describe what you are thinking, provide your perspective, and describe your joy! Give the child a running dialogue of what you are experiencing. This helps the child understand your inner experiences and reinforces that the interaction is a two-way street. You will find over time that the child learns to enjoy sharing this experience—meeting your needs, as well as you meeting his. It becomes more fun doing it together and sharing the experience, rather than doing it alone and just focusing on himself.

The process of reciprocity goes through many layers of complexity as the child develops. This is a long developmental process that requires ongoing daily practice. It is important that we start highlighting this objective as soon as possible and make it a routine way of interacting. This training is not age-dependent, so it can start at any age!

The world is a two-way street #2

Teaching the process of reciprocity, which was detailed in the previous post, is the cornerstone of human relating. The child on the spectrum, in order to function effectively in our social world, should have this skill developed as soon as possible. Much learning and development occurs through social reciprocity. Like all of us, the children have their own right to choose to be as social as they want to be. Whether we are introverted or extroverted, all of us need to know how to co-regulate with others.

This is not about forcing the children to be social butterflies, but teaching them how to relate with others so they can learn and relate with them. It is not about forcing the children to make friends or to be popular. It is about giving them the necessary tools to regulate effectively in our social world, which they cannot avoid. It is about giving them the tools to make that decision. Making a true choice means having the tools necessary for each option to be obtainable. Knowing how to engage reciprocally and co-regulate with others allows you to pattern your relating around your true social interest. It allows you to go about your daily living, relating with family and friends, working alongside co-workers, and dealing with the numerous people you come into contact with throughout the day.

Teaching the process of reciprocity and all of its components does not develop in once-a-week therapy sessions with a psychologist or speech pathologist. It is developed through numerous interactions in the typical daily routine. All children learn this process through thousands and thousands of daily interactions presented in their normal daily routine. This process is shaped over years of constant mentoring and practice at the hands of parents, teachers, friends, and relatives. It is naturally woven into the social fabric of our society. It is one of the basic human functions that provide the foundation for many other functions and skills. It gives the child the necessary tools for other interactive skills. The greater this development, the happier and more successful the children will be throughout their lives.

When writing about this subject I always get several adults on the spectrum arguing about the right not to be social if they choose not to be—that interacting is draining, and the child should not be forced into being a social butterfly. I totally agree. The amount of social relating should be a personal decision patterned by your own social interest. That should be an individual choice. However, this is a social world and learning to co-regulate with others is a basic function of living successfully around others. Whether we choose to have friends, get married, and participate in social events is a personal decision, but we all have to co-exist with others to meet our own individual needs.

Given the necessity of this function, it is important to incorporate these principles into your normal daily interactions as early as possible. The younger the better. Turn everything you do with your child into a two-way street— what I call "we-do" activities. All daily activity becomes a vehicle for teaching reciprocity. Doing things together, referencing each other, coordinating actions together, and sharing the experience with each other. Teach the child that all interactions require this "dance" of continually referencing each other in order to stay coordinated with one another and meet the needs of both of you.

For parents and teachers, this mentoring comes naturally for neurotypical children. We do it intuitively, with minimal conscious thought. However, since it doesn't come naturally for children on the spectrum, we have to learn to highlight and spotlight the individual procedures for teaching this process. The previous post gives some basic ideas for how to do just that. Once you learn how to frame activities and daily interactions to spotlight reciprocity, it will become a natural process for both of you. For those of you who would like even more information or development in this area, I refer you to look into Relationship Development Intervention (RDI). You can find more information about RDI at www.rdiconnect.com.

Teaching teens to "fit in"

How far do we go to teach people on the spectrum to fit in? We have seen how focusing on conformity can tear away at their identity and self-esteem. However, in order to live in our social culture, we need to be able to co-exist with others, so that we can live effectively among each other.

We all need to learn how to fit in to the culture we live in. We all need to conform to certain standards of social conduct, personal appearance, co-regulation with others, and so on. We are doing the kids a disservice by allowing them to stray too far from the general norm. As much as some adults wish the world would be more tolerant of their differences, our culture will only bend so far. Yes, I think tolerances for social differences should always be promoted, but people with disabilities still need to learn standard social norms and unwritten rules. They will not be able to survive independently without this knowledge.

Given that, many adults on the spectrum are very angry with feeling that they have to conform to neurotypical expectations and the stereotypes that go along with having ASD. Conforming comes at great cost to their identity and self-esteem. That is why it is so important to first listen to what the person defines as issues he wishes to change, and then help him develop strategies to better co-regulate with our world. Many of these adults know where they want to go; they just want supportive assistance to help them get there. We need to let them define the goals and dreams for support, not just assume we know what direction they need to go in. If we are a working partner with them, they will use us as a trusted guide. They need us to provide ongoing feedback on how they are fitting in and offer strategies to help, but also allow them to pattern the supports they need to get there. We need to lessen both the anxiety and the anger that these individuals experience with the "helping" professionals.

What does interacting consist of?

To effectively interact with another person, we have to subconsciously process multiple information simultaneously. This multitasking has to be rapid and fluid since the information is fleeting and quickly changing. Let's take a look at what simple interaction consists of.

Listening to the person

1. Listening to the words that the person is saying.

2. Reading the facial expressions, tone and fluctuation of voice, gestures, and body posture to help interpret his thoughts, feelings, perspective, and intention. What does he actually mean?

3. Comparing what is being said to what we know from past experiences we have had with the person and the situation being discussed.

4. Interpreting what is being said based on the situation (context) for which we are interacting.

5. At the same time that we are listening, we are also formulating how we are going to reply.

Talking to the person

1. Thinking about what to say and how to say it, and producing the right words.

2. Predicting how what we say may affect the other person, and what consequences it will have for us. "I better not say that, it may hurt his feelings!"

3. While talking, monitoring the nonverbal communication of the other person to read how he is reacting to what we are saying. "Looks like he is getting defensive (bored, doesn't get it, etc.)."

4. Thinking about what we are saying, as we are saying it, while monitoring how the person is receiving what we are saying.

As can be seen, during interaction the brain is rapidly processing multiple information simultaneously. This requires simultaneous communication between the various brain centers, most of it occurring subconsciously with minimal effort. However, for many on the spectrum, this integration does not occur naturally and smoothly at the subconscious level. They have to think it through, consciously processing this information. Consequently, this processing is very taxing and has to be done sequentially (focusing on parts of information at a time), not simultaneously. They miss a good portion of this information, often rendering their interactions awkward and out of sync with the rest of us. Interaction simply requires too much multitasking of often very vague, invisible information for people with ASD to process effectively. Consequently, they struggle with social interaction.

Intellectual vs. emotional processing: explaining the social cognition differences between our two worlds

In this message I describe how we (neurotypical and ASD) relate on different planes. These different levels (intellectual vs. emotional) are based on different styles of processing, which make it difficult for us to relate on common ground. When we can acknowledge and respect the differences in processing, we can bridge the two worlds for better relating.

Most people on the spectrum are intellectual (objective) thinkers, processing things analytically based on facts and details. Most neurotypical (NT) people, especially women, are emotional (subjective) thinkers, processing information emotionally (seeking the emotional meaning of the information). We look for the overall emotional meaning that the information has for us. The emotional context is the glue that gives information meaning to many NT people. This helps add meaning to the central coherence (overall meaning). NT people do not naturally perceive facts as detail, devoid of emotional meaning. They naturally look for the overall emotional meaning to interpret the facts. This is why we often do not see the facts or details very well. They are filtered, or biased, by our emotional interpretation.

People on the spectrum have stronger associative and procedural memory (factual memories) than NT people. They are very good at remembering factual detail because it is how they process information. Now, that doesn't mean they don't feel or remember strong emotions that are associated with an event, just not the emotional meaning the event has on them. For example, if an event had strong feelings attached to it (e.g. pain), they may remember the strong feelings that were associated with the information (associative memory). However, they would be weaker at remembering the emotional meaning (since they don't tend to process information that way).

NT people tend not to focus on concrete detailed facts about an event. We tend to remember the episodic memories of the event. Episodic memories are the emotional meanings that the event has for them. Because we tend to process information emotionally, rather than intellectually (factually), we tend to remember the emotional meaning (episodic memory) of the event. We tend to easily forget the factual details of the event, but hold on to the overall emotional meaning the event had for us. Without the emotional meaning, the event has little importance to us. For example, if you and I were to have gone to an amusement park many years ago, I would probably have forgotten most of the details of the event. However, I would keenly remember the emotional meaning the event had for me (we had fun together!). I would have only vague memory of the sequential details of what we did, but I would remember that we had a lot of fun doing it together. I would remember the fond memories of having lots of fun experiencing the event together. I would hold on to the emotional meaning of the event and forget most of the factual details. Most likely a person on the spectrum would hold on to many of the factual memories while the emotional, experiential memories might fade.

These differences in emotional versus factual/intellectual processing explain many of the differences in social relating. NT people tend to interact emotionally with one another, while most people on the spectrum tend to interact intellectually. Again, the differences in how we process information tend to pattern how we interact. When relating with others, NT people emotionally filter most of what is being said; they are reading between the lines, looking for the emotional meaning. We immediately interpret what is said by how we read the person's thoughts, feelings, perspectives, and intentions. This sharing of experiences with others holds strong emotional meaning for us. The emotional meaning provides the backdrop for interpreting the facts.

This has a strong impact on what motivates us to relate with one another. Most NT people tend to relate with others because of the need for emotionally connecting with others. People on the spectrum tend to relate more around an intellectual interest. They enjoy relating with others when the interaction is centered on a common interest that they can intellectually relate to. People on the spectrum interact more to seek and share information and facts, for instrumental reasons. They can get very excited about relating when it is around an intellectual endeavor that interests them. However, the conversation is usually very fact-related. The topic of conversation is the main interest, not sharing emotional experiences with another. They are not usually interested in small talk, sharing how each other's day went, simply hanging out, and spending time interacting about how each other felt about things. If the conversation doesn't seek or share information, there is not much need to converse.

Now, with NT people you can see some of these differences between men and women. NT women tend to relate more for emotional reasons, whereas NT men tend to relate around a common interest. Women can go out for dinner and spend hours simply relating, talking about whatever. Men, on the other hand, have to have an activity (golf, football, etc.) or intellectual topic (e.g. politics) to talk about. Men feel uneasy with simply chatting (sharing) with no specific topic to center them. This difference is what causes conflict between men and women! Women often complain that men do not (emotionally) read them right. They expect men to read between the lines and get what is emotionally important for them. Many often don't get it!

Emotional reasoning also has it downfalls. It tends to make NT people less reliable when remembering the facts of an event. We tend to see what we want to see and cloud the facts with what we expect to see. Factual memory is a much stronger asset for people on the spectrum. They focus on details and are much more reliable in remembering the facts. There are pros and cons to both types of informational processing. Emotional processing, as much as it gives strong meaning for NT people, can also cloud our thinking. We often misjudge the actual facts because we tend to read too much into them. We immediately start interpreting our experiences in terms of our past episodic/emotional memories to give meaning to the experience. In doing so, we often misjudge the true intent of others, or the meaning behind what is truly happening. We often read intent into what people say or do that may not really be there, and we tend to look for underlying messages that are often not intended.

This explains why many NT people misjudge the actions of people on the spectrum. We tend to emotionally misread intent behind their actions that is not really there. This causes NT people to get upset at some of the comments and actions of people on the spectrum, when there is actually no intent to hurt their feelings or affect them in any way. So, this results in two primary problems: (1) people on the spectrum cannot read the emotional meaning behind the intent of what we say, and (2) NT people attach emotional meaning to what the person on the spectrum says, when it is not really there (they mean literally what they are saying). As people on the spectrum say, if NT people would say what they mean, and mean what they say, we would get along just fine!

These differences in emotional reasoning and intellectual reasoning provide two unique styles of processing. We simply relate on different planes (emotional and intellectual). It is too bad that people cannot be strong at both of them. However, these two different modes of processing explain why we experience the world so differently from each other. To help bridge our two cultures, both parties need to get a better understanding of how each other processes information, so we can better understand how each of us experiences the world around us.

RELATING ON TWO DIFFERENT PLANES: LITERAL VS. PERSPECTIVE TAKING

Neurotypical (NT) people, when interacting naturally, look for the intent and perspective of others to give meaning to their words. We read between the words to understand the thoughts, feelings, and perspective of others. We are looking at intent: why are they saying what they are saying? We frequently read more into what is being said than the literal words. However, people on the spectrum tend to speak very literally ("What I say is what I mean") with little inferring or reading between the words needed.

Since NT people are used to inferring intent in people's actions, they automatically tend to assume intent even if the person is not projecting it. For people on the spectrum, if their intent is not clear or obvious, NT people will project (or infer) intent to them. Of course, this inferred intent often does not match what the person on the spectrum truly means. This gets everyone into trouble. On the one hand, the person on the spectrum is not reading the hidden meaning of NT people, and, on the other, NT people are misreading too much hidden meaning behind the literal words of those on the spectrum.

Difficulties behind communication

- NT people speak with multiple meanings and intentions, often with hidden meaning. Rarely is our communication literal to the word. Also, NT people usually assume that the same process occurs for people on the spectrum. So, they often infer certain perspectives and intentions in the person with autism that are not there. For example, the person with autism is often blunt and literal, saying it as it is! This often strikes NT people as rude and disrespectful, even though there is no intent on the part of the person with ASD to be rude and disrespectful.

- In turn, people on the spectrum speak very literally, often meaning exactly what their words are saying. Consequently, they often read the language of others very literally, missing the hidden meaning between the words (perspective and intention of others).

So, we are speaking on different planes. NT people are speaking on a perspective-taking plane of interaction, and people on the spectrum are speaking on a literal plane. No wonder there is frequent misunderstanding! NT people are used to inferring intention and perspective into people's words and actions. They read too much into the intent of people on the spectrum. They read intent when that intent is not there. We NT people have just as much problem reading the thoughts, feelings, and perspectives of those on the spectrum as they have with us. We are relating on different planes, both often missing the intent of the other.

When talking with adults on the spectrum, this issue arises a lot. It is central to them living comfortably with others. This misunderstanding on both sides leads to major problems in communicating and relating. When relating with those on the spectrum, don't assume they understand your perspective. Clarify and verify meaning. In order to ensure the other person understands what you mean, clarify literally what you mean and then verify that the other person understands. For children, this is the responsibility of the adult. However, as children become older, they have to take on that responsibility, since most people that they run into are not going to understand their differences. The same tools that we use to help the child understand, they have eventually to take on themselves if they wish to successfully co-regulate socially as adults.

For adults on the spectrum, I recommend using a "clarify and verify" approach. Always assume that you might be misinterpreting others, or others are misinterpreting you. If you take this position, you are always asking to make sure you got it right, or verifying whether the other person perceives you right. Again, assume that others may read more into what you are saying. Take the extra steps to clarify what you mean and then verify if they understand. When giving a response to a NT person, explain yourself and the reason for your answer. This way you leave nothing to the imagination. If you don't give an explanation for your answer/statement, NT people may assume more meaning to what you say.

NT people usually do not take language literally. They will usually read more into what you are saying, trying to understand the "why" behind your words. If you give a response and then clarify it with an explanation, it helps us to understand how you think and feel. If you don't specify the "why," we will intuitively read the more than what is there, but will often be wrong. We are programmed to look for it, to see the hidden meaning.

Why do people avoid me?

Neurotypical (NT) people—those of us not on the spectrum—often convey much of their meaning and intention through the use of nonverbal communication (facial expressions, body language, gestures, tone and fluctuation of voice, etc.). Since people on the spectrum have difficulty reading this nonverbal language, they have difficulty grasping what we are expecting. Consequently, their social responses are often out of sync with what we expect. Since this is confusing for us, it makes us feel uncomfortable. Thus, we tend to avoid those that we feel uncomfortable relating with.

In addition, people on the spectrum not only have a hard time reading the nonverbal communication of others, but they also have a hard time expressing themselves nonverbally. Their facial expressions, body language, tone and fluctuations of voice often do not match how they feel and what they intend to project. NT people rely on reading this nonverbal communication to understand the thoughts, feelings, perspectives, and intentions of others. We look past their words to read between the lines. Consequently, when interacting with people on the spectrum, NT people are looking for the nonverbal cues for understanding. However, when the nonverbal communication is not consistent with the person's verbal statements, it can be really confusing for us. This can cause NT people to be uneasy when interacting with people on the spectrum. Since it is very difficult to read the thoughts, feelings, and perspectives of the person with autism (theory of mind), it makes the NT person uncomfortable. NT people often avoid interacting with people they cannot "mentally" read. Like everyone else, we tend to avoid things that make us feel uncomfortable.

In summary, the lack of ability on both sides to adequately read the nonverbal communication of each other leads to great discomfort in relating with one another. The problems in communicating and relating is a two-way street. We both have difficulty reading the thoughts, feelings, and perspectives of the other, and therefore we both feel uncomfortable interacting with each other. However, once both parties understand why we are uncomfortable, it lowers the anxiety and helps us understand each other better.

Emotional relating (sharing subjective experiences)

Emotional processing (theory of mind) is the ability to "read" the thoughts, feelings, and perspectives of others. This involves the ability to understand what others are subjectively experiencing, so we can understand how they are acting. We look for the hidden meaning behind what people say and do. We do not take language literally but read between the lines. This is the basis of relating for neurotypical (NT) people, those of us not on the spectrum. As much as this is the nature of our (NT) social processing, it can also cloud our thinking. We quickly infer intent, often misjudging the actual facts, because we read too much into them. We often misjudge the true intent of others or the meaning behind what is actually happening. We can get overly jealous, read alternative motives, and over-exaggerate the intent of others, which may ruin friendships, relationships, and even cause wars. So, even though we are blessed with the ability to "read" the thoughts, feelings, and perspectives of others, we are often not very good at it.

This also explains why many NT people misjudge the actions of people on the spectrum. We tend to emotionally infer intent behind their actions that is not really there. People on the spectrum are often very literal, with little emotional body language. NT people often read too much intent into their behavior; they misinterpret the behavior as rude, mean, cold, and indifferent. There is no intent to hurt their feelings or affect them in any way. So, emotional processing both helps and hinders theory of mind. It allows NT people to interpret the emotional meaning in the actions of others, but can also distort the interpretation if the emotional meaning being inferred is incorrect. NT people need the emotional cues to infer intent. Since people on the spectrum often do not give off accurate emotional cues, NT people often misinterpret the intent.

Part of the problem with NT people misinterpreting the actions of people on the spectrum has to do with the lack of nonverbal communication. Theory of mind relies on the person having the ability to read nonverbal communication (facial expressions, body posture, fluctuations and intonations in voice, etc.). NT people rely on intuitively interpreting nonverbal communication to read the thoughts, feelings, perspectives, and intentions of others. Nonverbal communication is the language of "emotional relating." Now, people with autism are thought to be weaker at both receptively reading nonverbal communication and expressively using nonverbal communication. If people with autism use less nonverbal language, or use it differently, then NT people are going to have a hard time reading their thoughts, feelings, and intentions. Theory of mind works much better between people of "like minds."

So, the inability to adequately read the thoughts, feelings, and perspectives of each other goes both ways. People on the spectrum have a hard time reading our mental and emotional states, and we misinterpret (or read more into) their mental and emotional states. Just like people on the spectrum feel awkward interacting with us, we also feel very uncomfortable interacting with them. Neurotypical people are used to relating with people whose thoughts, feelings, and perspectives they can interpret accurately. When we cannot read these emotional cues, because either they are not there or we do not understand them (e.g. when the body language does not match what is being said), then we feel uncomfortable and tend to avoid interacting and relating with people on the spectrum. So, when both parties are not in sync with being able to read the internal emotional states of each other, the relating tends to break down. This helps explain why it can be so difficult for those on and off the spectrum to relate with each other.

Theory of mind: having empathy and sympathy for others

From a developmental model, theory of mind (the ability to read the thoughts, feelings, perspectives, and intentions of others) comes from back-and-forth emotional interactions between the parents and child. It is the early interactions of the parents and child engaging in emotion-based, back-and-forth interaction that invite the child to look for and read the feelings, perspective, and intentions of the other person. Theory of mind grows further in pretend play with the parent, where both are acting out roles of the characters. In pretend play, the child projects thoughts, feelings, and perspectives into dolls and other toy figures. Pretend play gives the child a safe avenue for exploring perspective taking and experimenting with social behavior.

For neurotypical children, the development of perspective taking (theory of mind) unfolds naturally through daily social interactions. However, for children on the spectrum, this process does not develop naturally. Also helping this process for NT children is the brain's drive for central coherence. With central coherence, the brain is looking past the detail to read the overall picture—the relationships between the parts. The brain is rapidly inferring hidden meaning beneath the words and actions of others. This drive to seek overall meaning underlying the individual parts is what provides the foundation for perspective taking.

In addition, recent research has pointed to "mirror" neurons in the brain that allow us to watch what others are doing and experience it as if we are doing it ourselves. This allows us to empathize with what others are thinking and feeling and to understand what the other person is experiencing as if we are experiencing it ourselves. These mirror neurons are not as efficient in people on the spectrum.

It appears that empathy, for NT people, comes from:

- The ability to interpret nonverbal communication (facial expressions, body language, and fluctuations in voice) to read the thoughts, feelings, perspectives, and intentions of others.

- The brain's natural tendency (central coherence) to look past the words and actions to understand the overall meaning (experience) of others.

- The mirror neurons in the brain that allow the person to vicariously experience what others are doing as if he is experiencing it himself.

All three of these functions seem to be impaired in people with ASD. This tends to limit what we call empathy, perspective taking, and theory of mind. Empathy—being able to read what others are experiencing and using this information to predict how they will act—is different from sympathy, which is the ability to feel for what another person is experiencing, once we understand what the person is going through. I think people on the spectrum have impaired ability to empathize (accurately read the mental states of others), but good sympathy for others, once they understand what the other is experiencing. They have good ability to feel for the needs of others, but have difficulty reading the nonverbal information. Once someone explains to them how the person is feeling, or they deduce it by the context of the situation, they may have strong sympathy for what the person is experiencing. They simply have difficulty reading it.

There have been reports of both children and adults on the spectrum who are supersensitive to feeling the emotional states of others, even to the point of being overwhelmed by the sensation. Almost like the sensing of an emotional aura, similar to that reported in animals. This is often interpreted as having strong empathy. However, although people on the spectrum can sense emotional states, they usually cannot identify and label what the emotions are or connect them to specific events. In other words, they sense the emotional vibes but do not understand what the emotions are, or cannot use the information to understand what the other person is experiencing. These emotional vibes can come in very strong and overwhelm the person on the spectrum, often scaring them.

Empathy requires sharing "like" worlds!

People on the spectrum often say that NT people do not have good empathy, because we often seem cold to their struggles. They have a strong argument for this. We have poor ability to read the internal states (thoughts, feelings, perspective, and intentions) of those on the spectrum, because their nonverbal language is different from ours. Since our ability to read mental states comes mostly from nonverbal communication, and we struggle with the lack of, or different, nonverbal communication of people with ASD, NT people have difficulty reading the mental states (thoughts, feelings, perspectives, and intentions) of those on the spectrum. Most NT people have difficulty empathizing with people with ASD. Since our brains are wired a little differently, we both experience the world a little differently. Part of empathy has to do with "like minds" reading "like minds." The person is assuming that the other is processing and experiencing the world in a similar fashion. We interpret the other's actions, facial expressions, and body language by comparing the communication to our past experiences relating with this person, as well as with others. Empathy is not being able to actually "read" the thoughts and feelings of others; it is inferring these experiences from the person's words and nonverbal communication. Since we tend to experience the world a little differently, as well as communicate our experiences differently, we both struggle with empathizing with each other. However, once we are aware of how the other person is experiencing the event, we can both have great sympathy for each other.

Clarify and verify

When relating with people on the spectrum, it is very important that we always clarify and verify that they understand what we are communicating. Because our language is vague and filled with subtleties, people on the spectrum are often not correctly reading the meaning and intentions behind what we are saying. They may not be getting the gist of what we truly mean. For those of us who frequently relate with people on the spectrum, we know that we have to be very literal and to mean what we say and say what we mean. However, this is often very hard to remember. Much of relating involves making assumptions that people know what we mean. And since many people on the spectrum are bright and have good speech, we assume that they understand what we are meaning. Their communication differences are often hidden. Since they have trouble processing nonverbal communication, they have a hard time reading our thoughts, feelings, intentions, and perspectives.

The same goes for us in reading the thoughts, feelings, and intentions of those on the spectrum. Since we are used to interpreting these mental states in others by their nonverbal language, we are used to automatically reading between the lines and inferring certain meaning and intent in the other person. Now, since people on the spectrum are not good at using nonverbal language, they are not easily understood by people off the spectrum. We often read more into what they are saying, or not saying, by inferring intentions that are not there. Or we misinterpret the intentions behind the often blunt, literal language of people on the spectrum. So, this misunderstanding goes both ways.

To make communication easier to understand, both parties need to get better at clarifying and verifying that we understand each other. We need to get in the habit of not assuming the person understands, and always clarifying what we mean and then verifying that they understand. The same goes for understanding them. We need to seek further clarification and verify that we understand what the person with ASD is meaning. We need to take what they say very literally, without inferring additional intent that is not there. So, we have to get used to double-checking that we both understand each other. If we think that there is hidden meaning in the statement, than we have to clarify and verify it with the child.

I see this misunderstanding so frequently with children at school. They are often confused because they do not understand what is expected, but are assumed to understand because they may have good language skills. Teachers, aids, administrators, and peers often assume that the children can read these invisible meanings and expectations, and thus are intentionally being rude, disrespectful, and noncompliant. If we take the time to clarify what we mean and verify that both parties understand, then these difficulties often subside. Not only does the child have a better understanding of what is expected and how to do it, but the teacher also gains a better view of what the child is struggling with.

How to clarify and verify

Many adults on the spectrum report that when they try this approach, many NT adults read this clarifying as being disrespectful or condescending, as if they are questioning the value of what we are saying. I think one of the ways to present the need to clarify, without sounding as if you are questioning the validity, is to present how you interpreted what they said and then ask if this is accurate. For example, say something like, "I am not sure I understand you correctly. I hear you say _____. Is this correct?" This is what I call "clarify and verify" communication. First you ask for clarification and then you verify if you understand it correctly, usually by repeating what you understand so the person can verify if it is correct.

This is what I teach my staff to do with the children. I tell them not to assume the child understands expectations. Clarify it for them specifically and then ask them to verify what they understand us to be saying.

Now, as the child becomes a teen and young adult, he has to learn to do the same. He has to empower himself to take the responsibility of (1) knowing that he has a hard time understanding the true meaning and intentions of others and to always clarify and verify what was said, and (2) assuming that other people will also misinterpret him so to double-check to make sure they understand. Many adults on the spectrum can avoid some of the awkwardness of social miscues by learning to clarify and verify that they understand and the other understands them.

They need to learn a few scripts such as "Let me see if I understand you right," "I hear you saying _____," "Let me clarify that you understand that _____," "If I hear you right, you are saying _____," and so on. Get used to clarifying what you are meaning and verify what you are hearing. This takes away the confusion and increases understanding, so there is less misinterpretation on both sides. If you are a parent or teacher, try to build this into your daily interactions with the kids. If you are a person on the spectrum, try to use this approach to make sure everyone understands. Life will be a little easier if we do.

Chapter 10

TEACHING RELATING SKILLS

In this chapter we are going to discuss relating skills, which are different from social skills. The differences here are that "social skills" usually involve teaching discrete social behavior (sometimes called scripts). These usually consist of "how to" skills: saying please and thank you, introducing yourself, ending a conversation, taking turns, and so on. Social skills training often consists of teaching concrete social rules and static behavior scripts for how to act in specific situations. You act this way in these situations.

Teaching social skills may help the person script his way through simple social situations, but may often leave him lost when relating with others. Relating is not a mechanical "say this and act this way." Relating with others requires the ability to continually appraise, evaluate, and monitor both your own behavior and that of the person you are relating with. Relating also includes sharing "internal experiences"—sharing your thoughts, feelings, and perspectives on how you are experiencing the event you share together. Dr. Steven Gutstein (Gutstein *et al*. 2000, 2002a, 2002b, 2009), founder of Relationship Development Intervention (RDI), was instrumental in introducing us to relating "functions" as compared with social "skills." These functions are mental dynamic processes that provide the foundation and meaning to when, where, and how we use these social skills. They consist of the functions that allow us to share experiences with others. They are not static social skills, but dynamic processes that allow the child to share pleasurable moments with another; reference another for information; read the thoughts, feelings, perspectives, and intentions of others; stay in tune with what others need while coordinating actions together; and regulate the dynamic flow of reciprocal interaction (the dance of relating with another). These are cognitive and emotional processes, rather than behavior skills. Most of these concepts are consistent with many of the social/emotional developmental models of development (DIR, RDI, Denver Model, Son-rise, etc.). My training has been more involved with Greenspan's (DIR) and Gutstein's (RDI) models.

FEELING "SAFE AND ACCEPTED"

Communicating love and acceptance!

If you are a parent or teacher, you are a significant other in the child's life. You are his protector, provider, and mentor. We have already discussed how individuals with autism experience continuous stress and anxiety as a result of their strong sensory, cognitive, and social challenges. Their nervous system is continually taxed, on high alert, and on guard. It is very difficult to feel safe and accepted when they are close to fight or flight. Suspiciousness and apprehension permeate their daily routine. For the child to feel safe with you, and trust following your lead, you need to communicate clear understanding and acceptance, while validating his feelings and vulnerabilities. He needs to view you as a companion and working partner with him.

In order for the child to feel safe in your presence, you need to understand and support his vulnerabilities (sensory, cognitive, social, emotional, etc.) and accept him for who he is. We need to meet the child where he is at. Accept, value, and seek to understand how he sees the world and continue to seek understanding of what he is attracted to and feels safe with. These are the child's comfort zones, where he feels safe and competent. Know what sensory preferences he is attracted to, what interaction strategies he feels the safest with, what tends to calm and soothe him, and what activities he feels the most competent engaging in. Identify, respect, and value these comfort zones to validate the child, helping him feel safe and accepted by you. Only then can he begin to feel safe engaging and sharing experiences with you.

It is important that your child feels loved and loving in order to feel safe and able to relate with you. For children on the spectrum, feeling loved and loving often looks different to how it looks for neurotypical children. They may express love by smelling your hair, lightly tapping you, or snuggling tightly into you. They may avoid physical affection, but love to chant, repeat the ABCs, or sing with you. Usually the way to the young ones' heart is through their senses. Include yourself in your child's preferred sensory attraction and he will become drawn to you.

At first you may have to follow his lead, become part of his world, and simply "hang with him," providing no direction and just being there. Be safe, non-judgmental, and nondirective. Allow him to feel safe in your presence, to feel valued for simply being him. Show enthusiasm for what he values and become part of his play and exploration. Help him feel safe and engaged with you. This may take a lot of work, over numerous opportunities, to gain his trust. However, the child will not learn to relate with you until he feels safe engaging with you.

"I love you rituals!"

Becky A. Bailey, in her book *I Love You Rituals* (2000), explores the importance of simple interactive routines that we use to communicate love and acceptance. These "I love you rituals" are usually repetitive, rhythmic interaction patterns that we use to emotionally connect with our children. They may be simple hand play such as patty cake, chanting a specific nursery rhyme during a daily routine, or singing a song around a task you are doing. It may include simply cuddling before going to bed, a little interactive play while taking a bath, or playing peek-a-boo with the towels when unloading the clothes dryer. Whether it is rocking together, cuddling on the couch, singing simple songs you made up together, or chanting a familiar nursery rhyme, pick two or three of these to use consistently, repeating them each day during predictable routines of the day. Familiarity breeds a feeling of safety, security, and predictability.

Children on the spectrum are often attracted to rhythmic sensory patterns. Some love movement, some deep pressure touch, and others rhythmic songs or vocal noises. Build predictable "I love you rituals" around these sensory preferences which help your child feel safe and loved. Becky A. Bailey's book gives hundreds of possible "I love you rituals." Use these special routines as moments of unconditional love. These routines become familiar and predictable patterns that encode episodic memories of love and acceptance. Use "I love you rituals" to add bonding to normal daily routines, to engage your child in interactive play, and to soothe your child when scared or anxious. Use them to help him become emotionally connected with you.

Some parents do not feel that their children love them or understand and accept their love. Sometimes we have to look very closely to see these expressions, because they often look radically different from how other children receive and express love. Does your child love you? I guarantee it! If you love and support the child, he will love you. Does he know how to express it? Maybe not, or often not in the same way we do. However, all children communicate in their own way. Look very closely and you will see it in an eye gaze, a special touch, vocal utterances, or some other subtle ways. Allow him to express it by pairing your love in simple repetitive interaction patterns, like the "I love you rituals."

Prompting eye contact

The easiest way to induce anxiety in children with autism is to prompt them to look at you. Often when children are trying to listen to what you are saying, prompting them to look at your eyes will make them anxious and interfere with them being able to listen to you. There are three primary reasons for this:

1. Many children have auditory processing problems. Research has shown that people on the spectrum often look at your mouth. This would make

sense if they need to look at your mouth to better understand what you are saying.

2. Some children use peripheral vision to view things. For them, direct vision is too intense and overwhelming, so they look with their peripheral vision. When they are looking at you, they will appear to be looking away from you. Many adults on the spectrum have told me that they become overwhelmed by the intensity of looking directly into your eyes. It feels very intimidating, very scary.

3. Some children cannot multitask two senses at one time. They can either listen to you or look at you, but not both at one time.

So forcing a child to look at you is not increasing his understanding, but often inhibiting it. It totally overwhelms and distracts him.

Like most all of us, looking at someone is much easier when we do it of our own volition. It is intimidating when someone prompts us to look at them. Same goes for all communication. We have found that children with ASD will look at you more frequently when indirectly invited to, not told to. Use the following tips and you find the child looking at you more often:

*   When talking to the child, position yourself so you are in front of him and at eye level. When your face is in his field of vision, it will get his attention better.

*   Use fewer words and more nonverbal language w hen communicating. Use more animated facial expressions and exaggerated gestures to communicate. This invites the child to reference your face to obtain the information needed. Use words to augment your nonverbal language, while conveying most of the information nonverbally. I animate my facial expressions which draws the child's attention.

*   When the child stops referencing you, try pausing briefly until his attention returns. Often the break in the interaction invites the child to check back with you to repair the breakdown.

So invite facial referencing, but do not demand eye contact. And please do not grab and turn their face to you.

Please do not turn my head!

Please, please, please do not let teachers, professionals, or any other well-intentioned adults prompt eye contact by physically turning the child's head and saying, "Look at me!" It is bad enough if you are verbally prompting the child to look at you, but physically turning the head is a physical assault on his security. He will have difficulty building trust in referencing you if you force eye contact. Nothing increases fear and anxiety more than someone grabbing your chin and turning your head to face them. It is intimidating and threatening. If you want children to feel safe, accepted, and competent in your presence, do not pressure eye contact or any other interaction. Share, relate, and invite, and you will eventually gain trust and reciprocity! "Work with me, trust and respect me, and I will reciprocate! Force yourself on me, and you will lose me!"

Qualifier! Safe touch vs. forced touch

I want to clear up any misinterpretation about the previous post on "Please do not turn my head." I don't want anyone to misinterpret that as meaning that touch is not good. On the contrary, I promote "safe hands" and warm touch to help the child to feel safe, accepted, connected, and engaged. Touch is a basic human need; however, we do need to respect comfort zones, especially with those children with tactile defensiveness.

For children who are not tactile defensive, I will often use a soft touch to the side of the head when drawing their attention and providing warm affection. For some children, I can invite facial referencing with soft touch to the cheek. This is totally different from grabbing the child's chin and physically turning it toward me. Grabbing can be perceived as very threatening and intimidating to the child, and reduces their trust in your touch. You want your touch to represent safety, not force. Use your touch to invite engagement, rather than pressure it.

In my discussions regarding "comfort zones," of course the tolerance and acceptance of physical touch varies greatly among children on the spectrum. This is where you have to know the child well, and invite touch, rather than force it. I have not seen a child yet who cannot establish trust in touch if it is not imposed on them. Even children with strong tactile defensiveness can learn to trust and enjoy human contact when it is not forced.

I don't trust following your lead!

For many children on the spectrum, uncertainty is their greatest fear! When the world is chaotic and confusing, scary and painful, uncertainty is your worst enemy. Novelty is an attraction for most young children, driving their curiosity and thirst for learning. However, for many children on the spectrum, familiarity and predictably are the only things that help them feel safe. High anxiety is the result of this underlying insecurity, leaving the child constantly on guard in anticipation of the next assault of uncertainty waiting around the corner.

If you are this child, what do you do to guard yourself and keep yourself safe? When the world is confusing and scary, your senses are overwhelming, and people are unpredictable, how do you survive? You try to control everything around you to make your world as predictable as possible and you aggressively fight any attempt by others to change that. Does that make you feel happy? No! However, it is not about feeling happy; it is about escaping fear! You become motivated to escape and avoid uncertainty at all costs! It becomes a survival need, not a drive for happiness.

Since you cannot read the intent and actions of others, their guidance pushes you into continuous uncertainty. The more you resist, the harder they push, pushing you into the scary void of uncertainty. How can you trust someone who pushes when you are scared, who pressures you into fear? You can't! You resist in panic; you kick, hit, and bite in protest. You build a wall of control that breeds further suspicion and distrust. You anticipate and interpret the approaches of others as possible threats to your security. You cannot trust something that you do not feel safe with.

For a parent, how do you build trust in a rigid wall of fear and insecurity? When your guidance is met with fear and fight? The answer lies in "stop guiding." You cannot guide those who do not trust! They cannot follow your lead if they do not trust you. When your guidance elicits fear and fight, you cannot lead and teach. Stop prompting, instructing, pushing, pressuring, and forcing compliance. It only breeds further fear and stronger distrust. As a parent or teacher whose role is to guide and direct, nothing makes you feel so inadequate and fearful as the child who adamantly resists your lead.

You have to build safety and acceptance first, before you can develop trust in following your lead. The child has to first feel safe in your presence before allowing you to guide him into uncertainty. To establish this trust, you have to back up and stop trying to prompt, instruct, direct, and force compliance. You have to first follow the child's lead, become a valued partner in his zone of comfort. If he fears uncertainty, then let him lead. Once he feels safe with you sharing his comfort zones, then you can gradually try to stretch these comfort zones.

Make the bulk of your interactions centered on what helps your child feel safe, engaged, and competent. What helps him feel safe and what engages him? What is he attracted to and what does he feel competent doing? Value what he values, and build yourself into those experiences. Be an active element in his world, one that he values and feels safe with. Learn what interaction style he feels safe with and is attracted to. Does he prefer slow, soft, and gentle interaction or an exciting, animated style? What types of experiences attract him (movement, deep pressure, music, video games, baseball statistics, etc.)? If the child likes to hum and rock, then hum and rock together. If historical facts help him feel competent, then become a historian! Become excited about what excites him! Stop leading for a while and be a follower. Establish trust before becoming a guide.

The secret is "affect"—sharing emotion together! Turn his world into a sharing experience. Become part of his play and make it a "we-do," doing it together and sharing the experience. Be excited and share emotion around the engagement. Affect, the sharing of emotion, is the glue that cements safe engagement. Whether that be gentle, soothing affect, or animated, excited emotion, let him lead and then become emotionally attached to it.

These strategies will teach your child to feel safe and accepted by you. However, this alone will not teach him to trust following your lead. Once he feels safe sharing emotional engagement in his activity, with him leading, then you start expanding his comfort zones by adding small variations into what you two are doing. Simply expand by adding small variations, creating small amounts of novelty (uncertainty) to his familiar play. Keep the variations small but fun! Gradually add more and more bits of variations (uncertainty) while he stays feeling safe and engaged with you. If he pulls backs and resists, back up and re-establish safe engagement again. More than likely the variation was a little too much for him. Back up and make it simpler. Keep the emotion sharing going (animated facial expressions, excited voices, etc.) to build the emotional connection (essential for trust). Gradually expand more and more by adding small variations to what he already feels safe with. Gradually adding safe novelty, with the child trusting your guidance, will teach him to feel safe following your lead. Once he feels safe with your guidance, he will trust following your lead.

EXAMPLE

I had a little six-year-old girl, Jamie, who loved to sing while rocking side to side. She knew several nursery rhymes and children songs that she would chant or sing over and over as self-stimulation. She used this singing as a way of arousing herself, as well as to zone out and escape the activity around her. She was a lovely girl; she would briefly look at you, then look away and return to singing. Obviously singing was a valued activity for her. She self-initiated singing and used it frequently throughout the day. She felt enjoyment from singing; it calmed and organized her.

To help build an emotional connection with Jamie, I became part of her world. I kneeled in front of her and started singing and rocking in unison with Jamie. I simply copied what she was doing and stayed in her field of vision. Every time Jamie looked over at me, I would smile and nod my head. I animated my expressions and actions so as to draw her attention, without overwhelming her. I knew that, for many children on the spectrum, imitating what they are doing often draws them into attending to you. So I simply copied what she was doing, becoming an active element in her play. It was safe and engaging. It wasn't long before Jamie became more interested in the engagement and would reference me for longer periods of time.

When Jamie felt safe with me being in her activity, I started to gently clap my hands as we sang and rocked together. This novelty startled her at first, as I expected it to. I wanted to throw in a simple variation to create mild uncertainty (uneasiness), but not too much to overwhelm her. After the initial startle response, Jamie became used to it and started to watch my hands. I think she liked the visual, rhythmic movement.

I incorporated this variation first into what I was doing, not what she was doing. We continued to sing and rock, while I gently clapped.

When Jamie relaxed and felt comfortable with this variation, I reached out to gently take her hands and clap with her. She pulled back and turned her head away, briefly interrupting the singing. I made the mistake of not telling her why I was going to touch her. The uncertainty was too much for her. I immediately backed off and returned to simple singing, clapping, and rocking. Once she felt safe again, I made a smaller step. I brought my hands closer to hers and said, "Jamie, clap" as I clapped my hands near hers. I used this to ease the transition to take her hands. I did this a few more times before reaching out my hands to gently take hers in mine, while softly saying, "Take hands." She didn't pull back so I quietly clapped her hands in rhythm to the singing. She initially stopped singing and rocking, but she did not pull her hands away. She allowed me to gently clap her hands while I sang and rocked. She appeared a little anxious, but did not pull away.

Within ten seconds she was back to singing and swaying, while letting me clap her hands to the singing. Her faced relaxed and I could tell that she liked the sensory feeling of clapping her hands to the rhythm. She allowed me to put in a variation, but also followed my lead. This was a big step. We continued this for another few minutes, then we took a break. I had to go back to the table since we were having her annual IEP meeting. She went back to her solitary singing and rocking.

After the meeting I was demonstrating again for the teacher and para-pro how I was using the singing and rocking to socially and emotionally connect with Jamie. I immediately started imitating the singing and rocking that Jamie was doing. After a minute of this, I reached out my hands and said, "Jamie, clap." She looked up and placed her hands in mine. Again, she allowed me to take her hands and clap to the singing. After a minute I removed my hands and immediately said "More" and placed my hands out. She placed her hands in mine and we clapped again. I did this clap, stop, invite for five trials. I was adding in another variation, but one that required her to communicate back to reinstitute the clapping. She now had to communicate that she wanted to continue by placing her hands in mine. I stayed face to face, at eye level, with Jamie so she could easily reference my joyful facial expressions. We wrote a goal and objective into the IEP to include this interactive play at least four times a day, simply using the song she was singing to engage her in clapping. She loved this interaction and would eagerly move toward staff to do it.

We started using this preferred interactive play to reinforce participation in other simple tasks. We would use a "now and next" picture sequence, using a photo of the non-preferred activity (e.g. coloring) followed by a photo of staff and Jamie clapping. She looked forward to these "now and next" sequences because they always ended with singing/clapping. Over time, this singing and clapping became a good tool to transition between activities and for expanding her interaction around other activity. It wasn't long before a few other kids wanted to do it also!

EMOTION SHARING! THE GLUE FOR SOCIAL ENGAGEMENT!

Emotion sharing! Making it safe!

Research is showing that most developmental learning occurs through relating with others. This includes social, emotional, and intellectual development. For normal development, emotion sharing provides the fabric for this interpersonal learning to occur—emotion sharing is defined in its early stages as the ability to reference another to share pleasurable moments. This emotion sharing becomes the glue for further bonding with others and a desire to be like them and learn from them. Unfortunately, due to sensory processing issues, emotion sharing can be very chaotic and overwhelming for many young children. It often frightens them, leading them to escape and avoid it. Whereas this emotion sharing is a natural developmental progression for neurotypical children, it is not part of the hard wiring for many children on the spectrum. If it is initially part of their structure, the interfering sensory sensitivities override it.

Developmental theory also states that this emotion sharing is key to further development of social referencing (referencing others for information and experience sharing), reciprocity (doing for and with others), and perspective taking (reading the thoughts, feelings, and perspectives of others). Unless this emotion sharing process is strongly established, further social and emotional development is hampered. Consequently, since emotion sharing is very difficult for children on the spectrum, this process is often impaired, which significantly impacts further social and emotional development.

Developmental models (Son-Rise, RDI, DRI, etc.) have recognized and incorporated early strategies for developing this emotion sharing process. Stanley Greenspan (1998, 2009) emphasised the importance of showing emotion as the attraction for emotional bonding. Steven Gutstein (Gutstein *et al.* 2000, 2002a, 2002b, 2009), founder of Relationship Development Intevention (RDI), augmented the importance of this affective connection by including multiple objectives around establishing emotion sharing as fundamental to developing further relating skills. The key is making emotion sharing safe enough so the child (1) feels comfortable experiencing it and (2) desires to initiate and maintain it. Many of these models start out by following the child's lead and becoming involved in what they are initiating. If the child is naturally seeking something on his own, it must have value for him and naturally motivate him. If you include yourself in that activity and build emotion sharing around it, the child learns to enjoy sharing the experience with you and thus begins to enjoy interacting with you. These simple activities then can be expanded on to build more complex engagement skills.

For young children, building opportunities for emotion sharing usually consists of placing the child in a simple and enjoyable interaction play in which pleasure can be shared. These activities are better if the main element in the play/interaction is the parent. This way, the child is more likely to reference the adult, since the adult is regulating the pleasure. I find that using the child's sensory preferences is a great avenue for building in simple interactive play. The stimulation is naturally enjoyable for him and being part of that "feel good" stimulation provides good opportunities for sharing pleasure. If you can build simple back-and-forth play patterns around what feels good to the child, he will be more naturally attracted to you and reference you to share pleasurable moments. In my experience, if I build simple back-and-forth, repetitive, rhythmic patterns around their sensory interests, the children feel safer engaging with me, and more readily reference me to share pleasure. When engaging with the children, we (1) position ourselves face to face and at eye level, so our faces are naturally within the children's easy vision, (2) use animated facial expressions and exaggerated gestures to attract their attention, and (3) use the enjoyable sensory patterns (rocking, swaying, chanting, singing, etc.) to invite the children to reference us to share these pleasurable moments. If the children love movement, we build engagement around simple movement activities. If they like deep pressure stimulation, then we build interaction around activities that include deep pressure. If smelling is their main sense, then we use smelling as the main element of play. We simply do it together, face to face, at eye level, using animated facial expression to get their attention, and share the experience.

Each child is different in their level of comfort in initial emotion sharing. Some like strong animation that arouses them. Others will become overwhelmed by such stimulation and need more subtle animation to match their sensory tolerances. Start in the child's "just right" comfort zones, teach that it is safe to share pleasurable emotions with you, and calm and organize him through his sensory preferences. Do not demand or direct eye contact or emotion sharing; invite him through these "feel good" sensory play patterns. Make it fun and safe to reference you to share pleasurable moments and to enjoy seeing that you also enjoy sharing the same experience. It becomes shared enjoyment around stimulation that feels good. Once the child enjoys sharing pleasurable moments, this emotion sharing becomes the glue to motivate the child to expand and learn to engage in reciprocal, back-and-forth interaction, reference you for information, and co-regulate interaction and other social and emotional development.

Teaching "emotion sharing"

In developing the ability to relate with others, the first process to foster is emotion sharing, the ability to share emotional experiences with another. If you can build the function of emotion sharing, all other social relating processes become easier. Emotion sharing is the underlying motivation for experience sharing, the natural ability to share mental/emotional experience with others.

To foster emotion sharing, you want to make your face the center of attention. When sharing pleasurable moments, your face must be within the child's field of vision for him to reference your emotional expression. By framing daily activities so your face becomes the most important object of vision, you are setting the stage to teach emotional relating. In doing so, it is important to invite emotion sharing by being in close proximity, face to face, at eye level. Do not force the interaction, demand eye contact, or turn the child's head to look at you. This does not mean "being in their face," which can intimidate the child. It simply means that you are within his field of vision and at eye level. This *invites* referencing your face, not forcing it. We want the child to want to reference you, to do it of his own volition, not to be prompted or forced. We want to stay within the child's comfort zones to establish safe referencing of our face to share pleasurable moments.

Make your face attractive by animating your facial expressions, making sure not to overwhelm the child. By doing so, the child is eventually drawn to find enjoyment referencing your facial expressions and sharing pleasure with you, not only to enjoy the excitement of the activity, but also to experience sharing the pleasurable moment with you. Throughout the day, build frequent opportunities for emotion sharing into all your day-to-day interactions with the child. Use animated expressions and inviting vocal noises, fun sing-song rhymes, and exaggerated gestures to display and entice emotion sharing.

Use sensory motor play to promote emotion sharing!

For young children, building their sensory preferences into your interactive play is very important for drawing them in to your reciprocal interaction. Using these sensory preferences is also important for helping the child feel safe and secure relating with you.

Emotion sharing (facial gazing to share pleasurable moments) is the first step in establishing strong emotional relating skills. It builds the foundation for further motivation to reference others for information and sharing experiences. Emotion sharing consists of ongoing reading of the emotional states in others, as well as sharing your emotional states with them. Whereas this comes naturally for most children, it does not come naturally for children on the spectrum. For children on the spectrum, sharing emotions can be very overwhelming. Their own emotions can be very scary for them, so trying to read those in others can also be overwhelming.

Many children on the spectrum are very sensory-based. They are very tuned in to their sensory sensitivities, as well as their sensory preferences. They often are attracted to and seek out the sensory stimulation (movement, tactile, visual, auditory, etc.) that feels good to them. This stimulation tends to calm and organize their nervous system, as well as excite and interest them. They are attracted to sensory patterns, which are often repetitive, rhythmic patterns of movement (rocking, swaying, twirling swinging), visual (reflections, visual movement patterns, light patterns, color patterns), tactile (deep pressure pulsating massage, stroking patterns, hand games, and other touch patterns), auditory (humming, singing, chanting, music), and proprioception (climbing, crashing, squeezing, pushing, pulling, etc.).

To help foster stronger emotional relating, parents can use the child's sensory preferences in simple sensory motor play. By building simple, back-and-forth, reciprocal play around these sensory preferences, it attracts the children's attention and interest, and invites safe, emotional engagement. By pairing yourself in activity that feels good to the child, it promotes the child to reference your emotional reactions and to share his pleasure with you. If the child likes movement, then you build yourself into simple movement play (swinging, rocking, running, etc.), or if he likes strong proprioception, then you build interactions around rough-housing, or push/pull type interaction. These repetitive, sensory motor play patterns invite back-and-forth, emotional interaction. They teach the child to feel comfortable emotionally relating with you, following your lead in simple play, and co-regulating in back-and-forth, reciprocal interaction. By doing so, the child learns to enjoy referencing your emotional reactions and sharing his with you.

Appendix B contains instructions on how to implement sensory motor interactive play and a list of possible play patterns to choose from. Pick two or three of these play patterns (or create your own) and then try doing them two to three times a day to engage in reciprocal, emotion-sharing play.

Relating with young, nonverbal children!

Every child has a preferred interaction style. This is the interaction style that they feel safe and comfortable with. What interaction style does your child respond best to? What does he feel safest with? What will best facilitate engagement?

Often children's sensory preferences will dictate how interaction should be given. Do they respond best to an upbeat animated style, or a slow and calm style? If they are sensory-defensive, they often get overwhelmed by excited, loud, animated people, and respond best to slow, calm, and quiet interaction. If they are sensory seekers, they tend to like more upbeat, quick-paced, animated interaction, which alerts them.

The three main tools for interacting are your hands, voice, and physical presence (body posture and facial expressions). How does the child respond to touch? Does he seek out and respond best to physical contact, or pull back and avoid any touch? What type of touch does he respond best to? Soft, light touch, or rough and deep pressure touch? How can you use your touch to calm and soothe him when upset, and to excite him when under-aroused? Does he pull away from touch or draw into your attention when touched? Do you initiate touch or invite it and let him control it? Touch is the most intimate human contact we can provide. It is important to know how to give it.

Your voice also has prime importance. The words used, the length of sentences, the speed of speech, and the tone and volume of voice all have major importance. Many children on the spectrum have auditory processing problems and strong auditory sensitivities. Many respond better to soft, slow, quiet voices. Others need loud, exciting voices to keep them stimulated. Many respond well to sing-song, chanting type speech, and enjoy rhythmic vocal patterns. Other children like only short phrases, spoken in slow, quiet voices, and become totally overwhelmed with fast-paced, excitable types of voice patterns.

Next, your physical presence and facial expressions play a major role. What is the child's need for physical space? Does he have a large physical space, and feel uncomfortable if you get to close to him? Or, does he like to cling, crash, hug, or climb on you? Does he get overwhelmed by animated facial expressions and exaggerated gestures, or does he perk up and attend to animated interaction styles?

These preferences can seem inconsistent depending upon the state of the child's nervous system. When he is calm and organized, he may respond well to touch, loud voices, and animated interaction. However, when his nervous system is stressed and drained, he may pull away from such intensity and want more space, quieter voices, and limited touch. We need to match the level of interaction to the state of the child's nervous system.

Overall, once you identify his sensory preferences, you can identify how to combine your touch, words, and facial expressions to help your child feel safe, accepted, and engaged with you. Teach people around your child how to relate with him in a way that he feels safe and engaged with. In Appendix C you will find a questionnaire for identifying the types of interaction styles, sensory preferences, and your child's social and emotional comfort zones that will help foster stronger emotion sharing.

Please, all I want is to play with my child!

Play is the major avenue for parents to connect with their children, share pleasurable experiences, and teach valuable life lessons. Through play, parents share emotional experiences with their children, transfer desired social values, and teach perspective taking and basic relating skills. Enjoyable play is as important for meeting the emotional needs of the parents as it is a valuable tool for the children. From the early moments of sharing pleasure around simple sensory motor play patterns to the later, more complex symbolic pretend play activities, play becomes the main avenue for both connecting and learning. Over the years, play becomes a major avenue for transferring the cultural knowledge of the elders down to their children.

Cooperative play is foreign to many children on the spectrum. They often appear indifferent or actively resist attempts by others to share in their play. Because of sensory issues and processing difficulties, trying to regulate the unpredictable uncertainties of cooperative play is simply too overwhelming. It is much safer to engage in isolated play that is totally under their control, extremely predictable, with minimal uncertainty. When the children reject their parents' attempts to engage them in this basic developmental ritual, it can be emotionally devastating for the parents. This indifference can lead to feelings of rejection, inadequacy, and loss of the basic parent/child emotional connections.

The early learning, social skills, and companionship that develop from play are very important for developing the foundation for later, more complex relating skills. Social processes such as joint attention, sharing, turn taking, referencing others for learning, understanding the thoughts, feelings, and perspectives of others, and co-regulating actions to stay coordinated in activity with others are established in these early play patterns. Without these early learning skills, social and emotional development is greatly inhibited.

What if your child passively, or actively, resists your attempts to engage him? What can you do to promote active engagement, so the child will feel safe and find it enjoyable? The following strategies have been shown to help foster safe engagement.

1. *Let the child lead!* Join the child in what he is doing! Do not try to guide or direct; simply join in with what he is doing and follow his lead. Become an element in his play. We know the child already finds this activity motivating, and feels safe because it is familiar, predicable, and he is controlling it. Sometimes children will resist the intrusion into their ritualistic play. If this is the case, be a passive observer, simply watching with minimal interaction. Once the child can tolerate you in his space of play, then proceed to engage by describing what you see, labeling what he is doing, and anticipating what is happening. Do not ask questions, give directions, or try to vary what he is doing. Simply watch and describe what you are experiencing.

2. *Imitate, animate, and playfully intrude.* Once the child is comfortable with you watching and describing, start to include yourself in the play. Begin by imitating what he is doing. "That looks like fun…let me try!" If the child is simply stimming, then imitate and copy his stimming (e.g. rocking, hand flapping, twirling string, etc.). If he is engaging in repetitive object play, then do the same right next to him (or better yet at a 45-degree angle so he can see you better). Imitate what he is doing, both actions and vocalizations. Many children on the spectrum are attracted to those who imitate them. You are valuing his world and establishing a connection.

Once the child is comfortable with this, add in animated emotion sharing: "That's cool!" "We did it!" "Awesome!" Use animated facial expressions, exaggerated gestures, and excited vocalizations. Reach out your hand for a gentle "high five." Again, do not question or direct; simply share in what he is doing. Many children on the spectrum are attracted to animation, as long as it is not directing them. This emotion sharing will become the glue that motivates further cooperative interaction.

Anticipate and comment on what he is doing: "Oh, it looks like we are going to hit that tree with your car! Watch out, tree!" Begin to apply meaning to all his actions and vocalizations. Each time the child makes a response, reply by assigning meaning. Each time the child looks up at you, show animated emotion. Each time he says something, respond (even if he didn't mean to communicate).

3. *Become a part of the play!* Next, slowly become an element in the child's play. By becoming an element in the play, you provide a playful intrusion. Now, instead of playing alongside him, you are playing *with* him. Again, try not to direct or control, just follow his lead. Frequently celebrate "doing together" with "high fives" and declarative statements: "We rock!" "Awesome!" "We did it!" Keep assigning and describing meaning to what he is doing and saying.

4. *Start adding simple variations.* Start expanding on what he is doing. Take what he is doing and add a little to it. If he is pushing his truck, put a barrier in front of it: "Uh oh, looks like a tree fell in the way" or "Watch out for the lady walking across the street," as you include a figure to walk across the street. Slowly expand on his actions, as well as adding to the theme of what he is doing. If he resists you expanding on what he is doing, then start with imitating his actions, then expand on your actions. This is less threatening because you are not affecting his actions, only yours. Build in anticipations. "I wonder what would happen if _____." Pause to give the child a chance to respond. If there is no response, simply do the action and comment on what happened: "Oh no, I am going to hit that tree!"

5. *Be sure to celebrate frequently!* Frequently throughout the play, pause briefly to celebrate by giving five, with animated emotion. Have fun and share the emotion. Try to stay in his field of vision so he can easily see your play and emotion sharing.

6. *If he resists, back up a little and make it simpler.* Each time you expand on what you do, if it is too big a change and the child resists, back up to where he last felt comfortable. Take it a little more slowly and make the change a

little smaller to keep it safe. You want to slowly stretch his comfort zones, while keeping the interaction fun.

7. Once the child is engaging in back-and-forth cooperative play with you, you can gradually expand the complexity of play (object play, functional play, pretend play, etc.). (This will require a later post.)

Remember, when encouraging cooperative play, start off by allowing the child to lead, keep it safe and simple, respect his comfort zones, and build in frequent emotion sharing. Be patient! It may take time for the child to feel comfortable, but it is worth it in the end. To teach cooperative play, I recommend multiple sessions throughout the day—at least three to four times a day if possible.

Follow their lead, animate, and imitate!
(Summary of guidelines)

Young children with autism often avoid the attempts by others to engage them. Since they do not understand how to read, react to, and coordinate interaction with others, it can be scary and something to avoid. Imitating the children's actions and vocal noises often attracts their interest and attention, providing a common ground to connect. By imitating their actions, the interaction has predictability and meaning. Also, it communicates that we value what they value. Sometimes we first have to enter their world, in order to gradually entice them to share our world. The following are step-by-step guidelines for successful engaging.

1. Follow his lead.

    a. For the young, difficult-to-engage child, start by following his lead.

    b. Take whatever he is doing and become part of it. Sit/stand face to face so it is easy for him to reference your face and actions.

    c. Become part of his fun, but do not try to direct it.

    d. Mimic his actions and wait for him to notice.

    e. When he references you, show animated emotion.

    f. Comment on what you see him doing and attach "emotional meaning" to it.

    g. By following his lead, and not directing, you are allowing the child to pattern his own comfort zone.

2. Use animation.

   a. Highlight your engagement with animated facial expressions and exaggerated gestures.

   b. Animation attracts attention and makes it easier for the child to read your actions.

   c. Animate facial expressions to attract attention and spotlight emotion sharing.

   d. Animation makes it easier for the child to read your emotions and be attracted to them.

   e. Wait for a response to your actions, and then expand on those with emotion.

3. Become part of the play!

   a. Slowly involve yourself in his play; become part of his enjoyment.

   b. Work face to face with animated emotion.

   c. Create opportunities for reciprocal, back-and-forth, interaction.

   d. Take any reactions the child gives back and expand on them.

   e. Close as many circles of communication as possible, attaching emotional expression to them.

   f. Expand back-and-forth interaction into turn taking, sharing actions, etc.

4. Add variations and expand play.

   a. As the child becomes more comfortable with your engagement, slowly start adding variations and expand what the child is doing.

   b. Imitate what he did, and then add a little to it.

   c. Add an extra element into his play (e.g. place a person in their train, add a car to it, place a barrier in its way, etc.).

   d. Spotlight with an animated emotional response ("Oh…wow! Look at the conductor!").

   e. By doing so, you slowly expand the child's play skills, as well as teach the child to co-regulate with you.

   f. Gradually teach the child it can be safe and fun to follow your lead.

5. Expand play and interaction.

   a. Over time, gradually expand from object manipulation play to functional play, and then to pretend play.

   b. Imitation leads to reciprocal interaction, to sharing and turn taking.

   c. The child learns to reference you for information, to stay coordinated in action with you, and to share pleasure with you.

   d. The child learns to feel safe following your lead, learning from you, and sharing pleasure with you.

Teaching emotion sharing through "we-do" activities!

Relating is about doing together! You cannot learn relating skills without numerous day-to-day "doing together!" Learning social skills (scripts) in isolation to normal day-to-day activities (doing them together) will not teach effective relating skills. Relating is about navigating the back-and-forth "dance" between two people around a shared experience. Fortunately, our normal day-to-day, routine activities provide numerous opportunities for "we-do" activities, where you are doing them together, sharing the experience together.

Basic guidance for "we-do" activities

1. Start with simple activities that the child already knows how to do and enjoys doing.

2. Do the task together, both taking active roles.

3. Work face to face, at eye level, to maximize facial gazing.

4. Use fewer words and more nonverbal communication (animated facial expressions, exaggerated gestures, etc.).

5. Use your words to share (thoughts, feelings, perspectives, etc.), not direct.

6. Focus on reciprocal interaction, engaging together, and sharing pleasurable moments (emotion sharing).

7. Frequently celebrate doing it together (e.g. high fives, thumbs up, etc.).

A "we-do" activity is any activity where you are doing it together, both playing an active role, with the focus on sharing the experience. Focus on emotional relating, not task performance. Create opportunities for recripocal, back-and-forth, emotion sharing. Position yourself so your face is easy to see. Use fewer words and more nonverbal communication (animated facial expressions, exaggerated gestures, exciting vocalizations) that will invite the child to reference your face. When the child references your face, show pleasurable expressions and frequent gestures (high fives, thumbs up, etc.) to invite emotion sharing. Have fun and teach the child to feel safe sharing emotion with you, both in expressing and reading emotional communication. The child with autism needs a lot of practice at reading, feeling, and sharing emotions. Relating is about sharing emotional experiences with another. Start early and practice often.

Try to pick activities where it is easy to build in back-and-forth, reciprocal interaction. Try to give the child a small role to play, even if you have to do 90 percent of the activity yourself. This could be putting clothes in the clothes dryer together, or sitting your child on your lap, facing you, and playing simple hand games. Whatever the activity, make it fun, and show and share emotion. Expect your child to check in with you (reference your face) to stay coordinated and to share pleasure together. If he disengages, then try pausing or making a stutter step or vocal noise to draw him back in again. Periodically throughout the event pause to celebrate doing it together. Give high fives, thumbs up, and animated expressions.

Build these "we-dos" into as many daily activities as possible. Don't do for him, do with him, using the activity as a vehicle to share emotion around. Play water games in the bath tub; brush teeth together while making funny faces in the mirror or take turns brushing each other's teeth; when loading the clothes washer, place each article of clothing over his head for him to remove excitedly and give back to you to put in the washer; eat ice cream together while taking turns feeding each other the ice cream, etc.

Three-step social reward! Celebrate rather than praise!

This is my contribution to the field of positive reinforcement. I learned years ago that teaching reciprocal reward, where both parties are reinforcing each other, is much stronger than simply praising the child. When doing "we-do" activities, use reciprocal reward, where the both the child and parent are actively praising/rewarding each other! The child is both being rewarded as well as rewarding (returning the praise). This makes the child an active participant rather than a passive recipient. A common example of reciprocal reward is giving five! If the parent puts his hand out allowing the child to slap his hand, then the child is an active participant in the celebrating. The parent opens the celebration and the child completes it by slapping his hand. Rather than praising the child, the parent is encouraging them to celebrate together.

Verbal praise is nice, but "Good job, Johnnie" tends to go in one ear and out the other, with minimal excitement. There are a few reasons for this: (1) words are fleeting, in and out quickly, and often do not stick, (2) the child is not actively involved in the reinforcement process (passively accepting the praise), and (3) it is used so much that the praise loses its enthusiasm and becomes artificial.

I also learned early on that by pairing three types of praise (physical, gestural, and verbal) the mutual reward is doubly effective. The mutual emotion sharing solidifies the relating, both giving and receiving in mutual celebration. It is reciprocal reward built around emotion sharing, translated into a three-step behavior strategy that is easy to do and understand.

It is much more effective to celebrate, than to praise. We celebrate by using a three-step social reward consisting of (1) physical contact in the form of "give five or ten," (2) a gesture of approval using "thumbs up," and (3) verbal declarative statements such as "Awesome!" or "We rock!" In addition, the child is actively engaged in the reinforcing process. He is reinforcing you as much as you are reinforcing him. The reward is reciprocal rather than the child passively accepting praise. The art of reciprocal reward, where the child is actively engaged in giving five, thumbs up, or knuckles, makes the social reward doubly effective. You are reinforcing each other, doing it together, celebrating and sharing the experience.

To further augment the three-step social celebration, use animated facial expressions, exaggerated gestures, and an excited voice. Make it fun, exciting, and reciprocal, with the child actively reinforcing you, as you are him. Celebrate companionship, sharing the experience of doing it together. It will not just increase the desired behavior but make the child feel safe, accepted, and competent relating with you.

I promise you, if you learn to celebrate rather than praise, the child will not only seek you out but joyfully follow your lead.

Three-step social reward! Tool for emotional engagement!

The reason I refer to the three-step social reward as celebrating, rather than praising, is because it focuses more on developing emotional relating skills than task performance skills. Since the reward process is reciprocal, with both parties actively rewarding (celebrating) each other, the essence is on sharing a pleasurable moment, via emotion sharing. By giving ten (physical), thumbs up (gesture), and declarative statement ("We rock!," "We did it!" etc.), the focus is on doing it together and sharing the moment. Affect is the glue that gives strong episodic memory to the celebrating. It teaches the child to (1) feel safe sharing emotion with you, (2) feel connected (emotionally attached) to you, and (3) reciprocate (share, co-regulate) interaction.

To augment the social/emotional learning of the three-step social reward, try these guidelines:

1. Get face to face, at eye level, when celebrating! You want your face to be easy to reference. When giving ten and thumbs up (or knuckles), bring your hands up close to your face, so the child is referencing your facial expression when celebrating.

2. Use fewer words and more nonverbal communication (animated facial expressions, exaggerated gestures, and excited vocalizations). Use words only in short declaratives ("Awesome," "We rock!" etc.).

3. Focus on "we," rather than "you." Take the focus off how well he did and celebrate doing it together and sharing the experience! This reduces task performance anxiety and draws attention to relating and celebrating companionship.

Using the three-step social reward not only reinforces the task performance skills you are teaching, but builds strong social and emotional skills in emotion sharing! It is learning through relating! Have fun! Share the moment!

Reading nonverbal communication: use less speech to say more!

Many of the social and communication challenges people on the spectrum have are related to difficulties in reading the nonverbal communication that makes up 80 percent of our interactions. They listen to our words very literally and have extreme difficulty reading the nonverbal communication (facial expressions, gestures, body posture, and fluctuations in voice) that are associated with these words and which provide the perspective, meaning, and intentions behind what is said. Most sharing of thoughts, feelings, and perspectives (which is the essence of relating) occurs through nonverbal communication.

When our children are young, we focus heavily on teaching them to speak (or use other forms of expressive communication). Many do become very efficient at speaking and literally communicating their needs, thoughts, and perspectives. However, they do not learn how to read the others to understand what they are truly saying—to read between the words to get what they mean. In the early years, infants and toddlers first learn to communicate nonverbally before ever learning to speak. The parent and child learn to communicate and relate with vocal noises, animated facial expressions, gestures, and other nonverbal actions. The child can read our facial expressions and voice fluctuations to share an experience with us. Children learn how to relate before learning to speak. In fact, this motivation to relate becomes a strong incentive for learning to talk.

This reading of nonverbal communication does not come easy for most on the spectrum. Instrumentally, we often teach them to talk before they learn how to relate nonverbally. We teach them the words before teaching them how to read the hidden meaning behind the words. As they get older, the children become bound to spoken words and tied to reading them literally. Unfortunately, since our spoken words are rarely used literally, they are often lost when relating with others.

It is important to teach the child how to reference faces to more effectively read the nonverbal communication. They need to reference faces for information. Since children on the spectrum are stimulus-bound on the spoken word, they cannot listen to you and look at you at the same time. Many children look away to hear what you are saying. They cannot do both at the same time. Those with auditory processing problems may need to look at the mouth to better interpret what you are saying. They are not able to both hear what you are saying and read your nonverbal communication at the same time. They are usually missing all the added hidden information.

To help teach the child how to read nonverbal communication, we must say less and communicate more through nonverbal language. Most facial gazing will occur when we use fewer words and more nonverbal language. Use fewer words and more animated facial expressions and exaggerated gestures to communicate. I do not prompt eye contact, just invite it. I let the child have complete choice and control in choosing to look at me. When inviting the child to relate with me, I tone down the verbal speech and increase the use of nonverbal language (facial expressions, gestures, etc.). I have to make a conscious effort to say much less, to get them to reference my face and actions for information and meaning. They have to pay attention to my nonverbal language to understand what is needed. This is not easy for people at first. We are used to talking way too much to direct the children, rather than simply relate with them. To help foster the child to both read nonverbal language as well as expressively use nonverbal communication, build the following into your daily interactions:

- Try to say less and communicate more nonverbally. Highlight your nonverbal language; use animated facial expressions, exaggerated gestures, and excited vocal noises to communicate.

- Use speech as secondary to augment your nonverbal language. Let the child reference your nonverbal communication first before adding words to augment it.

- When doing an activity together, get used to not verbally prompting the child through steps but use more head nodding, gestures, and facial expressions to signal whose turn it is, what to do, and when to do it. Get used to nodding your head "yes" to signal "go" or "your turn," and shaking your head "no" to signal "not yet" or "wrong way."

- This limiting verbal speech requires the child to check in with you to read your nonverbal communication.

- Most importantly, make sure to highlight emotion sharing since affect is the motivator for relating.

- At first the child may resist stopping to reference you and may simply charge ahead without checking in. Stop the action at this time and wait for the child to reference you again before moving forward. This can be frustrating for the child at first, so be patient and hang in there.

- Throughout the day, slow your interactions down and learn to use more facial expression and gestures to highlight what to do, and when to do it, and celebrate doing it!

Essentially, teaching children to read nonverbal communication starts with teaching parents to say less and highlight their nonverbal language. This is hard to do and requires a lot of practice. You need to learn to refrain from speaking first and lead with your nonverbal language. First show it, let them reference it, and then say it. Use words to augment what you are doing, not direct what you are doing. Get their attention, animate it, pause for them to read it, and then add words to augment it. It takes a lot of time and practice, but it will become natural for both of you over time.

Does your child "check in" with you?

For children to relate and learn from you, they have to be able to reference you for information: what to do, how to do it, and when to do it! The majority of early learning comes from social learning—learning by observing and following the lead of those more experienced than ourselves. Most learning occurs through interacting with others. Whether we are simply watching others or engaged in ongoing interaction, most learning comes through our relating with others.

Socially, we also need to reference others to stay connected during interaction. We need to continually check in with them to read their thoughts, feelings, and perspectives, to see if they understand us, and to stay coordinated with them. Without social referencing, we would never be able to co-regulate interaction or activity with others. We would each be following our own path, without referencing the needs of others.

There are different types of social referencing. We reference others to share pleasurable moments, understand their perspective, make sure we are safe, gain information (what, when, and how to do something), stay coordinated together, and assess how well we are doing. For example, if a parent is taking a child into a new social situation, the child may first look up at the parent to make sure it is safe to enter. The parent doesn't have to say anything; the child can read it. Once he is assured he is safe, then the child will reference the parent again for information on what to do. While doing it, he will also check in for feedback that he is doing it right and for information on what to do next. The child will also reference the parent to share their emotional reactions with them and to see if the parent is experiencing the same thing. Through this continual referencing, the child learns how to tackle new situations and become more competent.

Although this social referencing is natural for most children, it is difficult for children on the spectrum. They often do not recognize that the other person has value to them, or that others have thoughts, feelings, and perspectives that differ from theirs. They don't realize that the other person has information that is valuable to them, that they can learn and do better by referencing those around them. Consequently, they don't learn to share their experiences with others, to share their thoughts, feelings, and perspectives with others.

How are your child's referencing abilities? Does your child check in with you frequently during interaction and activity? Does your child continually reference back and forth between the activity and you to (1) make sure it is safe, (2) find out what to do and how to do it, (3) stay connected with you, (4) gain feedback on how he is doing, (5) share the emotional experiences with you, and (6) stay coordinated with you in the back-and-forth interaction. During new situations, will your child reference you to pace himself to stay regulated, or does he simply jump in and "do," with little regard to appraising what is needed and how to do it? Does he look to you for information, guidance, and ongoing feedback on how he is doing? Does he reference you to see if you are enjoying yourself and staying engaged (connected) with him? Don't feel bad if he does not. This deficit is common in people on the spectrum. It simply does not come naturally to them. You have to make it an objective and teach it. Some suggestions that may help:

- Engage in frequent "we-do" activity, where you share and take turns, help each other out, and coordinate actions together. This can be any daily activity from playing catch, playing with a toy, doing laundry together, shopping—anything where the two of you are doing it together.

- Position yourself so that your face is easy to reference—face to face and at eye level. I usually try to position myself at a 45-degree angle to the child so he can easily view both the activity and my face.

- Try to use more nonverbal communication (animated facial expressions, exaggerated gestures, excited vocal noises) and fewer words to guide and share emotion. The less you say, the more the child has to reference your face for information. Use words not to prompt and direct, but to share your thoughts, feelings, and perspectives.

- Slow down and ensure that your child checks in with you frequently for clues on what to do and when it is his turn, to share emotion with you, and to stay coordinated with you.

- Teach the child to check in with you before taking his turn and once he completes his turn (before you take your turn). Frequently use shaking your head "yes" to signify it is his (or your) turn and "no" if it isn't. Also use this time to share emotional reactions. If the child impulsively moves on without referencing you, pause and stop the action to cue the child back to reference.

- Create moments of uncertainty by leaving out information, pausing and hesitating, or creating simple barriers or breakdowns in the interaction. This requires the child to reference you to find out what to do or to repair the breakdown.

- I find that by positioning myself within the child's field of vision and using animated facial expressions, excited vocalizations, and celebrating (give fives, thumbs up, etc.), the child is eager to reference me. When emotion sharing is attractive, it is motivating to reference. Each child is different, but that frequently works for me.

The secret here is that you do not want the child referencing out of compliance, but because it has value for him. Once you frame referencing (how you position yourself and structure the activity) and make it rewarding to do so (emotion sharing), referencing will start to become natural. The greater referencing abilities he has, the greater potential for learning and for relating!

Dance with me! Teaching your child to stay coordinated with you

Once the child begins to reference you for information on what to do and how to do it, the next step is to teach him to use those referencing skills to stay coordinated in action or activity with you. Co-regulation is the back-and-forth checking-in and the referencing of the actions of others to stay coordinated in activity with them. In its most complex form, it requires both the referencing of your physical actions as well as your mental experiences (thoughts, feelings, perspectives, and intentions).

When two people are relating in an activity or simply talking, the relating is always a back-and-forth "dance," with both partners referencing each other to stay coordinated together. We all have experienced relating with others who do not seem to "get it," seem to either dominate the interaction or have poor awareness of not staying in sync with you. It is as if they are not referencing you or reading you correctly, to stay coordinated with you. We feel uncomfortable because the back-and-forth interaction does not flow smoothly. It appears one-sided with minimal acknowledgement of your needs. To effectively engage in back-and-forth, well-coordinated interaction, we have to be able to continually reference the other person to stay synchronized with them (both physically and mentally).

This usually requires the referencing and reading of nonverbal communication, but it also requires being able to continually shift attention back and forth from their actions to yours, so you both can stay coordinated. This joint attention can be a difficult process to pick up. It takes a lot of practice for it to become a strong function. In teaching the child to co-regulate, you want to teach him to continually reference you and pattern his actions to stay coordinated with you. He needs to continually reference you to pace himself to stay connected and in sync with you. The child must continually shift his attention back and forth from the task to you to stay coordinated with you in the activity.

Co-regulation requires the child to reference you to determine what, when, and how to act, and then match his actions with yours. He must monitor both yours and his own actions to pace himself to stay synchronized with you. This is very difficult for children on the spectrum. They tend to march to the beat of a different drummer, without referencing or pacing themselves to stay coordinated with their partner. Usually the partner needs to continually follow the child's lead to keep the activity regulated. This becomes a major barrier to creating and maintaining friendships. Other children lose interest if the child cannot stay coordinated in back-and-forth, give-and-take interaction.

Once you have established the child referencing you for information, then start requiring the child to stay coordinated with you in simple action patterns. We often start by doing parallel actions side by side, such as walking together side by side. In doing so, the child needs to continually reference you (check in) to stay side by side as you walk down the sidewalk. Walking together is often a first step in teaching co-regulation. We usually start on a sidewalk and walk side by side. If needed, we hold the child's hand. Usually the child has already learned that he needs to wait for us to shake our head "yes" to start the movement and to restart the action when it has stopped. The child learns that shaking your head "no" means "not yet" and shaking your head "yes" means "go!" If the child starts to walk a little too far ahead, the parent stops and pauses until the child references the parent and backs up to be alongside them. Once the child starts to continually reference you to stay side by side, then you periodically stop (expecting the child to notice and stop also), walk a little faster, or slow down a little to require the child to continually reference you to stay coordinated. From there you gradually let go of the hand so the child has to coordinate on his own.

Throughout the day you do simple activities with the child, where you expect the child to reference and pace himself by following your lead. If the child gets off course, you simply "pause the action" until he recognizes he is off course, stops, and regains coordination. When you notice the child is not referencing you, then pause or change your pattern to see if he regains the coordinated action. Once the child learns to stay coordinated in walking, then we move on to more complex co-regulating, such as riding a bike.

Next, we step up to co-regulating more complex coordination, such as passing a soccer ball back and forth. The child has to reference how hard or soft you pass the ball, and try to match his actions with yours. He has to learn how to reference you to learn when to pass the ball (waits for you to shake your head "yes") and to pass the ball to your feet (accuracy) and at a pace (speed) that will get it there, but not too hard that you have to go chase it. This requires him to match the pattern and speed that you use and monitor his own responses to stay coordinated. We teach the child to "two touch" the ball: one touch to stop the ball and the next touch to pass the ball. Often the child starts out by wildly trying to kick the ball back without stopping it first, bringing it under control, and then referencing you to see if you are ready. The child usually gets excited and tries to kick the ball hard before stopping it first. At that point the parent pauses the action and demonstrates how to stop the ball, pass it, and pace the pass. This is where it is important for him to initially reference you to shake your head "yes" to pass it back to you. The parent will always interrupt the action, model the correct response, and only let the action continue if it is done correctly.

This back-and-forth rapid referencing to stay coordinated in actions is the beginning of co-regulating. From there we use more and more nonverbal language (animated facial expressions and exaggerated gestures) to communicate information on what we are thinking, feeling, and contemplating during the actions. At this time the child moves from referencing you to stay coordinated with you, to referencing you to understand what your inner experiences are. In this state, co-regulating takes on the continued reading and monitoring of another's thoughts, feelings, perspectives, and intentions. You need to become skilled at using your facial expressions and actions to communicate your inner thoughts and feelings. This is when true relating begins—the sharing of experiences with another.

For further information and activity ideas on emotion sharing, social referencing, and co-regulating abilities, I recommend that you visit the official website for Relationship Development Intervention (RDI), www.RDIconnect.com, or read any of Steven Gutstein's books (Gutstein *et al.* 2000, 2002a, 2002b, 2009).

Chapter 11

PEER PLAY AND COMMUNITY INCLUSION

God, I would love to play!

Hi, my name is Jake!

Every day at recess I play in the sand. I love letting the sand sift through my fingers! It feels so soft as it slowly falls through my fingers and back down to the ground. I love to watch the way the sand looks falling through my hands and fingers. I can change how I do it so it falls in different patterns. I love the feel and calmness of doing it over and over again. It makes me feel safe and good. Occasionally the recess lady will ask me if I am OK. I usually say nothing and do not look up.

This sand play feels so good to me, and it allows me to avoid the chaos on the playground. I try to avoid the playground; not because I don't want it, but I just cannot make it work. I look out at the kids all running, climbing, swinging, and chasing each other. They must be having fun. They are all shouting and laughing. If they are laughing, they must be having fun! How do they do it? What is their secret? Why can't it work for me?

God, I would love to play!

I love to do these things! I love to run, climb, and swing. I especially love to laugh! I know how to do all these things, but I don't know how to do them with others! I don't know how to talk to and play with others. I watch what they do, but I just don't "get it." I don't understand. How do they do it? How do they know what to say, what to do, how to play the game? I just don't get it! I don't understand the rules, what they want, how to "do it together." They must know what to do and when to do it! I simply do not get it!

God, I would love to play!

I have tried over and over, but it doesn't work. It doesn't make sense to me. I know how to swing, run, climb, and I can talk. But it doesn't work. I can't seem to do it with them. When I have tried, I think I am doing it right! I watch and do what they do. But it somehow is not right. They look at me and laugh. I like to make them laugh, so I do it again! But then they either push me down or walk away from me. I don't understand that! What did I do wrong? Am I supposed to push back? Is this the fun? So I try to push back, then they yell for the recess lady. She pulls me away and yells at me! Why? I don't get it. I see them pushing each other, and they pushed me. Why can't I push them? Why don't they like that?

I listen to what they are saying. Often their words come too fast. They talk back and forth so fast I can't understand what they are saying. I try and say the same words, but they look at me funny. I try to do what they are doing, but I must not do it right. I cannot tell if they like me or not. I just don't get it! I want to, but I don't "get it!" So, I stay to myself, quietly sifting sand. After all, I do feel safe in being alone. And I do love the feel of the sand. It is predictable, I have control over it, and it feels good.

God, I would love to play!

At home I have an imaginary friend. Her name is Sally. I have a swing set and slide at home. I play with Sally all the time. We swing together, climb together, and sift sand together. She follows my lead so it is easy to do. She accepts me, she doesn't laugh at me, and she doesn't tell me what to do, or run from me. But how I wish I had a real friend! I watch the boys next door through the fence. Sometimes they stop and look at me. I look away. I am too scared. I know I can't do it! I only fail. How can I learn to do something I don't understand?

Yesterday we had a meeting at school. Maybe I did something wrong, I don't know. The teacher tells my mother that I am a loner, that I don't like being with the other kids. That I push them to the ground, and that they are scared of me. I am confused. I have not done anything to anyone. I just want to "fit in." I want to play! I want to yell and laugh, climb and swing with them. But I can't, I am dumb, I am not good enough. I could see my mom cry! I don't want my mom to cry. I am no good! They don't understand!!

God, I would love to play!

Today was different. I ate my lunch alone as usual. I went outside and played with the sand. It was nice outside and the sand felt good! As usual the other kids were playing on the playground. But today a girl came up and said "Hi." She told me her name, but I said nothing. I was scared! What did she want? She asked if she could play in the sand with me. I said nothing. She talked softly and slowly. Her voice felt good, soft, friendly. She sat near me and watched what I was doing. I didn't understand. She started to sift the sand like me! I looked up and she smiled! She didn't laugh, but she smiled! Somehow I knew that was good! She said "This feels good!" and did what I was doing. I am not used to that. It did not make sense, but it felt good. She liked what I liked! We didn't say much, but we did it together! She asked me what I do with the sand. I didn't say anything. I wanted to, but could not find the words. I just started to sift the sand another way. Again, she did it with me. Again, I was surprised, but it felt good. How different this was. I didn't have to watch her, to do what she was doing, to make myself do something I didn't know how. She liked what I was doing! She liked doing it with me! I don't know what this means, but it feels good!

God, I love to play!!!

The bell rang and we had to stop. I didn't want it to stop. I didn't want it to end! I was happy here with her. I was comfortable with her. She thanked me and asked if we could do this tomorrow. I could not speak. I did not know what to say. Does she really want to play with me? Will she actually come back tomorrow? I forgot her name! I am scared to ask.

Back in class I sat at my desk. I could not hear the teacher. I could not do anything. The teacher was talking, but I could not tell what she was saying. The girl was sitting up in front of the room. I now remember her sitting there before, but never talked to her. I felt good, but scared. Will she play again tomorrow? How can I tell? Before I knew it the bell rang again! It was time to go home. I just sat there. She turned and saw me. She smiled and came to me. "See you tomorrow!" she said. I looked at her, but could not speak. It didn't seem to matter! She smiled and left the room. It felt good!

God, I love to play!

The best social mentors are other children. With a little guidance, children can be very accepting and great mentors. The use of peer mentors is growing. Teaching other children how to play, in a non-threatening way, can facilitate play skills and eventual friendships. We simply need to start in children's comfort zones, where their skills are at. Children on the spectrum need to feel that others value what they like, and to first follow their lead. To play with them, so they can eventually learn to play back. With the right facilitation, the children can grow greater interaction and play skills. In turn, the other children learn to understand, accept, and even value playing with them. Acceptance is about understanding and valuing what others do. It is not just about teaching the child on the spectrum how to play like others, but also teaching the others how to play like him. Often you will find that they learn from each other and develop better play skills. Please support the use of peer mentors and teaching other children how to play with our children.

Facilitated play with peer mentors

Many of you who read the previous post, "God, I would love to play," saw a glimpse of your own children there. For some of you, that was a sad moment. However, the last paragraph was a clue to an open door. That little girl was a peer mentor who volunteered to make friends with Jake, the little boy. This was third grade. It was the beginning of a friendship that, last I heard, was still going four years later.

Also, within that same year, once the children saw the gains that Jake was making, two other children volunteered to be peer mentors (friends) with Jake. The nice thing about starting this young is that the peer mentors really want to be friends, so these become true facilitated friendships. It is amazing how effective it is to work with peer mentors. With Jake we worked one-on-one, with only one friend at first. He first learned how to co-regulate play with one person, instead of entering into the chaotic world of group play. This is a mistake I think many social skills groups make. They pair kids up with peer mentors, but often in group activities, which are way too advanced for the children's current abilities. Children on the spectrum have major difficulties processing even individual interaction and become totally overwhelmed trying to regulate several kids at one time.

The nice thing about starting with third graders is that they are so accepting, with a little understanding. They are mature enough to follow a few directions, but also are very pure in their interactions. Give one or two directions and then allow the mentor to freely engage, rather than script the interaction. In this case, Molly jumped at the chance to be Jake's friend. She didn't know how, but she wanted to be his friend. We told her that Jake was much like every other boy. He wanted to play with others but had difficulty understanding how. He had difficulty understanding how other people think and feel, so he also had difficulty understanding how to play with them. Jake thinks a little differently from others. He has the same desires but has trouble speaking to others.

We discussed with Molly how Jake would probably not talk at first, but that did not mean he didn't want to play with her. We simply asked Molly to play alongside Jake, do what he was doing, and simply talk about how she felt doing it without trying to direct it, change it, or prompt other activity. We asked her to say only one-sentence statements at a time and to not expect a response back. It was OK to simply sit and play with him (parallel play) with minimal interaction. We had Molly practice (role-play), with me playing Jake. The only additional suggestion was for Molly to smile whenever Jake looked her way. This was natural for Molly anyway. She was a friendly girl. It was amazing how easy it was for Molly to do. It was as if it was natural for her.

After two weeks of playing with Jake in the sand, we decided to expand it to the playground (swings, jungle gym). We knew Jake liked to swing, climb, and run; it was just that he could not do it with others. We didn't want to do it with the other kids on the playground, so we set it up for Molly and Jake to go out later in the afternoon for 15 minutes' "extra" recess. We figured we would need to teach some type of "safety" tool for Molly to help transition Jake into other activity. During the second week in the sand box, we had Molly start reaching out her hand to Jake (for him to touch) when she approached and when they ended the play. She was also encouraged to do this when Jake seemed to "freeze" during play. We wanted to establish an easy, safe form of physical contact. This also solidified the companionship. Jake appeared to feel safe with Molly, so this helped solidify it.

After two weeks we decided to take the play to the swings and jungle gym. Since Jake already knew how to play on the equipment, we didn't have to worry about teaching him to use them. Our only instruction for Molly was to start in the sand box, then reach out and take Jake's hand, say "Let's go swing," and then gently stand up. If Jake stands up with her, then go over to the swings and swing together. As we thought, Jake hesitated a second but then went over to the swings with Molly. He jumped on one swing and Molly right next to him. Jake had the biggest smile. As they swung together, Molly was asked to simply say "Swing" each time she went forward (which we role-played together). If Jake spoke at all, Molly was instructed to repeat the word back. And sure enough, Jake was happy as could be and he hollered out "Swing!" Molly immediately repeated "Swing!"

This facilitation progressed pretty quickly to climbing, riding the rocking horses, teeter-totter (seesaw), and going down the slide. They learned to take turns and follow each other's lead. As Jake was feeling safe and comfortable playing with Molly, we gradually recruited two boys to be additional peer mentors. This allowed us to build from one-on-one play to playing with two or three children. For each of the two boys, we gradually added one at a time into

Molly and Jake's play. This way Jake felt safe enough having Molly there and the boy would simply follow their lead. Eventually, when the boys felt comfortable with Jake, we allowed them to play with him without Molly.

These three friends became Jake's peer group. We started having them play in groups of two or three together, also inside playing computer games, board games, and bowling. Jake was really good with the video games, so that was really inviting to the boys. He also loved Transformers, which was also a favorite of one of the boys. We asked Jake's mother to start arranging play dates at home, with only one of the kids at a time. His mom was taught to sit down with Jake and his friends and make a list of activities that they all liked to play. From this list, mom and Jake would sit down and plan out each play date and would preview the night before the activities they were going to play and for how long. Also, mom helped remind Jake of any social rules that she could think of. They also reviewed this list just prior to the play date.

As time goes on, you can see that with a little planning we can expand these friendships to different children, activities, and settings. This cannot be done effectively without peer mentors and facilitated play. They just have to start where the child feels safe (comfort zone) and gradually stretch the play once the child feels comfortable. We start by allowing the child to lead, and then gradually teach co-regulation as he becomes more comfortable. When this type of peer facilitation is started early, it is actually pretty easy for both the child on the spectrum and the peers. They seem to be more natural at it, more genuine with wanting to be friends. It is a nice development to watch!

Jake and Molly: peer mentorship

With the last two posts, I hope people see that teaching play skills does not start with trying to teach the child how to fit in, to do something foreign to them, that will only confuse them. They don't "get it" and often stumble and fail. If you noticed in the case here of Molly being a mentor for Jake, it was about teaching Molly how to fit in with Jake, not Jake learning to fit in with the rest of the kids. This is a big difference in the way we try to teach social skills. We usually focus on teaching the child on the spectrum how to play with neurotypical children. However, we often forget that we can do better by first teaching the neurotypical children how to play with the child on the spectrum. Start in the child's comfort zone, follow his lead, and allow him to feel safe with other children. This approach, I feel, is the more effective way to teach social relating. Once the child starts feeling safe with the peer, then we can work on allowing the peer to direct more of the play. The child first has to feel safe and accepted before he can risk and grow.

Being a peer mentor—a more clinical name for facilitated "friend"—is not as hard as many may think. Children make great mentors when given a little awareness and coaching. Many children love helping others, and often enjoy the unique qualities of the child with special needs. They simply need a little coaching in how to play with the child and what some of child's different behaviors mean. Nothing complex, just some simple awareness of how your child thinks, feels, and communicates. In this case, Molly was a friendly, perceptive child who had shown an interest in Jake from the beginning. It works out best to pick someone who is friendly by nature and loves to help. You always want to ask for volunteers and not for a child to do it. Although you may get several children volunteering, I feel it is often best to start with one "friend"—one mentor who can make the initial connection with the child, enter his comfort zone, and establish the social connection. It is hard enough for the child on the spectrum to process interacting with one person, and much more confusing in a group of several children.

When teaching peer mentors how to play, we usually start by having them simply follow the lead of the child and let him pace the play. We try to teach them to say short phrases that describe what they are doing, rather than questioning and instructing. We may role-play and practice a little. However, many children are naturals at facilitating play. At first, adults should be watching and coaching as needed. Know what your objectives are (follow lead, safe non-demanding statements, back-and-forth turn taking, etc.). Start where the child is at, in their comfort zone, allowing him to lead. This is more comfortable for the child, establishing a trusting connection. Sometimes the two children naturally start to stretch the play, and sometimes it takes more coaching and facilitating. However, if you pick the right child, their natural tendencies are often better than ours. Do not move on to adding other children until you see good back-and-forth, reciprocal play between the two. Once that happens, gradually add one child at a time. However, keep it very simple and be ready to facilitate.

If you pick friendly, caring peers, you can hardly go wrong with this type of facilitated play. The children love being mentors, and the child develops friendships that can often last years. Once the child feels comfortable playing with one or two peers, other children start to feel more comfortable playing with the child. The peer mentors now become mentors to bridge the play with the other children. They learn to mentor and coach the other kids. It can be great fun and valuable lessons can be learnt by both the child on the spectrum and the peers.

Facilitated play should be built into the IEP as early as possible. It should be an ongoing goal for all the school years, becoming more complex as the child ages. Parents need to list this as one of the highest-priority goals, monitor the implementation and progress, and encourage the school along. Build in peer mentors who become friends over time, both inside and outside school. As needed, pull in a speech and language pathologist, school social worker, or psychologist to help frame this experience.

The joy of feeling connected

It is so interesting how the old view of autism was of someone who was indifferent and disinterested in people and only attracted to objects. Of the hundreds of children I have met over the years, I have yet to find a child who does not desire to connect with others, when given the right opportunity and feeling safe in doing so. Even in the most severe states of impairment, where social avoidance can be strong, I have found a deep desire to connect, but a strong fear of doing so. Once I find the avenue to communicate and established safety in my approach, the child is naturally attracted to connect. When you cannot understand the interaction, do not know how to relate or communicate, find socializing overwhelming, or have experienced multiple negative consequences trying to connect with others, you will withdraw and avoid contact.

Every child has an avenue to "connect" with you. It may be hard to see at first, but once you understand the child (what they are attracted to, what they feel safe with, what their preferences are), you can easily connect and build emotional attraction to relate. Just like the rest of us, no two children on the spectrum are alike. They all have their own unique qualities, preferences, and ways of interacting with the world. We all have a desire to feel safe and accepted with those around us, and to feel competent in connecting with others. It is finding the right approach, the right method, pace, and rhythm of interaction, to help the person feel connected. If you observe, listen, and meet the child at his level, you will connect with him. Once you have an understanding of (1) what he fears, (2) what he is attracted to, and (3) what his preferences are, you can build a strong social and emotional connection.

It often means inviting the interaction, but then letting the child lead it to feel safe. It may require finding the right pace and rhythm to the interaction, to synchronize with the way the child relates with the world. It also means finding the right ways to use your hands (touch), voice, and facial expressions to establish safety, as well as the right intensity (calm and slow, or animated). It often requires us to initiate, but not pressure, direct, or demand a response.

We also need to understand what the child is attracted to. This may be the main "topic of interest" for the child with Asperger's, or the sensory preferences that seem so inviting to children with severe cognitive deficits. Each child has preferences that attract them and offer avenues to build safe relating around. I may build reciprocal interaction around talking about historical details of each president for the child who gleams when discussing his favorite topic, or engage in rhythmic sensory movement play for the child who is attracted to a pattern of movement. It is about meeting the children where they are at, what they are interested in, and what they feel safe with.

Once the connection is established, you can gradually stretch greater interaction (relating) skills. You will also discover that natural desire to connect with others, when it is safe and accepting to do so. You will not only *see* it, but *feel* it. It is joyful for both you and the child. Connection is a shared experience that brings joy to both parties. When it is rejected, we are approaching it wrong, with the wrong attitude, or the wrong style, or being too demanding. Observe, listen, and follow the child's lead and you will find the connection.

Teaching social skills: the missing link!

Historically, teaching children on the spectrum how to "relate" has focused on teaching them social skills. The focus has been on teaching the children appropriate ways to interact. However, this training is often scripted and appears mechanical when it occurs. Even with good social skills training, the children have difficulty reading the subtleties of interacting so will always be a little out of sync with others. Since neurotypical children often feel uncomfortable with these differences, they may reject the child, either by isolating him or teasing him. However, we seem to miss half of the equation. Relating is a two-way street. Not only do children on the spectrum have difficulty reading and interacting with typical children, but typical children also struggle with reading and interacting with kids on the spectrum. So, it only makes sense that we need to teach both parties how to feel comfortable relating with each other. It simply doesn't work out well to teach only one side of the relationship.

When it comes to social skills, we seem to feel that the one who needs training, or changing, is the child on the spectrum. They have to learn the skills necessary to regulate in neurotypical interaction. Although we can teach the children many important social skills, they are always going to interact a little differently, because their brains process information differently; they simply think and relate differently. If we try to make the kids into something they are not, they will never feel comfortable with others. We cannot make them something that they are not, nor should we try. So, if they are going to be accepted by other children, we have to teach typical children how to relate with kids on the spectrum. Awareness and understanding are key to helping typical kids feel comfortable relating with our children. How can they accept those who they do not understand how to relate with? We need to put as much emphasis on teaching both children to understand and relate with each other.

The best time to start is in the early years. From kindergarten on, we need to provide (1) awareness training to the entire class on what autism is, as well as (2) awareness training about the individual child. This also can be done by sharing the qualities of all the children in the classroom that make them unique, focusing on the children's strengths and interests, as well as vulnerabilities. However, it is important that neurotypical children understand why the child may act differently, why it is difficult for him to interact the same way, and how they can interact effectively with the child on the spectrum. Focus very heavily on the child's strengths, as well as his difficulties. Talk about what can help the child feel safe and accepted, and how they can help the child fit in. Let the children talk about their own anxiety about relating and fitting in. Talk about how hard it is for children on the spectrum to read the thoughts, feelings, and perspectives of others, and how to help the child learn to share, take turns, and coordinate interaction. Talk to them about saying exactly what you mean and meaning what you say. Help them to understand that the child will not understand how you feel unless you tell him. Talk about being upfront and frank about letting the child know how to respond, rather than chastising him for responding differently. Teach how to be concrete in describing and explaining things to the child. Teach the children how to read and interpret the unique behaviors they may see from the child. Kids can be very accepting when they (1) understand the child's actions and intentions, and (2) are guided in how to facilitate interactions with the child. My experience is that once the children feel comfortable with the child on the spectrum, they often enjoy his strengths and preferences. The teacher should profile the interests of the child, which are often something that interests his peers.

From this understanding, teachers, aides, and support staff should set up and facilitate reciprocal interaction and cooperative play skills between the classmates. If the children feel "safe" with the child with autism, they will feel free to ask questions about behaviors and differences as they play. They can learn to support the child in cooperative play and to truly include the child. Children will learn to enjoy the child on the spectrum, and will often feel pride in helping him. Children can be the best social skills teachers, when taught to facilitate. Adults cannot teach children how to relate with other children. Children need to mentor each other, with the guidance of adults. As each year goes on, the social relating skills become stronger and more accepting, as they mature and develop stronger relationships. The only way to truly protect the child from bullying and to teach true inclusion is to build a strong, understanding, and accepting social network to support the child from year to year.

Parents need to rally together, provide the awareness training in the classrooms, help facilitate the social understanding for all the children, and guide and direct supportive interaction. You will find it rewarding for both your child and the other children.

Teaching young children to play with peers

Kelly, one of our members, asked a question that I know is of interest to many others with young children on the spectrum.

Kelly's question

How do you get your four-year-old to interact with other kids? He prefers to watch them. He is OK with his cousins. He doesn't ask them to play. He hits them, even me, and other family members for attention. Please help me.

AUTISM DISCUSSION PAGE

Many four-year-old children on the spectrum have major difficulties playing with other children. They do not have the skills or processing abilities to coordinate back-and-forth, reciprocal play. They cannot read the give-and-take, social pragmatic cues often needed for cooperative play with other children. I think it is great that he wants to observe the others playing, which shows he has interest in what they are doing. I would try to sit with him and quietly narrate what you see the other kids doing. This way you can describe for him what the other children are doing to gradually increase his understanding.

Pressuring him into group peer play will probably overwhelm him at this time. For kids on the spectrum, it is difficult enough to learn to play with one other child, and very difficult to play with a group of children. How you would start teaching social play depends on what his current skill and interest levels are. It would depend on his current social skills, play skills, social interest level, cognitive abilities, and language skills. Each one of these variables plays a part in peer play.

Peer play is very dependent on two primary skills: social skills and play skills. Both follow predictable developmental paths. For example, the child first has to learn "parallel play" skills (playing alongside another child) before learning "cooperative play" skills (coordinating back-and-forth play with the other child). Also, the child first has to develop "functional play" skills (using the toys in a functional manner), before he can learn "pretend play" (imaginative play). Just encouraging or pressuring the child to play with peers will not teach these skills. Doing so will overwhelm the child and increase the likelihood of failure and other children rejecting him, and the possibility of destructive behavior resulting out of frustration.

I would recommend the following:

1. Try to elicit the help of a speech and language therapist, psychologist, or social worker to help you design strategies for encouraging play skills and social skills. They will understand the developmental sequences for each skill (social, communicative, and play skills).

2. Work with him playing with you. He has to learn to cooperatively share in give-and-take, back-and-forth interaction and activity with you first. He must learn to share, take turns, reference you, and coordinate action with you first, before introducing another child.

3. Once he learns to play cooperatively with you, then add a peer into the play. During this play you want to frame the activity and facilitate the play, making sure the activity is very simple and it is easy to pattern the play. You need to pick both the play partner and activity with care. You need a peer who will be tolerant and easy to guide, as well as an activity that is easy to facilitate and that both children are already familiar with. You will need specific objectives to work on (e.g. sharing, taking turns). Again, the speech therapist can help with that.

4. Until then, do not pressure group peer play if the child (1) does not feel comfortable with it and (2) cannot regulate it. It is good that he likes to sit on the outside and watch the other children play. I recommend that you sit with him and narrate what the others are doing. This will increase his understanding of what he is observing.

5. It is important to stay within the child's comfort zones and slowly stretch him. For most children on the spectrum, it is mentally and emotionally draining to try to process and regulate peer interaction in group play. What comes naturally for other children has to be thought through and figured out by children on the spectrum. This can be very taxing and overwhelming.

6. Provide exposure with other children to gauge social interest. If the child is displaying no interest in wanting to play, encourage but do not pressure. That will only create increased problems, acting-out behavior, and peer rejection. Not all children are going to want to be social, and no amount of forcing will change that; it will most likely make their avoidance worse.

7. Realize that developing social play skills can take years to develop, with very careful planning. You have to teach skills in sequence and build on each one. As you progress, it is important to develop a few good friends (peers) to play with who will help facilitate his engagement.

8. When your son hits others for attention, it signifies that he does not know how to initiate interaction appropriately. So you will need to teach other, more appropriate, ways of initiating interaction (e.g. touching others on the arm instead of hitting them).

I hope this helps. Teaching social play skills is very complex, takes a lot of work, and has to be paced by your child. Take it slow, gradually stretch, but let the child pace the development.

Play dates

Most parents with children on the spectrum want to encourage cooperative play to foster eventual friendships for their children. However, simply pushing the children into unstructured play with two or three children often results in failure. Learning how to co-regulate interaction and relate with other children is a complex process that takes a lot of structured, facilitated learning opportunities. I usually recommend parents start with short, one-on-one play dates. Play dates can be planned ahead of time, previewed and reviewed with the child in advance, and then facilitated to maximize success. I recommend doing the following for maximizing peer play (or what some call "play dates"):

1. Developing peer play is a long and complex journey that needs to begin within the child's comfort zones, start simple, and build gradually. Relating with others can be very taxing and draining for your child. It requires extensive thinking and multitasking. Keep the initial play dates brief and consisting of a very simple activity that is easy to regulate. If you think your child usually does fairly well for only 45 minutes, then start with short, 30-minute play dates to maximize the chance of success.

2. If you do not know any children to invite for play dates, ask the teachers at school if there are any children who your child expresses an interest in or vice versa. Try to pick a child who may have similar interests and/or disposition. Keep it to only one child. Trying to regulate interactions with multiple children is extremely difficult for our children.

3. Try to find out as much about the peer as possible. Talk to the parents and make a list of likes, dislikes, and favorite activities. Try to identify a few activities that the children will have in common and can be used to build the play dates around. The simpler the activity, the better. Long complex activities, with multiple steps, may tax your child too much. Use activities your child is familiar with. This way, the child already feels competent with the activity and allows you to focus your attention on facilitating social play, rather than teaching how to do an activity.

4. Plan ahead and preview what is going to happen. Make a list of what possible activities the child and his friend are going to play. Try to schedule out the play date, with possible substitute activities if things do not go right. Always have a Plan B ready.

5. Discuss the following with the child ahead of time:

   a. what he can expect to happen (lay out the sequence of events)

   b. what will be expected of him

   c. how long it will last

   d. how he might handle any anticipated problems (sharing, taking turns, choosing activities, not getting his way, etc.).

6. Based on past play dates, discuss any problems he had and how he should handle them in the future. If possible, role-play them. Also role-play any new games or activities so he is familiar with them.

7. Prepare the activity the night before, and then review everything again just before the event.

8. During the activity, observe closely and help scaffold the activity as needed. Let the activity flow naturally, unless you see little signs of difficulty. When you see possible problems (a breakdown in regulation), provide subtle redirection to help repair the breakdown. Anticipate and look for the early signs; redirect and facilitate before problems erupt. It is easier to anticipate problems and provide accommodations and support to minimize them than it is to solve the problem once the child becomes dysregulated.

9. After the play date is over, sit down with the child and review how it went. Talk about what went well and what snags may have occurred. From your observations, pick one or two possible problems you saw and review these with him. Discuss how he may want to handle them next time (taking turns, sharing, taking turns choosing activity, etc.). In the future, try to have one main objective (social skill) that you are working on to help develop greater cooperative play skills.

10. Make a journal with a page for each play date. Make an outline form by dividing it into two sections to fill out with the following information:

    a. Preparation: list of potential activities, Plan B, potential problems with possible solutions.

    b. Post-activity: what activities were played, what worked well, what snags occurred, and what to try next time.

11. If you notice that the friend is perplexed about or uncomfortable with your child's behavior, then explain to the friend why your child is acting that way. Children feel most uncomfortable when they don't understand what is occurring and how to react to it. However, most children are flexible when they know what to expect and how to react.

12. Do not be quick to move on to multiple players and/or unstructured activities, until you build that into your play dates. Once your child seems to be building the cooperative play skills needed to co-regulate with one friend, then build in less structure and less facilitation to see how he does handling the give-and-take interaction and repairing breakdowns in regulation. Take it slowly to maximize success. I see the greatest failure in moving too quickly into the unstructured, multiple peer play activities,

similar to what you would find on a playground. This type of unstructured play requires way too much regulation for most of our children to handle effectively.

Organize play around common interests!

When looking for peers to develop friendships with, focus on your child's strengths and preferences. Often their selective interests that they are so passionate about (video games, sports statistics, cars, history, etc.) can be topics of interest to other kids. In school we try to build the child's interests into both academics (e.g. write about their favorite action figure) and social curriculum (peer activity around interests). By focusing on their areas of interest, the children shine and feel more competent. It will still be important to provide peer awareness to the other participants about specific behaviors that may seem odd (dominating the conversation, arguing a point, trouble taking turns, etc.) and for an adult to facilitate the play. Usually if the other children also have strong interest in that area, they will appreciate the child's passion and knowledge in that interest.

In school these special interests can allow the child to shine, both to their peers and themselves! Encourage the speech and language pathologist, social worker, or psychologist to use the child's special interest to build objectives into the IEP for developing social skills and facilitating peer play. If possible, keep the group to two or three children to make it easier for the child to handle the interaction. If one is available, have a teacher's assistant facilitate the group, model and guide cooperative participation, and keep notes on what the child is doing well and what needs to be worked on. The assistant can explain any questions the peers have regarding the child's mannerisms and encourage each person to share information about themselves and to highlight their strengths. Accenting the child's strengths and interests not only increases his motivation and self-esteem, but also makes him more attractive to other children. By highlighting the child's strengths, the other kids see him in a strong light!

After school, involve the child in extra-curriculum activities involving his special interests. Kids on the spectrum do better in play that is structured and well organized. They do best when socializing around a specific topic or activity. The topic or activity (video games, art, games, models, etc.) provides understanding and predictability for what he can expect to happen, what is expected of him, and a topic to relate around. Try to find outside activities around the child's favorite topic of interest. Clubs and organized activities provide adult supervision to facilitate structured play. They often have predictable schedules of events and common rules and expectations that become familiar and predictable for the child. They are also easy to preview ahead of time and to review afterwards. During these activities, the special interest or topic provides concrete avenues for the children to talk about and relate around. This is much easier for the children to regulate. A great organization for kids on the spectrum is Boy or Girl Scouts. Many kids join local troops or troops for children with special needs. They have organized meetings, work on very concrete and organized projects, have a predictable code of ethics, and have strong visual rewards (badges) the children can earn for all completed projects.

In addition, clubs and organized groups centered on common interests, provide the child with exposure to peers of similar interests he can invite to come over for individual play dates. He can strike up potential friendships that can extend away from the group activity. Also, parents can connect with other parents to organize and facilitate play dates. It works nicely when the child develops "safe" friends that he can both socialize with in these group activities and connect with outside the group. Other possibilities are church groups and activities put on by your local autism support groups. Many local recreational programs have inclusion policies, as well as adaptive recreational programs. In addition, many community education programs and private fine arts programs have become more user-friendly for children on the spectrum.

Supporting children in community (social) activities

Many of the children have had negative experiences engaging in community activities (social groups, clubs, sports, dance, scouting, etc.). Often their behavior is too unacceptable, they are teased or bullied, or they simply are lost in not understanding what is expected. Consequently, out of frustration, protection, or embarrassment, parents stop encouraging community (social) engagement. Although this is totally understandable, the children miss out on valuable social/ emotional learning experiences.

Many community activities fail because we put the children in situations that are way over their head. If the children do not understand the unwritten social rules, do not know what to expect or what is expected of them, or cannot display the needed skills to participate appropriately, they often engage in disruptive behavior that leads them to being rejected, teased, or bullied. Like any activity, we need to make sure that the demands of the setting do not outweigh the child's current abilities to handle them. Most likely, if the child is acting out, then the demands (social, cognitive, sensory, and physical) are greater than the child's current ability to handle them. Consequently we need to either (1) lower the demands (modify and simply the activity) and/or (2) build in greater assistance (facilitation) to help support the child in that given situation.

Most children on the spectrum are not going to fare well being thrown into a dynamic social activity with typical peers. The complexity of the unwritten social rules, dynamic reciprocal interaction, and coordinated roles will be way too sophisticated for their abilities. When such inclusion is going to take place, you need to know what the children's comfort zones are and their current abilities to co-regulate cooperative interaction with others. Usually it is best to either have an adult facilitator overseeing the activity and coaching both the child on the spectrum and the other children and/or elicit the use of one or more peer mentors who are recruited to coach the child during the activity. To help make such activity successful, it is good for the parents to do the following:

1. Visit the activity ahead of time to observe and note the general routine, the expectations for the child, the unwritten social rules, and what challenges may be anticipated. What are the common interaction patterns between the children? What are the physical/behavior demands of the activity? What skills does my child need to know? Who is leading or facilitating the activity? What sensory, cognitive, and social demands will my child experience?

2. Next, talk to the person who is leading, coaching, or facilitating the activity. Let them know your child's current skill level, his vulnerabilities, and the conditions your child needs to feel safe, accepted, and competent. Find out from this person what accommodations can be made to ease the adjustment, lessen the stressors, and support engagement. Also let the adult leader know what cues your child shows when getting overwhelmed, and how to best support your child during these times. If needed, offer to assist the leader in the activity to help support your child and facilitate successful engagement.

3. If possible, ask the leader if any of the children can be encouraged to be a peer mentor—someone who can help coach the child in appropriate engagement, facilitate interactions with others, coach the other kids in how to support your child, and protect them from teasing and bullying. If not, maybe a sibling or friend can also attend with the child to provide support during the activity and be a mentor and model for the child.

4. Make sure you prepare your child ahead of time. Before the event, talk about what the child can expect, what is expected of him, how long it will last, and what to do if he becomes overwhelmed. If possible, ask the leader what the sequence of activities will be in the next session, so you can anticipate what the child will need and prepare him ahead of time. This gives you a chance to anticipate what he may struggle with, and help him role-play and practice cooperative interaction. It gives you a chance to think about what guidance you will also want to give the leader or peer mentor in how to support your child during the activity.

5. If possible, have the child visit the activity simply as an observer, so he can see what it is going to be like before being expected to participate in the group. This may take one or more visits to accomplish. If you think

this is too big a step, ask the group if you can take some pictures or video so that you can start the exposure at home.

6. Make a small picture book of the activity, with a picture of the leader and pictures of the events in the sequence of activities. This way, you can review it through the week and each time prior to going. Again, some people make short videos of the child doing well in the event and replay them frequently between sessions. This helps to ingrain episodic memories of being successful.

7. If the child cannot handle ongoing participation in the activity, start small and gradually increase the exposure. Allow him to participate for short periods of time and then let him sit out along the side with you until he rebounds. Let him regroup and then try again for another short period. Gradually stretch his comfort zone while feeling safe doing it. Stay patient and supportive. Make sure you have an easy escape in case you have to quickly exit the event. I recommend discussing with the child what he can do if he starts to feel overwhelmed and reviewing this frequently so that he can feel safe in knowing that he can "escape" when needed.

8. If your child has some coping tools (fidget toys, sensory items, etc.) that he uses to stay calm during events, then encourage him to use them during the activity to handle his anxiety. We want to give him (1) what to do during the activity when he feels a little anxious and (2) how to escape and rebound when feeling overwhelmed. The best way to lower anxiety is for the child to know what to do when anxious. This avoids the anxiety of worrying about becoming overwhelmed.

9. Observe the activity as much as possible and make notes of what is working well and what skills your child needs to learn (sharing, taking turns, initiating conversation, joining in, etc.). Have one or two objectives that you are working on so you stay focused on teaching the social skills that your child will need to successfully engage. Following each event, review how it went, what good things happened and what challenges occurred, and brainstorm ways of dealing with the challenges.

10. Framing these community events by collaborating with the leaders, facilitating peer supports, simplifying the demands, and previewing, practicing, and preparing the child will help make community inclusion more successful.

Not all activity needs to be with neurotypical children. Many sporting events are too dynamic for children on the spectrum to successfully regulate. Fast-paced team sports that require processing multiple information simultaneously may be too difficult to handle. However, special needs adaptive sports can provide the same quality experience, but with lesser demands and greater accommodations. Local autism support groups should have a high priority on developing clubs, sports, scouts, and other social/community activities for children on the spectrum to safely participate together. If the family or child does not yet feel safe engaging in typical community inclusion, then develop special needs activities. During these activities recruit peer mentors to engage with the children and help regulate the activity. Local support groups should be setting up activities such as sports, dance, scouting, social skills groups, and bowling for the children, and working with local community recreational programs to offer such activities for their children.

Always remember, in encouraging such activity, start within the child's current comfort zone and slowly stretch participation, while you map out the challenges and strategies for helping your child successfully participate. Do not force children into activities that are too demanding for them. Let them pace themselves as they begin to feel more and more competent engaging with others. Always be aware of and respect their vulnerabilities and preferences, and always validate the anxiety they may feel. Yes, we may need to nudge them along a little with guided participation and proactive support, but do not force participation in overwhelming situations.

Keep it fun, keep it simple, and maximize success.

Part V

THE EMOTIONAL WORLD ON THE SPECTRUM

Chapter 12

IDENTIFYING, LABELING AND CONTROLLING EMOTIONS

It is not news to parents and teachers that many children on the spectrum have a very difficult time controlling their emotional reactions. They often overreact to minor snags, have difficulty regrouping once upset, or show no emotional reaction at all. Many people on the spectrum report being scared of their emotions. They often come on without warning, with little reason, and hit like a tidal wave. The children can have a hard time identifying and labeling their emotions, so they often interpret them as threatening. When emotions occur, the person does not feel in control of them and hence feels very vulnerable when they occur. Consequently, the child can feel very anxious in anticipation of emotions and panic once they start to occur. Since the child's explosive reactions usually upset others, he subsequently fears experiencing emotions. This chapter will look at helping the child identify, label, and control his emotions.

Teaching children to identify and label emotions

Many children on the spectrum have difficulty identifying and labeling their emotions. Consequently, the children have difficulty understanding them, often fear them, and feel helpless in controlling them. When you cannot label your emotions, you have difficulty appraising the nature and intensity of them. Many children on the spectrum overexaggerate the threat of their emotions, and therefore panic and overreact. So learning to control emotions must first start with adequately labeling them.

Before children can learn to control their emotions they first have to learn how to (1) identify and label their emotions, (2) connect them to external events that produce them, and (3) be able to judge the intensity of the emotions.

Begin by helping your child learn to identify and label the four basic emotions: happy, sad, angry (mad), and scared. I also add "calm," since it is an emotional state that I use frequently when teaching emotional regulation. When teaching emotions, try to use common daily experiences to spotlight these emotions. Identify and label all emotions you observe in your child, yourself, and others. Spotlight and label emotions wherever and whenever you get a chance.

1. Verbally label out loud your own emotions: "I feel sad that my friend Sharon moved. I will miss her."

2. Spotlight and label the emotions you see in others: "I think that man feels angry because he dropped his groceries!"

3. Label the emotions you see in your child: "Johnny, you look really happy eating your favorite ice cream."

Try to stick with the four or five basic emotions until they are learned. Instead of saying "frustrated," say "angry": instead of saying "depressed," say "sad." Keep with just the basic emotions. Otherwise, we confuse the child. Once the child gets good at identifying these emotions, you can slowly add others. Children often do well using visual "emotion faces" (picture chart) to help identify the basic emotions. Figure 12.1 provides an example of an emotion chart. You can purchase these charts commercially or download emotion pictures online. Once the child can connect the basic emotions, start having him identify and label them himself.

| Happy | Sad | Angry | Scared |

Figure 12.1 Emotion chart

It can be fun to use mood charts to talk about how you are feeling. Most young children start with the basic four-mood chart. Parents and teachers use the chart to help the children rate how they are feeling. Over time, we have them talk about how the emotion feels and when they usually feel it. We talk about how their body feels and, as they get older, how they are thinking at the time (connecting their thoughts to their emotions). These charts can be small and portable so adults can carry them around to use them in a variety of settings. Pair labeling how you feel with pointing to the appropriate face. Appendix D provides a similar feelings chart, which is also available to download from www.jkp.com/catalogue/book/9781849059947/resources.

1. Use the basic emotion chart in the morning, afternoon, and evening and have your child identify and label how he is currently feeling. Also talk about how that emotion feels and connect the event that is contributing to the feeling, so the child knows why he is feeling that way (what events are connected with that feeling).

2. Once you feel that the child is beginning to label emotions, pause and let him identify the feeling. When you and your child see others displaying emotion, instead of identifying the emotions for him, see if he can figure it out: "I wonder how that man is feeling because he dropped his groceries." If he does not reply, say, "I wonder if he is happy, sad, angry, or scared?" If he is young, only give two choices. Once the emotion is identified, talk about what events and behavior led you to that conclusion.

3. When watching television or videos, pause the show and talk about the emotions you think the actors are feeling, and connect the emotion to their actions. Again, allow the child to identify if the person is happy, sad, angry, or scared.

4. Look at pictures in magazines and talk about the emotions the people are expressing.

Feelings inventory

Once the child can accurately label the basic emotions, start making a "feelings" inventory, listing what common events usually elicit the given emotions. This helps the child learn how to connect his emotions to external events and build associative memories to categorize emotions with events. Figure 12.2 provides an example of a feelings inventory.

"Feelings" inventory

Happy
Eating ice cream.
Playing with Game Boy.

Sad
Kids teasing me.
Jimmy going away to college.

Angry
Julie playing with my Game Boy.
Telling me no when I want something.

Scared
Trying something new.
Going to the dentist.

Figure 12.2 Feelings inventory

Once the child can label the four basic emotions, then tie them to external events that elicit the emotions. Again it helps if you get used to thinking out loud. As with labeling emotions, now you label the emotion and immediately connect it to the event that is eliciting the emotion. "Mommy is angry because the eggs fell on the floor." The same basic situations apply: (1) label and connect your emotional reactions, (2) label and connect emotions you see in others, and (3) label and connect the emotions you see in your child. "You look sad. It can be sad when you lose something you really like." Appendix D provides a feelings inventory chart.

Four steps to identify emotions!

For children on the spectrum, emotions can come on suddenly with little warning. The children often cannot identify the emotion or connect it to the event triggering the emotion. The same time we are teaching the children to label the emotion, it is important that we also help them connect the emotion to a specific event. It then becomes easier to teach the child that the emotion is fleeting and short-lived; it will come and go as the event causing it subsides. Often, under intense emotion children panic and do not understand why they are feeling that way, that it will not last long, and that they will be safe while experiencing it. Try using these four easy steps to identifying emotions:

1. *Label.* Label the child's emotion: "Johnny, you look scared!"

2. *Connect.* Connect the emotion to the event: "Maybe you are scared because bowling is new for you."

3. *Validate.* Validate that the feeling is OK: "It is OK to feel scared when you are trying something new!"

4. *Reassure.* "Let me help you. Once we do it together, it will become familiar and less scary."

When this approach is used, we are (1) identifying and labeling the emotion for the child, (2) connecting it to the event causing it, (3) validating that it is natural to feel the emotion, and then (4) reassuring and supporting the child through the emotion.

You can help teach the child to read emotions by playing simple games involving guessing the emotions. Play charades where the two of you take turns guessing the emotion that the other is demonstrating. My favorite is making feeling faces in front of a mirror. There are also many commercial board and card games around for labeling and expressing emotions.

Once the child can accurately label the emotions, also talk about what the people are thinking and doing. Eventually, you want them to connect their emotions with their thoughts and actions. This will come later.

Teaching degrees of emotions

As the child becomes more competent in labeling the basic emotions, start working on rating the intensity of the emotions. Kids on the spectrum are often absolute—very black and white, all or nothing. They either feel happy or unhappy, with no degrees in between. They are happy or mad, and usually at high intensity. The concept of relativity is very difficult for them to understand. Their absolute, black and white thinking affects their emotional overreacting to relatively minor snags. They live in a world of extremes. Teaching them to rate the intensity of their emotion helps them to (1) more accurately appraise the intensity of the emotion, (2) more adequately appraise the threat of the emotion, and (3) eventually choose what coping skill to master the emotion. Once they learn these three functions, their anxiety level decreases and their panic reaction subsides.

The teaching of intensity starts off with only two degrees: "little bit" and "a lot"—I am either a "little bit" happy or "a lot" happy! This starts where they are at with the two extremes. Then once they get used to doing that, we add a middle step: "little bit, somewhat (or so-so), or a lot." As the child gets older, we add even more degrees, like the five-point scale below to rate his emotions. The child gets used to labeling his emotions by the number he rates them by. As parents identify and label emotions throughout the day, they are attaching a numerical rating to them. *The Incredible 5-Point Scale* has become a popular tool introduced by Kari Dunn Buron and Mitzi Curtis (2012) Using a portable five-point scale can be a great visual reference tool when practicing emotional rating. Figure 12.3 provides an example of an emotions rating scale, Appendix D also provides a copy of this emotions rating chart.

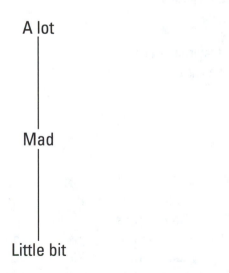

Figure 12.3 Emotions rating scales

Rating common events: feelings inventory

Making a "feelings (emotions) inventory" helps the child associate daily events with the intensity of emotion. The parents and child identify what events the child commonly experiences in his daily routine. This helps give him concrete reference points to associate with each level of intensity: "Feeling #4 (angry) is like what I feel when my sister takes my toys." This way he associates intensity with concrete daily events. He keeps a journal, adding more and more events into each numerical category. This also gives the parent/teacher a tool to help the child stay regulated. When a snag happens unexpectedly, the adult helps the child accurately appraise the intensity of emotion (or threat). So the adult may say, "I bet that is a level 3," for events that might automatically create a panic attack, helping the child realize it is not that big a deal. Sit down after an episode of emotion and re-evaluate how realistic the initial appraisal was. Then add it to the list to review and preview. Figure 12.4 shows a five-point emotions rating inventory. (Appendix D provides a blank rating inventory.)

5	Furious	Other kids bullying me. Breaking something.
4	Angry	Sister taking my toys. Computer freezing up.
3	Upset	Activity cancelled. Task that is difficult.
2	Irritated	Too much noisy activity. Having to wait.
1	Annoyed	Others interrupting me. Having to share with sister.

Figure 12.4 Emotions rating inventory

Adding ways to cope

Lastly, the chart expands out to include coping skills for each level of intensity. This teaches the children *how* they should behaviorally respond to the appraisal. The parent/teacher and child sit down and develop coping skills for mastering each level of intensity. It can also be fun to list these common daily stressors on index cards, with the intensity rating and coping skills on the back. Then each day the parent and child choose a couple of cards to role-play and practice. They can take turns demonstrating the emotion, rating its intensity, and practicing the coping skills for that level. The child gradually becomes competent labeling, appraising, and coping with their emotions. At this point the child's general anxiety level decreases, and his panic fight-or-flight reactions subside. The child begins to cognitively appraise the emotion and behaviorally master it. Figure 12.5 adds the column for which coping skills to use when dealing with each level of emotion. (Appendix D provides a blank coping skills chart.)

5	Furious	Other kids bullying me. Breaking something.	Walk away. Get help quickly!
4	Angry	Sister taking my toys. Computer freezing up.	Take a break. Ask for help.
3	Upset	Activity cancelled. Task that is difficult.	Deep breath, count to ten. Ask for help.
2	Irritated	Too much noisy activity. Having to wait.	Deep breath. Positive self-talk.
1	Annoyed	Others interrupting me. Having to share with sister.	Positive self-talk. "I can handle this!"

Figure 12.5 Emotions rating scale with coping skills

Emotions are scary!

The emotional world on the spectrum can be very scary! Emotions are often all or nothing, either turned-off or coming on like a freight train! When emotions hit, they often hit hard, going from 0 to 100 fast, with little warning. Since the children often cannot identify and associate with these emotions, they frequently report that they feel detached from their emotions. The emotions come on without warning and are difficult to label and connect to a cause, which leaves the person unable to control them. Like sensory overload, these emotions can overwhelm the children and leave them feeling totally helpless and in a panic! You cannot control that which you cannot define, label, and understand. The panic sets off the "fight, flight, or freeze" response, igniting outward acting-out or withdrawal and shutdown. Over time, any emotion sets off a panic reaction or fear of being overwhelmed and out of control. Then the least little snag can set off a panic reaction.

This is why it is important to help the children feel safe and accepted at times of heated emotion. They need to feel that those close to them understand the turmoil. We need to communicate understanding and acceptance at a time when the child is flooded with emotion. Offer assistance but do not pressure them to accept it. Communicate that you are there to keep everyone safe and minimize other interaction unless invited by the child. Some children will let you soothe them if the procedure is rehearsed ahead of time. However, often the children want to be left alone, because any outside support is too overwhelming. During these times we need to tone the world down, lessen all stimulation, and remove all demands. Don't fuel the fire! Take away the oxygen, and the fire will subside. What the child needs to realize is that the emotion will go away! It will not last long. He is safe with you, and together you will ride the tide until it is gone. If the child fears the reactions of others, then he will panic under emotion.

Don't hide or disguise it! Spotlight and feel it!

Most of the time we want to intervene early when our children start to get upset. We try to interrupt and protect them from stress so they will not get anxious and/or melt down. This is understandable. No parent likes to see their child suffer during times of emotion. For children on the spectrum, because they have difficulty identifying, labeling, and controlling their emotions, feeling emotion can be scary and cause panic. Any intense feeling can bring on panic, and trigger their fight-or-flight response. Since they feel vulnerable and helpless with their feelings, just a small amount of anxiety can set off panic. They do not know the difference between feeling a little bit anxious and intense anxiety. Once they start to feel emotion, they panic, which escalates the intensity. Consequently, parents want to shield the child from this panic, and often try to disguise, redirect, and ignore the emotion.

However, the children need to experience the feeling of being upset—that it is OK, will not last long—and to feel what it is like to master the emotion. I tell parents to first teach the child that he is safe and secure with you during times of emotion. Don't try to shield or avoid the emotion; let him safely feel it. Instead of quickly "fixing" the situation, help the child feel the emotion, reassure him that he is safe, and then help him identify and label the emotion. Let him safely experience the feeling with your support. Once you see the emotion coming, spotlight the emotion ("Wow…that is scary!") and tie it to the external event: "I bet having that bug land on you was scary!" Then guide him through it so he feels himself master the conflict (emotion) with your guidance. The children cannot learn to regulate their emotions and realize it is OK to feel anxious or scared until they safely feel themselves master the emotion. They need to feel the uneasiness to feel the mastery. You want them to feel competent in the face of emotion. So don't avoid it—spotlight it. Don't try to distract and hide it. Afterwards, it is good to review what happened, and how it was initially scary, but how "we" tackled it OK. The children learn to trust following your lead, to first face their emotions and then identify, label, and tackle their emotions. This cannot happen unless we slow down, and let them "safely" experience the emotion. By providing safe, repeated experiences of feeling and mastering emotional situations, the children learn to feel competent facing their emotions.

Kids also do not realize that emotions are fleeting: they come and go quickly, and will not last long. Children live in the moment, and feel that it will last for ever! It is important that we spotlight (1) what the emotion is, (2) the connection to the external event, and (3) that it will not last long. It is easier to ride the tide when you know it will not last long. Recognize and identify the emotion for the child, reassure him you will keep him safe, and then let him experience himself master it. With guided participation, help him master the anxiety. Once it ends and the child calms, then review the event and let him put words to the experience. Emphasize how we have feelings attached to almost all experiences; that they are sometimes strong, but do not last long. Spotlight how the child mastered the emotion and successfully handled the conflict.

Now, some children in the middle of the storm (meltdown) are too upset to have anyone try to calm them. They need everyone to back off, avoid talking, and allow them to calm on their own. For these children, you want to use these strategies during the build-up phase of emotional turmoil, before the volcano erupts. Even after a meltdown, once everyone is calm, it may be helpful to go back and talk through the events, identify the emotions, and discuss how tehy safely tackled the emotions. This way, the children eventually learn to feel safe with emotions, making it easier to face them.

Emotional regulation: teaching children to master their emotions

I am sure that 90 percent of parents on the Facebook page have experienced emotional regulation problems. For most children on the spectrum, emotional experiences can be very unpredictable, overwhelming, and scary. Whether it is happiness, frustration, fear, or anger, their emotional reactions can be unpredictable, either under-responsive (showing minimal emotion at all) or overreactive (blowing it out of proportion). They can be emotionally flat one moment, with frequent mood swings the next. Learning to regulate your emotions requires strong impulse control, the ability to understand and label the emotions, and the ability to match the correct emotion at the right intensity to the present situation.

We are not born with good regulation. Infants rely on their parents to regulate their emotional and physical needs. Research shows that it is through the infants' dependency on his parents to meet his physical needs as well as regulate his emotions that he eventually learns to regulate his own emotional responses. The world is very chaotic, scary, and frustrating for the young, fragile nervous system. Young children are totally helpless and dependent upon the loving hands of the caregiver to soothe and regulate their physical and emotional needs. The parent holds, rocks, feeds, and regulates all the child's basic needs. This consistent external regulation eventually becomes internalized through the loving guidance of the caregivers. Through the guided participation of the parents, the child gradually learns to regulate his own needs and emotions.

Unfortunately, many children on the spectrum have difficulty giving up control and allowing others to regulate them. Because of strong sensory sensitivities and their fear of novelty and uncertainty, they often do not seek out the support and regulation of others. They may actively resist the attempts of others to help soothe them. This leaves them going at it alone in the midst of the emotional storm. Emotions become something to fear and escape in panic. Without this external soothing, they have a hard time feeling what it is like to be regulated in times of stress. This establishes a strong sense of vulnerability and terror in the face of emotion. Since they do not learn to feel safe in allowing others to regulate them during emotions, they struggle to learn effective emotional self-regulation.

For such children, it is important to become a source of soothing and support during times of distress, to teach the children to trust following your lead during times of vulnerability. This is not an easy task to do, but a fundamentally pivotal point in relating with others. We need to teach the children to socially reference us for safety and security, to trust following our lead in helping them master their emotions. Once the children feel comfortable trusting our guidance during times of stress, then teaching self-regulation can occur through the coaching of the mentor (adult). By supporting and guiding the children during times of stress, we can teach them not to fear their anxiety, but to feel competent tackling the anxiety. This is not an easy task. Some children actively resist the help of others. It takes time and patience to make this work.

How to help

In times of stress, intervene early before the child becomes too overwhelmed to follow your lead. Stay calm, kneel down to his level, and gain his attention. Stop the action, acknowledge and validate how he appears (angry, frustrated, etc.), then lead him in a calming routine (deep breathing, counting, deep pressure, etc.). It is best to practice the routine when calm so the child will feel comfortable following your lead during times of stress. Stay supportive, validate his feelings, and reassure him that he is safe. Do the calming routine with him, modeling and pacing his actions. If needed, briefly lead the child away from the source of stress to a quieter area to use the coping skills to calm. Do them together and praise cooperation. Continue to validate, reassure, and attempt to use the coping skill until the child calms down. Once calm, talk about what upset him, build in extra support, and then briefly return to the event to try to master the problem. Returning to the event, if possible, is important for two reasons: (1) so that the child does not learn that he can escape all stressful situations by acting out and (2) to allow the child to see that he can get anxious, learn to master the uncertainty, and conquer the fear. However, never force returning to the event if the child is actively resistant. Slow it down, talk him through it, stay right with him, and tackle it together.

If the child refuses to follow your lead, then simply stay nearby and reassure him he is safe, while letting him work his way through the emotion. This is often common if we do not catch the child early enough to intervene when he is more responsive. Continue to work on practicing calming routines when the child is calm, and role-play situations that commonly upset him. It also may be beneficial to reward the child for allowing you to assist him in using the coping skills when upset. Keep with it; eventually he will begin to feel safe in allowing your assistance.

Steps to helping your child master his emotions!

1. Identify and practice a calming routine together.

2. When upset, intervene early in the behavior chain.

    a. Recognize early signs of agitation.

    b. The longer you wait, the harder it gets.

3. Get the child's attention.

    a. Stop the action.

    b. Get face to face, eye level. Not in their face, just at face level.

4. Support to calm.

    a. Verbalize what you see: "Wow, you really look angry to me."

    b. Use gesture and verbal prompt, "Calm down."

    c. "Take a deep breath;" do it together.

5. Engage the child in a calming routine.

    a. Lead the child in a calming routine (deep breathing, positive statements, deep pressure, etc.).

    b. Do it together, guiding the child.

6. Stay calm.

    a. If needed, move to a quieter area.

    b. If needed, restrict the child's space and movement until he is calm.

7. Return to the problem/challenge.

    a. If possible, return to the problem.

    b. Slow it down and work through it together.

    c. Help the child to master the problem.

Calming strategies

There are a variety of self-calming tools that people can use to calm and regulate themselves. Every child is different and we each have our own calming strategies. Help your child practice several strategies. Over time he will learn to rely on two or three techniques. At first, the child will not be able to calm on his own. It is important to find some calming strategies that you can do with your child; doing them together will allow you to guide the child through the strategies. Over time, by following your lead, the child will eventually begin to use self-calming strategies. Before trying these strategies when upset in the heat of the moment, practice them when the child is calm.

Calming strategies with your assistance

- Deep pressure massage.
- Neutral warmth deep pressure wrap.
- Rocking together.
- Singing, chatting, nursery rhythms together.
- Clapping hands to music.
- Dancing together.
- Sensory motor interaction patterns.
- Deep breathing together.
- Deep pressure palm squeezes.
- Chanting positive self-calming statements.
- Bouncing on trampoline, rhythmic movement.

Each child has his own unique sensory channels that you can often use to calm and soothe him. That may include counting or saying the ABCs if these are special interests of your child, singing nursery rhythms, reading quietly together, applying calming sensory input, or simply sitting quietly together. Rhythmic, repetitive patterns built around the child's sensory preferences can often be successfully used to calm him. As the child becomes older and more capable of regulating himself, then self-calming strategies are developed.

Self-calming strategies

- Physical outlets for energy release: jumping on trampoline, playing drums, riding exercise bike, pushing/carrying, swinging, working out, most physical activity.

- Self-stimulation: fidget items, chewing gum, deep pressure palm squeezes, humming, repetitive hand movements, etc.

- Relaxing techniques: deep breathing, slow rocking, muscle relaxation, meditating, solitude, sleeping, calming self-stimulation.

- Organizing thoughts: writing in journal, diary, feelings book, problem-solving sheets, self-calming statements.

- Favorite activity: listening to music, reading, drawing, focus on topic of interest.

Practice calming routines

Before attempting the coping skills in the heat of the moment, teach and practice them when calm. Role-play and practice the strategies together.

1. Determine a calming routine: deep breathing, positive statements, deep pressure, simple rhythmic movement, etc.

2. Practice the routine. Practice the routine when calm. Role-play it over and over.

3. Do it together using guided participation.

4. Develop a "social story" using it.

5. Start simple; build gradually.

6. Make a hierarchy of low- to high-anxiety provoking events. Start with mild conflicts.

7. Tackle them together!

It is very important to practice the coping strategies when calm, before coaching the child to use them when upset. It is hard to teach new learning when someone is upset. Make a list of common situations that cause stress for the child, and write them on index cards. Every day pick a couple of examples to role-play and practice using the calming skills. Do them together, have fun, and practice, practice, and practice. Next, make a list of least to most anxiety-provoking events for the child. Make a list of low-level frustrating events, moderate-level, and high-level stressors. Start with the mild events and coach the child in using the coping strategy to tackle the anxiety. Do them together, focusing on the successful mastery of the event. Once the child is successful at mastering the lower-level stressors, then move up to the moderate level. Do not attempt the high-level stressors until the child feels competent using the skills for the moderate level.

Using calming routines in the heat of the moment

Before tackling situations that provoke anxiety, preview how to use the coping skills in that situation. Then enter the situation and help guide the child through it, using the coping skills as needed. Once the event ends, sit down together and review how it went, focusing on how he handled it!

1. Preview and review.

    a. Preview the coping strategy before going into the event.

    b. Review how it went after the event.

2. Tackle it together.

    a. Look for times to use the routines. You might also create little situations of stress to spotlight and practice the strategies.

    b. Use them yourself to model for the child: "Wow, I am little scared— 'calm down,' deep breath."

    c. Do it together, talk it through while modeling.

3. Celebrate mastery.

    a. Celebrate mastering it together! "We did it!" "We rock!"

    b. Review it later; use competency book (journal, picture book) to log the experiences.

Be on the lookout for situations that may cause stress for your child. Prepare the child by previewing what to do (use a coping skill) if he starts to get upset during the event. Talk about what he can expect, and what will be expected of him. Talk about any anticipated problems, and practice how he (and you) can handle them if problems occur. This way, in the midst of the event he will already be prepared for you to coach him in the calming strategy, if the need arises. After the event, review how it went! If there were problems and you two tackled them together, review it and celebrate how you mastered it.

An additional tool is for you to model using the same coping skills when under stress. The child first gets to see how you successfully use the strategies for daily stress. Either create situations of stress for yourself, or use them when stress occurs naturally. During these events highlight the emotion and model the coping. Think out loud while you label your emotion, take a deep breath, reassure yourself, and model the coping strategy. By thinking out loud you enable your child to share the experience of what you are feeling, know that you are safe, and watch you successfully tackle the emotion.

Common elements in handling intense emotion!

During emotional overload the child is often overwhelmed, feeling very vulnerable, and entering in the fight-or-flight panic mode. Although every child is different, there are some common elements to consider when helping your child through these intense emotions.

1. Each child is different; however, it is important to help them feel safe and accepted during the emotion (even if we do not like the behavior). Our goal is to acknowledge that they are overwhelmed, reassure them that they are safe, and validate that they are accepted. We do not have to accept their behavior (especially aggression or property destruction), but we can validate the feelings behind it. At the time when they are overwhelmed with emotion, their cognitive coping skills collapse and they feel very scared and vulnerable.

2. Usually, showing little emotional reaction and keeping verbal interaction to a minimum is best during high emotions. When our emotions also escalate, it almost always fuels the fire. Also, for most children their communication skills often collapse during the escalation, both receptively (understanding what you are saying) and expressively (talking about their feelings). Do not expect them to reason with you at these times. Say very little and do not ask them a lot of questions. They cannot process, and reasoning just further taxes their mental energy. Many children may find repetitive, rhythmic chants or simple songs soothing. Often a familiar sing-song chant can help calm. Otherwise reassure the child he is safe and try not to say much at all.

3. Remove all task demands and requests for action. When they are in panic, fight-or-flight mode, they cannot focus or reason through any demands.

They need to back off and rebound. We need to reduce the stimulation and cognitive demands on them. If they need to follow through with something, wait until they calm down, then go back to it. Lower the demands, as well as the stimulation. Some children need to totally leave the situation to isolate themselves until the fury calms down.

4. Respect the child's comfort zone. Some children may need to be by themselves with minimal interaction; others welcome support in soothing. It is extremely important to know what their comfort zone is. Some children will withdraw and shut down, wanting little interaction. Some children will seek out and calm to deep pressure stimulation (holding, squeezing, messaging, rocking, etc.); some want you nearby but not touching or talking. Some will calm to repeating the ABCs or chanting their favorite nursery rhyme. Often slow, rhythmic patterns (rocking, singing, chanting, etc.) can soothe the nervous system. Also know what *not* to do. Know your child's comfort zones and respect them.

5. Have a plan! Whatever little strategies seem to work, use them every time. Develop a calming routine. Sameness represents familiarity, which represents predictability. There is security in predictability. It helps calm the fury. Uncertainty and unpredictability will fuel the fire. At the time, when they are overwhelmed by emotion, they need familiarity and predictability. It helps them feel safe and secure, even during times of chaos.

Reactive vs. receptive state of mind

Daniel Siegel (2012), in his book *The Whole-Brain Child*, describes how when the children are on guard, defensive, or angry, they are in a reactive state of mind. They interpret everything negatively and are not receptive to the positive. In the heat of the moment, it is not time to rationalize, scold, or counsel the children. They are too reactive (emotional) to look at things rationally. They are operating from their emotional brain, not their thinking, reasoning brain. Some children are in the "on guard," reactive state of mind most of the time. Because of either biological makeup or past experiences, they do not feel safe, are on high alert, and are always looking for the negative. They walk through life with filtered glasses on, looking for and interpreting things in a negative light. Usually these children have poor self-esteem and tend to look for negative intent from others.

I see this a lot in children with autism. Not necessary the negativism (although in some yes), but being emotionally reactive and less often in a receptive state of mind. Children on the spectrum will often freak when things don't go according to their expectations, and view every little change as a threat to their existence. Uncertainty drives them nuts. They need predictability and have to control everything they do to maintain that predictability. They are on guard and anxious, and panic quickly when things don't go according to plan. They are quick to react from the emotional part of their brain, with little mediation from the thinking brain. Research has shown that individuals on the spectrum have a higher level of stress (anxiety) chemicals in their nervous system, even during a resting state. These high levels of stress chemicals leave the nervous system on high alert for threat! When they are hyper-vigilant for threat, these children are going to be looking for the negative and be prepared to react quickly to stay safe (reactive state of mind). They are going to react quickly and intensively, often overreacting to the conflict.

This hyper-reactive state is natural given their sensory, social, and social processing difficulties. Between sensory bombardment and overload that leaves their nervous system vulnerable to insult, and the constant difficulties understanding and regulating with others, their nervous system is on high alert and ready to react, to stay safe. This hyper-alertness is an instinctual mechanism in the brain to be on guard when possible threat is near. The brain is ready to "fight or flee" at any moment. When the possibly of sensory insult and social discourse is frequently present, the nervous system becomes conditioned to be in a reactive mode most of the time.

What to do

- Know your child's state of mind. Know what state of mind (brain) your child is operating from. What is he like when receptive and what is he like when reactive? When he is in a defensive, reactive state, then it is not the time to command and demand. It is only going to push his panic button. It is not the time to tell him "what and why" because he is not receptive to listening. Listen to his perspective, and validate his feelings, before trying to negotiate. Try not to reason verbally with him, or convince him that he is wrong or should do things differently. Wait until the child is calm and in a receptive state to collaborate.

- A good portion of angry outbursts from children occur when adults ignore this principle and try to demand and direct, scold, or counsel the child when he is in emotional turmoil. As Dr. Ross Greene, author of *The Explosive Child*, explains, most problems don't come from a rigid and inflexible child alone, but when a rigid/inflexible child meets a rigid/inflexible adult. We have to be the flexible one to bring the child to a flexible (receptive) state.

- It is important to help the child feel safe, accepted, and competent throughout the day, so his nervous system is less defensive and more receptive. Help the child obtain a receptive state of mind, and keep him there. Understand and respect the child's comfort zones, and help him feel competent stretching these comfort zones.

- In the heat of the moment, when emotions are flying, respond to the feelings first, then the behavior. When the child is upset or emotional, do not try to scold, counsel, demand, or teach. As we have discussed before, acknowledge and validate the feelings behind the behavior first before dealing with the behavior. You don't have to agree with the behavior, just validate the feelings behind it. Once the emotion subsides, then collaborate. Of course, if the behavior is dangerous, you have to block and interrupt the behavior, but then focus on tackling the feelings, before discussing how to deal with the behavior. The child is not in a receptive state for cognitively reasoning what he should have done, or how bad he is.

- The first steps of intervention should be to protect first (interrupt and protect), then help the child feel safe. Once you acknowledge and validate his feelings, then reassure him that he is safe. Only when he is calm and receptive can you bring in the thinking part of his brain!

- How do we move the child from "reactive" to "receptive?" First, attune yourself to where the child is at in the moment. He is acting from his emotional brain, so we need to attune to this state in whatever helps to soothe him. It may be deep pressure touch, soft singing, rocking together, giving him a favorite stuffed animal, or simply leaving him alone until the emotions subside. Attune yourself with where he is at, and only move on once the emotions subside and he feels safe and accepted. When he starts to calm down, and appears more receptive, then you can discuss the episode. For some children this may be 30 minutes later, and for some hours later. Never scold him for being upset. You can discuss his behavior, but always validate how he feels. "I can understand how Johnny taking your toy would make you mad, but you cannot hit him when you're mad. Let's look at what else you can do to get your toy back."

Remember, when you forget and immediately go into your parenting (directive) mode, when you see the child dig in his heels, you are probably ignoring the emotional brain and trying to deal with his thinking brain. Back up and start where he is at.

Regulating young children

Identifying, labeling, and gauging emotions are all fine, but what about the child who is too young or not able to learn these strategies? Many young children do not have either the impulse control or the cognitive abilities to process their emotions. These children cannot sort out their feelings and will only spiral deeper into them until they become overwhelmed. For them, the longer they are focusing on their emotions, the more overwhelmed they become. For these children you may want to try the "interrupt, ignore, and redirect" model. You interrupt the emotion, say little about it, and immediately focus attention on what to do. With this strategy, you want to immediately get the child out of the emotional reactive part of the brain to the thinking/acting part of the brain. In doing this, you stay matter-of-fact, spend little time dwelling on the emotion, and direct the child to do one of a couple of options (coping skills or alternative actions). If possible, it is good to give the child a choice. For example: "Johnnie, I know you are mad because the toy you want is not there. You can either play with toy A or play with toy B. Which one do you want?" Or, if you are working on coping skills: "Johnnie, I know you are upset because the game got cancelled. You can either do deep breathing with me or do our exercises to calm down" (both of which are practiced when calm). Once calm, then you problem-solve together. This type of strategy requires that you stay calm, matter-of-fact, and directive. The child senses that you are calm and in control, and this provides an immediate sense of safety and security. This strategy does the following:

- It immediately directs the child's attention away from the emotion and into an action or making a choice between options. It activates the thinking part of the brain to focus on what to do.

- It immediately directs focus on what to do, which lessens the panic. It provides security from the predictability in knowing what to do. It pulls the child out of the scary feelings of hopelessness and being overwhelmed, and into immediate predictable action before the child becomes too overwhelmed in the emotion.

- By teaching a couple of concrete coping skills (deep breathing, counting, self-talk, physical exercise), this can provide the child with a sense of power over the emotion as he knows what to do immediately upon getting upset. It provides the child with tools for managing the emotions. Usually these coping skills are first taught when calm and then later used in the heat of the moment.

- Most children on the spectrum do better with structure, predictability, and routine. If you teach a couple of routine scripts (coping skills), they can lessen the emotion by activating the routine. When Johnnie starts to get upset, he immediately knows to count to ten and do deep breathing. It provides comfort in routine and predictability, as well as interrupts and distracts the emotion.

As the children mature, we still want to teach them to recognize, label, appraise, and connect their emotions in order to understand and feel safe with them, as well as regulate reactions to these emotions. For example, as the child gets older, he can use the steps above to initially check (inhibit) his emotional reaction to stay calm, then identify and appraise the emotional situation and problem-solve his way to mastering it.

Don't assume "no emotion" when you don't see emotion!

Reading emotional states in others is a struggle for many on the spectrum. Also, expressing emotion can be a struggle for many on the spectrum, at least in the way that neurotypical (NT) people express emotion. The ability to accurately express emotions (external expression of emotion that accurately matches the emotion being experienced) is an ability that fluctuates extensively, even within NT people. Many people appear cold or indifferent when in actuality they feel very deeply. They are just not strong in accurately expressing the emotion, so others often misinterpret how they are truly feeling.

This is very true for many on the spectrum. They often have a "flat affect" expression, meaning they appear not to be emotionally reacting. Their facial expressions and body language do not match the feelings they are experiencing. NT people often misinterpret them as "not caring," cold and indifferent. This can be very irritating for NT people, and very problematic for the person on the spectrum. Social relating is difficult to begin with for them, so when others are interpreting their flat affect as "not caring"—or, worse yet, "not feeling"—then relating becomes even more difficult. People become hurt and angry, and in turn respond back very hurtfully. This happens very frequently among family members, when parents and relatives begin to interpret their loved one as cold, indifferent, and unloving.

So, for family members and others close to people on the spectrum, please do not interpret them as unfeeling and assume you are accurately interpreting their emotional experiences. You must look deeper than their facial expressions and body language and learn their unique expressions of emotion. Emotions are there, often very intensively; however, you may have to further clarify and verify to get an accurate picture. Even with that, many on the spectrum have difficulty verbally reporting their feelings, and may become agitated when others question them about what they are feeling. So, tread lightly and respectfully, and never assume they are not feeling! More than likely they are feeling more intensively than us.

I can feel it, just not understand it!

I see this all the time. Many people on the spectrum, both children and adults, can be very sensitive to the emotional states of others—even to the point of being overwhelmed! Often they feel the emotions around them much more intensively than neurotypical people do. They can be hyper-sensitive to the emotions of others. However, even though they can strongly sense an "emotional aura," they are usually unable to label or identify it. Or some may have a hard time distinguishing between their own emotions and the emotions they feel around them. They just feel overwhelmed by strong emotion. This can be scary for them. To intensively feel it, but not be able to label or understand it, is scary. Many animals have this sensory ability. It is truly a sensory perceptional experience, rather than an intellectual one.

Emotional sensitivity with poor intellectual understanding

In the post above we discussed the strong sensitivity that people on the spectrum often have to the emotions of others. They can *feel* these emotions, but have poor ability to identify, label, and understand them. This sensitivity to the emotional aura of those around them can be overpowering and scary. Many on the spectrum feel it strongly in eye contact and thus are overwhelmed when looking into the eyes of others. They also can feel it in the emotional tones of those interacting around them. Why is this? Why can they be oversensitive, but yet have a poor ability to identify, label, and understand these feelings?

My theory falls back on the "weak connectivity" model of autism. In this model, many of the differences in processing can be explained by the weak neurological connections between the different brain centers, which interfere with the centers being able to communicate simultaneously with one another. This leads to poor brain integration. The right side of the brain is the emotional, intuitive, subjective reasoning part of the brain. The left side is the more factual, logical, intellectual thinking part of the brain. If the two sides are not integrated well, then they tend to operate independently without good ability for the left side to intellectually interpret the experiences of the right side (emotional experiences). When these two sides are integrated well, then the experiences of the right side (emotions) can be easy identified, labeled, evaluated, understood, and controlled. The left side of the brain acts as the "interpreter" and appraises, evaluates, and muffles the impact of this emotional intuitiveness. With many on the spectrum, there is poor left/right brain integration, so the emotional sensitivity cannot be adequately interpreted by the logical part of the brain.

In addition to the poor right/left brain integration, these strong, impulsive emotional reactions are also due to poor neuropathways from the upper, thinking part of the brain (frontal cortex) and the lower, more emotionally reactive part of the brain (limbic system). The frontal cortex is what allows us to check our immediate emotional reactions, inhibit our primitive impulses, and think before we act. When the neuroconnections between the frontal cortex and limbic system are weak, then the child cannot inhibit and tone down his emotional responses. These emotions overwhelm the brain before the thinking brain can control them. This can be very scary. The emotions come on like a tidal wave and overwhelm the child.

Many on the spectrum have a strong fight-or-flight mechanism, which quickly interprets uncertainty with panic. We all have this mechanism, but for people on the spectrum the threshold is lower and the panic reaction sets in faster. Since the strong emotional reactions overwhelm the thinking part of the brain, this uncertainty sets off a panic response and fear sets in. This same response can be set off by strong emotions from others. The emotions of others become very scary, since the left side of the brain cannot quickly interpret the strong emotion. Their left side of the brain is not adequately interpreting intellectually what is happening with their feelings. So they get these strong emotions, but have poor ability to identify, label, connect them with their source, and control them. They feel somewhat detached from their own emotions. It is as if they come on fast and intense, like a tidal wave, yet the child has no control over them. For children on the spectrum, this is very scary and sets off the fight-or-flight panic response. This panic, in turn, weakens their ability to cognitively interpret (identify and label) their emotions even more. So, for these children, both their own emotions and those of others are confusing and scary.

The weak neurological integration between the two sides of the brain also makes it hard for the person to distinguish if they are responsible for the emotions they are feeling. This is why the child will feel upset about the emotional reactions of others, even though the emotions are not connected with them. They just feel all these emotions, whether their own or those of others, and find it hard to differentiate between the two. Very confusing, very overwhelming! It is important that we recognize this when we see children on the spectrum overreacting to emotional states in others. It is not well understood by many in the field, and often not recognized at all.

Strengthening brain wiring to control impulses/emotions!

Recent brain research has identified that many on the spectrum have weak neurological connections (neurological pathways) between the different brain centers. These weaker connections make it more difficult for the different brain centers to communicate with one another. This has a major influence on the way we process, interpret, and respond to information. This also has a major impact on why many people on the spectrum have emotional regulation difficulties and poor emotional control problems.

In a very simplistic view, the brain has an emotion center (limbic system) and a thinking center (frontal cortex). The emotion center is part of the primitive center deeper in the brain, which experiences raw emotion. It is the part of the brain that provides immediate raw emotion and the fight-or-flight reaction. The thinking center (prefrontal lobes) provides us with the ability to immediately inhibit our raw emotion long enough to appraise and evaluate the actual degree of threat, and taper down our emotional reaction. It allows us to control our impulses, by overriding our primitive raw emotions. This inhibiting, appraising, and overriding ability of the cortex is only possible if the neurological pathways from the thinking center to the emotion center are strong enough to keep the emotional impulses in check.

Now, if these communication pathways are underdeveloped and weak, then the thinking center cannot rapidly inhibit the emotional response long enough to appraise and override the reaction. Hence the person's emotions go from 0 to 100 quickly. They overreact, and also take much longer to calm down. The overwhelming emotional tidal wave quickly sets off the fight-or-flight response, which in turn overpowers the thinking center's ability to inhibit it. The person reacts more from the primitive survival (emotion) center than from the thinking (appraising, evaluating) part of the brain. In order for the brain to be able to cognitively appraise, assess, and evaluate what is needed, it has to be able to inhibit the immediate response from the emotion center (limbic system).

In normal development, the limbic system (emotion center) exists at birth. The thinking center (prefrontal cortex) is the slowest to develop, gradually developing through childhood and early adulthood. This is why infants and young children have poor impulse control and weak ability to regulate their emotions. As the nervous system matures over the years, the thinking center develops and exerts more control over the emotion center. The person becomes better able to inhibit his impulses, appraise the situation, plan a course of action, think about the consequences of his actions, and monitor and evaluate the effects of his behavior. However, in autism, if the neurological connections are underdeveloped (or overdeveloped) and the communication is weak between these two centers, the thinking center will not be as able to immediately inhibit the strong reactions from the emotion center. The person is more likely to act on impulse, even though he can tell you later that he shouldn't have. He is more likely to be overwhelmed and emotionally reactive. Also, when he cannot be confident that his thinking center will inhibit these reactive emotional responses, he is more anxious about being emotionally reactive. This increased anxiety further hinders his thinking brain's ability to inhibit and control the reactive emotion center. The person becomes anxious and apprehensive when experiencing emotion and panics easily from fear that his emotions will overwhelm him. He cannot trust that his thinking center will be able to control his emotional responses. This insecurity leaves him feeling vulnerable in any situation that may overwhelm him.

Given the nature of this weakness, how can we help? Research on brain plasticity has shown we can strengthen neurological pathways by exercising them. If that is true, then we should (in theory) be able to strengthen the neurological pathways that connect the thinking center to the emotion center to become better able to inhibit and control our emotional reactions. We can do this in children by activating the thinking center early enough to inhibit the emotion center. By practicing "think before we act" strategies, we can strengthen the neurological pathways that allow the thinking center to inhibit and override the emotion center. We can help the child strengthen this ability in several ways:

- Continually model for the children how to think things through, how to stop and think, before acting. Model how to accurately appraise how threatening a situation is, assess what is needed, plan a response, and execute and monitor our actions. Parents can do this by thinking out loud as they go through the day—slowing things down and thinking out loud how they appraise and evaluate what to do and how to do it. They can think out loud as they face simple challenges in their daily routine.

- In addition, parents can help the children learn to think their way through things, to stop and think, as the children do things throughout the day. Do the activities with the child, slow them down, and think it out together (talk it through). We need to develop self-talk strategies to gradually develop internal thinking. Appraise what is needed, how to do it, and monitor how well they are doing. Model how to appraise, monitor, and evaluate. This process activates the thinking center of the brain, making it stronger and more automatic in response. We need to activate the thinking center to inhibit the emotion center. We need to practice this strategy throughout the day to ingrain activating the thinking center as habit in all daily activity. This will strengthen the thinking functions to become better at inhibiting the reactions from the emotion center.

- Parents can also help the child practice and role-play using these thinking (problem-solving) strategies for situations that commonly cause strong emotional reactions for the child. We do this by making a list of common, frustrating situations for the child. We write out each one on an index card. On each card we describe what the problem situation is. Next, we make a problem-solving worksheet with four questions on it: (1) What is the problem? (2) Why is it a problem? (3) What are possible options? (4) What are the possible effects of each option? This is essentially a "think it through" problem-solving worksheet. Then each day we pick a couple of problem cards and use the worksheet to think them through. In addition, as new situations crop up, we write them on index cards and add them to the stack of cards to practice. This way we are using real-life situations that are common for the child. This is a very laborious approach at first, but it teaches the child to think out solutions to common problems in their life, and teaches him to stop and think before hitting boiling point. It becomes easier and quicker as times goes on. Start by practicing a self-talk script, such as "stop, think, act," which will initially inhibit (check) the emotional impulse long enough to activate the thinking brain. Then use a brief 3–5 question outline to think it out. Three different types are presented below. However, you can create any 3–5 question outline that is specific to helping your child. These outlines give scripted routines that can be learned and ingrained as cognitive appraisals.

Appraising event	Problem-solving	Appraising threat
1. What can I expect?	1. What is the problem?	1. What could go wrong?
2. What is expected of me?	2. Why is it a problem?	2. How likely is that to happen?
3. What do I need to do?	3. What are my options?	3. How bad would it be if it did happen?
4. What problems may occur?	4. What are the consequences of each option?	4. How do I respond if it does happen?
5. How will I respond if problems arise?	5. What option to try?	

Write out these outlines on small laminated cards that can be put in the child's pocket. Start by practicing them at home by role-playing situations and thinking them through. Once the child feels comfortable with the strategies, then begin to use them in actual situations.

- Next, the parents and children need to identify the first signs of apprehension and agitation, so that they can intervene early, help the child stop and think, and activate the thinking brain center early enough to inhibit their emotional reactions. We often ignore the early signs and jump in with advice once the child is full blown! Then it is too late. Know your child's early signs. It is very important that this process is activated early in the emotional chain so that it is easier for the child to inhibit the emotional reaction before it becomes overwhelming.

- You cannot teach a new response in the heat of the moment. This is why it is important to role-play and teach the coping skill when the child is calm and organized. Once the child can instill this problem solving competently during practice sessions, then we start programming little snags into the child's day that will present the "just right" challenge (a little anxiety) so the child can practice using his thinking strategies. We make a list of common situations that causes anxiety for him, starting with minor snags. He first learns to use these skills under manageable situations before trying to tackle more problematic events. With the parents' help in scaffolding these events for success, the child becomes stronger in using his thinking brain to inhibit and control his emotional brain.

As the child learns to activate his thinking center more quickly and efficiently, he strengthens the neurological connections between the brain centers and becomes more confident in controlling his emotional impulses. Don't expect this to occur overnight. It needs frequent and long-term practice to develop these neurological connections.

"Pace" his behavior to regulate his emotions!

Many children on the spectrum have problems with both emotional and behavioral regulation. They tend to be "all or nothing" in everything they do. Many are very scattered and disorganized, jumping into things full force with little forethought, then exploding when things do not go right or someone blocks what they are doing. They have (1) poor ability to check their impulses, (2) impaired ability to judge what is needed, (3) the tendency to act without thinking, (4) difficulty monitoring their actions to stay coordinated, and (5) poor ability to evaluate the effectiveness of their actions. They tend to jump in and go 100 miles an hour, exploding in emotion when things don't go well. Emotionally, these children tend to be all over the place, usually at the extreme ends.

If this describes your child, you are not alone. Many children on the spectrum, especially young ones, have these characteristics that make life hard for both them and their family. Once children become emotionally dysregulated, they become overwhelmed and fall apart quickly. They may be hard to calm and take a long time to rebound. They may fight those who attempt to calm and soothe them, further increasing the stress and anxiety of everyone. As the child gets older, these emotional extremes can become serious and dangerous.

Emotional regulation and behavioral regulation go hand in hand. One parallels the other. When the children are calm and organized emotionally, they are usually calm and organized behaviorally. Consequently, by regulating their behavior, we can also regulate their emotions. So, if your child tends to jump in too quickly, move too fast, and lose it quickly, pacing his actions will help keep him calm and organized. This will also help him "stop, think, and act" by staying regulated enough for the thinking part of the brain to kick in.

Pacing is a method of keeping the child acting in a calm and organized fashion, moving at the right speed to stay regulated and referencing what is needed to stay coordinated. If he jumps in too quickly and moves too fast, then he cannot monitor his actions to stay coordinated. By helping your child pace himself, he can better appraise what is needed, slow himself down, and stay coordinated with what is needed to be successful. By slowing himself down and staying regulated, he will also stay emotionally calmer and be less likely to melt down.

With pacing, the parent helps set the speed and tempo of action so the child stays regulated. To do this, the parent does the task with the child, right alongside him, setting the pace, and teaching him to match it. The child learns to pace himself by referencing and following the lead of the parent. The parent sets the expectation that the child will do it together with them, staying coordinated together, and matching their lead. By keeping the child behaviorally regulated, you keep the child from becoming emotionally dysregulated. These referencing and coordinating actions are important skills to learn. They not only help the child stay emotionally and behaviorally regulated, but are fundamental for all other cooperative play/social skills. There are some basic principles that you have to use when engaging in regulatory activities:

1. Clearly define the boundaries and expectations before the activity begins. Children who have regulation problems need to have boundaries and expectations that are very clear and concrete. For example, pick a simple activity such as going for a walk together. The boundaries and expectations are (1) staying on the sidewalk, and (2) walking beside each other (not running up in front, or going off the sidewalk).

2. Once you define the boundaries, you need to frame the activity to ensure the child stays within the boundaries. You might have to hold hands at first to increase likelihood of him staying with you.

3. Teach your child to reference you (check in with you) to stay coordinated. When walking, stop frequently and teach your child to look at you to see when to start walking again. I usually shake my head "no" to signify not yet, and shake my head "yes" to mean go. This teaches the child to inhibit his impulse to immediately go. It teaches him to stop, look, then wait to act.

4. If the child starts to stray from the boundaries (walking off the sidewalk or getting ahead of you), then pause the action. Stop, pause, and wait for the child to return to within the boundaries (back alongside you). As stated above, shake your head "no" until the child is back, then shake your head "yes" to move forward. It is very important for the child to feel the boundaries by not letting him step too far outside them. If you let

him go too far, then it is hard to reel him back in again. This can take some time to teach. The child may test your limits at first. You have to hold your ground and not go further unless the child stays coordinated with you.

5. Provide ongoing positive interaction while walking together. However, if you have to stop the action because the child is stepping outside the boundaries, simply prompt the child back again; avoid scolding, coaxing, or counseling. Simply hold your ground, repeat the prompt, and wait the child out. If the child becomes too dysregulated, simply stop the activity and try again later.

6. It is important to start with a simple action such as walking together, so that there are not a lot of elements to the task to distract the child from the objective of staying coordinated with you. Essentially, you are teaching the child to pace himself by following your lead.

Once the child can do a few simple activities, such as walking together by pacing with you, then start using these procedures in a variety of activities that require the two of you to do it together, taking turns and coordinating actions together, with the child following your lead and referencing you to pace himself. You have to set the pace and then continually keep the child matching that pace; otherwise the action is stopped until the pace is re-established. This will help teach the child to slow down, check his impulses to move too fast, monitor his actions to stay coordinated with you, and keep his emotions organized. As these skills develop, you will notice the child becoming more and more regulated in both his behavior and emotions. Plus, when he starts to become dysregulated, he will be more likely to follow your lead to stop, check his impulses, and slow himself down.

Chapter 13

SHUTDOWNS AND MELTDOWNS

There are many aspects of autism that make the world chaotic and scary; however, emotions are probably one of the scariest. Children on the spectrum feel emotions very intensively, but often do not feel as if they have any control over them. They have difficulty identifying the emotions and connecting them to external events, and often become overwhelmed by them. These emotions come on like a tidal wave with little warning, leaving the children feeling helpless and vulnerable. Consequently, they frequently panic at the first signs of strong emotion. Hence, the beginning of a meltdown!

This panic reaction is natural when you feel helpless at dealing with emotions. Losing emotional control is very scary, so any sign of anxiety may set off a fear reaction. Making matters worse, these children often have a hard time rebounding after the episode is over. This leaves them vulnerable for the emotion charge to explode again. They often need extended time to fully recover after intense emotion. We typically think that once the child calms down he is fine. However, the emotion is lingering for some time following the event. Following a meltdown, try to minimize demands and overload for a couple of hours if possible.

As we have already mentioned, the nervous system for many on the spectrum is very fragile and vulnerable to continuous build-up of stress chemicals. Their systems are often anxious and on high alert. Just regulating the normal daily demands (sensory, social, cognitive, etc.) causes extensive accumulation of stress chemicals in the nervous system. For all of us, as the stress chemicals accumulate, our coping skills begin to break down. Unfortunately, for many children their body awareness is not good enough to sense the build-up of stress. They do not feel themselves getting stressed until they reach boiling point. Then, unfortunately, panic sets in and what few coping skills they have fall apart. This lack of feeling the build-up is why they appear to go from 0 to 100. Once at boiling point, the least little snag can set them into a frenzy.

As we all know, the meltdowns can be frightening and unpredictable for both them and us. They are like a volcano exploding, releasing all the built-up stress chemicals. Once the stress chemicals hit boiling point the fight-or-flight reaction sets in, and the immediate release of these chemicals is paramount. For some children, if the build-up is gradual, the brain will begin to shut out stimulation to avoid overload. The child will begin to shut down, limiting the amount of stimulation that the brain is experiencing in order to avoid being overwhelmed. These children will often appear very calm, but in a daze, unresponsive, or "out of it." This will often happen in school as the stress chemicals begin to increase. They will start to zone out, sometimes engage in calming self-stimulation, or even lay their heads down and go to sleep. This is a sign that they are overwhelmed. Unfortunately, we think that they need further prompting, so we increase our directing without being aware that we need to back off and give them time to rebound. Figure 13.1 shows the build-up of stress to the panic fight-or-flight response.

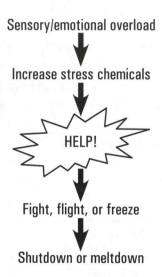

Sensory/emotional overload

Increase stress chemicals

HELP!

Fight, flight, or freeze

Shutdown or meltdown

- Confused, overwhelmed, scared!

- Overload of stress chemicals

- Breakdown of coping skills

- Elicits fight/flight/freeze response

- Meltdowns: tantrums, aggression, self-abuse to escape/reduce stimulation

- Shutdown: withdraw, shut out stimulation in order to rebound.

Figure 13.1 Progression of stress build-up to fight, flight, or freeze response, leading to shutdowns or meltdown

This diagram shows the effects of gradual build-up of stress chemicals. Autism is a bioneurological condition that leaves the nervous system fragile and vulnerable. Much of what our nervous system processes smoothly and effortlessly (the sensory, social, cognitive demands of the day) is very insulting and taxing for children on the spectrum. Their nervous systems are running on high, anxious and insecure. They become overwhelmed easily, which sets off the brain's panic button—the fight-or-flight reaction. If the stress comes on slowly enough, the nervous system will try to shut down, minimizing stimulation to avoid overload. If this is ineffective, or stimulation comes on too fast and strong, the child may melt down.

Accumulation of stress chemicals

Research has shown that individuals with ASD have higher levels of stress chemicals in their nervous system. Even when in a relaxed state, their system has increased levels of stress chemicals. This is because their nervous system is continually taxed and drained throughout the day. Running on high wears it down and makes it more prone to overload. Most mild snags for us can be major stressors for those on the spectrum. Most daily tasks at school take much more mental effort for children with ASD.

For all of us, stress chemicals accumulate in the nervous system as we go through the day. For children on the spectrum, these chemicals accumulate quickly. As the stress chemicals accumulate, eventually they hit boiling point, setting off the brain's fight-or-flight response. Figure 13.2 provides a graph of how stress chemicals can accumulate as the day goes on at school.

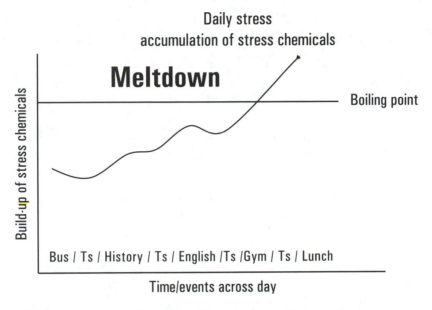

Figure 13.2 Progression of stress build-up to fight, flight, or freeze

Most of us can feel when we are getting stressed, so we often pull back and/ or engage in coping strategies to lower the stress chemicals. Our brains can sense the build-up of stress chemicals, cueing us that we need to pull back and take a break, so that we do not reach overload. People on the spectrum often have poor internal body awareness and do not feel the stress chemicals build-up. Consequently, they may be unaware that they are getting stressed until they hit boiling point. Unfortunately, by that time their coping skills have often collapsed.

Shutdowns vs. meltdowns

Both research and self-reports from adults on the spectrum have demonstrated that the brain has the ability to shut down slowly if stress chemicals are building too fast or stimulation is overloading the brain. This is the brain's defense mechanism to protect itself from overload and reaching boiling point. However, if this function does not work properly, and/or the stress chemicals are building too fast for the brain to avoid, meltdown is probable. So, when you see the child shutting down, immediately recognize the vulnerable state of defensiveness the brain is in. Withdraw any demands and allow the child to escape and rebound. Table 13.1 shows the differences between shutdowns and meltdowns.

Table 13.1 Differences between shutdowns and meltdowns

Shutdowns and meltdowns	
Shutdowns	• When stimulation becomes too overwhelming the nervous system shuts down to rebound. • Child may become lethargic, limp, stare or close eyes, and become unresponsive.
Meltdowns	• The stress chemicals reach boiling point, coping skills collapse, and the child acts out to escape/avoid situation and reduce anxiety. • Hitting, kicking, pushing, throwing, slamming, biting self, head banging, etc. all provide proprioceptive stimulation, which releases stress chemicals.
If stress chemicals increase gradually, shutdown is likely; if chemicals build quickly, meltdown may occur.	

When meltdowns occur, children often seek out strong proprioceptive input. This is strong input into the joints and tendons that tends to release stress chemicals and organize the nervous system. This will be seen in stomping feet, body slamming, head banging, throwing things, biting, and hitting self or others. Any strong physical exertion will provide the proprioception that is needed to release the pent-up stress chemicals. When stress chemicals hit boiling point, they have to come out! They explode in proprioception, seeking an immediate release of stress chemicals to rebound.

We know that proprioception will help calm and organize the nervous system. Knowing that stress chemicals build easily and quickly for children on the spectrum, we need to provide frequent avenues of proprioception throughout the day to continually release stress chemicals as they build-up. Proprioception can be provided with physical, gross motor activity (jumping, throwing, climbing, pushing/pulling, etc.) or by more subtle means of chewing gum, squeezing a squish ball, or wrapping stretch bands to the legs of the chair that the child can press his feet into. For other examples, please see ideas for sensory diet in Chapter 6 on sensory issues. At school, the child will need frequent breaks to rebound and release stress chemicals to avoid them accumulating to boiling point. Ask the occupational therapist to build in sensory breaks into the daily school routine.

Common causes of meltdowns!

There are many potential causes for meltdowns; however, the following are common causes:

1. Sensory overload: too much and too intense stimulation, setting off fight-or-flight panic reaction. As the children's senses are very sensitive and not filtered and integrated well, the more sensory "noise" in the environment, the greater stress for the child. If there is too much stimulation, or the stimulation is too intense, the brain becomes overwhelmed and panic sets in.

2. Information overload: too much information coming in too fast. Many children have delayed informational processing. Having to process multiple information simultaneously can overwhelm them. Information coming at them too fast or too much over time can overload the brain. We need to slow it down, break it down, and keep it simpler. These kids struggle with multistep directions and any multitasking of information.

3. Emotional overload: sudden, intense, and mixed emotions that come on suddenly and set off a panic reaction. Many children become overwhelmed by strong emotions, both their own and those of others.

4. Task performance demands: too many demands or too hard demands will push the child into panic. Many children have strong task performance anxiety, so ongoing prompting, instructing, and task demands will tax and drain the brain. If the child feels pressed, you risk a meltdown. We need to let the children pace themselves, and give frequent periods of rest to rebound.

5. Sudden changes or shifts in expectations. Once the child has an expectation set (expects things to be a certain way or occur a specific way), sudden snags or changes can set off immediate fright! The child's sense of safety and security is dependent on the predictability of what they expect. When the world matches what they expect, they are usually fine. When snags occur, their world falls apart.

6. Intense frustration: rigid need to have what they want (actually perceived by them to *need*), when they want it. If the expected outcome does not occur, they become overwhelmed with emotion. May start out as a tantrum, but become flooded with emotion and panic sets in setting off the fight-or-flight response.

7. Lack of communication skills. For nonverbal children or those with limited verbal skills, the immediate frustration of not being able to communicate what they want or need can set off intense rage. This often gets better as the child develops better communication (whether speech, signing, PECS, electronic communication devices, etc.). It is very important to find any means of communicating as early as possible.

8. Unable to "control" everything around them. The fear of uncertainty and need for predictability create a rigid need to control everything they do and that occurs around them. When forced to follow the lead of someone else, they panic, creating great stress and often meltdowns.

When the brain has difficulty processing the world around it, and has difficulty communicating its frustrations, tremendous stress can be expected and emotional turmoil will result. It is important that parents and teachers make a list of the potential stressors and build in strategies for supporting the child's vulnerabilities. The Fragile World on the Spectrum, located in Appendix E, provides a good summary of the different stressors and ways of supporting the child.

Differences between tantrums and meltdowns

It is very important for parents and teachers to understand the differences between tantrums and meltdowns. Although they can consist of similar behavior (yelling, screaming, crying, dropping to the floor, flailing, hitting or biting self, etc.), it is important to distinguish between the two. Why? Because it has major implications for how we interpret the behavior and how we intervene to help the child.

Tantrums

Characteristics of tantrums:

1. Child has some control over the behavior.

2. Child chooses to engage in the behavior.

3. Usually occurs specifically as a result of wanting something or escaping something he doesn't want.

4. Can end quickly once he gets what he wants.

5. Child can focus on others around him, often looking at them, yelling at them, and drawing their attention to himself.

6. Child looks for reactions from others when being disruptive.

7. Child may have the ability to talk and negotiate, although yelling and demanding.

8. If aggression is displayed, he will often seek out others to hit or kick, or get up and seek out property to disrupt.

Usually, the behavior is a means to an end (the child wants something or to avoid something) and the child acts out to get a specific reaction from others. Although tantrums can lead to the child being overwhelmed, they usually start under the control of the child. Tantrums often occur in nonverbal children when they lack other ways of communicating and getting their needs met. The child will often calm down once he gets want he wants or feels that he needs.

Meltdowns

Meltdowns usually occur when the child's brain is overwhelmed with stress chemicals and has reached the panic, fight-or-flight stress reaction. The stress builds up to the point that the brain is overwhelmed and loses the ability to cope. With meltdowns the child usually:

1. Appears to be in panic mode.

2. Does not appear to have control over his behavior.

3. Often cannot talk or problem-solve; loses ability to negotiate or reason.

4. Often cannot follow directions or argue; is too overwhelmed to engage.

5. Feels unsafe and appears to be reacting out of deep fear.

6. May have difficulty identifying the cause of emotion, or obvious "want or demand."

7. Is often experiencing sensory overload, too much cognitive stress, or ongoing social demands that tax and drain the brain.

8. Is often trying to flee or escape the situation around him, rather than seeking out attention. The child is seeking to escape what is overwhelming him, not seeking to gain something.

9. Usually does not hit, kick, or bite others unless others approach and attempt to calm or redirect him. Aggression often subsides when you back away, give him space, remove demands, and withdraw all interactions.

10. Can take a while to calm down (rather than calming immediately when he gets what he wants); needs time to escape and rebound.

11. Often expresses remorse for actions afterwards.

The child in a meltdown is reacting out of fright and fear. The fight-or-flight panic reaction is set off, and the child is (1) trying to escape the source of stress and (2) seeking proprioception (hitting, kicking, biting self, head banging, etc.) to release stress chemicals. He often does not want to interact with others, is not seeking their attention, and often wants to withdraw and isolate. However, if the child does not feel that he is safe, he may act out on property or others to get people to back off, or to release stress chemicals.

Intervening: tantrums

How we interpret the behavior (tantrum or meltdown) may affect the way we intervene. If the behavior appears to be a tantrum, we would want to:

1. Identify what function(s) the behavior serves (getting something he wants or trying to escape something he doesn't want). What is he trying to gain from the tantrum?

2. Try to focus on teaching the child more appropriate ways of getting his needs met (requesting, saying "stop," break cards, etc.). Provide an appropriate way of communicating the same thing that the tantrum does. Practice and role-play to teach the desired response.

3. During his early stages of getting upset, intervene quickly and coach the child to use his replacement behavior (desired response that was practiced).

4. Avoid giving in to the tantrum (to gain something or avoid something); prompt the desired response instead. If the child is throwing a tantrum to end a task he doesn't like, then say, "If you want us to stop then say 'stop.'" As soon as the desired response is given, immediately back off. You want to make sure that the tantrum behavior does not work and the desired response works immediately.

5. Minimize both verbal and emotional reactions to the negative behavior (stay matter-of-fact, no scolding, bribing, or counseling; minimal emotion), directing all attention to what you want him to do.

6. Reinforce the child for using the desired replacement behavior.

7. If the child refuses to respond, pull all attention away and walk away if possible (if not destructive or injurious). Ignore the behavior, but supervise to ensure safety. Once the child calms down, redirect him back to the task or to use the replacement behavior.

8. If needed (only if the above fail), implement a mild consequence (time out, loss of privilege, etc.) for not responding.

These are just basic starter procedures. If the above does not work, seek out professional advice. For more destructive aggression or property destruction, seek professional assistance to complete a detailed functional behavior assessment for designing safe and effective treatment strategies. Only implement the above for less aggressive tantrums (screaming, flailing, falling to floor, etc.) where safety can be assured.

Intervening: meltdowns

- When the child is melting down, typical behavioral techniques are not effective. The child is too overwhelmed to think, respond to directions, or reason with. He will not understand or respond to directions or consequences at this time. Punishing and threatening will only make things worse.

- Reducing meltdowns is most effective by designing preventative strategies for avoiding meltdowns in the first place. Identify the sensory, cognitive, and social challenges that overwhelm the child and build in proactive strategies for reducing the stressors. This usually consists of modifying the environmental demands to match the child's abilities, providing accommodations to lessen the stress, and teaching coping skills for dealing with the stressful situations.

- Redirection and intervention work best if we intervene very early in the behavior chain (at the first signs of getting overwhelmed), assist and support the child as soon as possible, and practice coping skills.

- Once in the heat of the moment, pull the child away from the situation, remove all demands, reduce all stimulation, and minimize questions or demands. We need to lessen the demands on the brain; let it regroup and reorganize.

- Focus on helping the child feel safe. Remove stimulation and demands, reassure the child that he is safe, and allow him space to calm down.

- Some children will let you help soothe them, but often they want no interaction. Respect their comfort zones.

- Program strategies usually consist of (1) lessening the stressors with modifications and accommodations, (2) teaching coping skills to deal with the stress and cope when first getting overwhelmed (say stop, present break card, leave setting, etc.), and (3) teaching a safe routine once overwhelmed (withdraw, pull away, immediately exit, rock and calm, etc.). Practice this routine until it becomes predictable and familiar. Then, in the heat of the moment, the child will feel safe implementing it.

Support the challenges to reduce the meltdowns!

Meltdowns and/or shutdowns are a sure sign that the demands of the situation outweigh the child's abilities to deal with them. Meltdowns are not the fault of the child, but a cue to us that we are forcing the brain into overload and that meltdown will eventually occur. Autism is a bioneurological condition that renders the nervous system fragile and vulnerable to stress and overload. All the normal sensory, cognitive, physical, and social demands of our typical day are overly stressful for the nervous system of those on the spectrum. This entire book has been devoted to understanding and supporting the cognitive, sensory, social, and emotional vulnerabilities that lead to this overload and contribute to meltdowns. If we identify and accommodate for all the sensory, cognitive, social, and emotional vulnerabilities, the child will have far fewer meltdowns. In Appendix E, the four pages of diagrams, Fragile World on the Spectrum, explain the stress–anxiety–meltdown connection, identify each area of vulnerability (sensory, cognitive, social, emotional, etc.), and outline strategies for each area of vulnerability.

I also use this document for planning treatment strategies and coping routines for stress, overload, and meltdowns. If the child is younger or more impaired, I use this document with the parents to analyze each area of vulnerability and build in positive supports for minimizing stress and maximizing engagement. This helps to provide a well-rounded treatment plan for supporting the child's overall daily living. For late teens and adults, I sit down with the individuals themselves and help them better understand their vulnerabilities, as well as how to use their strengths to work around them. They build their own support plan.

It is essential that a good plan for reducing meltdowns consists of proactive strategies for supporting each of these vulnerabilities, by:

1. *Modifying the environment.* Reducing sensory stimulation and task demands, and building in structure and predictability, using visual supports, providing a mental map, etc.

2. *Keeping the nervous system organized.* Plenty of rest, good nutrition, exercise, sensory diet, and plenty of breaks to rebound.

3. *Communicating understanding and acceptance.* Identifying and respecting the child's comfort zones, understanding and validating the child's struggles and feelings, letting the child set the pace of learning, and focusing on the child's strengths and preferences.

4. *Teaching coping skills.* Teaching the child better skills for coping with stress and empowering him to advocate for his own needs. As children become older, this includes increasing their awareness of their own vulnerabilities, and the ways in which to advocate and accommodate for them. (See page 339 for adult meltdowns.)

All the strategies in this book are designed to meet the needs of procedures 1–3 above. The companion book in this series, *The Autism Discussion Page on anxiety, behavior, school, and parenting strategies: A toolbox for helping children with autism feel safe, accepted, and competent*, goes into more depth about teaching coping skills for dealing with stress and anxiety, identifying the child's comfort zones and building a comfort zone profile, and developing strategies for matching the demands to the child's abilities. However, it all starts with outline provided in the Fragile World on the Spectrum in Appendix E.

Freeze, flight, fight response to overload!

You cannot force a brain to process faster than its wiring allows. Many children on the spectrum have delayed sensory and informational processing. Regardless of how bright the children are, they have difficulty processing multiple stimulation (information) simultaneously. This tends to (1) slow down the processing speed and (2) overwhelm the brain if too much information is coming in or it is coming in too rapidly. Our world tends to move way too fast for most of these children. Their brains are easily taxed and overwhelmed.

This is why we do not want to push, pressure, or force these children. More than likely they are still processing the information (demands), do not understand what is expected, or feel inadequate in performing what we are asking. When we push too hard, the brain becomes overwhelmed and panics. The wiring cannot handle being pushed faster than it can process. We cannot force it to process faster. The brain shuts down and freezes. For some children, this is easy to see. They will stop, stare off, and sometimes get glassy-eyed. The brain is trying to halt and process before moving forward. We may see that and continue to prompt the child to move forward, often because we are in a hurry. If we continue to pressure, the brain usually attempts to escape and avoid, by further shutting down to rebound. We often consider this as being noncompliant or oppositional. We then increase the prompting, often physically guiding the child, or become louder and more demanding. At that time, if the brain is not allowed to escape, it may melt down and the child then acts out. Then we the blame the child for acting out and further label him as defiant and oppositional.

Let the child pace the learning. We need to slow down, work with the child, and let him pace how fast we provide him with information, and how fast he can be expected to respond. Many children require 10–20 seconds or longer to process information before they are ready to respond. Be respectful, slow down and allow the child to process. If he freezes or does not respond, do not push or pressure—give time and support.

Window of opportunity!

In Chapter 2, in the section "Do you ever see that 'look'?" (See page 51), we discussed the freeze response that occurs just before the child becomes overwhelmed. This is when the child freezes, stares off, and may appear glassy-eyed or dazed. We all have seen that look. This is the moment when the brain is starting to get overwhelmed, freezes, and tries to block out further stimulation to avoid overload. At this moment, if we do not recognize the need to back off and instead continue to prompt, direct, or instruct, the child often becomes overwhelmed and loses all ability to cope. This is the moment of truth before the fury starts. It is also our moment of opportunity to quickly back off, remove all demands, and reassure the child that it is OK and he is safe. Read that look and support the child. Do not interpret this as noncompliance and defiance. This is the time to encourage the child to use his calming routine that has been identified and practiced.

As a parent or teacher, make sure everyone is aware of "that look" for your child. Make sure they learn to respect and support the child at this time, not command and demand! Communicate to the child that you read him well and he is safe and accepted to back away and escape to rebound. This is our chance to show the child we are listening to him and want to support him. Don't blow it! It is the essence of establishing trust.

The delayed effect!

How many of you see this? The child is fine at school, but explodes once he gets home!

Many people see this delayed effect once the child comes home from school. If the child is strong enough to hold it together at school, then the stress comes out as soon as he arrives home. The stress chemicals that accumulate during the day at school come out once the child is in a safe setting to release them. The child may appear fairly calm and organized at school, but he has learned to hold it together while building up this accumulation of stress chemicals. As discussed above, if the chemicals build slowly, the brain may go into shutdown to escape being overwhelmed. This mild shutdown will allow the child to appear calm and allows him to keep it together while at school. However, once home, the stress chemicals come reeling out!

When the parent approaches the school, the staff simply report that the child is doing well there. The school claims that the child does need any accommodations or extra supports. However, these children need the same supports (fewer demands, work broken down more simply, sensory diet, frequent breaks, physical activity, etc.) as the child who acts out frequently at school. We must realize that holding it in can be damaging to the nervous system and takes a great toll on the children. We need to identify the stressors, build in accommodations to lessen the stress, give frequent breaks to regroup, and provide a physical activity/sensory diet to release the stress chemicals as they are accumulating. We simply need to recognize what the nervous system needs to stay calm, alert, and organized, and not tax and drain the brain. Just because he looks good doesn't mean he is good!

This delayed effect is so common that schools need to take it seriously. Parents, I would approach the school team for help with this, and especially the occupational therapist who should clearly understand this phenomenon. All it takes is a few simple modifications and accommodations to support the child to reduce the stressors and release the stress so the child can arrive home feeling good about his day and about himself. However, you may need some of the professional team to interpret this effect for the teachers.

What do you do for your child once he comes home? How do you help him through this transition? Each child is different. Some children need to escape in isolation for an hour or so, some may need to take a nap, some rebound by engulfing themselves in a preferred activity (reading, music, etc.), and others need a heavy dose of physical activity. Whatever allows your child to release stress, regroup, and rebound should be a given as soon as he is out of school. Make this a consistent and predictable routine, so the child looks forward to it and knows it is coming.

At school, if possible, have the occupational therapist or school counselor work with the child to build in simple breaks, and teach simple coping skills for handling stress and staying calm and organized. Over the years, the child needs to learn how to identify what stresses his nervous system, gain awareness of how to advocate for accommodations he will need, and learn simple coping skills for managing the stress during his day. Starting now will help him build these needed skills. The other book in this series goes into more detail about stress and anxiety, and building coping strategies for managing them. Individuals on the spectrum will battle increased stress and anxiety throughout their life, so start early in empowering them to manage it effectively.

Why didn't I see it coming?

Have you ever noticed that meltdowns can appear out of the blue, with little warning? Everything seems to be going OK, then "BAMM!" they can hit!

We often are confused by being blindsided by a meltdown that simply comes out of nowhere, with little warning. "Where did that come from?" and "Why didn't I see that coming?" are two questions I get all the time. The child doesn't always show obvious signs of this stress. Believe me, he is often just as surprised!

Many children and adults on the spectrum do not feel the stress chemicals building up inside them. Their internal sensory receptors do not adequately provide the early feedback, giving them awareness that they need to act in order to reduce the overload. Also, even if they are aware of the stress, they do not feel safe to say anything about it.

Children on the spectrum generally have higher baseline stress chemicals in their nervous system. Their level of stress chemicals at a resting state (baseline) is already much higher than for neurotypical children. Consequently, it does not take much additional build-up of stress chemicals to reach boiling point. Also, be aware that the vulnerability to meltdown is much greater if the nervous system is being taxed due to poor sleep, fatigue, illness, or hunger. A minor snag may be easy to handle one day and set off a meltdown the next. Once we let the child withdraw, calm, and organize himself, be aware that it takes much longer for his nervous system to fully recover. So, just because he is no longer acting out or showing external signs of stress, his nervous system is still close to boiling point for some time after calming down.

Since the child may not look stressed, always be conscious of the accumulated stress chemicals that come from ongoing activity and transitioning throughout the day. The more the child does, the more that is asked of him, and the more he has to regulate social situations, the greater accumulation of stress chemicals. Once his nervous system becomes taxed and drained, a simple little snag can send him into a frenzy. Unfortunately, he may not be as aware of this process as you are. He doesn't feel it coming on until it is too late for him to do anything about it.

"But he was having fun!"

Remember, increased activity, social regulating, sensory stimulation, and performance demands will build stress chemicals, regardless of whether the experience is something the child likes or dislikes. We often associate meltdowns with the child experiencing something he dislikes or is fearful of. This is not true. Meltdowns often occur during or following fun and exciting events. During these times, the child and family often overextend the child and do too much. The child doesn't want to leave the event, nor do the parents. They are having loads of fun. However, the child is being strained by regulating all this fun and activity, and becoming drained just the same. Often I will have parents tell me, "We were having a great day; stringing together a lot of fun activities (especially in the community)." Remember, the child needs frequent breaks to rebound, regardless of whether the activity is fun or not. If there is a lot of novelty, social interaction, and sensory bombardment, he will need the breaks. Build them into your schedule, and keep the child organized and regulated.

Know the triggers and early signs!

To avoid the unexpected meltdowns, you have to be aware of the events that build increased stress chemicals for the child, how much he can handle, and be keenly aware of the early signs that he is getting dysregulated (since the child will not feel it).

Table 13.2 Common triggers and physical signs of stress

Triggers	Physical signs
• Tired, hungry, discomfort, sick. • Sensory overload. • Transitions. • Novelty, uncertainty. • Task-performance anxiety. • Pressure to socialize. • Unexpected change. • Unstructured social settings.	• Increased stimming. • Change in voice. • Increased motor activity. • Increased repetitive behavior. • Changes in body language (facial expressions, posture). • Perseverative behavior.

Table 13.2 provides a list of common triggers for stress and possible physical signs to look out for. Each child will have subtle signs that he is becoming dysregulated. By knowing these signs and realizing what type and how much activity the child can handle, you can help the child stay regulated. As you are planning your day, be conscious of how much activity the child can handle and if any common triggers might occur that may overload the child. Help him pace his day, building in frequent breaks and calming strategies to keep his nervous system calm and organized. When you are aware that you are stretching the child's comfort zones, look for those early signs. Try not to push it, but for sure look for those early signs. If you see them, pull back on the activity and give a break to rebound. As the child gets older, it is important to teach him what his early signs are, what they feel like, and how to pull back and recover. By learning how to cope with his own stress and overload, he will be less anxious by feeling more in control of these moments.

As the moment is building!

As stated earlier, the most effective strategies for reducing meltdowns are proactive strategies for reducing the chance of them occurring in the first place. By identifying, respecting, and supporting the child's physical, sensory, cognitive, social, and emotional vulnerabilities, we can prevent many of the meltdowns. When the demands of the current situation are greater than the child's abilities to cope with them, meltdowns are possible. Whenever the brain becomes overwhelmed with too much information coming too fast, the brain panics and goes into fight-or-flight mode. We need to reduce overall stress by accommodating for vulnerabilities. The previous chapters in this book identified and provided proactive strategies for accommodating and supporting the child's sensory, cognitive, social, and emotional vulnerabilities. Build in accommodations to support the child's sensory sensitivities. Make the world more understandable and predictable by providing a structured daily routine, keeping things concrete and literal, breaking things down, previewing ahead of time, and letting the child pace the action. Clarify and verify information and help the child navigate his social world. Try to avoid pressuring too much social interaction and keep interaction simple to avoid overwhelming the child. Understand that his brain has to struggle to understand and regulate the normal daily demands, and provide frequent breaks to rebound and regroup.

Have a preplanned routine!

Regardless of how well we build in proactive strategies, there will be times when overload occurs and the child will start to spiral. This is when understanding and recognizing the early signs (dilated pupils, becoming mute or hyperverbal, increased motor activity, increased stimming, repetitive vocal noises, etc.) allow us to act quickly to support the child. This is your last moment for holding off a fully fledged meltdown.

There should be a predetermined, predictable routine that consists of what helps the child feel safe and what tends to calm and soothe him. This plan should be developed with the parents, teachers, and child together. Based on the knowledge of what tools best calm the child (withdraw and isolate, rocking, music, reading, deep pressure, physical activity, etc.), build a step-by-step intervention plan to help calm and organize the child. Practice this routine with the child so that it becomes familiar and predictable when his mind starts to spiral out of control. For older children, role-play the situations that often present meltdowns and practice the calming routine. Then, once the routine is learned, always use this routine consistently during heated moments so it will become predictable and safe for the child.

In addition, write the routine down on a laminated card to give to others who may be in a position to help your child. Also, as the child becomes older, he can learn to hand this card to a first responder when he starts to dysregulate. When losing the ability to cope, the person often cannot speak effectively to tell others what to do. So it is good to have a card that he can simply hand to others that will instruct them in the routine.

When the countdown begins!

When the child starts showing the early physical signs of overload, implement the following:

1. Acknowledge to the child that you see he is getting upset. Do not ask questions or require him to think or respond. Simply acknowledge what you see and validate the child feelings. Reassure him he is safe. "Wow… you look upset to me! That's OK, let's go sit down over there and practice our deep breathing."

2. Immediately remove all demands, lower your voice, and speak in short phrases. Do not demand or command. Simply take him one step at a time through the predetermined (and practiced) calming routine. For some children, their auditory processing breaks down as they are spiraling. At home and in the classroom it can be more effective to have a picture sequence that reminds the child of what to do.

3. Assist the child in implementing the predetermined routine, step by step in order. Stay supportive and say very little. Remember to avoid questions and giving unnecessary directions. The child is having a hard time processing anything. Keep all attention on implementing the calming routine.

4. It is important that we communicate understanding and acceptance throughout the ordeal. The child needs to feel safe and accepted. Respect his comfort zones and stay consistent with the predetermined routine. I cannot emphasize this enough.

5. Once the child calms, be aware that it may take some time for the child to fully rebound. Even when he looks calm, his stress chemical levels are still very high and he needs extra time. Try to ease off demands for a while after calming down; provide extra support and watch for the return of early signs.

6. A short time later, if the child is able, debrief the situation with him, focusing on what worked and how he coped with the stress. Neither blame nor criticise. Brainstorm together any problems that may have occurred. Help the child feel stronger by working with the planned routine. The more empowered he feels, the more likely he will feel safe implementing the routine.

Possible calming tools

Most young children need help with calming themselves. They need adults to coach them by assisting them through the routine. For some children, it can be simply singing a nursery rhyme, chanting the ABCs, or repeating a calming phrase over and over. It may be allowing them to engage in their favorite self-stimulatory behavior or taking a break with a favorite activity (reading, music, etc.). Some children can be soothed by giving deep pressure touch or other calming sensory stimulation (rocking, bouncing, swinging, etc.). Table 13.3 provides a list of common calming strategies.

Table 13.3 List of possible calming strategies

Calming tools	
Slow and low	Slow down, lower demands, lower voice.
Deep pressure	Deep pressure to calm: hand massage, pillow press, neutral warmth, etc.
Proprioception	Proprioception to organize: joint compressions, stretching of limbs, body stretch.
Regulatory patterns	Rhythmic regulatory patterns to soothe: slow rhythmic rocking, swaying, bouncing, paired with soft rhythmic chanting.
Safe area	Safe areas to escape and rebound.
Relaxation	Relaxation procedures: deep breathing and muscle tension/relaxation.

For children who will accept help in calming down, two tools can often be calming. Gentle rocking and deep pressure is one tool that calms and helps organize the nervous system. Repetitive rhythmic patterns (chanting, singing, slow rhythmic movement, etc.) can also be calming. However, do not impose these techniques on the child. Many children are sensitive to touch and will find these techniques intrusive. Before ever using these techniques in the heat of the moment, practice them when the child is calm to instill them as safe calming tools, before trying them when he is upset. If the child finds them comforting, then and only then use them as part of his calming routine.

For children who want to calm on their own, simply give them space and time to escape to a safe area and engage in their favorite calming activity (self-stimulation, curling up in a blanket, reading, etc.). They just need time to recover and regroup themselves. Each child is different and including them in the planning is essential.

Deep pressure calming tools

Deep pressure tends to calm and organize the nervous system. It can be given in a variety of ways.

- *Hand hugs.* When first approaching the child, I will often provide deep pressure to the palm of his hand. I will cup my hands over one hand and provide pulsating deep pressure message into the palm of the hand. I usually do this while calmly reassuring him that he is safe. This is a quick and easy technique to use when first trying to calm the child.

- *Deep pressure massage.* This can be provided with rhythmic deep pressure massaging of the arms, shoulder and back, either by firm rhythmic stroking or by providing hand squeezes up and down the arms. This can be done standing, sitting, or lying down.

- *Neutral warmth wrap.* This can be implemented by sitting with the child between your legs and brought up tightly into you (their back to your chest). Wrap your arms around them in a tight bear hug and slowly rock side to side, while chanting or softly singing.

- *Shoulder/arm stroking.* This is often used in combination with a neutral warmth wrap. While the child is sitting with his back to your chest, firmly cup your hands on the top of his shoulders. While providing firm pressure, slowly move your hands down each arm and back up again in rhythmic strokes. Do not break your touch; keep it constant, firm, and consistent.

- *Pillow press.* Sit or lie the child down on a cushiony surface (couch, bed, mat, bean bag, etc.). With a larger pillow, couch cushion, or bean bag, provide deep pressure across the torso, arms, and legs, by gently but firmly pressing the pillow into the child in a slow pulsating fashion. Make sure to not cover his head or face, or cut off his breathing in any way. Again, only do this if the child is cooperative and finds this soothing. Do not force or impose pressure.

- *Deep pressure vests/blankets.* There are many styles of deep pressure vests that the child can wear to provide good calming input into his body. Also you can purchase weighted blankets (ask an occupational therapist) that the child can wrap up in.

Please see Appendix F for step-by-step procedures for hand massage, neutral warmth wrap, and pillow press procedures.

Reminder: These techniques can be intrusive and very uncomfortable for some children with tactile sensitivities. These techniques should be avoided for any child who actively resists their use. They should only be used if the child finds them soothing and you practice them when calm to teach their value.

What if it is too late?

Even with your best-laid plans, if you don't catch the child in the early stages of getting overwhelmed, he may be too far gone to listen and respond to the practiced routine. He may simply be too overcome with emotion to respond cooperatively. He is overwhelmed with emotion and losing all ability to cope. At this time, we need to remove all demands, lower stimulation, and, if possible, allow the child to escape to a quiet (safe) area to isolate and regroup. Once you see that the child is too upset to respond, acknowledge and validate that you understand and respect his need to avoid all stimulation and interaction, and need to think. Either remove all stimulation around him or move him to a safe area. If he tends to flail around or bang his head, then have him sit or lie on a bed, couch, or mat. Reassure him that he is safe, and that you will stay nearby to keep him safe. Respect his need for time and space, and simply let him calm on his own. At this time, he is out of control, and we need to communicate compassion and acceptance, while monitoring his safety.

Once the child has calmed down, give him some more time to rebound. Let him decide when he is ready to talk or rejoin the activity. Let him pace his own recovery. Once he is calm enough to talk, you might ask if he would now like to engage in the calming routine.

If the child is too aggressive or abusive to implement these strategies safely, then you should consider seeking professional help.

It is all about feeling "safe!"

In the heat of the storm, when emotions are flying, it is all about feeling safe! At the time when emotions are high, your number-one objective should be helping the child feel safe! When the child is overloaded and melting down, it can be intimidating if people approach him. Often our first objective is controlling behavior, but that usually fuels the fire. In our own anxiety, we often match the child's intensity in an attempt to talk over him, to immediately stop the rage. Then, when the child lashes out, we physically try to control the situation. It is hard for adults; we feel as if we need to control the situation, to stop it.

Try reminding yourself about safety: "feeling safe." The first priority is to help the child feel safe in his sea of emotions. This changes your whole approach and demeanor. You slow down, step softly, approach carefully, and lower your voice. The more upset the child, the quieter and calmer you have to be. You want to communicate to the child is that he is safe with you, that you will keep everyone safe! Don't question him, don't try to talk him out of his rage, and don't try to move him if possible. Simply pull everyone else away, give the child space, and say, "It's OK, you are safe! You are not going to get hurt, we'll keep everyone safe." Use the word "safe;" simply repeat, "Let's stay safe." Then, based on your knowledge of the child, focus all attention on helping him feel safe. Whatever that is for the child: giving him space, pulling away stimulation and demands, providing deep pressure massage, letting him rock, singing, soft talking, or simply saying nothing while standing nearby. Use the strategy that works best for helping that child feel safe. For the children who need their space, I simply stand nearby and let them know, "I am going to stay here to keep us safe!" Even if risk of injury warrants needing to hold the child, I continue to say, "I am just trying to keep us safe. We are going to sit here until we feel safe."

At this time, many people want to immediately make the child feel better, to not be upset, to talk them out of it. I find it is better to allow them to *feel* the emotion; to not jump in and make it better. Simply help them feel "safe" while experiencing the emotion. Let it happen; just reinforce feeling safe during the emotion. Allow them to use whatever soothing techniques work for them. Do not even try to process what happened until after the storm when everyone feels safe. You will find that this type of approach works 90 percent of the time: allowing the child to feel supported during the storm, and safe and accepted by those around him.

Safe areas

Many schools are starting to develop safe areas for children to go when needing a break and to regroup. These areas can be a separate room or small partitioned area in the corner of the room. I have seen large closets (with a curtain replacing the door) and small tents used to create safe areas. It is simply a small area with reduced stimulation and demands to give the children a chance to rebound and regroup.

These areas can be individualized for the child, but they often include items that tend to calm and organize. These might include large pillows, bean bags, stuffed animals, favorite toys, soft lighting, quiet music, small picture books, and fidget items.

The teacher may encourage the children to take a break when getting upset, and/or the children can have a "break card" that they present to the teacher when feeling the need for a break. These areas become associated with feeling safe and supported during the school day. They become the safe haven when the day gets rough. They reduce anxiety because the child knows that there is an escape when he needs it.

Sometimes it is best to say nothing at all!

For many children on the spectrum, as they are getting upset, their auditory processing skills collapse. Words become jumbled, confusing, and irritating! Their nervous system is in overload, and their emotions are spiraling. Trying to "talk" to them can add fuel to the fire and make them more agitated. We mean well, we want to help them out, calm them, and solve the problem for them, but our attempts seem to only add fuel to the fire. For these children we need to limit what we say, or say nothing at all. Depending on your child's ability to process language at that time, the following are suggestions:

- For some children who still maintain fair processing skills when upset, give clear statements about what the child needs to do. "Johnnie, go lie down on your bed" can give the child clear information on what he needs to do to calm, especially if the strategy was discussed ahead of time, practiced, and agreed upon. Have a consistent plan of action that is practiced and becomes routine. When the child's thinking skills are collapsing, giving a clear description of what to do can be effective. Do not focus on what the child is doing wrong, counsel him about his behavior, or try to teach more appropriate behavior at this time. It is not the time to teach, talk out of, threaten, or punish. Simply give information on what to do to cue the child into action. This only works if (1) the coping skill has been agreed upon and practiced, and (2) the child still has some degree of self-control left.

- For some children who have only partial processing when upset, try to avoid questions, directives, instructions, or counseling. Avoid any statements that direct the child to think or act. Simply use declarative statements that reflect, describe, ensure, comfort and soothe. For example, if the child is upset, say, "Johnny, you look really upset!" rather than "What's the matter, Johnny?" In the first statement you are describing what you see, not requiring him to respond. The second statement (question) requires him to process and come up with a response. This can create more overload and cause greater agitation. When you say, "Johnny, you really look angry!" you are (1) reflecting how you see he feels, and (2) inviting him to respond if he chooses to do so. It does not put him on the spot. It may be beneficial to provide reassuring and/or soothing statements, but do not direct the child to think or act. This provides interaction to support, rather than instruct.

- For the child who simply cannot process language at all when upset, you might be able to use pictures to convey information. If you have discussed and practiced using a couple of coping strategies, you can have pictures of these on a laminated card that you hand to the child to cue him on what to do. A simple picture can prompt a coping response, where words can aggravate the child more. For these children, auditory information (talking) collapses and visual information is easier to process.

- For many children who collapse very quickly and cannot handle any talking, it is better to say nothing at all. Your words add fuel to the fire and expect the child to process more, especially when he is already overwhelmed. Some of these children may still welcome you to help soothe them physically, but simply cannot process words. For this child, I would provide soothing, physical contact or movement, but say very little. Maybe sing a nursery rhyme or hum a soothing tune, but no language to process. You are simply using the tone and rhythm of your voice to help soothe the child. Then there are other children who cannot handle interaction of any kind. They may be very angry, confused, and overwhelmed, and simply cannot deal with interacting, period! For them, simply standing nearby may give them the sense of safety they need. Just knowing that you are there to keep them safe and support them is enough.

- Lastly, there are some children who simply need to be alone! Even your presence can overwhelm them. For these children, it is often better to pull back and give them lots of space to calm down on their own. You can provide them with a safe space and any objects (stuffed animals, bean bag, pillows, etc.) that might help them soothe, but give no interaction at all.

For many children, the type of interaction and amount of language will vary, depending on who is doing the intervening, where the problem is occurring, the time of day it is, and how far into the meltdown they are. The earlier you intervene in the build-up stage, the more processing capabilities they have. Also, a lot depends on the state of their nervous system at the time of their difficulty, and the type of stimulation going on around them. If they have had a stressful day, lack sleep, are hungry, or not feeling well, their processing ability will deteriorate even faster.

It is important to understand how your words, voice, and interactions affect your child when upset. Know what style of interaction, if any interaction at all, helps calm and support him. It is important for us to listen to, understand, and respect the child's tolerances. By doing so, we are helping him feel safe, accepted, and supported during his emotional storm.

Don't punish meltdowns!

Often we want to punish "bad" behavior. However, when the child is overloaded and melting down, his judgment, reasoning, and cognitive coping skills crumble. Punishing a child for true meltdowns is like punishing a child for having a seizure. His brain is in panic, fight-or-flight mode. In times like these, the child needs understanding, acceptance, and the opportunity to pull back, escape, and rebound. We also need to recognize that at the moment the demands of the situation outweigh the child's current abilities to handle them. We need to pull back and let the child de-escalate and reorganize. Keep everyone safe and feeling accepted. After the fury has calmed, then we need to debrief and look for what went wrong and what may be done differently in the future to avoid the meltdown. Punishing the child when he is out of control will only create anger, hostility, and further anxiety about becoming overwhelmed. The fear of melting down will create immediate panic when anxiety hits, increasing the likelihood of melting down.

Consequences (punishment) work if the child (1) has control over his behavior, (2) knows how he should act instead, and (3) makes the choice to act badly even though he knows how to act otherwise. If the child is overwhelmed to the point of activating his fight-or-flight response, his coping skills will fall apart and he will act to escape or avoid the stressful situation. Once the stress chemicals reach boiling point, the child will act in a way to (1) escape the stress and (2) release the stress chemicals. New learning cannot take place in situations of overload. We need to (1) reduce the demands that produce overload, (2) teach better coping skills to deal with the stress, and (3) teach another way of responding once overload occurs. This cannot be taught during the meltdown, but can be practiced and role-played when not stressed.

It is important that we do not punish meltdowns. If the child loses control, scolding, counseling, or threatening will only makes things worse. It is best to focus on the feelings behind the behavior and not the behavior itself. Acknowledge and validate that he is upset and that you will keep him safe. You can set boundaries and consequences for behavior, but at the moment of impact focus on acknowledging and validating the feelings, removing all demands and stimulation, and helping the child feel safe until it is over.

It is important to work with the child to understand his meltdowns, what causes them, and what can be done to avert them. We need to communicate to the child that we are a "working partner" with him, to collaborate on identifying and lessening the triggers, recognizing early signs of stress, and learning coping strategies for pulling away and calming when stressed. The child needs to feel that he is safe and accepted with us and that he can trust that we will support him through this scary process.

Meltdowns due to rigid/inflexible thinking!

Many children on the spectrum have rigid/inflexible thinking. Their thinking is very black and white, either/or, all-or-nothing, absolute thinking. The world has to be as they expect it. When the world doesn't match their expectation, all hell breaks loose! When the children don't get what they want, an event doesn't go as planned, or a snag happens that they weren't expecting, the world falls apart. They go from 0 to 100 quickly and a meltdown occurs. This happens most frequently with younger children, but it can occur well into adulthood.

For many young children on the spectrum, the world is very rigid and absolute. They have very rigid, inflexible thinking, and can only see the world in terms of their own immediate needs. For such children, you will face the following issues:

- The child can only see things based on his immediate need. His thinking is very rigid, with minimal ability to see options or to shift gears when things do not go his way. There is no other way but his way. The child doesn't have the cognitive skills yet to appraise the situation, understand the options available, evaluate the severity of the threat, or understand the effect his behavior has on others. The biggest problem is going to be the inability to shift gears, meaning that when things don't go how he expects them to, the world falls apart.

- Because the executive functioning part of the brain is not well developed, the child has poor ability to inhibit his impulses or to think before acting. So, immediate impulse becomes immediate behavior. This leads to two major problems: weak impulse control and poor frustration tolerance, resulting in frequent tantrums when the little snags happen without warning.

- Coinciding with the rigid/inflexible thinking is very poor emotional regulation. Emotionally, he will go from 0 to 100 quickly, with little ability to regulate his responses. Emotions come on like gangbusters and overwhelm the child with little defense. The child doesn't have the ability to cognitively appraise the severity of the situation and match his emotional response accordingly. Therefore he overreacts to simple snags, going from 0 to 100 with little warning. The world is very black and white, good or bad, happy or angry, with little middle ground.

Now, given the above problems, I would recommend the following:

- Once the child has an expectation of what is going to happen, it will be difficult for him to shift gears. So, the best thing to do is prepare him ahead of time. You need to:

○ get used to preparing him for what is coming up before entering into situations. Preview what he can expect, what is expected of him, how long it will last, and what is coming up next

○ lay out any boundaries for behavior before entering the situation, so he has the right expectation and you are not adding rules once the activity starts. You want to make things very clear and concise, very black and white. The more you set his expectation, the less he has to shift gears. If you have to add new rules or change rules in mid-action, give him some time to adjust to it, so he doesn't have to rapidly shift gears

○ give him warning before transitioning from one activity to another. Give him a few minutes' warning before ending an activity and let him know what is coming up next ("In a few minutes we need to stop playing the game and brush your teeth"). Then give him another warning one minute before the transition.

- When you have to add or change rules in the middle of the action, ease into it and redirect without demanding a quick behavior change. Try to avoid saying "no," which means "never and the world will end." Instead of focusing on what he is doing wrong, state what you want him to do. Demanding that he stop doing something or saying "no" doesn't tell him what to do, so it leaves him emotionally hanging without a way of responding. Focus on (1) gently redirecting him into what you want him to do, and (2) helping him out by providing gentle assistance in the right direction. It is not the time to counsel, explain, scold, or use reason. Just gently redirect without demanding and getting emotional.

- Be aware that your emotional reactions, especially arguing, will only fuel the fire. Trying to explain and reason in the heat of the moment will not work. The parent immediately freaks and they start to yell, become demanding, and try to force action. This will immediately make the child melt down. Stay calm, focus on what you want the child to do, and then gently help redirect the child to do it.

- Knowing that interrupting and directing your child will bring on tantrums, try to pick your battles. If you two are arguing a lot, most likely many of the issues are not worth the battle. The more arguing you do, the less positive impact you will have. Try to bite the bullet for many small things and save the intervening for more major issues.

- Since he cannot adequately appraise situations, you want to concretely explain things as they are happening so he sees the big picture. Detail out the situation, especially more subtle aspects that the child will usually miss. He is not going to see it on his own. You have to draw the bigger picture for him.

- Assume that you cannot prepare everything ahead of time, so emotional reactions are going to happen. You need to identify a calming strategy to do with your child to help him calm once he overreacts. Every child is different in what will help calm and organize them, but try to identify and practice coping skills that you and your child will do to help calm him down. I say *you and your child*, because the chance that your child will be able to calm himself is slim in the early stages, unless you simply leave him by himself and let the meltdown run its course. Although time out is frequently used in these situations, this can be scary for the children since they are left by themselves with overwhelming, scary emotions and no help to calm. This is why I don't usually recommend time out. I tend to look for a sensory motor regulatory pattern (see Appendix B), such as deep pressure or neutral warmth, to use as a calming technique. Practice this coping skill every day when the child is calm. Practice it so it feels natural for him when you try to use it in the heat of the moment. Also, try to catch him when he first starts to look upset, before he is so worked up that he will not accept the help.

- Watch your emotions and your language. Try to stay calm and avoid making demands. Try to redirect to what you want him to do. Focus on what you want him to do and then gently assist him in that direction. The more upset he is, the calmer you need to be. Now, saying that is so easy. Don't beat yourself over the head for getting frustrated, upset, and emotional. The situation you are in is very hard. You often feel helpless and angry when you see your child feel and act this way. It takes time and hard work to learn to stay calm in such situations.

I highly recommend parents read the book *The Explosive Child* by Ross Greene (2010). This is a great book for learning how to deal with the problems you are experiencing. There is a lot of information to absorb. Just remember, these problems will take time and patience, and there are no quick fixes.

Meltdowns around compulsive behavior!

One of the members on our page asked for suggestions to help her with her five-year-old son who was very disorganized, compulsive, and demanding. He was very anxious and driven to compulsive behavior as a result of this anxiety. He had to have what he wanted, the way he wanted it, and when he wanted it. He had to have control over everything, otherwise he would melt down. This is very common in anxiety-driven compulsive behavior in young children on the spectrum. The following are some possible suggestions I gave our member. For those of you with similar children, I thought this may be helpful.

MY SUGGESTIONS

I can give you some suggestions, but please take them with caution. I do not know your son and all the antecedent conditions that lead to his meltdowns.

1. With his anxiety level, plus medical problems, you may want to have him evaluated by a DAN (Defeat Autism Now) doctor who specializes in the biomedical treatment of autism. This is expensive, but can be worth it. If you don't have the money for that, try getting on one or two biomedical autism Yahoo message boards, blogs, or Facebook pages, and get advice from some of the parents on what natural supplements they use to treat anxiety.

2. Try to get a good sensory integration evaluation by a qualified occupational therapist for a sensory diet that can be used to calm and organize his nervous system. You may have a good occupational therapist at school who could help.

3. Try to keep him physically active. Physical activity is very good for calming and organizing the nervous system.

4. Right now your son's thinking is very black and white, rigid, and inflexible. When things don't go as expected, he immediately panics and melts down. Also, at age five, his ability to control his emotional responses is not very good. They come on quickly and overwhelm him before he has time to keep them in check. It will take time for his brain to mature enough to have better impulse control. The obsessive compulsive behavior is the only way to keep his anxiety in check. However, from a behavioral standpoint, it is not good to calm his meltdown by giving in and letting him engage in what he is upset about not doing. This will tend to strengthen his meltdowns. The longer he melts down, the more likely he will get what he wants. This makes the behavior stronger and more likely to occur. To help minimize the meltdowns, temporarily I would allow him to engage in the compulsive behaviors as long as they were not hurting anyone or infringing on anyone's rights. Instead of interrupting and telling him "no," causing him to get frustrated, I would pick my battles and let him engage in his compulsive behaviors to minimize frustration. Instead of frustrating him, setting off a meltdown, and then giving in, I would not interrupt the behavior unless I had to. Be flexible yourself, and let him engage in the compulsive behavior if it is not hurting anyone. Compulsive behavior serves the purpose of reducing anxiety. If the behavior is blocked and not allowed, the anxiety will increase and meltdowns will occur. Until he learns alternative coping skills for dealing with frustration and anxiety, it is best to avoid major frustration. Only interrupt behavior that

is too serious to allow. People may see this as giving in, but until we teach your son how to deal with frustration, then having a meltdown is the only mechanism he has.

5. For behaviors that you cannot allow, block and interrupt them, while redirecting him to what you want him to do—not simply telling him what he cannot do. Also, if possible avoid the words "no" or "can't," substituting what he can do or when he can have it. For kids with inflexible thinking, "no" means never and immediate panic sets in. If meltdown still occurs, you want to:

    a) Validate the child's feelings, "I can understand how _____ makes you feel upset. It is OK to feel upset." You do not have to agree with the behavior, just acknowledge and validate the feelings driving the behavior. Then prompt your child to engage in a preplanned strategy for calming when upset.

    b) Identify a plan of action for your son to keep him safe, and to calm him once a meltdown occurs (pull himself away to a safe setting, lie down, sit on sofa, allow deep pressure from you, or engage with you in a soothing interaction). Once this is determined, practice and role-play using the calming strategies at a time when he is not upset. It can be fun to role-play it; sometimes you model by being your son and having a meltdown, followed by you using the calming procedure. Then have him do it. This way, it makes the calming strategy more automatic and predictable to use when upset. Practice the calming strategy together and make it fun. Repetition will lead to greater likelihood of him using it when upset.

    c) Now, back to meltdowns. When he gets upset, validate his feelings to show acceptance of him (not his behavior), have him follow through with the calming strategies, praise him for calming, but do not allow him to get his way once you have told him no. Once he is calm, sit down later and review what happened, and praise him for calming himself with the strategy used (even if it took him two hours to calm).

6. Now, here is the fun part. You want to teach frustration tolerance. Make a list of the most common situations that cause the meltdowns for your son. List them in a hierarchy of least to most anxiety-provoking (least to most likely to cause a meltdown). Starting with the least anxiety-provoking event, role-play or artificially set the situation up to occur frequently. Preview what will happen (the frustrating event) and how he should respond; then practice it. Practice using the calming strategy and praise him for cooperating. As your son learns to handle the minor frustrations without meltdowns, keep working up your list of more anxiety-provoking events. Focus on praising when calm, even if it took a long time to calm. You want to focus on helping him feel competent at calming when frustrated.

7. It is also fun to make picture stories around the common events that upset him and how he can handle himself when upset. In addition to praising him for using the calming strategy during practice, when real-life situations arise, cue him in to what he "should do" (use the calming strategy) and praise for using it. After he has calmed, sit down later and review how he calmed down and was able to make it through the frustration. You want to focus on developing feelings of mastering the frustration.

8. For events coming up in his day that have common stressors for your child, preview ahead of time what is going to happen and how he should respond. Preview and possibly role-play it. During the event, coach him through the coping strategy and praise him for staying calm.

I know this is a lot of information at one time. However, at this time and based on his age, your son will have major frustration and meltdowns. We need to teach him to identify, practice, and gradually learn more effective ways to cope with the frustration. By doing so, we validate that you are a "working partner" with him, supporting and teaching him how to handle frustration.

Using the child's interests and strengths to help teach emotional regulation

In the build-up phase of a meltdown, you can sometimes use the child's interest to distract and get him to follow your lead to help regulate him. The following example shows how the parent uses the child's interest in the alphabet to temporarily distract her and lead her out of the stress.

Jaime, one of our members, had the following question:

 Jaime's question

The 64K question. She enjoys sign language, she taught herself through the *Signing Times* DVD series. Last night, when a flood of emotions/rage came on I had her stop and sign the alphabet, numbers and her name. It re-directed her momentarily and may (?) have decreased the rage that followed. This morning she was punching her wall as she dressed for school and I tried to go in and "soothe" her but she said "don't touch me." She didn't look like she trusted me. So I guess trust IS an issue. I've been so busy not trusting her that I never turned it around and thought she could feel the same. I know that she gets the most relief from deep pressure. When she's relaxed, she's usually wrapped tightly in a blanket. She's had a weighted blanket for years. And I know they use the weighted stuff at school. She even has one of those 'body sox'—I guess I should get the moth balls off of it? Thank you so much for your time and help!

AUTISM DISCUSSION PAGE

Jaime, the fact that she would sign the alphabet with you is a good sign that she will allow you to coach her when under stress. Yes, this temporarily distracts her and gets her focused on something outside herself in order to rebound. Being able to follow your lead in a regulatory pattern (signing the alphabet) can help her learn to regulate and gain control over her emotional reaction. At this time she does not have the ability to inhibit her impulses, so she needs to rely on someone else who she trusts to help her regulate. Since she accepted your coaching, this shows good potential for her. Now, whether she accepts your coaching or not will probably depend on how soon you intervene in the emotional reaction. If you catch her early enough, you can distract, focus attention on the signing, and keep her regulated. If she gets too overwhelmed, she may not be able follow your lead.

Let me take you through what I would recommend. Now, remember all I know about your daughter is the few sentences that you described above, so I may be off base.

1. Your daughter responded well to "focused distraction," as described above. This is a great tool for interrupting, getting focus on something outside herself, and following your lead to pace and calm her. The more situations in which the two of you use this technique to calm, the more responsive she will become to inhibiting her emotional impulses.

2. She enjoys deep pressure stimulation, which is good to calm an anxious nervous system. However, it sounds as if she doesn't like someone touching her when she is upset. If she likes to wrap herself in a blanket, then this may be a good technique to use to self-calm. Some people who need both deep pressure and intense stimulation will lie face down on a bed, with arms underneath them, and rock/roll from side to side. The rolling enhances the deep pressure and is totally controlled by the person.

3. It is nice to have both (1) self-calming techniques and (2) other assisted calming techniques (for times when she cannot regulate on her own).

4. Work closely with your daughter to teach her to (1) recognize when she is starting to get upset and (2) use calming techniques when she starts to feel herself getting upset. At first you may need to cue her in when you see her starting to get upset (she may not recognize it) and coach her to use the calming techniques.

5. To teach emotion regulation, first start with practicing the regulation when calm. Make a list of situations that frequently frustrate her. Write each one on an index card. Every day pick a couple of example cards and role-play them, practicing using the calming techniques. The best time to learn something is when you are not upset. She needs to practice and instill the techniques when she is calm and organized. Do them together, establishing the trust in both the techniques and following your lead. Do them together, have fun, and praise heavily.

6. Throughout the day look for situations of stress. When you see her getting a little upset, acknowledge how she looks, reassure her it is OK, and then redirect her into the calming strategies (signing alphabet, deep pressure). Do them together if she needs the coaching. Focus on the mastery she experiences. For situations that occur throughout the day, afterwards review how it went (when both are calm). If it went well, talk about how she (or both of you) mastered the frustration by using the coping strategies. If it didn't go well, discuss how maybe you need to start earlier or use a different technique. Add the recent situation to an index card to practice for the next couple of days.

7. Make a hierarchy of least to most frustrating situations. Make a list of low-level frustrating situations, a list of moderate-level frustrating activities, and a list of examples of high-level frustration. If she is not ready to use the techniques during the high-level frustrating situations, then start by providing frequent exposure to using the techniques for low-level situations. Once she feels competent using the strategies during these times, then move to moderate-level situations. Once these are mastered, move on to the higher-level frustrating situations.

8. It is important for her to feel the anxiety, not to cover it up. Acknowledge how she feels, validate that it is OK and that she is safe. She cannot feel the mastery without first feeling the anxiety that she is tackling. We want her to eventually feel competent in the face of anxiety, not to hide it. Through repeated, successful mastery of anxiety-provoking events, she will learn not to overreact to the anxiety. She will learn that (1) the anxiety is not as threatening and (2) she has the power to successfully handle it. This will help decrease the initial fight-or-flight panic that comes now when she starts to feel frustrated.

9. This is a good time to introduce a three-point emotion rating scale, with 1 being annoying, 2 being upsetting, and 3 being mad. She may need to learn different coping strategies for each level, based on the intensity of frustration. For example, counting, signing, or deep breathing for level 1 (annoying), self-hug wraps for level 2 (upsetting), and deep pressure rolling on the bed for high level 3s (angry). When frustrating events occur, ask her what numerical rating is it and then use that coping skill.

10. Most importantly, focus on the times when she conquers the frustration, focusing on the feelings of mastery and competency.

You can use any one of these strategies or all of them together, depending on what works for your child. The point is gradually teaching your child how to feel safe with her emotions by learning to control them.

Adult meltdowns

Some of the adults on the spectrum who are fans of the Autism Discussion Page want to discuss some of the adult issues. Several of you mentioned dealing with meltdowns. So here are my thoughts! Please comment and share your experiences.

Many of the strategies for dealing with meltdowns in children are similar for adults. However, adults are expected to implement their own strategies, advocate for themselves, and be aware of their own stressors and overload. The strategies for adults on the spectrum need to be a self-management plan, rather than one that a parent or teacher designs and implements. So, what was once an externally designed plan needs now to become a self-managed plan.

Start with your nervous system! Your nervous system is fragile and more likely to be vulnerable to stress. It is important that you eat well, exercise regularly, and get plenty of sleep. Make sure you don't skip meals; eat mini snacks and keep a nutritious diet. Try to give yourself 30 minutes of exercise daily. Exercise is important for regulating your nervous system. And, of course, you need plenty of sleep and rest breaks during the day. Since your nervous is more fragile, it will become taxed very easily if you are hungry or fatigued.

Sensory overload

- Adults on the spectrum need to be keenly aware of their own tolerance levels to avoid overload. This includes sensory sensitivities, social tolerances, informational overload, and mental energy levels. You need to know what types of stimulation to avoid, and how to make modifications and advocate for accommodations in your work and living settings. Be aware of what sensory stimuli in commonly visited settings are irritating to you, what may overwhelm you, and how you can accommodate and adapt to them. Modify the environment if you can; if not, build in adaptations to cope.

- Make your daily settings sensory-friendly. Try to make modifications to your home and work setting (softened lighting, muffled noise, partitioned work area, etc.) to make the environment as sensory-friendly as possible. At home, even if your family will not make modifications, try to make one room of your home sensory-friendly for you to escape to when you need to rebound.

- If you are going to new events, try to visit the setting ahead of time if possible, to check out the setting and evaluate the sensory bombardment you may experience. This way, you can figure out what accommodations you may need. Plan ahead for all events and review before going.

- Keep a sensory "toolbox" (sunglasses, rim hat, gum, ear plugs, MP3 player, fidget items, etc.) at home, at work, and in your car. Don't wait until you start to feel stressed to use your tools. Always appraise the settings you are in; be proactive and use these tools and coping strategies to avoid accumulating stress that will lead to overload.

Social overload

- Monitor your social demands. For most adults on the spectrum, interacting can be very taxing. So, know what your limits are. For most individuals, interacting one on one with someone you know can go OK for short periods of time. However, trying to regulate in a group conversation or navigate a group activity can be very taxing and overwhelming. Try to avoid such activities, or only stay in them for short periods of time. Know your limits. If you are at parties, try to find the least active area that will minimize the amount of social contact you have. Let people come to you, rather than you mingling around the room. That way you can control the level of interaction you have to regulate.

- At work, know your physical and social environment well. Group meetings where you have to present or interact extensively will be very taxing for you. Try to arrange your social interaction to be brief and familiar. Try to avoid the crowded coffee room, cafeteria, and social stops where others may put you in the social hot seat. Try to get an individual office or partitioned work area. Listen to music to block out conversations and background noises.

- If you are a parent or live with others, you will need to give yourself a spot to get away to regroup. Home should be a safe setting where you can be yourself and meet your sensory, social, and emotional needs so you can regroup for the next day.

Processing overload

- Try to avoid work tasks that require a lot of multitasking. Try to do one task at a time, and break longer tasks into simpler steps. Keep a very organized home and work area; give everything a predetermined spot and keep it there.

- Develop consistent routines and schedules throughout your day to keep yourself organized and reduce confusion. Map out your day (time and events) and leave yourself plenty of time between events. Many people on the spectrum have a difficult time judging how much time tasks will take. Then they get rushed and anxious, increasing chances of overload. This strategy ensures that you complete necessary tasks, and allows you to relax and regroup between tasks.

- Remember that your mental energy, as you move from one task to another, will drain easily. Plan frequent breaks to rebound and re-energize. Again, don't wait until you feel taxed to take breaks. Proactively schedule in frequent breaks to avoid being taxed and overwhelmed. Once you start to get tired, your energy drains more quickly, and overload can set in before you have a chance to react.

- The more taxing the event, the more time you need to rebound and re-energize. If you are going to a highly taxing event, don't plan another event immediately afterwards. For highly taxing social events (concerts, parties, etc.), you may need to spend the next day doing very little. If you know you are going to go out socially on Friday night, take a good portion of Saturday to regroup.

Escape and rebound

- Always have a means of escape if you feel yourself being overloaded. This can be to the bathroom, outside, your car, or a separate area away from the group. It is best if you give yourself these breaks periodically throughout the event to proactively minimize overload. Remember, it is not wise to wait until you start feeling stressed to react. It may be too late!

- When going into any new setting, map out a means of temporary escape if needed and to take breaks to regroup. Also, arrive late and leave early to avoid overload. Keep a sensory tool with you to help you regroup once you escape.

- Learn the early signs that your body is telling you that stress is building up. Many adults on the spectrum report poor awareness of the bodily cues that they are getting stressed. They do not have good self-awareness of their internal states, which tell us that we are starting to get stressed. This is important in order to be able to pull out of stressful situations before becoming overwhelmed. To be able to avoid meltdowns effectively, you have to be aware of when you are in the beginning stages of build-up. There is new work being done with meditation and mindfulness exercises to help adults become more aware of their bodily sensations and to lower their stress levels.

- Identify and practice a few relaxation coping skills (deep breathing, positive self-talk, fidget item in pocket, gum, etc.) to help relax your nervous system while in high-stress settings. Distraction (music, mental tasks, etc.) can help you block out some unwanted stressors.

- Lastly, when feeling a meltdown coming, escape as soon as possible. It is important to leave immediately. It is better to flee than act out! Get away and engage in your favorite calming strategies. You can always apologize later. You do not have time to problem-solve at this time. Your coping skills are minimal and decreasing quickly. If needed, carry a small card that explains why you are leaving (escaping). You may not have the words to explain. Just get out, escape, and rebound!

I hope some of these suggestions help. Please feel free to share your experiences and add additional recommendations on the Facebook page.

Part VI

PUTTING IT ALL TOGETHER

WHERE TO GO FROM HERE

This book explored four main areas of vulnerabilities (cognitive, sensory, social, and emotional) that cause major stress and anxiety for those on the spectrum. My aim was for the reader to walk away with a good understanding of how the person on the spectrum processes information and experiences the world. For parents, teachers, and caregivers, I hope that you have gained a better understanding of how your child is experiencing the world, as well as possible strategies for helping him to feel safe, accepted, and competent facing these challenges. I hope you have gained greater awareness of how to help build on your child's strengths, accommodate for his vulnerabilities, and foster healthy development.

There is a lot of information in this book. What do you do with it, and where do you start? In the appendices I have provided three documents to summarize the areas of vulnerabilities (Appendix E, Fragile World on the Spectrum), allow you to complete a brief assessment of where your child is at (Appendix G, Core Deficit Assessment), and then develop a profile of how to help your child feel safe, accepted, and competent (Appendix H, Comfort Zones Profile). The Comfort Zones Profile is a great tool to give teachers, professionals, caregivers, friends, and relatives in the child's life, to help guide them in supporting your child.

The first document, Fragile World on the Spectrum (Appendix E), consists of four pages of diagrams that explain stress, anxiety, and meltdowns. The second and fourth pages of this document also summarize the different areas of vulnerabilities and challenges for children on the spectrum, and list common strategies for accommodating and supporting these challenges. I frequently use this document to explain the core areas that produce stress and anxiety for the children, as well as the effects this stress has on the child's nervous system. The second page gives me a comprehensive summary of the children's main areas of vulnerabilities. It frames my assessment, like a checklist, so I cover all the areas and develop a comprehensive understanding of how the child experiences the world. Once we complete our assessment, I use this page to summarize which challenges the child experiences and how they interrelate with each other. It provides the parents and/or the individual with a comprehensive view of what we need to focus on to help him feel safe, accepted, and competent in his daily living. On the fourth page, we use this chart to develop a comprehensive plan of strategies to support each one of the main areas of challenges. We pick and choose which areas are priorities and which strategies to use. We develop a comprehensive menu of interrelated strategies that will help support the child to be all that he can be.

The second document, Core Deficit Assessment (Appendix G), provides a brief screening tool for each one of these four areas of vulnerability (sensory, cognitive, social, and emotional). As I go through each domain (sensory, cognitive, social, and emotional) with the parents (or individual), we rate how prevalent each item is and give concrete examples of how these qualities are expressed in their child. This screening tool is a good starting point for identifying items of interest for developing proactive strategies. Also in Appendix A, Sensory Evaluation, I provide a more detailed assessment tool for further defining the child's sensory profile. These documents are also good to give to professionals that you seek out for assistance.

Finally, the third document is the Comfort Zones Profile (Appendix H), which you can use to summarize the sensory, cognitive, social, and emotional strategies for helping your child feel safe, accepted, and competent. This document helps frame a comprehensive profile of how to support your child in all settings that he regularly attends. It also has a section for listing your child's strengths, preferences, and interests, with ideas on how to build these qualities into learning and relating experiences. Give this document to the school and add it as an addendum to the IEP (individualized education program). Give the document to caregivers, professionals, and relatives who frequently support your child. You can add and subtract any information to this profile that is important for supporting your child. This document can later be used and modified by the children themselves to advocate for their own needs.

Between these three documents you can continually reflect on what progress is being made, determine what objectives to work on, add new strategies, and update new information for helping your child feel safe, accepted, and competent!

Appendices A, C, D, G, and H are available to be downloaded from www.jkp.com/catalogue/book/9781849059947/resources and they have been marked with a ★.

Where to go from here?

Facebook page!

As stated in the introduction, this book is a collection of articles (posts) that I share on the Facebook page, Autism Discussion Page (www.facebook.com/autismdiscussionpage). This Facebook page has more than 50,000 members (parents, teachers, professionals, and adults on the spectrum from all over the world) who comment, give suggestions, and share their valuable experiences. We continually review each of these articles while exploring and sharing ideas and learning from each other. On this page I also provide more than 40 PowerPoint slide presentations in the photo section of the page, which provide narrative slides relating to these topics. People can post questions, give suggestions, and share their valuable experiences with others. This book, together with the second book below, provides a manual for the page. Between the posts, comments, slide presentations, and discussions, this page provides for multifaceted, continued learning opportunities.

The second book: The Autism Discussion Page on anxiety, behavior, school, and parenting strategies: A toolbox for helping children with autism feel safe, accepted, and competent

This book is part of a two-book series compiling all the educational articles found at our Facebook page, Autism Discussion Page (www.facebook.com/autismdiscussionpage). This book provides information on the four main areas of core differences. The second book goes into more specific issues of stress and anxiety, teaching coping skills, effective discipline, tackling challenging behaviors, using strengths and preferences, teaching and mentoring strategies, building daily living skills, tackling issues at school, and empowering yourself and your child. Between the two books, you have a comprehensive toolbox of strategies for supporting your child is all areas of life and in all settings!

Good luck! Please join us at the Facebook page (Autism Discussion Page) and become part of the journey!

Appendix A

SENSORY EVALUATION

Name: Born: Age:

Residence: Date of assessment:

Target behaviors (issues) of concern:

Circumstances surrounding behavior (precipitating events, consequences (reactions) to the behavior):

Does behavior occur in a chain?

Medical concerns (seizures, allergies, constipation, utis, diabetes, reflux, ulcers, etc.):

Medications:

Communication skills:

Vision/hearing:

Tactile

☐ Dislikes being touched.
☐ Resists hugs and kisses.
☐ Is fearful when others approach.
☐ Withdraws or hits when approached or touched.
☐ Rubs spot after being touched.
☐ Exhibits clingy behavior.
☐ Tries to handle or touch everything/others.
☐ Resists others holding hand.
☐ Insists on large personal space.
☐ Prefers to be in corner, under table, behind furniture.
☐ Likes/dislikes tight clothing.
☐ Layers clothing.
☐ Pushes up pant legs, sleeves, shirts.
☐ Strips off clothing.
☐ Will only will wear certain texture of clothing.
☐ Removes tags, collars, or cuffs.
☐ Frequently adjusts clothing or bedding.
☐ Insists on something wrapped around wrist, arm, and finger.
☐ Dislikes being barefoot.
☐ Insists on being barefoot.
☐ Walks on toes.
☐ Spits out/rejects certain food textures.
☐ Is a picky eater.
☐ Resists grooming: face washing, bathing, shaving, hair combing, tooth brushing, nail cutting.
☐ Has a high tolerance for pain.
☐ Over- or under-sensitive to hot or cold.
☐ Dislikes wearing hats.
☐ Craves deep pressure.
☐ Engages in persistent hand-to-mouth activity.
☐ Mouths objects or clothing.
☐ Rubs or plays with spit, feces.
☐ Persistently has hand in pants or pants pocket.
☐ Sits on hands/feet.
☐ Pushes or rubs body against objects/walls/people.
☐ Insists on holding an object in hands.
☐ Rubs fingers against hand or other fingers.
☐ Masturbates frequently.
☐ Engages in self-injurious behavior: scratches, pinches, rubs, hits/slaps, pulls hair, bites hand/wrist/arm.

Comments:

Proprioceptive

☐ Has poor muscle tone.
☐ Has weak grip.
☐ Tires easily.
☐ Is passive unless encouraged or assisted.
☐ Has slurred speech.
☐ Is clumsy/awkward.
☐ Is awkward getting on and off furniture.
☐ Is overly rough with objects and people.
☐ Likes to rough house, wrestle.
☐ Flaps hands, claps, jumps, hops, stamps feet.
☐ Bites, chews on objects.
☐ Presses or bangs wrists.
☐ Climbs in inappropriate places.
☐ Pushes or leans heavily against people or objects.
☐ Slams furniture, pounds on wall, throws things.
☐ Hits, slaps, or bangs head.
☐ Bites self.
☐ Grinds teeth.
☐ Butts head or body into things.
☐ Hits, kicks, pushes objects/others.

Comments:

Vestibular

☐ Tenses or becomes irritable when moved.
☐ Displays gravitational insecurity.
☐ Has poor balance, is anxious when moving.
☐ Drops to floor when anxious or walking distance.
☐ Is hesitant on stairs or ramps.
☐ Resists being moved by others.
☐ Resists participating in movement activities.
☐ Loses balance easily.
☐ Falls or trips easily.
☐ Holds on to staff, railing, wall.
☐ Prefers to sit on the floor.
☐ Bumps into things, has difficulty walking around things.
☐ Rocks frequently.
☐ Jumps, twirls, spins, or bounces.
☐ Wags head.
☐ Paces, seeks frequent movement.
☐ Likes to swing.
☐ Likes movement activities.
☐ Waves or flicks finger(s) near eyes.
☐ Has spurts of running.

Comments:

★

Auditory

❏ Is sensitive to loud noises.
❏ Can hear frequencies that others cannot.
❏ Can hear humming of lights, electrical wires, other breathing that others cannot.
❏ Speaks loudly.
❏ Hums constantly.
❏ Covers ears with hands.
❏ Is distracted by background noises.
❏ Becomes agitated in large group activities.
❏ Is a very noisy person.
❏ Listens to TV or music at loud volume.
❏ Becomes agitated, disruptive in noisy activities.
❏ Relaxes when whispered to.
❏ Loves music.
❏ Has frequent ear infections.
❏ Sometimes "tunes out" or "turns off" from world.

Comments:

Visual

❏ Is oversensitive to sunlight.
❏ Is oversensitive to bright lighting.
❏ Squints frequently, looks down a lot.
❏ Becomes overwhelmed with strong visual changes.
❏ Flaps hands, usually around eye level.
❏ Rolls head, usually from side to side.
❏ Enjoys staring at lights.
❏ Enjoys turning lights on and off.
❏ Enjoys things that spin or turn.
❏ Plays with hands in front of eyes.
❏ Presses eyes with hands, usually at corners.
❏ Has difficulty moving from one surface to another.
❏ Is a page turner.
❏ Loves shiny or reflective objects.
❏ Loves mirrors.
❏ Has poor eye contact.
❏ Appears to stare through people.
❏ Is fascinated with fans, things that spin.
❏ Eyes tire easily/quickly when reading.

Comments:

Smell/taste

❏ Smells everything.
❏ Will not eat without smelling food first.
❏ Likes to smell others' hair.
❏ Loves the smell of cologne or perfume.
❏ Dislikes smell of cologne or perfume.
❏ Has strong emotional reactions to smells.
❏ Becomes disorganized, irritable in activities with strong smells.
❏ Avoids things with strong smells, especially cleanser.
❏ Frequently smells hands/fingers.
❏ Is a very picky eater.
❏ Dislikes certain textures or taste of food.
❏ Loves only strong tasting food.
❏ Eats only bland food.
❏ Puts everything in mouth.
❏ Chews on string, clothing, and fingers.
❏ Has many allergies.
❏ Will spit out foods does not like.

Comments:

General reactions

❏ Poor frustration tolerance.
❏ Needs to control all activity and interaction.
❏ Inability to delay gratification.
❏ Poor attention span, distractible.
❏ Noncompliant, resistant to direction.
❏ Unpredictable emotional outbursts.
❏ Constantly moving, difficulty sitting still.
❏ Difficulty with transitions between activities, places, and people.
❏ Generally anxious, easily upset, disorganized.
❏ Becomes overwhelmed with highly stimulating activities.
❏ Becomes upset with change in routine.
❏ Needs rigid schedule.
❏ Seeks constant attention or reassurance.

Comments:

★

Stimulation person seeks/craves:	Stimulation person avoids:
Touch:	Touch:
Proprioceptive:	Proprioceptive:
Vestibular:	Vestibular:
Auditory:	Auditory:
Visual:	Visual:
Taste/smell:	Taste/smell:

Stimulation that tends to calm and organize:

Tactile:
❏ Brushing.
❏ Deep pressure massage.
❏ Neutral warmth, wrap.
❏ Sandwiching, pillow press.
❏ Lotion or talc rub.
❏ Rolling therapy ball over body.
❏ Deep pressure stroking down arms, legs, or back.
❏ Sandwiching between mats or bean bags.
❏ Wrapping: blankets, towels, clothing (spandex), Ace bandages.
❏ Snuggling in bedding or large pillows, or stuffed animals.
❏ Sleeping/lying in sleeping bag.

Also alerts:
❏ Brisk rubbing.
❏ Tickling.
❏ Rubbing with different textures.
❏ Finger painting.
❏ Finding objects in sand, bean, rice, etc.
❏ Water play.

Proprioceptive:
❏ Joint compressions, head compressions, finger stretch.
❏ Full body stretch.
❏ Chew gum.
❏ Squeeze "stress ball" or squishy ball.
❏ Physical relaxation/isometric exercises.
❏ Weights vests, ankle/wrist weights, backpacks
❏ Vibration less than 110 Hz.

Also alerts:
❏ Bending, reaching, stretching activities.
❏ Lifting, carrying, push/pull, stacking.
❏ Any gross motor activities: hop, skip, run, jump, climb, crawl, creep, scoot, march, stomp, clap, squeeze, tug, hang on.
❏ Trampoline.
❏ Kick/bounce/throw ball.
❏ Dancing.
❏ Any physical exercises, exercise bands, push-ups, resistant exercises—isometrics in chair.
❏ Vacuuming, sweeping.
❏ Outdoor work, pushing lawn mower, sweeping garage, raking.
❏ Mat time, rough-housing, wrestling.
❏ Arm wrestling.
❏ Leap frog, tug-of-war, wheelbarrow walking.
❏ Jumping and crashing on the bed or bean bag.
❏ Healthy, chewy foods (e.g. celery, carrots, apples, nuts, fruit leather, beef jerky), thick liquids requiring straw (milkshakes, smoothies, gelatin, pudding).
❏ Rolling/kneading dough/clay.

★

(Stimulation that tends to calm and organize *cont.***)**

Vestibular
- ☐ Slow lateral swinging.
- ☐ Slow rocking.
- ☐ Passive bouncing on trampoline—sitting.

Also alerts:
- ☐ Swinging.
- ☐ Turning, rotating, spinning.
- ☐ Most gross motor movement: jumping, running, bouncing, crawling, etc.
- ☐ Trampoline.
- ☐ Scooter boards, wagon rides.
- ☐ Sitting on therapy ball to watch TV or do work.
- ☐ Playing on slides, swings, seesaws, trapezes, rings, ladders.
- ☐ Dancing.

Helps to provide proprioceptive stimulation (organizing) following vestibular (arousing).

Auditory/visual
- ☐ Soft music.
- ☐ Minimize light and noise.
- ☐ Environmental tapes.
- ☐ Ear plugs, head phones/mp3 to block out noise.
- ☐ Sunglasses to minimize light.
- ☐ Lava lights or relaxation lights.
- ☐ Screening walls at work areas to help minimize stimulation.

Taste/smell:

Treatment planning:

Sensory diet: Modulate (increase/decrease) arousal

Alerting activities: **Calming activities:**

★

List accommodations/adaptations needed (ear plugs, sunglasses, etc.):

Schedule of sensory activities (list activities at specific times during the day):

Meltdown/crisis times (calming/organizing techniques, quiet area to escape—soothing music, large pillows, squeeze objects, etc.):

★

Appendix B

SENSORY MOTOR REGULATORY PATTERNS

Purpose: Calm and organize nervous system.
Promote emotional attunement.
Establish "facial gazing" and "emotion sharing."
Establish adult as soothing support when distressed.

1. Use very simple interactive activities, such as peek-a-boo, "I am going get you," rocking back and forth, sandwiching/squishing with bean bag, etc. that provide repetitive, rhythmic interaction patterns.

2. Sit (stand) face to face, at eye level, with close physical contact. This allows you to regulate activity, keep the child focused, and encourage facial gazing.

3. Add rhythmic sing-song or chatting (like "Row, row, row your boat") to the rhythmic pattern. This uses your voice, touch, and facial expression to engage the child.

4. Use exaggerated gestures, animated facial expressions, and exciting vocal noises to engage the child, establish facial gazing, and share enjoyment.

5. Your primary objective is to establish facial gazing so that the child can reference your emotions. Start the rhythmic pattern and establish facial gazing. If the child averts his gaze (turns away), hesitate and pause the interaction until the child returns gaze, then immediately restart the pattern. If needed, you can stutter or exaggerate the movement, slow it down or speed it up, or raise or lower your voice to draw the child's gaze back to you.

6. You can greatly enhance the emotion sharing by spotlighting the exciting part of the pattern. Hesitate, pause, exaggerate, or draw out the moment just before the climax (just before dropping, tickling, etc.). For example, in peek-a-boo, just before showing your animated face, draw out the words "peek, aaaaaaaaaaa, boo!" This creates anticipation and excitement.

7. Stay with the same pattern for a while to create a sense of predictability and familiarity. As the child becomes comfortable with the pattern, you can add simple variations to the pattern. Keep it very simple at first and add small variations to provide novelty and excitement. If the child seems too anxious at the change, back up to the previous pattern.

8. Try to pick only a few patterns to start with. Keep them simple and do them the same way at first so that they become familiar and predictable for the child.

9. Eventually you will feel the child start to help regulate the activity. As you hesitate, the child may actively attempt to regulate the pattern.

10. It is important that you lead the activity, as much as possible, so the child learns to feel safe following your lead. For children who actively resist this, you may have to let the child lead and slowly teach the child to feel safe following your lead.

11. Remember what your objectives are. You are focusing on establishing "facial gazing," "emotion sharing," and "engagement."

Most importantly, engage the child and have fun!

Sensory motor regulatory patterns

1. Rocking, swaying, or dancing together. Standing or sitting, hold the child's hands or arms, and rock, sway, or dance in a simple rhythmic movement. Chant or sing.

2. "1,2,3…bop!" Gently clap hands and tap cheeks. Take his hands in yours, clap them softly together to the count of "1..2..3" and "bop!" tap his hands to your cheeks. Then repeat to his cheeks.

3. Peek-a-boo, using the child's hands or feet. Animate your facial expressions and voice.

4. Leg presses. Lie the child down. Kneel in front of him and bend his knees so they are up in the air, with your face between them. While counting to three, bounce his knees slightly. Chant "1..2..3…pause/hesitate…PRESS!" and press his knees down and in toward his chest. Allow your face to follow so it comes in close to his gaze.

5. Blowing up a balloon. The adult blows up a balloon with animated expressions. Gently let air out on the child's hand or neck, make squeaky noises while letting air out, or let go of balloon to fly around the room. Variation: have the child press against your cheeks as you blow. In addition, tie the balloon and gently tap it back and forth.

6. Blowing bubbles, face to face, while the child touches, claps, or tries to catch them. Get close, wait until the child references your face before blowing the bubble.

7. "Up…up…up…drop!" With the child lying down, hold his arms and gradually lift his upper body with stuttering pauses ("up…up…up"). Hesitate, then let the child drop them back down with animated excitement.

8. "I am going to get you, get you, get you!" Then tickle, poke or kiss the child.

9. Rocking/rowing back and forth. Sit facing each other, holding each other's arms. Slowly rock back and forth (to "Row, row, row your boat"), or pull each other (stretch) back and forth.

10. Crash, fall, or jump together into bean bags. Stand side by side, count to three… pause… and fall together. Lie there a moment and tickle each other.

11. Push the child backwards into bean bags. With the child's back to the bean bags, count 1, 2, 3 and push him to fall backwards into the bean bags. Cuddle and tickle together on bags.

12. Pillow press with bean bag or large pillow. With the child lying down, chat, "I am going to get you!" and squish him with a bean bag. Keep your face close to his for emotion sharing.

13. Friendly pillow fights. Use animated faces and excited vocals to create anticipation.

14. Sit and bounce together on therapy balls. Hold hands and bounce or sway together. Add excitement by creating a chant and falling off!

15. Toss a ball back and forth, or try to hit each other with a soft ball.

16. Clapping hands or drumming to music. Get face to face, take his hands and clap them to a simple beat, with animated singing.

17. Swinging. With the child in a swing, stand in front of him, take his legs, and swing him back and forth. On the way up, hold and pause to elicit anticipation, then let him drop and swing back. Variation: As he swings, grab his feet each time he comes back. Variation: pretend to be kicked each time the child comes back at you.

18. "This is the way the cowboy rides!" Sit the child on your knees, facing you. Take his arms and gently bounce him on your knees. Start with "This is the way the lady rides," then "gentleman rides," then "the cowboy rides" as you increase the intensity of bouncing.

19. Making a sandwich. Make a sandwich with the child as meat. Lie the child on a large pillow or couch cushion. The child pretends to be his favorite meat. Pretend to spread mustard, ketchup, pickles, etc. on him in tickling fashion. Next place another large pillow on top of the child and pretend to eat him.

20. Rolling prone on ball: Lie the child prone on a ball. Holding his hands, roll him back and forth to "Row, row, row your boat." Pause and go faster for "merrily, merrily, merrily, merrily, life is but a dream" and roll the child off ball into your arms.

21. Bounce and fall off ball. Kneel in front of the child. Hold the child and bounce him on a ball to "Humpty Dumpty." Pause and draw out "h…a…d…a…g…r… e…a…t…" and bounce the child off on to a bean bag to "FALL!"

22. Rolling ball on the child: With the child lying down, roll the therapy ball over his body and sing (to rhythm of "Mary had a little lamb") "We're rolling out the cookie dough, cookie dough, cookie dough, (repeat) …(pause/hesitate)…and bouncing it to pieces (bounce ball on the child)."

23. Swinging. Hold the child's legs and swing back and forth while chanting. After a few swings, swing the child up and hold…pausing (sharing excited facial expressions) and letting him drop.

24. Making a hot dog roll. Lie the child on one end of a roll-out blanket. Pretend to make a hot dog roll. Put on mustard, ketchup, relish, etc. and then roll him tight in the blanket…and pretend to eat him.

25. Sit the child on top of the back of a couch that is up against a wall. To "Humpty Dumpty," when you get to "had a great…(pause/hesitate)…FALL," pull the child so he slides down the couch to the cushion.

26. "Wheels on the bus." Sit the child on your lap. Hold his arms and rotate to "Wheel on the bus go round and round," then back and forth to "Wipers go swish, swish, swish," then bounce to "people on the bus go up and down."

27. Using face paint, sit face to face and paint each other's faces.

28. Sit with your child in front of you. Let the child brush and "do your hair" with ribbons, curlers, barrettes. Make funny faces and excited statements.

29. Sit side by side in front of a mirror. Take turns tracing each other's face on the mirror.

30. Sit face to face and feed each other ice cream out of a bowl. Use an animated face and excited vocal to "emotion share."

This is only the beginning! Use your creativity and improvise as you go along. Any simple interactive games can be adapted for facial gazing, social referencing, and emotion sharing.

Appendix C

CHILD ENGAGEMENT QUESTIONNAIRE

Child's name: Respondent:
Child's age: Date:

This child is being considered for a program to encourage social referencing, cooperative play, and reciprocal interaction. We are trying to gather information regarding the type of activities your child prefers, what he will participate in with you, what type of preferences the child has, and what type of guidance he will respond the best to.

Motivation for engagement

Does child seek out interaction with others?

Does child seem interested in what others are doing?

Does child respond positively when invited by others?

Does child welcome others' involvement in his play?

Does child initiate interaction/play with others?

Does child draw attention of others to things that excite him?

Level of engagement

Will child allow others to closely watch what he is doing?

Will child allow others to actively participate in what he is doing?

Will child allow others to add variations or lead the activity?

Will child actively follow the lead of another in activity?

Does child need to control the interaction/activity and actively resist the lead of others?

Will child share toys in parallel play?

Will child engage in reciprocal, back-and-forth play?

Will child attempt to stay coordinated with others in activity?

Will child engage in pretend play?

Type of engagement

What are different types of activities child will engage in?

Play activities:

Household tasks:

Personal care (toileting, dressing, bath, etc.):

What is the favorite activity to engage child?

How long will child engage in activity/interaction with you?

Try and list at least three activities that will most likely encourage your child to engage with you:

Experience-sharing abilities

Does child reference others to share pleasurable emotion?

Will child turn to others for soothing when scared or upset?

Will child reference the face of others for information?

What conditions elicit the best eye contact/facial gazing from the child?

Will child engage in back-and-forth referencing facial expressions to share emotion and clarify/verify actions?

Following the lead of others

Will child follow your lead in simple activities?

How does child respond to:

Verbal instruction:

Gestures:

Demonstration:

Physical guidance:

Visual strategies:

Does child respond better to an animated/excited approach, or a calm, quiet approach?

What is the best way to prompt and guide the child?

★

Sensory profile

Touch

What type of touch does child seek out?

What type of touch does child avoid?

How does child respond to (+ likes it, - dislikes it, +/- inconsistent):

Light touch?	Firm, deep pressure?	
Touch to face?	Hands?	Head?
Shoulders/back?	Arms/legs?	Stomach?
Types of touch: Stroking?	Massaging?	Hugging?
Kissing?	Caressing?	

What type of touch calms/soothes child?

What type of touch alerts child?

Will child allow you to touch him during fun activities?

Does child allow touch to guide and direct him?

Movement

What type of movement does child seek out?

What type of movement does child avoid?

What type of movement calms: slow, rhythmic, rocking, side to side, etc.?

What type of movement alerts: fast, intense, jerky, etc.?

Does child like to be picked up and swung around?

Does child like chase games?

Does child like run and jump play?

How does child respond to:

Slow movement:

Fast movement:

Rhythmic moment:

★

Linear, circular, spinning:

Positions: standing, sitting, prone, etc.

Proprioception

Does child like rough-housing, wrestling?

Does child enjoy push, pull, hitting, kicking type of activities?

Does child like falling, crashing into things?

Auditory

Does child have any sensitivity to noise: loud noises, frequencies, and specific noise?

Does child seek out auditory stimulation: likes loud, stimulating noise, vocal stimulation?

Children on the spectrum often respond well to rhythm and rhyme. When interacting with the child, does he enjoy it when you:

Sing:

Chant:

Use an animated voice/facial expression:

Hum:

Use a sing-song voice:

General

What stimulation does child seek out?

What stimulation does child try to avoid?

What stimulation tends to calm and soothe child?

What stimulation tends to excite and alert child?

Does child tend to engage in any self-stimulatory behavior?

Does child have any obsessive interests/passions?

What are child's favorite activities?

What helps child feel safe?

What are child's fears?

★

Appendix D

FEELINGS CHARTS

Feelings chart

This chart is used to start teaching children to label their feelings in the moment. Periodically throughout the day, ask the child to identify the picture/emotion that best defines how he is feeling. This is also good to use during events to identify how the child feels so he starts to connect the feelings to the events.

Feelings inventory

This chart has the child identify what common events create the given feeling for him. The child starts to not just label the emotions but also to connect the emotions to common events in their day.

Emotions rating scale

This chart uses a five-point rating scale to teach children to rate the degree of intensity of given emotions. Many children are all-or-nothing thinkers with little awareness of the degree of relativity of emotions. This chart teaches them how to gauge the intensity of emotions by rating them from one to five.

Emotions rating inventory

This chart helps the child to identify common daily events that create the intensity of emotion for each rating. What events annoy him, irritate him, upset him, etc.? This helps the child connect his emotions to common events.

Coping skills inventory

Once the children can gauge the intensity of the emotion, then they can learn what coping skills they can use at each level of intensity. For example, the child may use positive self-talk ("I can handle this") or a protest statement ("Please stop that") when annoyed or irritated, and use deep breathing, leave and seek help, etc. at higher levels.

Feelings chart

Calm

Happy

Sad

Angry

Scared

★

Feelings inventory

Events that create the feeling

Feeling	Events that create the feeling
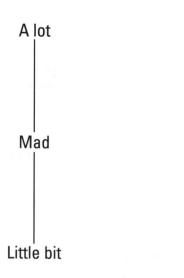 Calm	
Happy	
Sad	
Angry	
Scared	

Emotions rating scale

A lot

5	Furious
4	Angry
3	Upset
2	Irritated
1	Annoyed

Mad

Little bit

★

Emotions rating inventory

Events that create the feeling

5	Furious	
4	Angry	
3	Upset	
2	Irritated	
1	Annoyed	

Coping skills inventory

List coping skills for each level

5	Furious	
4	Angry	
3	Upset	
2	Irritated	
1	Annoyed	

★

FRAGILE WORLD ON THE SPECTRUM

My world is "confusing" and "overwhelming!"

Overwhelming environmental demands	→	Weak and fragile nervous system	→	Stress overload!	→	Fight, flight, or freeze!

- Too much, too fast!
- Too loud, too bright!
- I don't understand!
- What do they mean?
- I don't know how to act!
- What is expected?
- How should I respond?

- Sensory-defensive; overreacting to stimulation.
- Poor registration of information.
- Problems integrating senses.
- Becomes overloaded easily.
- Poor digestive and weakened immune systems.
- Areas of brain do not work well together to give meaning to event.

- Build-up of stress chemicals.
- Feeling confused, overwhelmed.
- Feeling frustrated, anxious and scared.
- Breakdown of thought processes and ability to regulate emotions.

- Shutdowns: withdraw; unresponsive; nervous system shuts down in order to rebound.
- Meltdowns: tantrums, aggression, property disruption, self-abuse, all in attempt to release stress chemicals and to escape/avoid stressors.

Please help me to understand and feel safe, accepted, and competent!

SOURCES OF STRESS

I don't understand! cognitive deficits

- Delayed informational processing.
- Difficulty processing multiple information.
- Focus on detail, often missing the big picture.
- Rigid, inflexible thinking.
- Problems processing rapid change, shifting gears.
- Difficulty planning, organizing and following a plan of action.
- Trouble understanding what is required.
- Must process too much, too fast!
- Needs simple, concrete, visual instructions.

Sensory overload!

- Too bright, too loud, too strong, too much!
- Difficulty integrating sensory input.
- Over- or under-aroused.
- Sensory overload!
- Physical demands too difficult.

Social performance expectations!

- Strong social anxiety.
- Difficulty reading and interpreting social cues.
- Impaired ability to understand intent and perspective of others.
- Hard to coordinate and repair interaction.
- What is expected?
- What is he saying?
- What does he mean?
- What should I say?
- How should I act?
- Interaction moving too fast!
- I don't want to stand out!
- Often unaware of how behavior is seen by others.

Confused! Overwhelmed! Frustrated! Scared! Anxious!

Poor emotional control

- Poor frustration tolerance.
- Poor self-control.
- Often anxious, easily upset, disorganized.
- Unpredictable emotional outbursts.
- Difficulty identifying, interpreting, and regulating emotions.

Communication

- Difficulty processing what others are saying.
- Problems reading nonverbal communication.
- Very literal; cannot read between the lines.
- Trouble formulating a verbal response.
- Problem communicating feelings, needs, and wants.
- Verbal skills deteriorate when upset!

Structured routine

- Demands of routine, too much, too fast.
- Transitions/change are hard.
- Difficulty understanding rules, roles, and expectations.
- Needs rigid schedule that is familiar and predictable.
- Avoids novelty and change.
- Difficulty with mediating time and schedules.
- Shifting gears unexpectedly.
- Unstructured time causes stress.

Stress reaction

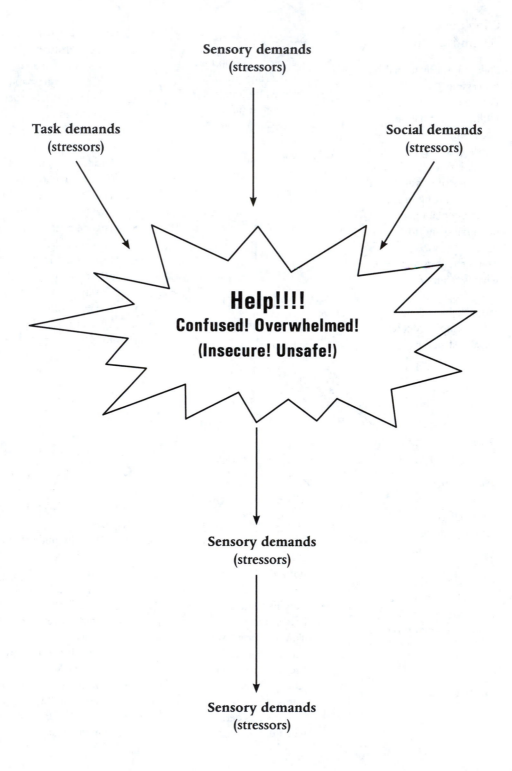

Stress reduction

Calm and organize nervous system

- Reduce stimulation.
- Provide calming input.
- Use deep pressure to calm.
- Use proprioception to organize.
- Provide slow vestibular as tolerated.
- Do physical activity to release stress chemicals.
- Use a sensory diet to calm and organize nervous system.

Reduce confusion

- Reduce demands.
- Slow down, one step at a time.
- Keep directions simple, concrete, with visual cues.
- Don't assume child understands; provide added support.
- Preview and review often.
- Ensure concrete beginning and end to tasks.

Reduce social demands

- Encourage and support, but do not pressure.
- Help interpret intent and expectations of others.
- Assume social anxiety.
- Role-play and/or guide through interaction.
- Use social stories.
- Use awareness training for peers.

Support when agitated

- Intervene/support at first signs of agitation.
- Remove demands, slow down, stay calm.
- Be supportive not punitive.
- Help child calm and feel safe.
- Coach alternative responses.
- Provide "safe area" to escape to when anxious.
- Help problem-solve if child is calm enough.

Structured routine

- Provide a consistent, predictable routine.
- Use a visual schedule.
- Slow down, space out activity.
- Tailor demands/expectations to maximize success.
- Minimize fatigue, sensory overload.
- Provide support for transitions.
- Prepare for novelty/change.
- Create patterned routine and demands to suit individual needs.

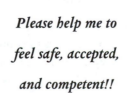

Please help me to feel safe, accepted, and competent!!

DEEP PRESSURE TECHNIQUES

Deep pressure massage

1. Procedure can be implemented in the sitting or lying position.

2. When giving deep pressure massage, use the palm of your hands, not your finger tips. Provide firm massage, not light touch. As much as possible, attempt to move your hands around the body without breaking contact (lifting hands from surface).

3. Provide massage to arms and legs by cupping your hands around the limb. Firmly squeeze (hug) the limb with your hands, for several seconds at each spot, as you slowly work your way up and down the limb. Continue firm pressure, massaging as you go.

4. Provide deep pressure to shoulder by cupping hands over the shoulder, and applying pressure for several seconds, massaging as you move around the shoulder.

5. Provide deep pressure to the back with the palms of your hands. Again, keep contact with the skin, as you massage down the back.

6. Do not force the procedure on the person. If the person is resistant, ease into it, a little at a time. Stop if the person actively struggles.

Pillow press deep pressure

1. Lie the person on their back, on a mat, sofa, or bed. Place their arms to their side.

2. Deep pressure stimulation can be provided with a firm pillow, cushion, or bean bag. Using the pillow, cushion or bean bag, provide firm pressure across the chest, abdomen, and arms. Mold the pillow around the body, to provide as much contact as possible. Avoid covering face and head.

3. Provide pressure with your arms. While always maintaining pressure, alternate from firm to gentle pressure. Provide firm pressure for 5–10 seconds, then gentle pressure for a few seconds; keep repeating pressure. Continues pressure for 1–2 minutes.

4. When finished with the chest/abdomen area, provide pressure across the legs, using same procedure.

5. Next have person roll over on their stomach and provide pressure to shoulder, back, arms, and legs.

Neutral warmth/wrap

1. Sit the person on the floor or on a mat.

2. If the person is tolerant, wrap him in a blanket, or sheet if it is too warm.

3. Sit behind the person and bring the person into you, providing as much physical contact as possible. Wrap your arms around him, providing a firm hug.

4. Slowly rock from side to side for approximately 5–10 minutes. Every few seconds alternate the pressure of the hug, while always maintaining some pressure.

5. For increased deep pressure stimulation, place a pillow across the chest and abdomen. This distributes pressure from the hug across the front of the body.

6. Do not force the wrap on the person. If the person is resistant, ease into it, a little at a time. Stop if the person actively struggles.

7. Often the person might relax back into your chest, putting a strain on your back when rocking. If this occurs, sit with your back against a wall.

8. For maximum effect, this procedure should be implemented several times a day. If the procedure is going to be used to relax someone who is agitated, it is important to introduce it to the person when they are calm. Once the individual is responsive to the procedure, then use it as a calming technique.

Appendix G

CORE DEFICIT ASSESSMENT

Name: Date: Age:

Informant: Evaluator:

I = Infrequent   O = Occasional   F = Frequent

Core deficit	I	O	F	Examples/ comments
Sensory deficits				
1. Either under- or over-sensitive to touch.				
2. Either under- or over-sensitive to sounds.				
3. Either under- or over-sensitive to light.				
4. Either under- or over-sensitive to smells/tastes.				
5. Shows apprehension in movement activities.				
6. Withdraws or hits when approached or touched.				
7. Becomes overwhelmed in loud or crowded settings.				
8. Dislikes certain clothing, or layers clothing.				
9. Resists grooming: face washing, bathing, tooth brushing, combing hair, etc.				
10. Has problems understanding/following spoken directions.				
11. Sometimes appears not to hear when spoken to.				
12. Frequently seeks out stimulation (touch, deep pressure, crashing, movement, smells, etc.).				
13. Is frequently on the move; overactive.				
14. Is frequently touching/grabbing/hanging on others.				
15. Is slow, sluggish, with little energy.				
Other:				

Core deficit	I	O	F	Examples/ comments
Cognitive deficits				
16. Displays delayed information processing; delay in responding.				
17. Has difficulty processing multiple information simultaneously.				
18. Gets confused with multiple-step directions.				
19. Needs tasks broken down into small steps.				
20. Has problems multitasking.				
21. Has a short attention span, concentration, is easily distracted.				
22. Has trouble starting and finishing tasks.				
23. Has poor planning and organizing skills; scattered.				
24. Often loses or forgets things.				
25. Has poor impulse control, acts without forethought.				
26. Has problems monitoring actions to stay coordinated with others.				
27. Doesn't understand the effects of his behavior.				
28. Has difficulty shifting gears with minor snags or changes.				
29. Shows rigid/inflexible thinking; can only see his way.				
30. Displays black and white, all-or-nothing thinking (cannot see gray areas).				
Other:				
Emotional deficits				
31. Displays intense emotional reactions; often over-exaggerated.				
32. Goes from 0 to 100 quickly, difficulty calming down.				
33. Seems to lose control, becomes overwhelmed.				
34. Has poor frustration tolerance (has to have it now!).				
35. Has trouble identifying/labeling emotions.				
36. Often appears anxious, scared, or apprehensive.				
37. Changes moods quickly, difficult to predict.				
38. Laughs or cries for no apparent reason.				
39. Becomes over-excited easily.				
40. Shows emotions that often don't match situation.				
41. Shows little emotion.				
42. Has difficulty recognizing emotions of others.				
Other:				

★

Core deficit	I	O	F	Examples/comments
Social/communication deficits				
43. Has difficulty communicating needs and wants.				
44. Gets frustrated when others don't understand.				
45. Has difficult time understanding spoken directions.				
46. Needs to have directions repeated several times.				
47. Gets upset when given directions.				
48. Has difficult time making friends.				
49. Has difficulty reading social cues.				
50. Shows poor regard for (difficulty reading) the thoughts, feelings and perspectives of others.				
51. Has to control all interactions.				
52. Has difficulty sharing and taking turns.				
53. Has difficulty coordinating back-and-forth interaction.				
54. Has poor awareness of how his actions affect others.				
55. Seeks out frequent attention.				
56. Seems anxious, apprehensive when interacting.				
57. Tends to avoid social contact.				
Other:				
Medical/psychiatric				
58. Eating or sleeping problems.				
59. Chronic infections, congestion.				
60. Digestive, gastrointestinal problems.				
61. Constipation, loose stools, etc.				
62. Allergies, arthritis, migraines.				
63. Mood swings, over-activity.				
64. Withdrawn, inactive, little interests.				
65. Rapid, pressured speech.				
66. Anxious, apprehensive, fearful.				
67. Compulsive, repetitive behavior.				
68. Hallucinations.				
69. Delusional ideations.				
70. Preoccupied thoughts.				

★

SUMMARY SHEET

If used in conjunction with functional behavior assessment, which core deficits impact the target behaviours in question?

For each core deficit area, list possible compensations, accommodations, or skills to teach.

Sensory:	Emotional:
Cognitive:	Social/communication:

Medical/psychiatric:

★

Appendix H

COMFORT ZONES PROFILE

Name: Age: Date:
Reporter:

Sensory profile

a.   Sensory stimulation the child avoids/is defensive to:

b.   Sensory stimulation the child is attracted to, seeks out:

c.   Sensory stimulation that alerts the child:

d.   Known sensory situations that overwhelm the child:

e.   Sensory stimulation that calms the child:

f.   Sensory accommodations, or sensory diet, currently used to support the child:

g.   Favorite sensory activities for engaging the child in interaction:

h.   Other:

Cognitive (information) profile

a.   Information processing problems the child experiences:

☐ delayed processing   ☐ processing multiple information
                                        simultaneously

☐ processing auditory information   ☐ processing visual information

Explain:

b. Best way to present information to the child:

Type: (visual, pictures, written, verbal, etc.)

How much? (Short phrases, broken down into small portions at one time, etc.)

How fast? (Needs 15–30 seconds to process, etc.)

c. Information (topics) that tend to be easy for the child? Difficult?

d. The child tends to have problems:

☐ concentrating   ☐ organizing materials   ☐ initiating a task

☐ staying on task   ☐ finishing task   ☐ turning in completed work

Explain:

e. Accommodations/supports that have worked well in helping the child learn:

f. Other:

Social profile:

a. What type of interaction style works best to:

Engage the child (animated, calm, non-demanding, slow-paced, physical contact, etc.):

Soothe the child:

b. Types of interaction to avoid with the child:

c. Types of interaction that overwhelm the child:

d. How the child handles interacting with:

Familiar adults:

Unfamiliar adults:

★

Other children:

Group activities:

e. The child's interaction skills:
Sharing:

Taking turns:

Following directions:

Referencing others to stay coordinated in action with them:

Sharing enjoyment with others:

f. Social situations to avoid for the child:

g. Accommodations and supports that help the child feel safe and accepted with others:

h. Other:

Emotional profile:

a. The child's general level of emotional stability (fairly calm, emotionally overreactive, etc.) is:

b. How the child expresses:
Excitement/pleasure:

Frustration:

Unhappiness:

Sadness:

Fear:

c. The child's abilities to:

Identify and label his emotions:

Control and regulate his emotions:

Calm after getting upset:

Situations that the child becomes overwhelmed by, or overreacts to:

d. Supports/accommodations that can be used to keep the child from becoming emotionally overwhelmed:

e. Best ways to calm the child when upset, overwhelmed:

f. Things to avoid when the child is emotionally overwhelmed, upset:

g. Other strategies that help the child feel "safe" in general, and in times of stress:

Other comfort zones (medical, dietary, physical activity, etc.) important to the child feeling safe:

Given the above information, the child functions the best under the following conditions:

The child struggles the most under the following conditions:

Summary of strengths and preferences

The child feels the most confident and learns best when we focus on his strengths and preferences.

★

a. The child's strengths include (what are his best qualities? What is he good at? What does he feel most competent doing?):

b. Favorite interests (topics, hobbies, music, activities, toys, etc.):

c. Ways of incorporating interests into learning opportunities. List any ways that have been used to incorporate the child's interests and preferences into learning opportunities (reading, writing, math, researching topic, etc.), to build social engagement around (peer play, group activities), and to soothe and cope with stress. Possible ways of expanding on these interests. Build the child's strengths, preferences, and interests into as many areas of learning as possible.

REFERENCES

Bailey, B.A. (2000) *I Love You Rituals*. New York, NY: HarperCollins.

Dunn Buron, K. and Curti, M. (2012) *The Incredible 5 Point Scale: The Significantly Improved and Expanded Second Edition; Assisting Students in Understanding Social Interactions and Controlling their Emotional Responses*. Shawnee Mission, KS: AACP Publishing.

Greene, R.W. and Ablon, S.J. (2005) *Treating Explosive Kids: The Collaborative Problem-Solving Approach*. New York, NY: Guilford Press.

Greene, R.W. (2008) *Lost at School: Why Our Kids with Behavioral Challenges Are Falling Through the Cracks and How We Can Help Them*. New York, NY: Simon and Schuster.

Greene, R.W. (2010) *The Explosive Child: A New Approach for Understanding and Parenting Easily Frustrated, Chronically Inflexible Children*. New York, NY: HarperCollins Publishers.

Greenspan, S.I., Wieder, S., and Simons, R. (1998) *The Child with Special Needs: Encouraging Intellectual and Emotional Growth*. Reading, MA: Perseus Books Group.

Greenspan, S.I. and Wieder, S. (2009) *Engaging Autism: Using the Floortime Approach to Help Children Relate, Communicate, and Think*. Reading, MA: Perseus Books Group.

Gutstein, S.E. (2000) *Autism Aspergers: Solving the Relationship Puzzle—A New Developmental Program that Opens the Door to Lifelong Social and Emotional Growth*. Arlington, TX: Future Horizons.

Gutstein, S.E. (2002a) *Relationship Development Intervention with Young Children: Social and Emotional Development Activities for Asperger Syndrome, Autism, PDD and NLD*. London,: Jessica Kingsley Publishers.

Gutstein, S.E. (2002b) *Relationship Development Intervention with Children, Adolescents and Adults, Social and Emotional Development Activities for Asperger Syndrome, Autism, PDD and NLD*. London: Jessica Kingsley Publishers.

Gutstein, S.E. (2009) *The RDI Book: Forging New Pathways for Autism, Asperger's and PDD with the Relationship Development Intervention Program*. Houston, TX: Connection Center Publishing.

Nason, B. (2014) *The Autism Discussion Page on anxiety, behavior, school, and parenting strategies: A toolbox for helping children with autism feel safe, accepted, and competent*. London: Jessica Kingsley Publishers.

Siegel, D.J. and Bryson, T.P. (2012) *The Whole-Brain Child: 12 Revolutionary Strategies to Nurture Your Child's Developing Mind*. New York, NY: Bantam Books/Random House.

Winner, M.G. (2003) *Thinking About You, Thinking About Me*. London: Jessica Kingsley Publishers.

Winner, M.G. (2008) *You Are a Social Detective*. San Jose, CA: Think Social Publishing.